Bonhoeffer's New Beginning

Praise for *Bonhoeffer's New Beginning*

"In mid-century Europe, totalitarians on both the left and the right sought to remake humanity, society, politics, morality, geography, and population. The scope of their hubris was astonishing, as was the body count they left behind. To accomplish their idolatrous, disastrous goals, everything was permissible.

In his important new book, Andrew D. DeCort demonstrates that Dietrich Bonhoeffer responded theologically in Nazi Germany to this mania for remaking the world through projects of political salvation at the point of a gun. DeCort shows that Bonhoeffer's biblical theology of creation, Christ, and resurrection precluded any human project to serve as our own creators and saviors by engineering a new beginning in human life. Instead, Christians at least, know (or should know) that we are called to respond to God's creative and reconciling action, and that we must do so in love of God and others.

This is a groundbreaking work, ranging exhaustively over the Bonhoeffer corpus and the secondary literature. It reveals a new dimension of Bonhoeffer's thought, and demonstrates once again that Bonhoeffer was always responding to the dangerous political and moral ideas around him with a disciplined theological and ethical response—a response that took him to his death.

Highly recommended!"—**David P. Gushee**, president, American Academy of Religion; Distinguished University Professor of Christian Ethics, Mercer University

"DeCort's *Bonhoeffer's New Beginning* takes on the profound and utterly inescapable problem of the 'new beginning,' the 'beginning again,' in the wake of devastation and catastrophe, and suggests that, and then shows how, Bonhoeffer engages in Christian theology in light of this problem. This book is a terrific vision, in my mind especially illuminating on some of the Christocentric elements in Bonhoeffer's work, and drawing on work in philosophy and political theory as well as Christian theology; it casts new light on our predicaments and the ways that Bonhoeffer may help us identify, understand, and confront them."—**Charles T. Mathewes**, Carolyn M. Barbour Professor of Religious Studies, University of Virginia

"DeCort's treatment of Bonhoeffer is creative. This study of Bonhoeffer, which includes analysis of other major figures like Friedrich Nietzsche and Hannah Arendt, takes an innovative turn to look at the concept of an ethics of beginning again."—**Reggie L. Williams**, associate professor of Christian ethics, McCormick Theological Seminary

Bonhoeffer's New Beginning

Ethics after Devastation

Andrew D. DeCort

LEXINGTON BOOKS/FORTRESS ACADEMIC
Lanham • Boulder • New York • London

Published by Lexington Books/Fortress Academic
Lexington Books is an imprint of The Rowman & Littlefield Publishing Group, Inc.
4501 Forbes Boulevard, Suite 200, Lanham, Maryland 20706
www.rowman.com

Unit A, Whitacre Mews, 26-34 Stannary Street, London SE11 4AB

British Library Cataloguing in Publication Information Available

Library of Congress Cataloging-in-Publication Data

Names: DeCort, Andrew D., author.
Title: Bonhoeffer's new beginning : ethics after devastation / Andrew D.
  DeCort.
Description: Lanham, MD : Lexington Books-Fortress Academic, 2018. | Includes
  bibliographical references and index.
Identifiers: LCCN 2018027566 (print) | LCCN 2018032097 (ebook) | ISBN
  9781978701007 (electronic) | ISBN 9781978700994 (cloth : alk. paper)
  | ISBN 9781978701014 (pbk. : alk. paper)
Subjects: LCSH: Bonhoeffer, Dietrich, 1906-1945. | Hidden God. |
  Suffering—Religious aspects—Christianity. | Ethics.
Classification: LCC BX4827.B57 (ebook) | LCC BX4827.B57 D394 2018 (print) |
  DDC 241.092—dc23
LC record available at https://lccn.loc.gov/2018027566

∞™ The paper used in this publication meets the minimum requirements of
American National Standard for Information Sciences—Permanence of Paper
for Printed Library Materials, ANSI/NISO Z39.48-1992.

Printed in the United States of America

For beloved Lily and brother Eyob (1997–2011)

Through you I learned that our encounters with
strangers are sacred gifts from God.
Thank you for two of the most precious
new beginnings in my life.

This is for me the end, but also the beginning.

—Dietrich Bonhoeffer's last words
before being hanged on April 9, 1945

Contents

Acknowledgments

This book is dedicated to my beloved Lily Atlaw DeCort. Thank you for so faithfully keeping your promise and unceasingly supporting me at every step of my writing. I have never met anyone like you with greater kindness, strength, and committed love. You are forever my righteous prize (Songs 2:2).

This book is also dedicated to brother Eyob, my saint of darkness and a shining exemplar of goodness, courage, and hope, some of whose story is told in chapter 1.

I wish to give special thanks to:

My parents, Joe and Jane DeCort, and my brother Joe DeCort III for your generous support, and Jason, Abby, Elizabeth, and your dear families.

Professor Jean Bethke Elshtain (1941–2013), my beloved PhD advisor. It was a great honor to be Professor Elshtain's final doctoral student. With her I have "joined the ranks of the nervous,"[1] while always remaining rooted in "this gratitude at being created," which I too hope "has worked its way into the very tissue of these reflections."[2] Like her *Public Man, Private Woman*, this is "a nasty book" in which I have "attempted to think 'really honestly' from the vantage point of" human devastation.[3]

Professor Donald N. Levine (1931–2015), who inspired me with his vision of education ("conversation about the meaning of life, as each sees some part of it, on behalf of everyone"[4]), mentored me in Ethiopian studies, invited me

---

1. Jean Bethke Elshtain, *Democracy on Trial* (New York: BasicBooks, 1995), xvii.

2. Jean Bethke Elshtain, *Who Are We? Critical Reflections and Hopeful Possibilities* (Grand Rapids, MI: Eerdmans, 2000), xvii.

3. Jean Bethke Elshtain, *Public Man, Private Woman: Women in Social and Political Thought* (Princeton, NJ: Princeton University Press, 1981), xi.

4. Donald Levine, *Wax and Gold: Tradition and Innovation in Ethiopian Culture* (Chicago: University of Chicago Press, 1965), xii.

to edit his final book on Ethiopia,[5] became a dear friend, and had the kindness to tell me on his death bed, "If I have any regrets at all, it is that I will not be able to read your dissertation." *Egziabher yestilign*, Gash Liben.

Bruce Ellis Benson, who was generously instrumental in moving this book to publication. Thanks for forgetting your jacket at the party; new beginnings sometimes commence in the most incredible ways.

Peter Kline, who generously painted the beautiful artwork for this book. Thank you for reintroducing me to Bonhoeffer through your eyes. Thanks also to Philipp Schütz for generous assistance with the cover design.

I agree with C. S. Lewis: "Friendship is the greatest of worldly goods."[6] I wish to thank friends who have been invaluable in the writing of this book, including Graham Smith, Thom Bernasol (*Volo ut sis!*), David Robinson, Stephen Scheidell, Matt Vega, Dave Schmidgall, David Ellis, Steve Andres, Ben Chleboun, Tanner Gesek, Stephen Sandoval, James Hoey, Anna Faulkner, and Dr. Matthew Robinson, my beloved friend for over twenty years. Matthew, congratulations on the forthcoming publication of your beautiful book, *Redeeming Relationships, Relationships that Redeem: Free Sociability and the Completion of Humanity in the Thought of Friedrich Schleiermacher* (Tübingen: Mohr Siebeck). We began, finished, and will walk onward together in redeeming relationship.

Stephen Scheidell and Dai Li, who generously compiled the indexes for this book and provided other important assistance.

My colleagues and students at the Ethiopian Graduate School of Theology, especially Drs. Desta Heliso, Theodros Teklu, and Seblewengel Daniel. May Christ guide us as we make a new beginning for public theology in Ethiopia.

Beloved friends in the Authority, Action, Ethics: Ethiopia (AAE) program at Wheaton College (2013–2016), especially Dr. Steve Ivester, Professor Daniel Haase, Roger Sandberg, David Robinson, Jenna Herskind, and Hannah Gross. What an extraordinary new beginning. You saved my life.

Our beloved family in Ethiopia, who so generously supported our new beginning here: Esayas, Eleni, and your *lejjoch*; Gash Atlaw and Ezra; Muluken Nega and Miheret Brook; Eden Gelan, Ermias Zeleke (1969–2017), Masresha Tamiru, Birukti Tagesse, Yonas Urgecha, Betty Kiros, Ruth Emmanuel, Hallelujah Lulie and Kidist Tekle, Nebeyou Alemu, Tekalign Nega and Tehitena Mesfin, Tsedale Lemma; and dear Wudenesh Tilahun and your beloved family.

---

5. Donald N. Levine, *Interpreting Ethiopia: Observations of Five Decades*, ed. Andrew DeCort (Los Angeles, CA: Tsehai Press, 2014).

6. C. S. Lewis, letter to Arthur Greeves on December 29, 1935, in *Collected Letters*, vol. 2, ed. Walter Hooper (London: HarperCollins, 2004), 174. I'm grateful to Dr. Jason Lepojärvi for locating this citation for me.

Professor Charles Mathewes at the University of Virginia, Professor Patchen Markell in the Political Science Department at the University of Chicago, and, above all, Professor William Schweiker at the University of Chicago Divinity School for very helpful comments on my manuscript. In his *Theological Ethics and Global Dynamics*, Professor Schweiker asks, "Is it not time to make our religious traditions responsible to their own best insights?"[7] This is what I have attempted to do with my religious tradition in this book.

The Institute for Christianity and the Common Good (www.iccgood.org) for generously covering the permissions fees for this book as part of our mission to share presence, strengthen theological education, and promote neighbor-love for the suffering. I'm particularly grateful to Joe and Karen DeCort, Graham and April Smith, the Herskind family, David Robinson, James Hoey and April Park, David Ellis, Tanner Gesek, and many others for making ICCG possible. Thanks also to Mike Gibson for his responsive editorial assistance. Your email blew me away.

Finally, I hope this book is read as an expression of gratitude to Dietrich Bonhoeffer for the gift and challenge of his life and writings.

The people named here and many others were in my heart as I wrote on gratitude as a practice of new beginning in Bonhoeffer's thought. With him, I say to you:

> To me it is as if I were experiencing now for the first time in my life what it means to be thankful to another person, what a profoundly transforming power gratitude can be—it is the Yes—this word so difficult and so marvelous, appearing so seldom among mortals—from which all this springs—may God from whom every Yes comes grant that we may speak this Yes always thus and always more and more to one another throughout our entire life.[8]

Andrew DeCort
April 3, 2018

---

7. William Schweiker, *Theological Ethics and Global Dynamics: In the Time of Many Worlds* (Malden, MA: Blackwell, 2004), 125.

8. Letter from Dietrich Bonhoeffer to Maria von Wedemeyer on January 24, 1943 (16:387).

Citations and Abbreviations

I will refer to Dietrich Bonhoeffer's writings in the following manner: title and date (when not a monograph), followed by volume and page numbers in parentheses. I will note instances where I modify the English translations of the German.

The italicized numbers below will serve as abbreviations for the volumes of Bonhoeffer's works in English and *Love Letters*:

1: *Sanctorum Communio: A Theological Study of the Sociology of the Church*. Edited by Clifford J. Green. Translated by Reinhard Krauss and Nancy Lukens. Minneapolis, MN: Fortress Press, 1998.

2: *Act and Being: Transcendental Philosophy and Ontology in Systematic Theology*. Edited by Wayne Floyd Jr. Translated by Martin Rumscheidt. Minneapolis, MN: Fortress Press, 1996.

3: *Creation and Fall: A Theological Exposition of Genesis 1–3*. Edited by John W. de Gruchy. Translated by Douglas Bax. Minneapolis, MN: Fortress Press, 1997.

4: *Discipleship*. Edited by Geffrey Kelly and John Godsey. Translated by Barbara Green and Reinhard Krauss. Minneapolis, MN: Fortress Press, 2000.

5: *Life Together* and *Prayerbook of the Bible: An Introduction to the Psalms*. Edited by Geffrey Kelly. Translated by Daniel Bloesch and James Burtness. Minneapolis, MN: Fortress Press, 1996.

6: *Ethics*. Edited by Clifford Green. Translated by Reinhard Krauss, Charles West, and Douglas Stott. Minneapolis, MN: Fortress Press, 2005.

7: *Fiction from Tegel Prison*. Edited by Clifford Green. Translated by Nancy Lukens. Minneapolis, MN: Fortress Press, 1999.

  8: *Letters and Papers from Prison*. Edited by John de Gruchy. Translated by Christian Gremmels, Eberhard Bethge, and Renate Bethge, with Ilse Tödt et al. Minneapolis, MN: Fortress Press, 2010.

  9: *The Young Bonhoeffer: 1918–1927*. Edited by Paul Matheny, Clifford Green, and Marshall Johnson. Translated by Mary Nebelsick and Douglas Stott. Minneapolis, MN: Fortress Press, 2003.

 10: *Barcelona, Berlin, New York: 1928–1931*. Edited by Clifford Green. Translated by Douglas Stott. Minneapolis, MN: Fortress Press, 2008.

 11: *Ecumenical, Academic & Pastoral Work: 1931–1932*. Edited by Victoria Barnett, Mark Brocker, and Michael Lukens. Translated by Anne Schmidt-Lange et al. Minneapolis, MN: Fortress Press, 2012.

 12: *Berlin: 1932–1933*. Edited by Larry L. Rasmussen. Translated by Isabel Best and David Higgins, with Douglass Stott. Minneapolis, MN: Fortress Press, 2009.

 13: *London: 1933–1935*. Edited by Keith Clements. Translated by Isabel Best, with Douglass W. Stott. Minneapolis, MN: Fortress Press, 2007.

 14: *Theological Education at Finkenwalde: 1935–1937*. Edited by H. Gaylon Barker and Mark Brocker. Translated by Douglas Stott. Minneapolis, MN: Fortress Press, 2013.

 15: *Theological Education Underground: 1937–1940*. Edited by Victoria Barnett. Translated by Victoria Barnett et al. Minneapolis, MN: Fortress Press, 2012.

 16: *Conspiracy and Imprisonment: 1940–1945*. Edited by Mark Brocker. Translated by Lisa Dahill. Minneapolis, MN: Fortress Press, 2006.

 92: *Love Letters from Cell 92: The Correspondence between Dietrich Bonhoeffer and Maria von Wedemeyer, 1943–1945*. Edited by Ruth-Alice von Bismarck and Ulrich Kabitz. Translated by John Brown. Nashville, TN: Abingdon Press, 1995.

Beginning

Initium ut esset homo creatus est—"that a beginning be made man was created," said Augustine. This beginning is guaranteed by each new birth; it is indeed every man.[1]

—Hannah Arendt

Beginning is fundamental for the world and human life. It is an event, act, idea, and aspiration that sources and shapes all that we are and do as storied creatures in reality. According to Aristotle, "The beginning is admittedly more than half of the whole, and throws light at once on many of the questions under investigation."[2]

Humans are beginners by birth. As Hannah Arendt observed, "With each new birth, a new beginning is born into the world."[3] We are conceived as newcomers who never were before but then begin from a beginning given to us by others that we did not make in a world we did not create. With astonishment, Søren Kierkegaard noted, "In *the moment*, a person becomes aware that

---

1. Hannah Arendt, *The Origins of Totalitarianism* (New York: Schocken Books, 2004), 516. I have decided not to amend Arendt and others' dated, gendered language. Arendt is referring to St. Augustine, *City of God*, trans. Henry Bettenson (New York: Penguin Classics, 2003), XII.15, 500, 501, in which Augustine attacks the Greek idea that "the human race had no beginning, no start in time" but turns in eternal cycles and argues instead that "novelties are possible, things which have not happened before and yet are not at variance with the ordering of the world" based on the claim that "it is not impossible for God to make something new, something he has not made before, and at the same time, because of his unimaginable foreknowledge, never to change his design."

2. Aristotle, *Nicomachean Ethics*, Loeb Classical Library, trans. H. Rackham (Cambridge, MA: Harvard University Press, 1926), 1098b5–7.

3. Arendt, *The Origins of Totalitarianism*, 599–600. On "beginning" and some of its philosophical genealogies, see Asher D. Biemann, *Inventing New Beginnings: On the Idea of Renaissance in Modern Judaism* (Stanford, CA: Stanford University Press, 2009), 24–25.

he was born, for his previous state . . . was indeed one of 'not to be.'"[4] This other-originated natality—this gift, which simultaneously gives and limits our capacity to begin—is the mysterious foundation for all of our lives and every beginning ever after. We are *begunners*, creatures who live between the passivity and activity of our beginnings.[5]

After birth, as Dietrich Bonhoeffer meditated from his dissident seminary, "Each new morning is a new beginning for our lives."[6] When we wake from sleep, we begin afresh and encounter the ever-new mystery of freedom in the various conditions, decisions, and stages of our lives. Indeed, as Arendt argued, "Because he *is* a beginning, man can begin; to be human and to be free are one and the same."[7] Thus, from childhood, we grow into agents with the fraught capacity and responsibility to make beginnings that change our lives, others, and the world around us. We confront the question of what we should do and who we should become, and we wrestle to make wise judgments at the decisive turning points in our lives, relationships, and vocations.[8]

These decisions—some as simple as "going out of your door"[9] or giving your number to a stranger—become beginnings that alter our identities and destinies in small and profound ways that often exceed our knowing. They variously fill us with joy and leave us traumatized.[10] Here the practice of gratitude and forgiveness—what Martin Luther King Jr. called the "catalyst creating the atmosphere necessary for a fresh start and a new beginning"—is pivotal.[11] Thomas Hobbes presciently observed, "There is no action of man in this life, that is not the beginning of so long a chayn of Consequences, as no humane Providence, is high enough, to give a man a prospect to the end."[12] Hobbes's insight points to the profundity of Jesus's prayer from the cross for

4. Søren Kierkegaard, *Philosophical Fragments*, trans. Edna and Howard Hong (Princeton, NJ: Princeton University Press, 1985), 190. See Annie Murphy Paul, *Origins: How the Nine Months Before Birth Shape the Rest of Our Lives* (New York: Free Press, 2010).

5. Thus, beginning is both given and chosen. James Baldwin points out the unjust burden of birth in a racist context in *The Fire Next Time*, writing to his black nephew, "You were born where you were born and faced the future that you faced because you were black and *for no other reason*. The limits of your ambition were, thus, expected to be set forever." See *Baldwin: Collected Essays*, ed. Toni Morrison (New York: The Library of America, 1998), 293.

6. Dietrich Bonhoeffer, "Morning Blessing: Devotion" from summer 1935 (14:864–65).

7. Hannah Arendt, "What Is Freedom?" in *The Portable Hannah Arendt*, ed. Peter Baehr (New York: Penguin, 2000), 456. She continues, "God created man in order to introduce into the world the faculty of beginning: freedom." See also Arendt, *The Origins of Totalitarianism*, 601.

8. See Jean Bethke Elshtain, *Public Man, Private Woman: Women in Social and Political Thought* (Princeton, NJ: Princeton University Press, 1981), 10–11.

9. J. R. R. Tolkien, *The Lord of the Rings*, single-volume edition (New York: Houghton Mifflin, 1993), 87.

10. For profound studies on trauma and new beginnings, see Bessel van der Kolk, *The Body Keeps the Score: Brain, Mind, and Body in the Healing of Trauma* (New York: Penguin Books, 2015), and Mark Wolynn, *It Didn't Start with You: How Inherited Family Trauma Shapes Who We Are and How to End the Cycle* (New York: Penguin, 2016).

11. Martin Luther King Jr., *Strength to Love* (Minneapolis, MN: Fortress Press, 2010), 45.

12. Thomas Hobbes, *Leviathan*, ed. C. B. Macpherson (New York: Penguin, 1985), 406.

all human initiative: "Father, forgive them, for they do not know what they are doing."[13]

We tell time with beginnings, celebrating birthdays, anniversaries, holidays, and other personal and public memorials. These times turn our thinking into thanking as we re-present our formative beginnings "with the mystic chords of memory"[14] and imagine new ones for our future.[15] Our days are "saturated with beginnings."[16]

We innovate and make revolutions in religion, politics, science, and technology. On the brink of the American Revolution, Thomas Payne famously wrote, "We have it in our power to begin the world over again. . . . The birthday of a new world is at hand."[17] Perhaps more radical still, the young Bonhoeffer wrote in his journal from Italy, "a *completely* new intellectual history started with Christianity from the very beginning."[18] We now find ourselves contemplating a "post-human" future.[19] Whatever we make of these specific cases, beginnings enable us to tell time and write histories as stories with a "before" and an "after" that often focus on "origins" and their complex implications for individuals, society, and the world.[20] These innovations and revolutions, in turn, have become fundamental for our epochal self-understanding as humans with planetary agency living in (late) "modernity."[21]

Even so, the deepest analysts in the Christian tradition have been vigilant to beginnings as profound temptations that entice and often betray human ambition and desire. In his autobiography, which narrates his fall from being "a little piece of creation" to an alienated ego torn apart inside himself and time, St. Augustine confessed, "I disdained to be a little beginner. Puffed up with

---

13. Luke 23:34.

14. Abraham Lincoln, "First Inaugural Address," in *The Collected Works of Abraham Lincoln*, ed. Rob B. Basler, 9 vols. (New Brunswick, NJ: Rutgers University Press, 1953), 4:272.

15. See Hannah Arendt, *The Life of the Mind*, ed. Mary McCarthy, one-volume edition (New York: Harcourt, 1978), 2:185.

16. Biemann, *Inventing New Beginnings*, 24.

17. Thomas Payne, *Common Sense* (Mineola, NY: Dover Publications, 1997), appendix. This is a fascinating text to read together with John Locke's famous statement, "Thus in the beginning all the world was *America*." See John Locke, *Two Treatises of Government*, ed. Peter Laslett (New York: Cambridge University Press, 1988), II, §49, 301.

18. From Bonhoeffer's diary in 1924 (9:105). See Larry Siedentop, *Inventing the Individual: The Origins of Western Liberalism* (London: Penguin Books, 2015), pt. 2, "A Moral Revolution."

19. See Yuval Noah Harari, *Homo Deus: A Brief History of Tomorrow* (New York: HarperCollins, 2017).

20. For example, Neil Postman in his brilliant *Amusing Ourselves to Death* (New York, NY: Penguin, 2005), 6, aims to tell "the story of the origin and meaning of this descent into a vast triviality." In *The Second Sex* (New York: Knopf, 1993), xlv, Simone de Beauvoir asks, "How did all this [sexism] begin?" On the structure of narrative, see Paul Ricoeur, "Emplotment: A Reading of Aristotle's *Poetics*," in *Time and Narrative*, trans. Kathleen McLaughlin and David Pellauer (Chicago: University of Chicago Press, 1990), 31–49.

21. See Michael North, *Novelty: A History of the New* (Chicago: University of Chicago Press, 2013), and Joshua J. Yates, "The New Cosmopolitans and The Problem of the Good World" (University of Virginia: Unpublished, 2009).

pride, I considered myself a mature adult."[22] Many centuries later, Kierkeg-aard continued this meditation, analyzing how the human in despair "wants to begin a little earlier than do other men, not at and with the beginning, but 'in the beginning.'" Such a soul and its society cannot rest in receiving itself as a finite gift after the beginning but must grasp to become "the infinite form" in the sovereign position of the Beginning itself, which all too easily evolves into what Augustine called "the lust for domination."[23]

We are maddened by a lust for beginning—to be first. Thus, in Bonhoef-fer's judgment on the precipice of Hitler's Germany in 1933, the appeal of the satanic tempter is precisely the promise of the beginning: "You are the beginning and you are the end, for you are in me. Believe me, the liar from the beginning: lie, and you will be in the beginning and will be lord of the truth. Discover your beginning yourself."[24] Ominously, eight years before, Hitler had published an article entitled "The New Beginning."[25]

In the wreckage of our beginnings, many of us ache for new beginnings after we suffer loss, failure, death, and devastation. Indeed, for our purposes, we might define "devastation" not simply as the condition in which we can-not begin again or at least fear that we cannot (destruction) but as the condi-tion in which we doubt that we *should* or that it is *worth* loving enough to try (nihilistic despair). Not all memorials are celebrations, nor are all origins good, as Arendt's title *The Origins of Totalitarianism* makes so grievously clear. Our commencements can be catastrophic.

Thus, religious communities repent and pray for revival. Citizens and public servants work for reform and renaissance, what Aristotle called the art of "beginning and begunning well."[26] As Alasdair MacIntyre famously observed, "Ours too is a time of waiting for new and unpredictable possibili-ties of renewal,"[27] even as we labor under the heavy burden of Machiavelli's realist wisdom: "Nothing is harder to manage, more risky in the undertaking, or more doubtful of success than to set up as the introducer of a new order."[28]

22. St. Augustine, *Confessions*, translated by Henry Chadwick (New York: Oxford University Press, 1998), III, v, 9.
23. Søren Kierkegaard, *The Sickness Unto Death: A Christian Psychological Exposition for Up-building and Awakening*, ed. and trans. Howard V. Hong and Edna H. Hong (Princeton, NJ: Princeton University Press, 1983), 68. See Augustine, *Confessions*, III, viii, 16.
24. *Creation and Fall* (3:28–29).
25. An editorial for *Völkischer Beobachter* on February 25, 1925.
26. Aristotle, *Politics*, Loeb Classical Library, trans. H. Rackham (Cambridge, MA: Harvard Uni-versity Press, 1932), 1277. I have altered the translation of τὸ δύνασθαι ἄρχειν καὶ ἄρχεσθαι, which I believe illuminates Aristotle's meaning.
27. Alasdair MacIntyre, *After Virtue*, third edition (Notre Dame, IN: University of Notre Dame Press, 2007), xvi.
28. Niccolo Machiavelli, *The Prince, A Revised Translation, Backgrounds, Interpretations, Mar-ginalia*, second edition, trans. Robert Adams (New York: W. W. Norton & Company, 1992), 17. In this same section, Machiavelli argues that violence or being an "armed prophet" is necessary for "innovators" to succeed.

Amid this risk, Jack Balkin is surely right that "a return to origins and to basic principles is a standard method for urging reform, and especially radical reform."[29]

More radically, then, some of us hope for a new beginning for our world as a whole as we face devastation and the terrible reality of evil. We hope, pray, struggle, and passionately wait for a miracle, a new creation begun again but freed from the hatred, violence, suffering, and death that so profoundly ravish the world as we know it now, including the "new worlds" we fantasize and fabricate.[30] The apocalyptic words "Behold, I am making everything new!" strike our ears with unforgettable force, whether we hear them as false hope, a subtle temptation, or the divine promise that gives us courage to walk on and make good of what we have started when everything seems lost.[31]

The brute fact that our consciousness is capable of conceiving such ideas—the beginning, beginnings in general, and a new beginning for ourselves, society, and creation as a whole—is astonishing and wondrous, the ecstatic beginning of philosophy according to Socrates.[32] Thus, Hannah Arendt called "our whole existence . . . a chain of miracles"[33] infused with "the pathos of novelty."[34] Indeed, some experience beginning as the trace of a gift hidden in our origins and housed in our memory, which promises everlasting newness when we pay attention and give thanks.[35] As Wendell Berry profoundly asks, "Who are we to say the world did not begin in love?"[36]

Whatever we make of them, then, beginnings are tremendously mysterious. They always elude our grasp for full comprehension and total control with deeper depths. As Thomas Mann narrated in 1933, our beginnings are ever accompanied by the words "'again' and 'farther,'" such that we ourselves are never truly (in) the beginning.[37] It was this infinite regress that provoked Hegel to interrogate, "The question with which we have to begin is: 'How are we to secure a beginning?'"[38]—perhaps in response to Kant's ponderous

29. Jack Balkin, *Living Originalism* (Cambridge, MA: Harvard University Press, 2011), 97.

30. See Willie Jenkins, *The Christian Imagination: Theology and the Origins of Race* (New Haven, CT: Yale University Press, 2011).

31. Revelation 21:5.

32. See Plato, *Theaetetus*, in *Plato: Complete Works*, ed. John Cooper (Indianapolis, IN: Hackett Publishing Company, 1997), 155d.

33. Arendt, "What Is Freedom?," 459.

34. Hannah Arendt, *On Revolution* (New York: Viking, 1969), 27.

35. See Augustine, *Confessions*, Book X.

36. Wendell Berry, "Some Further Words," in *New Collected Poems* (Berkeley, CA: Counterpoint, 2012), 360.

37. Thomas Mann, *Joseph and His Brothers*, trans. John E. Woods (New York: Knopf, 2005), 3.

38. G. W. F. Hegel, *Lectures on the Philosophy of Religion* [1827], one-volume edition, ed. Peter C. Hodgson (New York: Oxford University Press, 2006), 113. See also *Hegel's Science of Logic*, trans. A. V. Miller, ed. H. D. Lewis (Amherst, NY: Humanity Books, 1999), 67–78. To my knowledge, Plato, *Republic*, Book VII (533c), is the first to speak about "securing" (βεβαιώσηται) "the beginning" (τὴν ἀρχὴν) through "thinking" (διάνοια).

paradox, "The necessary being cannot begin to act, [but] the contingent being cannot act in a first beginning."[39] Meditation on the beginning uncovers the primal question, "Why is there something rather than nothing?," which exposes us to our radical contingency and givenness as creatures.[40] Thus, Arendt repeatedly returned to "the problem of beginnings—a problem because beginning's very nature is to carry in itself an element of complete arbitrariness" in which "there is nothing left for the 'beginner' to hold on to."[41]

Such vertiginous meditations led Bonhoeffer to claim that "the desire to ask after the beginning is the innermost passion of our thinking" because the beginning "is what in the end imparts reality to every genuine question we ask." The beginning is our "why." And yet, like a reef enveloped in an ocean of time and consciousness, our efforts to grasp the beginning "lose their strength in spray and foam."[42] We are after the beginning, in the middle between origin and end, begunners without autonomous knowledge or possession of either.

Thus, whether we probe the mysterious beginning of the world inaccessible to science or the foundations of reality or the philosophical coherence of the concept or our drive to initiate titanic turning points in history or the most ordinary exercises of our agency or radical hope for the future or our very births, falling in love, and the wondrous humility appropriate to them, there is always surplus and surprise in our beginnings, what Arendt called "a startling unexpectedness."[43] Plato insisted that "the whole risk of being human" and the "most important choice . . . in life and death" is found in how we choose to begin, such that he warned with great sobriety, "Let the one who begins

---

39. Immanuel Kant, *Reflexionen* 4219, quoted in Christopher Insole, *Kant and the Creation of Freedom* (New York: Oxford University Press, 2013), 105. Kant was a profound thinker of beginnings. See *The Critique of Pure Reason*, ed. and trans. Paul Guyer and Allen W. Wood (New York: Cambridge University Press, 2006), especially on the Third Antinomy, where Kant refers to "a faculty of absolutely beginning a state" (A445/B473), "an unconditioned causality that begins to act from itself" (A445/B473), and "an unconditioned original being" (A467/B495). Essential to the Christian notion of God's omnipotence is the paradox that God is able to make a voluntary new beginning, which endows finite creatures in God's image with the capacity for beginning, while transcending time, necessity, and randomness. Beginning is God's prerogative. See Søren Kierkegaard, *Journals and Papers*, Vol. 2 (Bloomington, IN: Indiana University Press, 1970), 2:1251 / Pap. VII A 181, and Amos Funkenstein, *Theology and the Scientific Imagination* (Princeton, NJ: Princeton University Press, 1986), 10–12.

40. See Martin Heidegger, "What Is Metaphysics?," in *Basic Writings*, ed. David Farrell Krell (New York: HarperCollins, 1993), 110, and Arendt, *The Life of the Mind*, 1:124. Lawrence Krauss's *A Universe from Nothing: Why There Is Something Rather than Nothing* (New York, NY: Free Press, 2012) is a scientifically fascinating and philosophically sophomoric attempt to answer this enduring question.

41. Arendt, *The Life of the Mind*, 2:207. Kant identified this before Arendt in his first *Critique*, A445/B473. See Biemann, *Inventing New Beginnings*, 23.

42. *Creation and Fall* (3:25).

43. Hannah Arendt, *The Human Condition*, second edition (Chicago: University of Chicago Press, 1998), 177.

not be careless about his choice."[44] Some have argued that beginning is fundamentally divine, the gift of God "In the beginning" and ever after, which is given and received anew in all of our beginnings that are beginnings of love.[45] Thus, Paul sang of Jesus with the early Christians, "He is the beginning" in whom "everything has become new!"[46]

To return to where I started, beginning is fundamental to the world and humanity. A strong case could be made that "beginner"—*homo inceptor*—is the most basic and inclusive description of who we are as creatures in our extraordinary universality and inexhaustible singularity. In one way or another, we are always beginning ever after we were nothing. As Arendt perceived so profoundly, "[Beginning] is indeed every man."[47] Indeed, in his last recorded words before his Nazi execution, Bonhoeffer testified that a new beginning lay hidden even in death itself: "This for me is the end, but also the beginning."[48]

This book is about the ethics of making new beginnings after devastation. I thank you for joining me in what was a challenging and beautiful new beginning in writing it—and now seeking to live after it.

---

44. Plato, *Republic*, Vol. 2, Loeb Classical Library, trans. Christopher Emlyn-Jones and William Preddy (Cambridge, MA: Harvard University Press, 2013), 618b, 619a–b.

45. Genesis 1:1; John 1:1. See Arnold Ehrhardt, *The Beginning: A Study in the Greek Philosophical Approach to the Concept of Creation from Anaximander to St. John* (Manchester: University of Manchester Press, 1968), and Kenneth Schmitz, *The Gift: Creation* (Milwaukee, MN: Marquette University Press, 1982).

46. Colossians 1:18 and 2 Corinthians 5:17. See Isaiah 41:4, 44:6, 48:12; Revelation 1:8, 17, 2:8, 21:6, 22:13. "Beginning" was a common title for Christ and a topic of reflection in early Christianity. See Peter C. Bouteneff, *Beginnings: Ancient Christian Readings of the Biblical Creation Narratives* (Grand Rapids, MI: Baker Academic, 2008), 69, 115, 171.

47. Arendt, *The Origins of Totalitarianism*, 616.

48. See the letter from S. Payne Best to George K. A. Bell on October 13, 1953 (16:468) and the appendix to this book for a brief study of how this final statement encapsulates Bonhoeffer's basic theological vision and ethics of new beginning.

Introduction

Our Overall Take on Human Life

The Problem of Morality and the Ethics of New Beginning

THE QUESTION AND ARGUMENT

Is it good to exist? Should life in the world with others be loved?[1] Should the conviction of goodness and the commitment to love serve as our fundamental orientation to reality? These are the questions at the core of this book. According to Charles Taylor,

> if you grasp our predicament without ideological distortion, and without blinders, then you see that going one way or another requires what is often called a "leap of faith." . . . What pushes us one way or the other is what we might describe as our over-all take on human life, and its cosmic and (if any) spiritual surroundings.[2]

I believe these questions penetrate to the heart of whether we should take normative ethics seriously and thus whether we should embrace a thick sense of moral responsibility for how we live as finite creatures in time, space, and language with others.[3] Conversely, these questions interrogate whether the moral life reduces down to mere preference, prudence, and power as Hobbes

---

1. "The other" or "others" will have an important place throughout this book. I intend this term to carry a triple valence: (1) the ordinary sense of "other people," (2) the more technical sense of singular persons who are not me/us or mine/ours (sometimes written "the Other"), and (3) "others" who are often ignored, stigmatized, excluded, oppressed, or annihilated. My thought has been deeply inspired by Emmanuel Levinas, though not without critique and alteration.

2. Charles Taylor, *A Secular Age* (Cambridge, MA: Belknap Press of Harvard University Press, 2007), 550.

3. On normative ethics, see William Schweiker, "On Religious Ethics," in *The Blackwell Companion to Religious Ethics*, ed. William Schweiker (Malden, MA: Blackwell, 2008), 6–7, and Wayne Boulton et al., "An Introduction to Christian Ethics," in *From Christ to the World: Introductory Readings in Christian Ethics*, ed. Wayne Boulton, Thomas Kennedy, and Allen Verhey (Grand Rapids, MI: Eerdmans, 1994), 2–3.

thought—the finite will as the origin and arbiter of value and order. As Taylor indicated, these questions ask about "our over-all take on human life, and its cosmic and (if any) spiritual surroundings."

In the pages that follow, I will test the answer to these questions with an experiment in moral science that I will call "universal entry." Universal entry would seem to devastate beyond hope the convictions that it is good to exist and that life in the world with others should be loved as our normative, overall take on human life. This exercise does so by exposing and centering in consciousness the injustices and horrors of the world in which we live and suffer and to which we contribute.

Thus, the problem of a new beginning for ethics and human life is introduced: *Can we begin again after devastating moral rupture?* Are we capable of and justified in making a new beginning that could redeem the goodness and love-worthiness of finite life with others in the world? Or does such bold initiative simply perpetuate the rupture from which we seek to recover? Or worse still, does such a "new beginning" expose us to the fact that all normative moral orientation is arbitrary and a matter of self-assertion and power and thus anarchic—without a grounding, guiding beginning from the fictitious "start," what Dietrich Bonhoeffer called "the murderous law of never-ending beginnings"?[4]

In response, I will argue that Dietrich Bonhoeffer's thought provides a coherent theological ethics of new beginning that enables us to affirm positive answers to these questions without ignoring universal entry's trial: *Yes, it is good to exist, and, yes, life in the world with all others should be loved, precisely as we practice universal entry as the scope of our moral consciousness and community in the world with and for others.* I will argue that Bonhoeffer's position revolves around his understanding of the beginning of ethics itself and God's initiation of a new beginning in the wake of our devastation, after which we may begin to follow imperfectly in this life and in which we may hope to begin again by faith in the next. (Part of the wager of universal entry and this book's argument is that we only truly learn to begin again when we learn to see, feel, and respond to the other's suffering. Thus, universal entry both problematizes morality and counterintuitively points the way to the ethics of new beginning.)

A tangential argument of this work is that the theme of beginnings and new beginnings leads us into the inner coherence and core of Bonhoeffer's thought, a claim I have not seen made in other Bonhoeffer scholarship. We will see that the real newness of this new beginning for Bonhoeffer is *the*

---

4. This is very close to what Arendt called "the problem of beginnings—a problem because beginning's very nature is to carry in itself an element of complete arbitrariness" in which "there is nothing left for the 'beginner' to hold on to." See *The Life of the Mind*, 2:2207.

gift and presence of the other person and thus the self's God-given liberation from its self-enclosure to begin again by welcoming, waiting on, and
responding to others in bonds of self-giving love and service. This is what
Bonhoeffer called "a new life in being there for others."

I will also argue, however, that Bonhoeffer's affirmative answer to my
opening questions comes at great cost and with great challenge. His theological ethics requires committing ourselves to a life of self-giving love and
service for others to the point of personal sacrifice, suffering, and death—
what he named "costly grace." That is, his ethics of new beginning requires a
responsible life of following after the new beginning founded by Christ, who
gives his life for others to the point of crucifixion. The new beginning and the
radical hope that Bonhoeffer's position makes available cannot be reduced to
mental assent, cheap consolation, and pernicious self-congratulation free of
personal commitment and sacrifice commenced and carried on by faith.

In the conclusion, I will directly address the crucial question of whether
the perceived absence of God in much contemporary thought and experience
destroys the plausibility of Bonhoeffer's position for people today, rendering
it powerless or of merely parochial interest. If God is not there—if God does
not begin—then Bonhoeffer's position is yet another false start and ultimately
falls apart. Here I will explore how Bonhoeffer interprets the death of God, as
well as the importance of faith and the risk of committing ourselves to God's
new beginning amid doubt, the call to self-giving love, and suffering.

I should note immediately that this book's argument is not that Bonhoeffer's position is true, although I believe that it is. I am content with arguing
that (1) Bonhoeffer's position enables us to affirm the goodness of existence
and the love-worthiness of life in the world with others in the face of universal entry, that (2) Bonhoeffer's position is more compelling than the other
thinkers with whom I will put him in conversation, and thus that (3) Bonhoeffer's description of a new beginning for ethics and human existence should
be taken seriously as a *vital option* for belief and practice amid our "midnight
within the moral order"[5] and "crisis of incoherence"[6] in which it is far from
obvious—perhaps desperately doubtful—that these founding principles of
morality and the moral life itself are real and worthy of our commitment.
Beyond that, like Kant, I am happy to leave room for faith because I am not
convinced that any of us can be argued into such fundamental commitments.

The basic datum that I will assume, but not argue, is that most nonpatho-
logical modern humans (I am tempted to say humans who live after Jesus and

---

5. King, *Strength to Love*, 55. David Gushee in *The Sacredness of Human Life: Why an Ancient
Biblical Vision Is Key to the World's Future* (Grand Rapids, MI: Eerdmans, 2013), 4, writes of "a
nauseating sense of insecurity and decay, both in our institutions and in their foundations."

6. Robert Bellah, *Religion in Human Evolution: From the Paleolithic to the Axial Age* (Cambridge,
MA: Harvard University Press, 2011), xix.

Paul and the universalizing moral revolution they initiated[7]) have a primitive intuition and yearning—perhaps even *need*—to affirm precisely this: that it is good to exist and that life in the world with others should be loved as our "over-all take on human life." Thus, if Bonhoeffer's position can make sense of and defend this intuition and a way of life that corresponds to it without collapsing into an anesthetizing consolation, it is, at the very least, worthy of serious interest, investigation, and perhaps—in the mystery of faith—converted conviction and practice.

Before turning to Bonhoeffer (chapters 3–5), after having discussed the moral gravity of this study and the trial of universal entry (chapter 1), I will set his position within the larger intellectual and historical horizon of four important moral philosophers: Friedrich Nietzsche, Hannah Arendt, Jonathan Glover, and Jonathan Lear (chapter 2). Their work significantly focuses on the question of making new beginnings for ethics in the wake of devastating moral ruptures, which is why I engage with these specific thinkers. I will argue that each of their positions is unable to plausibly redeem the principle that it is good to exist and that life with others in the world should be loved within a universal scope, and thus that they fail to provide us with the new beginning we need for ethics today.

This does not mean that their positions are obviously false; I think Nietzsche should be taken with particular seriousness. Life could simply be this tragic, this anarchic, this atrocious and unworthy of love, an endless struggle that Nietzsche pictured as "birds of prey . . . bearing off little lambs."[8] It does mean that *if* a position can be articulated that gives a coherent account of why these convictions can and should be affirmed as the source and foundation of our moral life, this position should be taken extremely seriously, both intellectually and practically.

To summarize, then, I understand this project as being situated within the broader Western liberal tradition, which is centrally constituted by the basic claims that individual persons are universally and equally valuable, that it is good to exist, and that life in the world with others should be loved and embraced with a deep sense of gratitude and moral responsibility as our overall take on life.[9] I interpret Dietrich Bonhoeffer's theological ethics of new beginning as making an important contribution to defending and extending this

---

7. See Siedentop, *Inventing the Individual,* especially part 2, "A Moral Revolution," and chapter 4, "The World Turned Upside Down: Paul." For a complimentary argument about universal human rights in the modern and contemporary context, see Samuel Moyn, *Christian Human Rights* (Philadelphia, PA: University of Pennsylvania Press, 2015).

8. Friedrich Nietzsche, *On the Genealogy of Morals,* ed. and trans. Walter Kaufmann (New York: Vintage, 1969), I, §13. See also III, §25.

9. Again, see Siedentop, *Inventing the Individual.*

moral tradition in the twenty-first century—"a strange and disturbing time in Western history"[10]—from within his Christian theological conviction.[11]

WHY BONHOEFFER?

In my reconstruction of Bonhoeffer's ethics of new beginning, I refer to some 220 different documents from his corpus, spanning diaries, letters, sermons, papers, lectures, articles, fragmentary notes, books, and other sources.[12] Before

---

10. Ibid., 362.

11. Already in 1928, Bonhoeffer wrote in his journal, "My theology is beginning to become humanistic; what does that mean? I wonder whether Barth ever lived abroad?" (10:64). Much later, in the midst of totalitarianism, Bonhoeffer argued in his *Ethics* (6:132) for an interpretation of Jesus as the "origin, essence, and goal" and "refuge" of the "higher values" of Western civilization, which he thought were now in danger of being destroyed. He summarized these values as "justice, truth, science, art, culture, humanity, freedom, and patriotism." See chapter 4 for further discussion. This is the textual foundation for what Charles Marsh calls "Bonhoeffer's abiding loyalty to the Western humanistic tradition and to the liberal ideals of toleration, justice, humanity, and reconciliation." See Charles Marsh, "Eric Metaxas's Bonhoeffer Delusions," October 18, 2016, www.religionandpolitics.org. See also John de Gruchy, *Confessions of a Christian Humanist* (Minneapolis, MN: Fortress Press, 2006), 27, in which this Bonhoeffer scholar locates Bonhoeffer within the tradition of Christian humanism. Even Bethge writes that Bonhoeffer in prison was preoccupied with "vehemently liberal questions." See *Dietrich Bonhoeffer: A Biography*, revised edition (Minneapolis, MN: Fortress Press, 2000), 889. At the memorial service for Bonhoeffer in London on July 27, 1945, Bishop Bell spoke of Bonhoeffer as a defender of "humanitarian and liberal ideals." See *Dietrich Bonhoeffer*, 931.

12. My task is not to situate Bonhoeffer in his biographical context or to trace the influences of his intellectual formation on our topic. I will assume a basic continuity in Bonhoeffer's fundamental thought, which I believe this thematic study demonstrates, while noting places where he modifies or changes his position where relevant (see chapter 4, note 153). The most comprehensive biography is Bethge, *Dietrich Bonhoeffer*. For a problematic but popular biography, see Eric Metaxas, *Bonhoeffer: Pastor, Martyr, Prophet, Spy: A Righteous Gentile vs. the Third Reich* (Nashville, TN: Thomas Nelson, 2010). The most recent biography is Charles Marsh, *Strange Glory: A Life of Dietrich Bonhoeffer* (New York: Knopf, 2014). Dianne Reynold's *The Doubled Life of Dietrich Bonhoeffer: Women, Sexuality, and Nazi Germany* (Eugene, OR: Cascade, 2016) focuses on Bonhoeffer's relationships with women, as well as his complex relationship with Eberhard Bethge. For various studies of Bonhoeffer's intellectual formation, see Peter Frick, ed., *Bonhoeffer's Intellectual Formation: Theology and Philosophy in His Thought* (Religion in Philosophy & Theology) (Tubingen: Mohr Siebeck, 2008). For interpretations of Bonhoeffer's early influences, see Michael P. DeJonge, *Bonhoeffer's Reception of Luther* (New York: Oxford University Press, 2017), Michael P. DeJonge, *Bonhoeffer's Theological Formation: Berlin, Barth, and Protestant Theology* (New York: Oxford University Press, 2012), Andreas Pangritz, *Karl Barth in the Theology of Dietrich Bonhoeffer*, trans. Barbara and Martin Rumscheidt (Grand Rapids, MI: Eerdmans, 2000), and Carl-Jürgen Kaltenborn, *Adolf von Harnack als Lehrer Dietrich Bonhoeffers* (Berlin: Evangelische Verlag Anst., 1973). For a study of Bonhoeffer's time in America and the influences of African American church and culture on his life and thought, see Reggie Williams, *Bonhoeffer's Black Jesus: Harlem Renaissance Theology and an Ethic of Resistance* (Waco, TX: Baylor University Press, 2014). For Bonhoeffer's later reception, see Matthew Kirkpatrick, ed., *Engaging Bonhoeffer: The Impact and Influence of Bonhoeffer's Life and Thought* (Minneapolis, MN: Fortress Press, 2016), and John de Gruchy, "The Reception of Bonhoeffer's Theology," in *The Cambridge Companion to Dietrich Bonhoeffer*, ed. John de Gruchy (New York: Cambridge University Press, 1999). For a helpful exploration of Bonhoeffer's immediate context in Germany, see John A. Moses, "Bonhoeffer's Germany: The Political Context" in the same volume.

turning to the larger discussion in chapter 1, a few more words are appropriate in response to the question, "Why Bonhoeffer?"

First, Bonhoeffer (1906–1945) lived through and passionately engaged one of the most horrific periods in human history: the First World War, the rise and rule of Nazism, the extermination of the Jews, and the devastation of World War II. Bonhoeffer himself was executed for treason as an enemy of the state by the Nazis in the Flossenbürg concentration camp on April 9, 1945. If we can expect sober realism that rejects world-denying escapism and naïve optimism from anyone, it is Bonhoeffer.

Nonetheless, second, throughout his life and writings, Bonhoeffer's thought exhibits profound courage and an enduring witness to fundamental hope that I believe remains illuminating, inspiring, and urgent for the twenty-first century. Bonhoeffer is a compelling witness to a way of life that is energized and oriented by the conviction that it is good to exist and that finite life in the world with others should be passionately loved without exclusion as our basic moral orientation to reality.[13] Bonhoeffer was not perfect and would have rejected any attempt to "canonize" him as a saint. But he stands out as an important exemplar for moral imagination and action today, what W. H. Auden called "a paradigm now of what a plausible Future might be."[14]

It is this simultaneity of sober realism and rebellious hope—of eyes wide open to human brutality and devastation, combined with penetrating vision into the promise of a divinely given new beginning that both exceeds human power and initiates human responsibility—that has drawn me to Bonhoeffer. I interpret Bonhoeffer's ethics of new beginning as a compelling response to Iris Murdoch's searching question, "How is one to connect the realism which must involve a clear-eyed contemplation of the misery and evil of the world with a sense of an uncorrupted good without the latter idea becoming the merest consolatory dream?"[15]

To give an initial glimpse into Bonhoeffer's critical yet hopeful sensibility and thought, I quote at length from a letter Bonhoeffer wrote to his friend Erwin Sutz about weddings in the midst of war:

> The chief characteristic of such occasions essentially rests in the fact that, in the face of these "last" times (I do not mean this to sound quite so apocalyptic), someone dares to take a step of such affirmation of the earth and its future. It was then always very clear to me that a person could take this step as a Christian truly only from within a very strong faith and on the basis of grace. For here in

---

13. See Bonhoeffer's lecture from November 19, 1932, "Thy Kingdom Come! The Prayer of the Church-Community for God's Kingdom on Earth" (12:285–97) and his letter to Bethge on May 20, 1944 (8:394).

14. W. H. Auden, "The Garrison," in *W.H. Auden: Collected Poems*, ed. Edward Mendelson (New York: Random House, 1976), 633–34.

15. Iris Murdoch, *The Sovereignty of Good* (New York: Routledge, 2001), 59.

the midst of the final destruction of all things, one desires to build; in the midst of a life lived from hour to hour and from day to day, one desires a future; in the midst of being driven out from the earth, one desires a bit of space; in the midst of widespread misery, one desires some happiness. And the overwhelming thing is that God says yes to this strange longing, that here God consents to our will.[16]

Finally, as I indicated earlier, reflection on new beginnings takes us into the core and inner coherence of Bonhoeffer's thought, but this theme remains virtually unexplored in Bonhoeffer scholarship. Indeed, while he repeatedly discussed the issue of beginnings (as we shall see), Bonhoeffer himself never produced a comprehensive analysis in a single place. Thus, I shall be doing for Bonhoeffer on beginnings and ethics something similar to what Bonhoeffer did in an early essay with regard to Karl Barth's interpretation of science: "Since Barth never has published any comprehensive treatment of our problem, we will have to use some single utterances of his and try to show the lines of connection with his whole thought, which sometimes Barth himself did not draw."[17] While the primary purpose of this study is not to interact with Bonhoeffer scholarship but Bonhoeffer himself and his arguments, I hope this study will make a constructive contribution to the ongoing interpretation and reception of his thought by showing the consistency, centrality, and power of his reflection on the ethics of new beginning and the fundamental gratitude, responsibility, and hope generated by this ethics for moral life today.

NOTES TO THE READER

Before turning to the body of this book, some brief notes to the reader may be helpful.

First, when reading an earlier draft of this manuscript, Charles Mathewes commented that my interpretation of Bonhoeffer is "new" in certain respects and sometimes divergent from other readings of his thought. Having carefully studied the entirety of Bonhoeffer's existing corpus, I have attempted to interpret Bonhoeffer's thought with rigor, thoroughness, and faithfulness. Whether my reading of Bonhoeffer is original and, if so, to what extent this is a virtue or vice, I leave to the judgment of scholars who have attempted to study Bonhoeffer's writings with the same care and comprehensiveness that I have.

---

16. Letter to Erwin Sutz on September 21, 1941 (16:220). For similar passages related to marriage and hope for the future, see letter to Gustav Seydel on June 23, 1942 (16:328); letter to Maria von Wedemeyer on January 17, 1943 (16:383); letter to Maria von Wedemeyer on August 9, 1943 (92:61–62); and wedding sermon for Renate and Eberhard Bethge on May 15, 1943 (8:82–84).

17. "The Theology of Crisis and Its Attitude to Philosophy and Science," written at Union Theological Seminary, 1930–1931 (10:463).

Second, I quote Bonhoeffer quite heavily throughout this book. This is both because I find Bonhoeffer's words so beautiful and because many of his writings may not be readily accessible to the reader within the large and expensive volumes of his complete works.[18]

Third, the chapters in this book are lengthy and demanding, especially chapter 5 on Bonhoeffer's practices of new beginning. Because that chapter attempts to present a coherent train of thought, I have decided not to break it up into shorter, separate chapters. This is perhaps unfortunate because I find that chapter most exciting for the overall purpose of this book: the practiced ethics of making new beginnings after—and perhaps still in the midst of or even heading into ("after")—devastation. Should this lengthiness become tiresome for a single reading, I encourage the reader to work through the major sections on Bonhoeffer's respective practices of new beginning one by one while keeping in mind the overarching argument of the chapter as a whole. The same can be applied to the other chapters.

Fourth, for readers who find themselves losing the forest for the trees as they make their way through the chapters that follow, I recommend skipping to the end of the book and reading "Beginning Anew" for clarification and perhaps fresh inspiration for making sense of the detailed arguments laid out in the body of the book.

Fifth, throughout this book, I intentionally make use of political-legal language in the context of theological, philosophical, and ethical discourse. I hope these overtones and their pregnant implications are kept in mind within my wider argument about the ethics of new beginning.

For example, in politics and law, a "foundation" is not an inert metaphysical entity or abstract idea but, originally, a novel act, an "initiative," "origination," "birth," or "fount," that is intended to ground and guide ongoing initiative and action that follows "after the beginning." Likewise, "precedents" are decisive events and judgments that come "after" or "out of" the foundation but "before" us now. As such, they give us guidance for interpreting and extending the founding "constitution" in a faithful way between the past and future, combining innovation with continuity.

Again, there are deep political-legal roots in our word "authority," which derives from the Latin *auctor* and profoundly combines senses of "founder/actor" and "author."[19] Most basically, "authority" is that grounding, guiding,

18. For accessible collections of his writings, see *The Bonhoeffer Reader*, ed. Clifford Green and Michael DeJonge (Minneapolis, MN: Fortress Press, 2013), *The Collected Sermons of Dietrich Bonhoeffer: Volume 1*, ed. Isabel Best (Minneapolis, MN: Fortress Press, 2012), and *The Collected Sermons of Dietrich Bonhoeffer: Volume 2*, ed. Victoria Barnett (Minneapolis, MN: Fortress Press, 2017).
19. See Hannah Arendt, "What Is Authority?," in *The Portable Hannah Arendt*, ed. Peter Baehr (New York: Penguin, 2000); Bonhoeffer, "The Führer and the Individual in the Younger Generation" from February 1933 (12:279); and Giorgio Agamben, "*Auctoritas* and *Potestas*," in *State of Exception*, trans. Kevin Attell (Chicago: University of Chicago Press, 2005).

energizing actor/act/action that provides the founding plot or storyline—the starting point and trajectory—for narrating whence we come, where we are heading, and thus who we are, what we should do, and who we should become "after" the beginning as we live into novel situations.

The authors who can most convincingly tell us *that* genesis story become our "authorities." And their stories "authorize"—for better or worse—various forms of identity, action, and moral order that we take to be recognizable, right, and worth following after now ("authoritative"), that is, whose beginning to accept as rightly founded and thus rightfully to be built on. Thus, "authority" differentiates whose narrative to continue writing with the authorship of our own lives and powers of beginning between past and future and whose narratives to discard as distraction, detour, and destruction.[20]

Likewise, in the political and legal context, "principle" does not mean a timeless, abstract proposition per se. As its Latin roots indicate (*princip-*), a principle is a "source" or "foundation" that is meant to launch and propel initiative and sustained action within a coherent but dynamic course or order. Machiavelli understood this well, and we can still hear this in our word "prince," which literally means the one who "takes (*capere*) first (*primus*)" or decides the beginning, like a captain (*caput*, "head") who "heads out" and "leads the charge" for the republic to follow. A principle, then, is a meaningful plot that shows us where to go and thus how to follow after as free citizens within a constitutional foundation.

Perhaps most significantly for this book, our word "rule" translates the Greek word *arché* (ἀρχή), which got translated into Latin as *princeps, principia*, etc. As Hannah Arendt never tired of pointing out, *arché* and *archein* ("to rule") originally meant "beginning" and "to begin." Thus, when translating Greek (political) philosophy, it is difficult to know when to translate *arché, archegon*, and *achein* as "rule," "ruler," and "to rule" and when to translate them as "beginning," "beginner," and "to begin."[21]

This actually makes a great deal of sense because the beginner is literally the one who decides—who "initiates" in the sense of *starts* but also *sanctifies* or *sanctions*—how we commence, where we are heading, and thus our trajectory and the game ("regime") we are playing ("ruling" or "being ruled by"). The beginner lays the foundation, sets the rules, decides precedents, and determines which principles are relevant in the order.

Here the beginner is not a "novice" in the sense of someone who is not serious or an "amateur." The beginner is the *ruler*, the one who initiates us

20. This indicates why it was impossible for the Romans to separate politics and religion. If "religion" is what ties us back (*religare*) to the founding origin, then religion is essential for politics because it tells us where we come from, who we are, and thus what we should do now. Politics becomes the work of building on the religious foundation.
21. I indicated this earlier in "Beginning," note 26.

and tells us how to measure whether we are on the right track as we exercise our freedom, just like the *auctor*. The beginner is the *prince*, and what follows after his or her beginning is the *principality*, the rule or domain of action that legitimately makes sense in light of where or how we started "in the beginning" (*en arché*).[22]

Thus, *arché* unsurprisingly shows up in some of our most important political vocabulary: monarchy (one-beginner/ruler), patriarchy (a father- or man-beginner/ruler), anarchy (no-beginner/ruler), etc. The one who is "arch-" is "in the beginning" and thus has the privileged position ("presidency" or "premiership") to decide how we *began* and thus how we (should) *begin* and thus whether and in what ways "we"—for example, "We the people"—have any real, coherent meaning at all or if, to the contrary, "we" are simply "anarchic," that is, *beginningless*: without "rule" and merely an inchoate mass of fragments. Thus, the beginner decides what counts as faithfulness and genuinely *new* (what *follows*) and what is simply deviant "novelty" and *old* (what is *fallen away, cut off,* and *dying*), perhaps often despite appearances.

These comments are not meant to be a clever word game or "language mysticism." To the contrary, they are intended to show the deep and profound importance and interdisciplinary relevance of "beginnings" and "new beginning" in our intellectual tradition and the practical world of action, politics, and law. When I discuss "the ethics of new beginning" earlier and in the chapters that follow, I hope these rich and fundamental resonances in our vocabulary—foundation, authority, principle, rule—are kept in mind not only for theological and ethical order but, as such, simultaneously for legal and political order as well.

When Bonhoeffer discusses and makes fundamental claims about "the beginning," who is privileged to begin, and thus how we should begin (or not begin) today, he is intentionally, if indirectly, tapping into this extremely elemental and consequential stream. In light of the pervasiveness of language about "newness," a "new Reich," "new realities," a "new epoch," and "new beginnings" in the rhetoric of Hitler, Nazi politics, and Nazified Christianity, we should recognize the radically important political-legal discourse to which Bonhoeffer was intentionally responding in his discussions of newness, beginnings, and the rule of Christ.[23] This becomes especially clear when we note that Bonhoeffer decided to lecture on Genesis 1–3 in Berlin during

---

22. The profound significance of the fact that Genesis and John begin with these words should not be overlooked or underestimated for what they are saying and attempting to do as founding, "constitutional" texts for theological-political communities.

23. For example, already on February 25, 1925, after his beer hall putsch and the banning of the Nazi party, Hitler published an editorial for *Völkischer Beobachter* titled "The New Beginning." See chapter 4, notes 33 and 34.

the fateful months before and after Hitler became chancellor of Germany in January 1933. He then wrote a long meditation on Psalm 119, largely focused on beginnings, during the time that Hitler declared "new realities" on behalf of the German Reich and initiated world war. Bonhoeffer's choices were not by accident.

In addition to Hannah Arendt, the thinker who has most influenced my thought on beginnings as a textual-hermeneutical and legal-political theory for faithful but new beginning is the American constitutional scholar Jack Balkin.[24] Balkin calls his position "living originalism" or "framework originalism," in which new initiatives—whether in law, politics, culture, and/or faith—must be rigorously *faithful* to the founding constitution ("originalism") while also, precisely in doing so, *growing* out of and *extending* beyond its initial scope to *redeem* and *perfect* its most originary principles ("living").

While I do not interact with Balkin's work in this book, I hope his framework of "living originalism" is kept in mind throughout as I discuss "the beginning," "following after," and "practices of new beginning" in Bonhoeffer's thought. Bonhoeffer was fiercely critical of "principles," which he understood as the human attempt to get "behind," control, and replace God "in the beginning." (This is isomorphic with his critiques of "religion" and "ethics."[25]) But it seems to me that Bonhoeffer's theological ethics follows a strikingly similar logic as the political-legal logic sketched earlier when it is understood that *God* alone is ultimately "in the beginning" and thus that *God* is the only rightfully sovereign beginner and ruler for us to "follow after," what Bonhoeffer calls *Nachfolge* ("following-after" or "discipleship") and *Nachdenke* ("thinking-after").

As we shall see, Bonhoeffer thinks that we are finite, fallen, and deeply fallible beginners who begin best—or only begin truly at all—when we follow after God's initiative, which is always newly for and with others in love. But Bonhoeffer never rejects our responsibility and fraught capacity to make beginnings, which would amount to what he condemned as "cheap grace." What we might call Bonhoeffer's *Christarchy* (he used the German *Christusherrschaft*[26]) or Christarchic ethics of new beginning points to the grave implications of the human attempt to possess our beginnings for ourselves and the fatal regime that follows from them, what Bonhoeffer named "the murderous law of never-ending beginnings." But it also points

---

24. See Jack Balkin, *Living Originalism*, and *Constitutional Redemption: Political Faith in an Unjust World* (Cambridge, MA: Harvard University Press, 2011). For several of the most relevant passages in Arendt's work on beginnings, see chapter 2, note 55.

25. See Dietrich Bonhoeffer, "Basic Questions of a Christian Ethic" from 1929, "There is no Christian ethic" (10:363).

26. *Ethics* (6:402).

to very empowering possibilities for our initiatives as beginners following after Christ with and for others.[27]

Sixth, I hope this book speaks to a broad audience that welcomes readers from beyond the Christian faith. (Patchen Markell, a nonreligious political scientist at the University of Chicago, commented that reading my book felt like visiting "an especially welcoming church.") But the question of audience becomes especially important in my attempt to answer my opening questions about the goodness of existence, the love-worthiness of life with others in the world, and thus our overall take on human life. What are the criteria for adequately answering—or at least responding to—these fundamental questions, and to whom will they be convincing?

Some of the criteria that are at work in my judgment, particularly the ability of an ethic to defend the value of all humans and to offer hope to all humans, as well as the wider creation, may appear inherently biased to my Christian convictions and thus automatically and unfairly invalidating of nontheological positions. In particular, I argue that the ethics of new beginning and thus adequate answers to my opening questions must speak not only to the living but also to the dead, to those who seem categorically beyond the limits of hope for a new beginning from within a nontheological point of view. I believe that a compelling, comprehensive ethics of new beginning must be able to speak to victims of violence and horrific evil—to people who have had their presence in the world and the gift of new beginnings unjustly annihilated, often by other humans claiming to make a "new beginning."

But I recognize that this conviction makes it tricky to put Bonhoeffer, a Christian pastor and theologian, in dialogue with nontheistic thinkers, who either reject the possibility of a God-given resurrection (Nietzsche) or remain silent about it and allow it to play no role in their respective ethics (Arendt, Glover, and Lear). As I will say again in the conclusion, what I ask is if an ethics that cannot offer an account of hope for the most terribly devastated people, now lost to our world, is also able to sustain a convincing account of the radical value of individuals and life itself *still in our world*. Is some account of a new beginning beyond the limits of this world necessary to defend a normative vision of moral reality within this world, especially a moral vision that defends and vindicates the dignity of all people, including the worst sufferers of our world?

In his *Works of Love*, Søren Kierkegaard wrote, "The true lover says: 'Hope all things; give up no man, for to give him up is to abandon your love for him—and if you do not give it up, then you hope. But if you abandon your

---

27. This makes sense of Bonhoeffer's statement in his unfinished drama from prison, in which his lead character says, "If the foundation crumbles, it's all over" but continues, "The foundation is deep and solid and good. You just have to build on it, not beside it, on the quicksand of so-called new ideas" (7:67–69). See the discussion of this passage in the conclusion to chapter 5.

love for him, then you yourself cease to be a lover.'"[28] If we give up hope for the most radically devastated, can we still claim to be lovers? And if we cannot be lovers of the most radically devastated (the doubly hopeless), can we still speak meaningfully of *ethics* in and for our world with others who suffer and experience horrific devastation without ceasing? As Jean Vanier writes, "If we are incapable of loving, what is left? There is nothing but despair, anguish, and the need to destroy."[29] This is the burden of universal entry.

What I will say for now is that I have attempted to interpret all of the nontheological authors in this book with care and seriousness, not as straw (wo)men to be opportunistically knocked down but as serious thinkers with whom to wrestle and learn. While I ultimately argue that their positions fail to offer an adequate ethics of new beginning, partially because of their inability to offer the hope of a new beginning for the most horrifically devastated and dead, I endeavor to present their positions with the honesty and critical engagement they deserve. As I have stated earlier, I also attempt to articulate and repeatedly emphasize how Bonhoeffer's ethics of new beginning and the radical hope it offers is not and cannot become a numbing consolation for the world-weary whose religious "hope" is ultimately an escape from reality and moral responsibility. As Bonhoeffer wrote from prison, "Only when one loves life and the earth so much that with it everything seems to be lost and at its end may one believe in the resurrection of the dead and a new world."[30]

Finally, if this book were longer, I would have liked to put Bonhoeffer's ethics in conversation with the evolutionary theory of "deep historians," "new atheists," and other thinkers like Daniel Lord Smail,[31] Frans de Waal,[32] Robert Bellah,[33] and Yuval Noah Harari.[34] Their work, which relies on the principle of natural selection and thus the fundamental role of violent predation in nature, poses a special challenge to my argument that it is good to exist and that life with others should be loved because they argue that competition and killing are original and indeed originary to animate reality from the beginning, well before humans come on the scene, and thus what Christians traditionally understand as "the Fall." If this is so, in what sense can Christians claim that

---

28. Søren Kierkegaard, *Works of Love*, trans. Howard and Edna Hong (New York: HarperPerennial, 2009), 239. See John Locke, *A Letter Concerning Toleration*, ed. James Tully (Indianapolis, IN: Hackett, 1983), 51: "The taking away of God, tho but even in thought, dissolves all."

29. Jean Vanier, *Community and Growth*, revised edition (Mahwah, NY: Paulist Press, 1989), 26.

30. Letter to Bethge on December 5, 1943 (8:213).

31. Daniel Lord Smail, *Deep History and the Brain* (Berkeley, CA: University of California Press, 2008), and *Deep History: The Architecture of Past and Present* (Berkley, CA: University of California Press, 2011).

32. Frans de Waal, *The Bonobo and the Atheist: In Search of Humanism among the Primates* (New York: W. W. Norton & Company, 2013).

33. Bellah, *Religion in Human Evolution*.

34. Yuval Noah Harari, *Sapiens: A Brief History of Humankind* (London: Vintage, 2011), and *Homo Deus*.

God is the good Creator and that God's creation and human life within it are worthy of love rather than a bloodstained field of struggle riven by Manichaean dualism that makes universal entry a moral nightmare? But alas, this book is long enough, and that remains work for another project.[35]

Now to the trial of universal entry.

35. See William Cavanaugh and James K. A. Smith, eds., *Evolution and the Fall* (Grand Rapids, MI: Eerdmans, 2017). This volume is worth reading but, in my opinion, ultimately fails to provide a compelling explanation for how God's goodness, predatory natural selection as the mechanism of evolution, and the origins of evil coherently relate.

Chapter One

The Trial

Universal Entry and the Problem of Morality

Does your heart break when their heart breaks?[1]

—David Gungor

DEVASTATION AND UNIVERSAL ENTRY

In his book *Human, All Too Human*, Friedrich Nietzsche argued,

> Every belief in the value and worth of life is based on impure thinking and is only possible because the individual's sympathy for life in general, and for the suffering of mankind, is very weakly developed. . . . Thus the value of life for ordinary, everyday man is based only on his taking himself to be more important than the world. . . . If he were able to grasp and feel mankind's overall consciousness in himself, he would collapse with a curse against existence.[2]

Is Nietzsche right? Is it necessary to be an impure thinker—one who does not "step out of himself" and thus "overlooks other men" in their suffering—to believe in the value of life? Does a pure mind—the mind that remembers and welcomes others in their suffering—lead to a despairing "curse against existence"?

These are vexing questions that interrogate whether serious, uncensored ethical reflection destroys itself and leads to devastating nihilism, the conviction that reality is morally vacuous, meaningless, and unworthy of love. As

---

1. The Brilliance, "Does Your Heart Break?" from the *Brother* album (2015). Used with written consent of the band.

2. Friedrich Nietzsche, *Human, All Too Human: A Book for Free Spirits*, trans. Marion Faber (Lincoln: University of Nebraska Press, 1986), 35.

Emmanuel Levinas wrote, "Everyone will readily agree that it is of the highest importance to know whether we are not duped by morality."[3] But is the examined life worth living?

This meditation on whether serious ethical reflection destroys itself has crystallized for me in a simple exercise, an experiment in moral science, which I have called *universal entry*.[4] In this exercise, I have interrogated whether my conviction about the goodness of existence and my capacity to love finite life with others in the world is perversely contingent on forgetting, deselecting, or denying the horrifying realities of other people's lives, suffering, and death.

Universal entry became for me a kind of Cartesian ethical meditation: "I realized that it was necessary, once in the course of my life, to demolish everything completely and start again right from the foundations, if I wanted to establish anything at all in the [moral] sciences that was stable and likely to last."[5] It was rooted in an enlarged practice of St. Augustine's prayer in his *Confessions*: "The house of my soul is too small for you to come to it. May it be enlarged by you."[6] And its basic sensibility was articulated by Kierkegaard, combined with James Baldwin:

> All the joy proclaimed in the world in which sorrow is not heard along with it is but sounding brass and a tinkling cymbal that tickle the ears but are repulsive to the soul. . . . This voice that trembles in pain and yet proclaims joy, this is heard by the ears of the troubled one.[7]

> There is a covenant of tears with God, and this covenant is not seen, is not heard, except by he who sees in secret and understands from afar, but it is a covenant in salvation with the God who will wipe away the tears. And there is a fellowship of sufferings with God, the secret of which is the assurance of an eternal salvation in the trustful understanding with God.[8]

---

3. Emmanuel Levinas, *Totality and Infinity*, trans. Alphonso Lingis (Pittsburgh, PA: Duquesne University Press, 1969), 21.

4. I began developing the idea of universal entry from experiences with the U.S. Embassy in Addis Ababa, Ethiopia. As all local applicants know, the U.S. Embassy only grants visas or "entry"—whether single or multiple—to people that it believes will enrich and strengthen, or at least not harm, the United States. The rest are denied entry and excluded. But what if our mind and moral consciousness were an embassy that granted *universal* entry to *all* applicants: to the poor, the sick, the oppressed, the suffering, the dying, even the dangerous? Would it still be any good to exist in such a universally welcoming govern-mentality or state of mind?

5. René Descartes, *Meditations on First Philosophy*, in *The Philosophical Writings of Descartes*, Vol. 2, trans. John Cottingham, Robert Stoothoff, and Dugald Murdoch (New York: Cambridge University Press, 1984), 12. This attempt to "start again right from the foundations" is not fully possible morally or hermeneutically, but Descartes's wider exercise and my adaptation of it can be useful.

6. Augustine, *Confessions*, Book I, v [6].

7. Søren Kierkegaard, *Eighteen Upbuilding Discourses*, ed. and trans. Howard V. Hong and Edna H. Hong (Princeton, NJ: Princeton University Press, 1990), 122.

8. Kierkegaard, *Eighteen Upbuilding Discourses*, 264. A song that communicates the internal struggle of universal entry is Sade's "King of Sorrow" from her album *Lovers Rock* (Epic, 2000): "I'm crying everyone's tears / And there inside our private war / I died the night before / All of these

But what was the point, the purpose, of *my* salvation if it did not permit me to behave with love toward others, no matter how they behaved toward me?[9]

The exercise of universal entry, which I rigorously practiced during the year when this book was conceived, went as follows. When I woke up in the morning in the safety of my bedroom, I called to mind people who start their day in the sleepless exhaustion of terror. When I put on my clothes, I called to mind people who have no clothes or only smelly, embarrassing rags. When I brushed my teeth, I called to mind people who have no running water and whose teeth throb with infections. When I ate my breakfast, I called to mind people who are malnourished, in excruciating pain from hunger, or numb from starvation. When I studied and wrote, I called to mind people who are in prison or have been killed for speaking openly on behalf of freedom and justice at the hands of oppressive regimes while their families languished without them. When I appreciated the beautiful snow fluttering down outside my window, I called to mind the homeless for whom snowflakes are a dreaded reminder of danger, frostbite, or death. When I spent time with my wife, I called to mind husbands whose wives have been raped and/or murdered in violent conflicts.

This experiment was grueling and exhausting. I constantly allowed my mind to be crowded with strangers, to say to sufferers, "I have you in my heart."[10] I found that goodness became a "demented icon," a subtle but searing sign of the evil in the world. All causes for joy simultaneously became reminders of sorrow, reflections of devastation: sleep, exhaustion; health, sickness; clothes, nakedness; friends, oppressors; food, hunger; safety, danger; success, catastrophe; sex, rape; memory, horror; hope, fear; presence, absence; life, death; love, hatred.

From the start, I attempted to be crystal clear about some crucial elements of this "experiment in moral science." First, this exercise of calling to mind others in their sufferings was not hypothetical, merely simulating fictional scenarios that do not exist in reality. To the contrary, the various examples mentioned earlier and countless others are real experiences for millions of real people around our planet each day, to say nothing of the dead. Thus, second, this moral exercise was not masochistic. It was not some self-deceptive infliction of torment by ratiocination—a masturbatory "mind game"—through which I derived some perverse pleasure. To the contrary,

remnants of joy and disaster / What am I supposed to do? . . . There's nothing anyone / Can say to take this away / It's just another day and nothing's any good / I wonder if this grief will ever let me go / I am the king of sorrows." When we open ourselves to others' pain, must we conclude, "It's just another day and nothing's any good"?

9. Baldwin, *The Fire Next Time*, in *Baldwin*, 310.
10. See Philippians 1:7.

this experiment was an anguishing attempt to welcome and wrestle with the realities of real people's lives and their implications for our most fundamental moral questions. Hence I gave this exercise the name "universal entry," signifying the willingness to grant all strangers and sufferers "visas" into the state of my mind without exception or exclusion, even to the point of consciousness becoming an asylum of sufferers, a mourning tent, a burial ground for the dead and dying.[11]

If we are willing to undergo the trial of universal entry and live with this radically enlarged moral consciousness opened to others in their devastation, is life in our world still any good and worthy of love? Or is our love contingent on our capacity to deny, deselect, and screen out the painful and sometimes horrific realities of other people's lives? And thus, is our moral conviction and energy sustainable only through a concealed inhumanity, an act of explicitly or inexplicitly judging that the devastation of other people's lives does not matter to us—or perhaps matter at all? This is what Nietzsche called the "impure thinker" who can believe in the value of life only because he "takes himself to be more important than the world." Otherwise, "he would collapse with a curse against existence."

These questions raise the question of whether our sense of moral order—of goodness, love, and ethical universality—is founded on a perversity: the affirmation of the goodness of life and love for the world based on the forgetfulness or denial of other persons in their devastation. Such a "morality" is perhaps the grossest privilege and injustice.

As we know, foundations so often are perverse throughout the world's politics, religion, and culture.[12] In our account of ethics' beginning and normative claim, when we dig to the bottom, are there destruction layers of buried devastation and death that scream against what we fabricate on them—sophistries of "goodness" and "love" and "moral equality"? As Nietzsche sneered, "how much blood and cruelty lie at the bottom of all 'good things'!"[13]

---

11. See Susan Sontag, *Regarding the Pain of Others* (New York: Picador, 2003), 115.

12. For examples across civilizations, see Robin W. Lovin and Frank E. Reynolds, eds., *Cosmogony and Ethical Order* (Chicago: University of Chicago Press, 1985). See also *Enuma Elish* in *The Babylonian Genesis*, ed. Alexander Heidel (Chicago: University of Chicago Press, 1963), 40–41, in which the earth and sky are made out of the corpse of a murdered god, and Hesiod, *Theogony, Works and Days. Testimonia* (Cambridge, MA: Loeb Classical Library, 2007). Note William Schweiker, "A Preface to Ethics: Global Dynamics and the Integrity of Life," *Journal of Religious Ethics* 32, no. 1 (2004): 13–37, 14: "[In Aristophanes's myth,] the world is born in violence and warfare." In the historical-political sphere, see Arendt, *On Revolution*: "The conviction, In the beginning was a crime . . . has carried through the centuries no less self-evident plausibility for the state of human affairs than the first sentence of St. John, 'In the beginning was the Word,' has possessed for the affairs of salvation" (pp. 10–11). See Jean Bodin, *On Sovereignty*, trans. Julian Franklin (New York: Cambridge University Press, 2008): "Reason and common sense alike point to the conclusion that the origin and foundation of commonwealths was in force and violence" (I.4, 238).

13. See Nietzsche, *On the Genealogy of Morals*, II, §3. Note Smail, *Deep History and the Brain*, 193: "One thing is for sure: *Homo* is a determined colonizer." Kevin Bales, *Disposable People: New*

STORIES OF DEVASTATION AND
THE CHALLENGE OF UNIVERSAL ENTRY

As I worked on this book, numerous stories from around the world concretized and intensified my demanding trial of universal entry. Often on a daily basis, I read about and saw pictures of the Syrian civil war, which is estimated to have killed some five hundred thousand people, mostly civilians, and made refugees of over ten million others, contributing to the most severe global refugee crisis since World War II.

I read about the horrific violence in the Central African Republic, driven by the struggle of Muslim and Christian militias to exterminate the other and control the country. I remember reading about a mother from C.A.R. who gave birth to a girl soon before her village was overtaken by militiamen intent on killing everyone. The woman had no choice but to take her newborn and flee through the jungle. But the baby got sick and died on their journey, and again this woman had nothing but a devastating choice: she had to dig a hole, bury her daughter, and leave her behind. And thus this precious newborn life was reduced to a terror-stricken memory in her mother's mind—a mother whose emotions, moral consciousness, and devastated grief are just as real and important as our own.

I followed the civil war that has unleashed so much devastation and death in South Sudan only a few years after its hopeful new beginning in 2011. An image after the massacre in Bentiu was especially horrifying and revelatory: a photograph of an industrial tractor scooping bloated or flattened bodies off the dirt road like a trash cleanup. In Bentiu and too many other places in South Sudan, life had been reduced to trash, and lifeless machines were being used to remove the human waste. This was only one horrific image among so many others of corpses dumped in piles of garbage, being eaten by birds, lying lifeless in churches and schools where they had been slaughtered, while the leaders of the opposing sides supposedly sought "peace" within the safety and luxury of the Sheraton Hotel in neighboring Addis Ababa.

The world has followed the rise of the so-called Islamic State in Syria and Iraq with terrorist activities now stretching to Libya, Yemen, Paris, and beyond. So many lives have been brutally murdered by ISIS, whether

---

Slavery in the Global Economy (Berkley, CA: University of California Press, 1999), 197: "What we often call the beginnings of human history are also the beginnings of bondage." Darrel Falk, "Human Origins: The Scientific Story," in *Evolution and the Fall*, ed. William Cavanaugh and James K. A. Smith (Grand Rapids, MI: Eerdmans, 2017), 7: "We have a long history of causing extinctions of other species. . . . This pattern of destruction . . . likely began tens of millennia ago as we conquered new land already occupied by our cousin species, the Neanderthals." Two other texts that have contributed to my thought are Sam Keene, *Faces of the Enemy: Reflections of the Hostile Imagination* (New York: Harper & Row, 1991), and D. L. Smith, *Less than Human: Why We Demean, Enslave, and Kill* (New York: St. Martin's Press, 2011).

through video-recorded beheadings, shootings into mass graves, or bombings in public areas. So many more have been made into powerless refugees with nothing left but misery, leading to the refugee crisis confronting Europe and the world mentioned earlier.

I followed the stories from Nigeria of ISIS-affiliated Boko Haram's kidnapping of hundreds of schoolgirls, massacring and scorching towns of people, and spreading general terror. I followed the Ebola crisis in Liberia, Sierra Leone, and Guinea, which infected over twenty-five thousand people and killed over ten thousand others—horrific enough on its own but also symbolic of collateral horrors, especially for children and the poor. On the opposite side of the continent, I followed the activities of al-Shabaab in Somalia, including the Westgate shopping center attack, which left sixty-eight people dead, and the invasion of a Kenyan university, which killed 147 Christians. Of course, al-Shabaab engages in assassination attempts, bombings, and other killings on a daily basis that are often not reported in Western media. Its most recent truck bombing left over five hundred civilians dead in Mogadishu.

More intimately, I followed developments in Ethiopia. In many ways, Ethiopia tells a story of hope after it was seared on the global conscience with the 1984 famine and its images of skin-and-bones starving children. For example, some of the Millennium Development Goals have been met, maternal and infant mortality have been drastically reduced, and Ethiopia now boasts one of the fastest growing economies in the world. Still, Ethiopia has again found itself in need of emergency food aid for almost ten million people amid the worst drought since 1984. Civil war has been avoided since the revolution in 1991, but the war with Eritrea in 1998 claimed over seventy thousand lives and Ethiopia has recently passed through a state of emergency in response to civil conflict in which hundreds were killed by security forces and over twenty-five thousand were imprisoned. Amid the new roads, glassy buildings, and boasts of booming growth, tens of millions of Ethiopia's one hundred million people still live on around $1.50 a day in miserable conditions.

Of course, it should be emphasized that many of these people stand as powerful witnesses of human dignity, resilience, and contentment even in the midst of extreme poverty and terrible suffering. But these people's lives and their sometimes smiling faces should not be romanticized. Often behind the cheerful surface there are stories of trauma, devastating loss, chronic pain, and explicit and implicit forms of abuse, oppression, and torture. For example, according to Gary Haugen of the International Justice Mission, "59 percent of women report being victimized by sexual violence, and . . . 68.5 percent of Ethiopian *girls* said they had been sexually abused."[14] These

---

14. Haugen and Victor Boutros, *The Locust Effect: Why the End of Poverty Requires the End of Violence* (New York: Oxford University Press, 2014), 53. See also Darsema Sori's gripping "Letter

struggles are strikingly captured in the title of Abbe Gubegna's 1963 Amharic novel *I Refuse to Be Born* (*Allewweledem*), a protest against birth itself in the face of extreme poverty, political oppression, and existential misery, as well as the name of the infamous neighborhood in Addis Ababa hauntingly called Errie Bekentu—A Cry for Help in Vain.[15]

This is to say nothing of the horrific memories of the Derg's "Red Terror," which massacred some five hundred thousand people and continues to haunt human life in Ethiopia. Streets and secret rooms contain around one million people with severe mental illness in a country with only one psychiatric hospital with some 150 beds.[16] In the capital city alone, the streets are inhabited by maimed and wounded elders, an increasing number of young women who survive through prostitution, and tens of thousands of children.[17]

I met one of these "street kids" soon before beginning my PhD at the University of Chicago, a thirteen year old named Eyob (Job). Eyob had been sent by his parents to the city from the countryside of Hadya to wander the streets and find a miracle or die. As a child, Eyob fell into an open cooking fire, and his head was terribly burned. Having no access to adequate medical care or financial means, Eyob's wound was never properly treated, got infected, and continued to expand throughout his childhood. The stench from Eyob's wound became so putrid that his family removed him from school, where Eyob had excelled, in order to shelter the family from shame: Eyob was seen as a sign of God's curse on them and thus had to be hidden from public visibility. Thus, Eyob was essentially reduced to invisible suffering in his parents' dwelling until they eventually put him on a pickup truck headed for the city and said goodbye.

On the afternoon of May 1, 2010, Eyob and I ended up somehow on the same street at the same time in Addis. After Eyob approached me to ask for money and I said no, he turned around to walk away, his hood slipped off, and I could see the terrible wound on the back of his head. After a moment of inner struggle, I ran after him, and I could not believe my eyes. Eyob's skull was so eaten away by cancer that I could see his brain pulsing through the oozing wound that was the back of his head. I have never seen a wound so

from Qilinto Prison," January 17, 2017, published online by *Addis Standard* at http://addisstandard.com/letter-qilinto-prison-will-not-falter-journalist-darsema-sori/.

15. See Yohannes Edemariam, "From an Ancient Cloud: Getting by in Ethiopia's Slums," *Harper's Magazine*, May 2007, 67–75.

16. Interviews with Dr. Maji Hailemariam, a postdoctoral fellow at Michigan State University.

17. See Sehin Teferra, "Agency and Sisterhood: A Feminist Analysis of Ethiopian Sex Workers' Experience of, and Resistance to, Violence" (Unpublished doctoral dissertation, SOAS, University of London, 2015), and Indrias Getachew, "Ethiopia: Steady Increase of Street Children Orphaned by AIDS" (UNICEF, January 2006). Note Lamentations 2:11: "My eyes fail from weeping, and I am in torment within . . . because children and infants faint in the streets of the city."

horrifying. It was literally eating away the life and dignity of this young man as he wandered the streets alone.

Over the next few months, my friends and I fought for Eyob's life, and I was privileged to get to know him well. I was deeply impressed by Eyob's intelligence and knowledge, his kindness and humor, his sense of God's love and the goodness of being alive. At the end of the fifth day that we waited at the Korean Hospital in vain for him to be seen by a doctor, he asked to use my phone and texted his brother, "God is love." He was always thinking of others and trying to help the people around him, especially other children in the burn ward once he was finally admitted. I discovered Eyob to be a powerful agent and witness of self-transcendent faith, hope, and love, not a powerless victim or object of pity. His dream was to become a pastor and professor and thus to share his story of suffering and healing with others for a more hopeful and just society.

But after securing the advanced medical procedures that Eyob so desperately needed and hearing the doctor's ecstasy-inducing promise of "Eyob can now live a normal life," Eyob's cancer returned, we sent him back to Hadya to spend his final days with his family, and he died in January 2011 at the age of fourteen.

Descriptively, Eyob's entire life from his earliest memories to his last days was dominated by excruciating pain and physical degradation; by social stigma, shame, and isolation; and then by the abandonment of his parents to wander alone in a big city begging for help from total strangers. I know there are many more Eyobs in Ethiopia and around the world today. Eyob was one, but he was one of many Jobs.[18] He is the one who most profoundly opened my mind to universal entry, my saint of darkness to whom this book is dedicated.

Closer to home, as I studied at the University of Chicago and worked on this book, I have intentionally walked some of the streets where almost eight hundred people were murdered in 2016. These stats are not merely horrific stories of just one person killing another but of families and communities ripped to pieces by histories of racism, poverty, hopelessness, and violence imbedded in American society, which plots the narratives of over 260,000 black men who have been killed in the United States since 1980.[19] So much could be said about this history and its continuing devastation in America.[20]

---

18. See Malala Yousafzai's Nobel Peace Prize lecture for 2014: "Though I appear as one girl . . . I'm not a lone voice . . . I'm many. I am Malala. But I'm also Shantia . . . I'm those 66 million girls who are deprived of education. And today I'm not raising my voice. It's the voice of those 66 million girls." Accessible online at www.nobelprize.org/nobel_prizes/peace/laureates/2014/yousafzai-lecture.html.

19. Jeffrey Goldberg, "A Matter of Black Lives," *The Atlantic*, September 2015.

20. See Howard Zin, *A People's History of the United States* (New York: Harper, 2005), and Michelle Alexander, *The New Jim Crow: Mass Incarceration in the Age of Colorblindness* (New York: New Press, 2012).

In the wake of this infinitesimal exercise in universal entry, I interrogate again: *Is it good to exist? Should life in the world with others be loved? Or are we duping ourselves with morality?* Is our sense of the goodness and love-worthiness of finite life with others predicated on editing out or forgetting the horrors that afflict and destroy the lives of real people every day— Nietzsche's "impure thinking" that "overlooks other men" in their suffering? When we dig beneath the surface, is our moral life perversely founded on excluding or selective concern for others' lives, sufferings, and horrors, without which we would "collapse with a curse against existence"?

When I practice universal entry in my moral consciousness, it is not only explicitly evil things that are devastating. It is also the explicitly good things— meals, fellowship with others, meaningful work, sex, play, and worship—that become demented icons shimmering with the suffering, catastrophe, and death of others. Do we suffer their presence? Or is our moral consciousness and community itself just another zone of selectivity, censorship, and exclusion because the sustainability of our morality is dependent on this, lest it crumble into dust and blow away in the winds of grief and nothingness? As St. Augustine wrote but here within a different perspective,

> So my life was to me a horror. . . . There was no rest in pleasant groves, nor in games or songs, nor in sweet-scented places, nor in exquisite feasts, nor in the pleasures of the bedroom and bed, nor, finally, in books and poetry. Everything was an object of horror, even light itself; all that . . . made me feel sick and repulsive. . . . I had become to myself a place of unhappiness in which I could not bear to be.[21]

It is from within the moral meditation of universal entry that we can revoice Albert Camus's penetrating claim in *The Myth of Sisyphus*: "There is but one truly serious philosophical problem, and that is suicide. Judging whether life is or is not worth living amounts to answering the fundamental question of philosophy."[22] In this context, the question of suicide is not raised primarily because of our own inability to discern or construct any meaning in our own lives or the universe, which could still betray narcissistic discontents.[23] To the contrary, here the question of suicide is raised by the suffering and devastation *of the other persons* and our inability to live with (1) a morality that is

---

21. Augustine, *Confessions*, IV, vii (12).

22. Albert Camus, *The Myth of Sisyphus*, trans. Justin O'Brien (New York: Vintage, 1991), 3. Note the central character's dramatic statement in Søren Kierkegaard, *Repetition*, trans. Walter Lowrie (Princeton, NJ: Princeton University Press, 1946), 114: "My life has been brought to an *impasse*. I loathe existence. . . . Is there no director? Whither shall I turn with my complaint?"

23. For a soft example of this, see the suicide note of Stephan Zweig, accessible online at http://booksproseandverse.blogspot.com/2013/11/stefan-zweig-suicide-note.html: "But after one's sixtieth year unusual powers are needed in order to make another wholly new beginning. Those that I possess have been exhausted by long years of homeless wandering."

sustainable only by selectively screening out others or (2) a moral consciousness that has become a crazed asylum of sufferers out of love for the world in which even goodness is a reminder of evil.

Whatever we may conclude about suicide itself vis-à-vis Camus, suicide as a response to moral devastation indicates the seriousness and intensity of the problem of morality. As I write these words and you read them, people are being violently murdered, raped and left for dead, displaced, and are languishing in poverty, inhabiting sewers, groaning in hunger, selling themselves to survive, committing suicide, and calling an end to life. These are realities for real people, not sadistic simulations.

On what basis, then, are our repeated claims and legislated norms about "human dignity" and "human rights" justified or remotely redeemable? Is it not the case that universal morality is secretly self-destructive, whether this leads to an act of suicide, the active embrace of nihilism, or the more implicit responses of boredom, therapeutic spirituality, the radicalization of sex and violence in entertainment and society, religious fundamentalism, racism, and the ubiquity of consumerism, leading to Pope Francis's claim that "the post-industrial period may well be remembered as one of the most irresponsible in history"?[24]

These reflections have focused primarily on recent world events and personal narratives in the Middle East and Africa. But as I have already indicated, this question of whether serious moral reflection destroys itself and leads to despair—what Nietzsche called "the problem of morality"—is also deeply rooted in Western civilization and came to a head in the wake of the horrific events of the twentieth century.[25] These events, especially the German Holocaust,[26] left Western thinkers reeling with the question of whether morality itself had simply imploded and forced us to face the purely fabricated nature of human "morality" as mere *mores*, empty conventions "constructed" on cultural preferences that can be made, unmade, and remade in all sorts of ways.[27] Are our fundamental moral convictions all arbitrary, all mere preference, prudence, and power, all anarchic—without any beginning to ground, guide, and energize us as we seek new beginnings today?

---

24. Pope Francis, *Laudato Si: On Care for Our Common Home* (Washington, DC: United States Conference of Catholic Bishops, 2015), §165. See Zygmunt Bauman, *Does Ethics Have a Chance in a World of Consumers?* (Cambridge, MA: Harvard University Press, 2009).

25. See Jonathan Glover, *Humanity: A Moral History of the Twentieth Century*, second Edition (New Haven, CT: Yale University Press, 2012), and chapter 2 for a discussion of Glover.

26. See Jürgen Moltmann, "European Political Theology," in *The Cambridge Companion to Political Theology*, eds. Craig Hovey and Elizabeth Philips (New York: Cambridge University Press, 2015), 3–22, who sees Auschwitz as the starting point for serious moral reflection.

27. For Nietzsche's concept of "the morality of mores," see *On the Genealogy of Morals*, preface, §4 and III, §9.

THE QUESTION OF THE
ETHICS OF NEW BEGINNING

In all of these contexts, the same urgent questions present themselves, questions at the heart of this book: How should we understand our moral condition as finite beginners? Are we qualified to make a new beginning for ourselves? If not, what are the sources of hope for a new beginning that can sustain our ethical vision and responsibility? Is there another new beginning that can justify and energize the foundational beliefs that it is good to exist, that life in the world with others should be loved, and thus that we should commit ourselves to others to the point of universal entry? Or are we left with Nietzsche's curse against existence and the nihilistic options of the impure thinker: indifference and self-preservation, boredom and consumeristic hedonism, or at best perhaps a sense of hopeless tragedy combined with a groundless commitment to serving "human rights" and the world's "progress"? What is the ethics of new beginning after devastating moral rupture?

As Socrates warned over two millennia ago, "Let the one who begins not be careless about his choice," for "this is the most important choice for him in life and death." Indeed, this beginning choice about how to begin is "the whole risk for a human being."[28] In chapter 2, I turn to explore four philosophical options for making a new beginning in response to the problem of morality.

---

28. Plato, *Republic*, Vol. 2, 618b, 619a–b.

Chapter Two

Four Options

The Problem of Morality and the Ethics of New Beginning in Nietzsche, Arendt, Glover, and Lear

> To see and to demonstrate the problem of morality—that seems to me the new principal task. I deny that it has been done in previous moral philosophy.[1]
>
> —Nietzsche

Moral philosophers have wrestled with the questions outlined in the previous chapter with particular focus and urgency in the modern West and beyond. Robert Pippin named "the historical problem of modernity" the question of "whether an origination, or new self-grounding in history is possible."[2] Similarly, Michael North describes modernity as "the time in which anomaly becomes the norm and revolution, therefore, a constant condition."[3] Asher Biemann adds, "To be sure, being in the midst of a difficult flux, without beginnings and without shelter . . . has become a familiar motif of our times."[4] Thus, William Schweiker has called "the work of reconstruction . . . the central business of contemporary moral theorists."[5]

It is within this search for new "grounding" and "reconstruction" in a time of "constant revolution" and "a difficult flux" that I turn now to survey some

---

1. Friedrich Nietzsche, *The Will to Power*, trans. and ed. Walter Kaufmann and R. J. Hollingdale (New York: Vintage, 1968), II, §263. Henceforth cited as WTP. Nietzsche wrote similarly in *Beyond Good and Evil*, ed. Rolf-Peter Horstmann and Judy Norman, trans. Judith Norman (New York: Cambridge University Press, 2005), "Isn't a moralist the opposite of a Puritan? A thinker, that is, who treats morality as something questionable, question-mark-able, in short, as a problem? Shouldn't moralists be—immoral?" (§228). Henceforth cited as BGE.

2. Robert Pippin, *Modernism as a Philosophical Problem: On the Dissatisfactions of European High Culture* (Malden, MA: Wiley-Blackwell, 1999), 3.

3. North, *Novelty*, 48, 182.

4. Biemann, *Inventing New Beginnings*, 23.

5. William Schweiker, "Loose Morals: The Barbaric 20th Century," *The Christian Century* 120, no. 10 (May 17, 2003): 36–38.

13

significant thinkers who directly addressed our problem of devastating moral rupture and the ethics of new beginning. What are their options, and can they offer a compelling solution?

Two points are worth noting from the outset. First, I read Arendt, Glover, and Lear's positions as quite similar to Nietzsche's (primarily rooted in the human will) and ultimately unable to overcome his "question-marking" of morality, especially when the trial of universal entry is kept in mind. Nevertheless, second, I see their respective positions as sufficiently distinct, as well as their analyses of the relevant ruptures compounding, to warrant exploring each of them in turn.

Thus, I ask afresh: What are the options for an ethics of new beginning after devastating moral rupture?

FOUR OPTIONS

Nietzsche: The Advent of Nihilism, the New Philosopher, and the Will to Power

As a radical moralist, Friedrich Nietzsche "question-marked" morality and interrogated, "Shouldn't moralists be—immoral?"[6] And like a paradoxical prophet, Nietzsche declared that Western morality's foundation had fallen apart and collapsed. According to James Davidson Hunter, Nietzsche was "the first to understand radical skepticism of this kind and its portentous implications for the Western world. Ever since Nietzsche, intellectuals have been grappling with the meaning of this rupture."[7] David Gushee echoes Hunter, calling Nietzsche "the first, and most influential, to explicitly abandon the whole legacy" of Christian theology and its "sacredness-of-life ethic."[8]

For Nietzsche, Western morality had been destroyed by nihilism, the condition in which the highest moral values contradict one another and thus lead to "the radical repudiation of value, meaning, desirability." Nietzsche calls nihilism the condition in which "'why?' finds no answer."[9] With his penetrating "evil eye,"[10] Nietzsche believes the "value" of—*the will to*—"truth" had

---

6. BGE, §228.

7. James Davidson Hunter, *To Change the World: The Irony, Tragedy, & Possibility of Christianity in the Late Modern World* (New York: Oxford University Press, 2010), 207. Polemarchus, Machiavelli, Hobbes, and others are important precursors.

8. Gushee, *The Sacredness of Human Life*, 5.

9. WTP, I, §1. In WTP, §§22–23, Nietzsche differentiates between passive nihilism ("decline and recession of the power of the spirit") and active nihilism ("a violent force of destruction"). For a wider historical perspective, see Michael Gillespie, *Nihilism before Nietzsche* (Chicago: University of Chicago Press, 1996).

10. Friedrich Nietzsche, *Twilight of the Idols*, trans. Thomas Common (Mineola, NY: Dover, 2004), Preface. Henceforth cited as TI.

unmasked the facts that (1) "God is dead";[11] (2) the idea of absolute "goodness" is a historical fiction used by the weak, resentful mass to manipulate the strong (the core argument of *Beyond Good and Evil: Prelude to a Philosophy of the Future*[12]); and (3) the real "genealogy of morals" is found in the most basic but disguised and suppressed drive in all reality: the will to power (the core argument of *The Genealogy of Morals*). Bitterly and hilariously, it was the will to truth—what Christianity had held aloft and even divinized—that had destroyed God and goodness as the basis of Christian civilization.[13] Morality secretly destroyed itself.

This was the context in which Nietzsche augured a coming catastrophe for European culture and morality. As he wrote in the manuscripts that were gathered into *The Will to Power*,

> What I relate is the history of the next two centuries. I describe what is coming, what can no longer come differently: *the advent of nihilism*. This history can be related even now; for necessity itself is at work here. . . . *For some time now, our whole European culture has been moving as toward a catastrophe*: restlessly, violently, headlong, like a river that wants to reach the end, that no longer reflects, that is afraid to reflect.[14]

For Nietzsche, we are like animals in the forest: we can feel the storm coming on, but we are too terrified "to reflect," sensing in our bones that "morality will gradually *perish* now." With this vision, Nietzsche names himself "the first perfect nihilist of Europe," the one who had already proleptically lived through nihilism's full catastrophic course and now passed to the other side, naming his kind "we firstlings and premature births of the coming century."[15] And what he found was that "the period of catastrophe" was really a fortuity because it represented "the advent of a doctrine that sifts men."[16] This "doctrine" is the will to power.

---

11. See Friedrich Nietzsche, *The Gay Science*, trans. Walter Kaufmann (New York: Vintage, 1974), §§108 and 125. Henceforth cited as GS. See BGE, I, §53.

12. BGE, II, §202: "[What] calls itself good is the instinct of the herd animal man." GM, I, §2: "Good, that is, of the first rank, in contradistinction to all the low, low-minded, common and plebeian."

13. BGE, I, §1: "*Why not untruth instead?* . . . It ultimately looks to us as if the problem has never been raised until now." See WTP, II, §202 and §399: "The will not to let oneself be deceived is of different origin [than believed]: a caution against being overpowered . . . one of life's instincts of self-defense."

14. WTP, Preface, §2 (emphasis added). Nietzsche foreshadows this passage in GM, III, §27: "Morality will gradually *perish* now; this is the great spectacle in a hundred acts reserved for the next two centuries in Europe." See BGE, I, §55.

15. GS, Book V, §343.

16. WTP, I, §56.

One of Nietzsche's decisive insights, which he believed should transform how we *will* and *value*[17] and about which he was consistent and unambiguous, was that the rejection of the Christian God is inseparable from the rejection of all traditional, normative morality, even if contemporary society is too stupid or cowardly to realize this. The rejection of Christianity leads to nihilism.

This claim is the heart of the "advent of nihilism" and the coming "catastrophe" described in the earlier passage. For Nietzsche, it is manifest—a matter so obvious that it is repeatedly overlooked—that when we abandon the "Christian God," we must also abandon "Christian morality" as well. This is because Nietzsche sees Christianity as a coherent system of thought in which God and God's will is the sole source of any morality that is binding on voluntary creatures with their endless capacity to make contradictory valuations. It is God who, as the creator, has "privileged knowledge" of what is good for us, and thus God is the "transcendent origin" of morality's truthfulness, worth, and "necessity." Thus, the "price" for getting rid of God is morally bankrupting in Nietzsche's estimate: "When you give up Christian faith, you pull the rug out from under your right to Christian morality as well. . . . If you break off a main tenet, the belief in God, you smash the whole system along with it: you lose your grip on anything necessary."[18]

But Nietzsche passionately and insightfully insists that we repeatedly fail to acknowledge this. As theology recedes, our intensified commitment to morality is really the hangover and suppressed triumph of the Christian imagination. Christian morality—especially its affirmation of the universality and equality of human worth, as well as the notion of intrinsic goodness—was so successful in shaping our common sense and institutions, Nietzsche argues, that we overlook how our "morality" is fundamentally *Christian*. And thus it is anything but obvious that we have any right, much less any obligation, to it once we have abandoned the Christian faith. Ironically, our self-supposed liberation from God turns into a dishonest, self-deceived intensification of Christianity's unique moral vision as we seek for new order and rights.

Thus, Nietzsche argues that most of us fail to appreciate "the problem of morality." That is, we fail to see that morality is *problematic*, that its right to make an authoritative claim on how we think, desire, and behave is something we have implicitly abandoned and thus is nonobvious and almost certainly false. Nietzsche's devious point is that *there is no genuine "problem*

---

17. In BGE, I, §3, Nietzsche defines "valuations" as "physiological requirements for the preservation of a particular type of life." See Friedrich Nietzsche, *Thus Spoke Zarathustra*, I, "On the Thousand and One Goals," in *The Portable Nietzsche*, ed. and trans. Walter Kauffman (New York: Penguin, 1982), 171: "Change of values—that is the change of the creators. Whoever must be a creator always annihilates." Henceforth cited as TSZ.

18. TI, IX:5, "Raids/Skirmishes of an Untimely Man"). Siedentop, *Inventing the Individual* has argued persuasively that Nietzsche was right and that liberal morality and its egalitarian values are fundamentally Christian in origin and justification.

of morality" once the Christian God is rejected; all that remains is the human will and its drive for power. Nietzsche writes, "Naiveté: as if morality could survive when the *God* who sanctions it is missing!"[19] In his absence, we are left with an arbitrary free for all as voluntary, willful "esteemers."

Based on this insightful line of argument, Nietzsche proclaimed that it was the task of "the new philosophers" and "men of the future" to "create new values," to inaugurate a new beginning for Western society and its "morals" based on his newly discovered "doctrine" of the will to power.[20] Thus, he calls "the gospel of the future" precisely "*The Will to Power*: Attempt at a Revaluation of All Values"[21] and names the "man of the future" the "Antichrist and antinihilist" who will triumph over God and nothingness by the sheer force of his will.[22]

These subversive neo-evangelists would undoubtedly be seen as oddballs and disturbers of the order like his "madman" and Zarathustra.[23] But Nietzsche was insistent that this new beginning work—this "revaluation" based on the will to power—was an essential task, a crucial spiritual vocation for human honesty, increasing power, and surviving devastation. Indeed, Nietzsche thought that this was the only option that could "take the place of this perfect nihilism," which had proleptically wrecked Western civilization, its moral foundations, and thus its will for life, its capacity to affirm existence as worthy of love—to answer the question, "Why?" In short, the "advent of nihilism" forces us to invent "*new values*," to become the sovereign creators of a new world.[24]

The preparatory deconstruction required for this new beginning is what Nietzsche calls a "more natural . . . attitude toward morality," which amounts to a new honesty about reality and society:

> Principles have become ridiculous; nobody permits himself any longer to speak without irony of his "duty." . . . What does it mean that the welfare of my neighbor *ought* to possess for me a higher value than my own? . . . What is the meaning of that "Thou shalt," which even philosophers regard as "given"?[25]

---

19. WTP, II, §253. See also GS, Book V, §343: "What must collapse now that this belief [in the Christian God] has been undermined—all that was built upon it, leaned on it, grew into it; for example, our whole European morality." See Hannah Arendt, *The Promise of Politics*, ed. Jerome Kohn (New York: Schocken Books, 2005), 51.

20. BGE, I, §42. See also BGE, II, §203: "Towards *new philosophers*, there is no alternative . . . who are strong and original enough to give impetus to opposed valuations and initiate a revaluation and reversal of 'eternal values' . . . the force that compels the will of millennia into *new* channels . . . whatever hidden, dreadful, or benevolent spirits have existed on earth will pale into insignificance beside the image of this type." See also GM, I, §17.

21. WTP, Preface, §4.

22. GM, II, §24.

23. See BGE, I, §43.

24. WTP, Preface, §4. See Hans Joas, "The Genesis of Values as Genealogy of Morality? (Friedrich Nietzsche)," in *The Genesis of Values* (Chicago: University of Chicago Press, 2001).

25. WTP, I, §121; II, §269. See BGE, II, §33: "The feelings of utter devotion, of sacrifice for your neighbor, and the entire morality of self-abnegation have to be mercilessly taken to court and made to account for themselves. . . . 'Aren't these perhaps—*seductions*?'" See BGE, II, §82.

After all, if God is dead, *who* could possibly stand in as the originator and guarantor of such audacious claims that so radically diverge from the survival of the fittest? Nietzsche thinks that our new beginning starts by admitting who and where we are as moral agents: the notion of binding responsibility and the priority of the neighbor is outdated and dishonest; only the will to power remains.

Thus, Nietzsche calls his *"chief* proposition" the principle that "there *are no moral phenomena, there is only moral interpretation of phenomena. This interpretation itself is of extra-moral origin."*[26] In other words, there are no moral *givens*, no self-revealing and self-grounding moral realities or facts beyond human fabrication.[27] The implication is striking and all-encompassing: "The origin of moral values is the work of immoral affects and considerations."[28] The track of morality is but the trail of violence, the path we have literally beaten with the plow of our will, what Nietzsche calls "fossilized violence." Thus, Nietzsche asks, *"Whose will to power is morality?"*[29] *not* "Whose morality is *before* or *beyond* the will to power?" His point is clear: *All* "morality" *is* "will to power," whether we recognize this or not; the relevant question is *whose* will wins and thus can pave the path of the future.

For Nietzsche, this is "the problem of morality," which he thought weak, Christianity hungover, modern people were too cowardly to face: morality itself is immoral (or, really, amoral); it is born and bred in the lust for power but forgetful and in denial of its true bastard origins, and its fabricated drive for "truth" ironically forces morality to discover this. When taken seriously, then, "mores" lead us back to that "original," raw state in which power is recognized as the determiner and only justifier of genuine *value* during our "mere moment . . . of no importance to the general character of the earth . . . between two nothingnesses . . . without plan, reason, will, self-consciousness, the worst kind of necessity, *stupid* necessity."[30] Nietzsche's conclusion is radical and all-encompassing: "Morality itself, in the form of honesty, compels us to deny morality."[31]

For Nietzsche, this is the "catastrophe" looming on the horizon but also the opening to the genuine breakthrough of "new values" or "revaluation," which marks our new beginning. Its heart is the self-conscious embrace and affirmation of the will to power or "active nihilism." If there is no truth or binding morality, we are free to make up the beginning and order that we ourselves

---

26. WTP, II, 258. Also in BGE, II, §108. See BGE, I, §2 and §231.
27. BGE, Preface: "[Perspectivism] is the fundamental condition of all life." Also BGE, I, §36: "Our world of desires and passions is the only thing 'given' as real."
28. WTP, II, §266. See GM, III, §9: "All good things were formerly bad things; every original sin has turned into an original virtue."
29. WTP, II, §274.
30. WTP, II, §303.
31. WTP, II, §404.

want and will. We are the founders and authors in the middle without beginning. The future is open; the world belongs to those who can master it.

Foundational to Nietzsche's new beginning, then, is what he calls the *"new world-conception,"* which denies any beginning to reality at all: "The world . . . becomes, it passes away, but it has never begun to become and never ceased from passing away. . . . Its excrement are its food."[32] The world has no beginning (an-archic) and thus no direction or rule, no plot to follow after, no law to orient and energize action other than endless motion. It is a circle. Thus, Nietzsche calls the world "a circular movement that has already repeated itself infinitely often and plays its game in *infinitum"*—"a monster of energy, without beginning, without end."[33] Indeed, the world and we ourselves are "the will to power and nothing besides!"—a kind of excremental cannibalism of power.[34]

Within such a "new world-conception," Nietzsche thinks that "a declaration of war on the masses by *higher men* is needed" in order to launch this new beginning after the rupture of nihilism.[35] Indeed, it is precisely *"suffrage universel"*—what Nietzsche calls "the system through which the lowest natures prescribe themselves as laws for the higher," which "commenced with Christianity"—that must be opposed as self-deceptive, weakening nonsense. In its place, "a doctrine" is needed that can work as a "breeding agent" capable of "strengthening the strong, paralyzing and destructive for the world-weary." Nietzsche goes so far as to insist on "the annihilation of the decaying races," which preserves "slavish evaluations." (Nietzsche, who hated Plato, is essentially following Socrates's claim in *The Republic* that the weak and sick should either be left to die or actively killed to secure the "virtue" of the polis.[36] This lends credence to Nietzsche's claim that *"suffrage universel . . .* commenced with Christianity." It certainly did not commence with Plato.) On the precipice of such a revolution, Nietzsche augurs, "The time for petty politics is over: the next century will bring the struggle for the domination of the earth—the *compulsion* to great politics."[37]

To accomplish this feat, Nietzsche declares, "We have to be destroyers!"[38] This "dominion over the earth" will produce a "higher type" of humanity

---

32. WTP, IV, §1066.
33. WTP, IV, §1067. In BGE, I, § 9 and §259, "Life itself is *essentially* a process of appropriating, injuring, overpowering the alien and the weaker . . . life *is* precisely will to power."
34. WTP, IV, §1067.
35. WTP, IV, §861–62. See WTP, II, §361.
36. See Plato, *Republic*, Vol. 1: Books 1–5, Loeb Classical Library, trans. Christopher Emlyn-Jones and William Preddy (Cambridge, MA: Harvard University Press, 2013), 407e and 410a.
37. BGE, II, §208.
38. Vis-à-vis Nazism's appropriation of Nietzsche, he encouraged "race mixture" as a way of intensifying power (WTP, IV, §862). But he calls for the opposite in BGE, §§200, 261, in which he describes mixing races as a source of "disintegration."

capable of self-creation in the face of the abysmal moral emptiness of reality. The "new philosopher," indeed, the "new European" is thus "forced to give himself laws, forced to rely on his own arts and wiles of self-preservation, self-enhancement, self-redemption" to accomplish this "great task" of starting over.[39]

Lest we be offended, Nietzsche offers a parable from nature to defend the "naturalness" of what he proposes: "That lambs dislike great birds of prey does not seem strange: only it gives no ground for reproaching these birds of prey for bearing off little lambs."[40] This parable illustrates the maxim that Nietzsche calls "the symbol and watchword reserved for the highest ranks alone as their *secretum*": "'Nothing is true, everything is permitted.'"[41] That is, if we ask what can "justify" such a new scheme of value and thus a new beginning for civilization constituted by predation, Nietzsche scornfully sneers back that our question betrays that we remain bewitched by Christianity and have missed the point of his "new language" entirely: "We no longer *believe* in morality, as they did, and consequently we have no need to found a philosophy with the aim of justifying morality."[42]

This is what Nietzsche means by "beyond good and evil." The very logic of "justification" has collapsed before the human will and been abandoned.[43] "Justification" is reduced to "strength," and strength is merely a measure of the will and its self-assertion driven by humanity's inherent egoism.[44] Birds of prey will do what they will. We may feel *pity* for the "little lamb" and not *like* the "great bird of prey," but that sentimentality gives no ground for claiming that one is "right" and the other "wrong." One is strong and the other weak. The strong wins and the other loses. That is the way of nature.

Nietzsche's conclusion is clear: "One must destroy morality if one is to liberate life."[45] This moral destruction will simultaneously mark our liberating new beginning in which enslaving virtues like "industry, modesty, benevolence, temperance"—resentful Christian qualities that lead to self-denial and diminishment—are obliterated. In our new beginning, what is needed is "a sovereign disposition, great inventiveness, heroic purposiveness, noble being-for-oneself"[46] because we are "condemned to *invention*."[47] Nietzsche declares,

39. BGE, §262.
40. GM, I, §13. See GM, III, §25 for Nietzsche's misogyny and repudiation of democracy.
41. GM, III, §24. Note Albert Camus's sobering commentary on this idea in *The Rebel: An Essay on Man in Revolt*, trans. Anthony Bower (New York: Vintage International, 1991), 5.
42. WTP, II, §415. See BGE, I, §4.
43. WTP, II, §401.
44. BGE, II, §§175, 244, 265, 284.
45. WTP, II, §343.
46. WTP, II, §358. See §276.
47. BGE, I, §12.

But true philosophers are commanders and legislators: they say "That is how it *should* be!" They are the ones who first determine the "where to?" and "what for?" of people, which puts at their disposal the preliminary labor of all philosophical laborers, all those who overwhelm the past. True philosophers reach for the future with a creative hand and everything that is and was becomes a means, a tool, a hammer for them. Their "knowing" is *creating*, their creating is a legislating, their will to truth is—*will to power.*[48]

Thus, it would seem that the "new philosophers" take the place of God. It is their (in)finite will that fabricates the future, that serves as the origin and law of value to which others must conform or be crushed. Preference and obligation, power and authority are elided, and theirs is the "creative hand" that can instrumentalize all else for their power-hungry purposes.

The one who can say *Yes!* to all of this is the "new philosopher" of the future, the author(ity/itarian) who brings the gospel of a new beginning for humanity freed of lies and self-denial in the nihilistic conflict of the highest values.[49] He is the ironically "pure thinker," not because his mind is concerned for others but because he is "beyond good and evil." As I indicated earlier, then, Nietzsche's "future," as he himself insisted, was really a return to the pre-Christian past and the aristocratic nobility of Greece and Rome.[50]

To sum up, for Nietzsche the problem of morality is not that the world is "evil" or that valuable persons' lives are violently ravished like lambs without redemption vis-à-vis the trial of universal entry.[51] There is no beginning, everything is cyclical, and nothing—and no one—is fundamentally *new* in Nietzsche's philosophy. Despite Nietzsche's language, there is no genuine newness or absolute value at all but only eternal recurrence, the snake eating its excrement. Thus, the real "problem of morality" is that we think and feel these things, that we remain trapped in these bewitching Christian moral constructs, which endow divine dignity in individual persons and thus an ultimate gravity to their fate. Once we have gone through the "catastrophe" of nihilism and realized that there is *no* intrinsic "value," "unity," or "truth" to life whatsoever other than what we impose on it, *then* we can remake our world as "new philosophers" and "new Europeans."[52] And thus we can begin again as we will. The world is ours for the taking and making. We invent and enforce our own beginning.

---

48. BGE, II, §211. See §253.

49. See BGE, I, §56.

50. See Siedentop, *Inventing the Individual*, Part I, "The World of Antiquity."

51. See Friedrich Nietzsche, *The Antichrist*, "Preface: Revaluation of All Values," in *The Portable Nietzsche*, ed. and trans. Walter Kaufmann (New York: Penguin, 1982), 569.

52. WTP, I, §12, B: "Once we have devaluated these three categories, the demonstration that they cannot be applied to the universe is no longer any reason for devaluating the universe."

Nietzsche's new moralist announced with the ecstasy of an oracle, "Oh! If you knew how soon, so soon now—things will be different!"[53] Nietzsche's new beginning was meant to be radical and world changing. Looking forward to the twentieth century (Nietzsche died in 1900), it appears that Nietzsche was disturbingly prophetic.

Arendt: Natality, Totalitarianism, and the First Consciously Planned Beginning After All Hopes Have Died

Against Nietzsche and the biblical Teacher, Hannah Arendt insisted that she had discovered something new under the sun.[54] According to Arendt, totalitarianism was fundamentally novel, as well as the life of each newborn child, who harbors within him- or herself the mysterious power of beginning something new by virtue of being born. This is what Arendt called our "natality," which could be warped into birthing something so neoteric and devastating as totalitarianism.[55]

The new world of totalitarianism was deeply Nietzschean, a world blitzed and brutalized by "a sovereign disposition, great inventiveness, heroic purposiveness, noble being-for-oneself."[56] And for Arendt, the advent of totalitarianism marked an "unprecedented crime"[57] and a "novel form of government"[58] far beyond traditional tyranny, perhaps analogous to the coming "catastrophe" that Nietzsche foresaw shadowing European civilization decades before.

In order to describe the devastation wrought by totalitarianism, Arendt reached for apocalyptic and biblical images. She described totalitarianism as an "iron band" that encompassed and wrenched the life out of existence, as a "sandstorm" that left reality buried in pulverized ruins.[59] In it, she saw a movement from "Hades" (for example, displaced persons camps for persons

53. BGE, §214.

54. See Ecclesiastes 1:9.

55. For the most crucial passages in Arendt's oeuvre on natality, beginnings, and *arché/archein*, see *Love and Saint Augustine*, ed. Judith Chelius Stark and Joanna Vecchiarelli Scott (Chicago: University of Chicago Press, 1996 [1929]), 29, 55; *The Origins of Totalitarianism*, 586, 591, 599–601, 612, 616; *The Human Condition*, 9, 176–78, 188, 224–25, 231; "What Is Freedom?," 456–60; *On Revolution*, chapter 1 (especially 27) and chapter 5 (especially 212–14); "Labor, Work, Action," in *The Portable Arendt*, 178–81; *The Promise of Politics*, 45; *The Life of the Mind*, 2:18, 29, 32, 110, 195, 198, 203, 207, 216. See Stephan Kampowski, *Arendt, Augustine, and the New Beginning: The Action Theory and Moral Thought of Hannah Arendt in the Light of Dissertation on St. Augustine* (Grand Rapids, MI: Eerdmans, 2008), especially 45–56.

56. Though Arendt's analysis of totalitarianism emphasizes its puzzling purposelessness and "selflessness."

57. See Hannah Arendt, *Eichmann in Jerusalem: A Report on the Banality of Evil* (New York: Penguin Books, 2006), 263, 267, 273, 283, 288. Henceforth cited as EJ.

58. See "Ideology and Terror: A Novel Form of Government," Chapter 4 of Part III of *The Origins of Totalitarianism*, especially 616. Henceforth cited as OT.

59. OT, 616. This seems to be an allusion to Isaiah 14:16–17.

"superfluous and bothersome") down to "Purgatory" (for example, Soviet labor camps ravaged by neglect and violent force) down to the depths of "Hell" (for example, Nazi concentration camps) where "the whole of life was thoroughly and systematically organized with a view to the greatest possible torment." This backward pilgrimage of damnation was orchestrated and enforced by totalitarian propaganda and terror.[60]

For Arendt, these biblical descriptions were apt because totalitarianism represented the systematic destruction of the human person through "total domination" and the fabrication of "living corpses," in the process of which "conscience as such . . . apparently got lost in Germany."[61] She went so far as to describe this as a "change of the nature of man,"[62] which was fabricated, first, by killing "the juridical person in man" through total arbitrariness,[63] then by murdering "the moral person in man" through "robbing death of its meaning as an end of a fulfilled life,"[64] and finally by destroying "the differentiation of the individual" in "his unique identity" by reducing humans to shaved, denuded numbers covered in "grotesque camp clothing" leading to "the nihilistic generalizations which maintain plausibly enough that essentially all men alike are beasts."[65] To grasp the enormity of this horror, Arendt named this destruction of the human condition "radical evil," which she thought was "previously unknown to us" and in which "there are neither political nor historical nor simply moral standards."[66] Here human existence—created "that there be a beginning" as Augustine wrote and Arendt never tired of quoting—is reduced to the "absolutely superfluous."[67]

Unsurprisingly, then, in the preface to the first edition of *The Origins of Totalitarianism* (1950), Arendt analyzed her moment in Western civilization as "the calm that settles after all hopes have died." She confesses that the destruction was so fundamental and far reaching that "we no longer hope for an eventual restoration of the old world order with all its traditions." Instead, in the swirling chaos of "the violence of wars and revolutions," we find ourselves amid "the growing decay of all that has still been spared." Indeed, Arendt went so far as to say that "there prevails an ill-defined, general agreement that the essential structure of all civilizations is at the breaking point."[68]

---

60. OT, 450, 453, 574.
61. EJ, 103.
62. OT, 619.
63. OT, 577–82.
64. OT, 582–83.
65. OT, 584–86.
66. OT, 572; see xvii. Note Arendt's later revision in her essay "Some Questions of Moral Philosophy," in *Responsibility and Judgment*, ed. Jerome Kohn (New York: Schocken Books, 2005), 95, 146, in which she discusses "the banality of evil." Henceforth cited as RJ.
67. OT, 573.
68. For Arendt's interpretation of "the end of tradition," see her essay "The Tradition of Political Thought" in *The Promise of Politics*, edited by Jerome Kohn (New York: Schocken Books, 2005).

With our civilization in ruins, Arendt thought that its moral tradition "can no longer provide the guidance to the possibilities of the century, or an adequate response to its horrors."[69] While denouncing both "Progress" and "Doom" as twin "articles of superstition," Arendt insists frankly that "all traditional elements of our political and spiritual world were dissolved into a conglomeration where everything seems to have lost specific value."[70] In such a state, Arendt thinks that we find ourselves confronted with "the irresistible temptation" to resign ourselves to "the mere process of disintegration" in which the world and our lives with others have "begun to appear lifeless, bloodless, meaningless, and unreal."[71]

These are powerful analyses: "all hopes have died," "the essential structure of civilization is at the breaking point," "everything seems to have lost specific value" such that we face the "irresistible temptation" of meaninglessness. This is the devastating moral rupture to which Arendt was responding after Nietzsche's advent of nihilism.

Still in the original preface, Arendt begins to indicate her response, which she will develop in her "Concluding Remarks" and I will characterize as her ethics of new beginning: she calls for humans around the world to forge a "new guarantee" protecting "human dignity," which she thinks "can be found only in a new political principle, in a new law on earth." Arendt insists that this "new law" and its "validity" must now "comprehend the whole of humanity," even as she immediately states that the law's power "must remain strictly limited, rooted in and controlled by newly defined territorial entities."[72] That is, Arendt argues that we must fabricate a universal law that protects *everyone's* "human dignity," even as we must remain worried about the resurgence of totalitarianism and thus build into the law limitations, namely, "newly defined territorial entities" checking and balancing one another.

Before turning to her "Concluding Remarks," we must note that Arendt's introductory response already presents a tension with her own critical analysis of the foundations of modernity with the French Revolution and its "Rights of Man" later in *Origins* and then in *On Revolution*. In the chapter "The Decline

---

Henceforth cited as PP. See also "Tradition and the Modern Age" in *Between Past and Future: Eight Exercises in Political Thought* (New York: Penguin, 2006). Henceforth cited BPF. See also "Some Questions of Moral Philosophy," 54.

69. OT, xxv. See PP, 38: "We live today in a world in which not even common sense makes sense any longer."

70. For Arendt's critique of "Progress," see *On Violence* (New York: Harcourt, 1972), 129, and *The Life of the Mind*, 2:155. Henceforth cited as LM.

71. OT, xxvi.

72. OT, xxvii. For a discussion of principles and beginnings, see *On Revolution*, 214ff. Henceforth cited as R. See Lucy Cane, "Hannah Arendt on the Principles of Political Action," *European Journal of Political Theory* 14 (January 2015): 55–75, and Marco Goldoni and Christopher McCorkindale, eds., *Hannah Arendt and the Law* (Oxford: Hart Publishing, 2012), especially chapter 8, "The Search for a New Beginning."

of the Nation-State and the End of the Rights of Man," Arendt writes, "This new situation, in which 'humanity' has in effect assumed the role formerly ascribed to nature or history, would mean in this context that the right to have rights, or the right of every individual to belong to humanity, should be guaranteed by humanity itself."[73] That is, if some theological account of history or some picture of timeless "nature" has been abandoned, "humanity" must step in to play the role of the moral lawgiver and thus also the guarantor of the "right to have rights." Similarly but for a different purpose to Nietzsche, humans must devise the possibility of there being a structure of moral obligation to ground and guide our new beginning.

But Arendt is deeply suspicious of this exclusively humanistic proposal. In fact, she avers, "It is by no means certain whether this is possible."

In Arendt's analysis, this move leads to a vicious circle of instrumentalism. She writes, "A conception of law which identifies what is right with the notion of what is good for—for the individual, or the family, or the people, or the largest number—becomes inevitable once the absolute and transcendent measurements of religion or law of nature have lost their authority."[74] Intrinsic value and right collapse, and they become contingent on the human will, which can then choose to *nill* the bindingness of the law and the rights of others. In this case, rather than the will responding to and thus being accountable to anything "out there," it now finds itself in the position of the inventor and legislator, as Nietzsche argued. The moral universe, then, hangs on human choice, which then becomes indistinguishable from the will to power and its instrumentalization. (Recall that Nietzsche said that the "new philosophers" make everything into "tools" for their purposes.) This is what Arendt later called "the problem of beginnings—a problem because beginning's very nature is to carry in itself an element of complete arbitrariness" in which "there is nothing left for the 'beginner' to hold on to"[75]—and thus nothing left to limit the beginner's novel self-assertion.

Pointing out the way in which "Christian theology provided the framework for all political and philosophical problems" up to modernity, Arendt quotes Plato's maxim, "Not man, but a god, must be the measure of all things."[76] Otherwise, when trying to make a new beginning for morality, we find ourselves in a curious situation, which she articulated later in *On Revolution*: "Those who get together to constitute a new government are themselves unconstitutional,

---

73. See Peg Birmingham, "The An-Archic Event of Natality and 'the Right to Have Rights'" in *Social Research* 74, no. 3, Hannah Arendt's Centenary: Political and Philosophical Perspectives, Part I (Fall 2007): 763–76.

74. See Arendt, PP, 51, and R, 159, in which Arendt discusses secularization and "the need for an absolute from which to derive authority for law and power." See *The Human Condition*, 154: "Utility established as meaning generates meaninglessness." Henceforth cited as HC.

75. LM, 2:2207.

76. OT, 379. See *Men in Dark Times* (New York: Harcourt, 1968), 82.

that is, they have no authority to do what they have set out to achieve. The vicious circle in legislating is present not in ordinary lawmaking, but in laying down the fundamental law." Here Arendt returns to the same point, now quoting Rousseau, that "to put the law above man and thus to establish the validity of manmade laws . . . 'one actually would need gods.'"[77]

But this is precisely what the declaration of the Rights of Man rejected and why Arendt sees it as an epoch-making "turning point in history." "It meant," she argues, "nothing more nor less than that from then on, Man, and not God's command or the customs of history, should be the source of law."[78] And thus, perhaps unsurprisingly and tellingly, Arendt saw "in the new secularized and emancipated society" a new uncertainty and anxiety emerging about the real existence of genuine "social and human rights," which had previously been guaranteed by "social, spiritual, and religious forces" "outside the political order." In this "new situation," calls emerged for stronger protections to guarantee the dignity and rights of individuals "against the new sovereignty of the state and the new arbitrariness of society," the fact that the order of society and the value of the individual were now recognized and ratified by law as the arbitrary construction of the bare human will on whatever scale. But in the declaration of the Rights of Man and moving forward, "no authority was invoked for their establishment" because all transcendent authority had been rejected and "Man himself was their source as well as their ultimate goal." (This is what Nietzsche saw as the hangover of Christian morality.) In short, "Man appeared as the only sovereign" but now devoid of "the grace of God." And for Arendt, "sovereignty" and "tyranny" on the human level are indistinguishable, as we saw so poignantly in Nietzsche.[79]

In this important section of *Origins*, then, it seems clear that Arendt is concerned and deeply critical. For her, "It is by no means certain that this" autonomous new beginning "is possible" or justified. Moreover, this human grasp for self-appointed "sovereignty" over the construction of the human condition stands as a crucial "turning point" in the movement toward the radical human hubris that led to the sandstorm of totalitarianism, which she thinks destroyed the moral traditions and structures underpinning Western civilization and led to its collapse.

Thus, for Arendt to suggest in her preface that "human dignity needs a new guarantee which can be found only in a new political principle," which will presumably be constructed and enforced by autonomous humans, even if within "newly defined territorial entities," seems to reveal an important tension and weakness in her thought. Her proposed new beginning seems to

---

77. R, 184.
78. OT, 369.
79. OT, 369. See R, 152.

require an optimistic embrace and even intensification of this autonomy and self-creation, which led to the time "after all hopes have died."

In her "Concluding Remarks" to the original edition of *The Origins of Totalitarianism*, Arendt implicitly deepens this tension. Again she names "the holes of oblivion and the world of the dying as the central issues of our political life."[80] We now live among—perhaps *are*—"men who, having lost their religious faith, are convinced that there is no sense in life and no difference between crime and virtue" like Nietzsche's "new Europeans" beyond good and evil. The (post-)totalitarian world is marked by "contempt for reality" and "the proud assumption of human mastery over the world," which ultimately destroys our "human dignity" as "cobuilders of a common world" in which our natality thrives.[81] In such a world, human equality has become perverse: "All men are equally superfluous."[82]

For Arendt, we find ourselves in ruins. Probing to the heart of her analysis, she judges that "the whole of nearly three thousand years of Western civilization" and its "comparatively uninterrupted stream of tradition, has broken down; the whole structure of Western culture with all its implied beliefs, traditions, standards of judgment, has come toppling down over our heads." And like Nietzsche, Arendt shines the spotlight on our "reluctance to admit this situation," preferring to pretend like our moral world is still intact. But Arendt is emphatic: "Whether we like it or not, we have long ceased to live in a world in which the faith in the Judeo-Christian myth of creation is secure enough to constitute a basis and source of authority for actual laws." She finds it even more ridiculous to think that we could still believe in a "universal cosmos of which man was a part and whose natural laws he has to imitate and conform" like the French revolutionaries claimed.[83] For Arendt, like Nietzsche, our moral foundations have collapsed, and honesty demands that we admit this.

Similar to Nietzsche still, Arendt acknowledges that the loss of faith in the Judeo-Christian myth of creation amounted to a loss of "ultimate meaning . . . which, because it lay at the very beginning, seemed secure" and thus secured the moral order against the arbitrariness of human willfulness and historical accident. Getting to the heart of the matter, myths of creation "assume that something was there, given, already established before human history actually began" such that "the direction of history was beyond human effort, its laws sprang from a transcendent source (or event) and could only be obeyed or disobeyed," rather than being made up and unmade by humans and their will

---

80. OT, 620.
81. OT, 622.
82. OT, 624.
83. OT, 625.

to power.[84] This *givenness* both endowed human existence with a transcendent *dignity* and also emplotted human history with a normative *direction*, which provided guidance for human *action*. But this is precisely what Arendt thinks the eighteenth-century revolutions implicitly or explicitly rejected, replacing this God-given beginning and theological emplotment of history with a notion of timeless "nature," which Arendt thinks has also become defunct in light of "man's mastery" and "emancipation from nature"[85] reaching for a divine kind of techno-planetary agency.[86] (This argument should be kept in mind when we look at Bonhoeffer's interpretation of Western history and its being "torn" from its "origin" in chapter 3.)

In Arendt's analysis, then, "our new difficulty" is precisely that "we start from a fundamental distrust of everything merely *given*."[87] Indeed, "the first disastrous result of man's coming of age," according to Arendt alluding to Nietzsche, "is that modern man has come to resent everything given, even his own existence—to resent the very fact that he is not the creator of the universe and himself." Having lost faith in God and the belief in the goodness and love-worthiness of God's creation, we are driven to replace God with ourselves and to remake reality as we wish. "In his resentment of all laws merely given to him," Arendt continues, "he proclaims openly that everything is permitted and believes secretly that everything is possible."[88]

Again, Arendt's response to this situation seems deeply tensioned, if not contradictory. On the one hand, in the final paragraphs of her "Concluding Remarks," she claims that the fundamental choice confronting human beings today is "the choice between resentment and gratitude as basic possible modern attitudes."[89] And it is clear that Arendt's choice is for this gratitude in the face of the sheer "givenness" of the world and human beings, what she calls "the miracle of being,"[90] which sources Arendt's deep *amor mundi*.[91] She writes (quoting Faulkner) that this fundamental affirmation of the givenness of human existence expects only "one's own anonymous chance to perform something passionate and brave and austere . . . into man's enduring

---

84. OT, 626. See 270. For Arendt's discussion of sacred beginning, authority, and religion in Christian and Roman thought, see *Love and Saint Augustine*, 48ff.; "What Is Authority?," §4; PP, 44ff.; R, 199; and LM, 2:203–17.

85. OT, 627.

86. OT, 588. See HC, 148 and 269.

87. OT, 627.

88. OT, 630.

89. OT, 630–31. See LM, 2:185: "How suggestive such affirmation can be as a solution for the apparent meaninglessness of an entirely secularized world."

90. OT, 604.

91. See PP, 203. It seems to me that "givenness" is something like God's "shadow" or trace in Arendt's thought, an insight from Patchen Markell.

chronicle"[92] out of gratitude for the gift of time, in which we are not alone but live with others with whom we discover and enact natality.[93] For Arendt, this gratitude for given time and shared space in which to speak and act with others is enough.[94] This passage, in turn, alludes to an earlier, magnificent statement, in which Arendt declares,

> This mere existence, that is, all that which is mysteriously given us by birth and which includes the shape of our bodies and the talents of our minds, can be adequately dealt with only by the unpredictable hazards of friendship and sympathy, or by the great and incalculable grace of love, which says with Augustine, "*Volo ut sis* [I want you to be]," without being able to give any particular reason for such supreme and unsurpassable affirmation.[95]

Thus, Arendt's final sentence in the original edition of *The Origins of Totalitarianism* quotes a triumphant passage from Scripture that celebrates human solidarity and hope after a miraculous deliverance from death: "Do thyself no harm; for we are all here" (Acts 16:28).

In the end, with her affirmation of "givenness" beyond the grip of totalitarianism's "iron band," Arendt seems to relax, if not renounce, the human drive for self-creation and sovereignty as our own beginning and rule. Her ethics of new beginning is founded in gratitude for what is given, which affirms human natality, plurality, and thus our limitations and mutually limiting relations with one another.

But as Arendt herself seems to admit, she acknowledges no one to be grateful *to* for these "givens" (gifts?). This is why we are unable "to give any particular reason for such supreme and unsurpassable affirmation." Arendt never allows God as first Beginner to play any role in grounding and guiding her ethics of new beginning other than tangential allusions in her less formal writings.

This leads to the profound tension in her ethics of new beginning. Arendt insists that, having left behind a theological account of history as well as a timeless order of nature, we must fabricate our own new, manmade beginning. She says, "We shall have to create—not merely discover—a new foundation

---

92. See Patchen Markell, "Anonymous Glory," *European Journal of Political Theory* 16, no. 1 (2017): 77–99. See EJ, 233, for a more measured and minimalist affirmation.

93. See "What Is Freedom?," 442. See also R, 174, in which Arendt describes the French view of covenant-making community as "the only reasonable hope for a salvation from evil and wickedness at which men might arrive in this world and even by themselves, without any divine assistance."

94. See her letter to Mary McCarthy, January 25, 1972, in *Between Friends: The Correspondence of Hannah Arendt and Mary McCarthy 1949–1975*, ed. Carol Brightman (New York: Harvest Books, 1996), 307 and LSA, 52: "Gratitude for life having been given at all is the spring of remembrance, for a life is cherished even in misery."

95. OT, 382. See LM, 2:104m and Margaret Miles, "*Volo ut sis*: Arendt and Augustine" *Dialog* 41, no. 3 (Fall 2002): 221–30.

for human community as such," which for Arendt amounts to history's "first consciously planned beginning, together with the bitter realization that nothing has been promised us, no Messianic Age, no classless society, no paradise after death." Indeed, Arendt thinks that we ourselves shall have to "devise" the "very measure, the yardstick of good and evil" in our creation of a new foundation for global human community, curiously echoing Nietzsche.[96] But all of this stands in striking contradiction to her affirmation of "givenness" as our new starting point for morality: "The conscious beginning of history of mankind will mean that nothing merely given can serve as a yardstick ... from now on man is the only possible creator of his own laws and the only possible maker of his own history."[97]

In the time "after all hopes have died," this seems like the only option for Arendt: either mankind will restart history on its own foundation and "rule together an overcrowded earth" or we will "perish."[98] In unresolved tension with our gratitude for what is given, we must go beyond it and remake it somehow into something else.

Arendt goes on to insist that the "new concept" of "crimes against humanity" must play the central role in this new global beginning,[99] which she links with the "one right" that she sees transcending our political rights as subjects of legal states: "the right never to be excluded from the rights granted by this community," that is, the right not to be "excluded from the whole sphere of legality where rights spring from the mutual guarantees which alone can insure them."[100]

But the problem as I see it, which is complexly interwoven with Arendt's tensioned affirmation and renunciation of "the given," is that Arendt does not say much here about where this "one right" comes from or what justifies it, much less what could redeem it, other than mere human fabrication, which she herself criticized and cautioned against. Arendt argues that "rights exist because we inhabit the earth together with other men ... rights spring from human plurality," an idea she will develop further in *The Human Condition*.[101] Nonetheless, despite Arendt's distinction between the concepts of the "human condition" and "human nature" and her principled agnosticism

96. OT, 627.
97. OT, 629.
98. OT, 627.
99. See EJ, 268.
100. OT, 628. See OT, 376 and 631.
101. OT, 629. See HC, 178. A fuller discussion of Arendt's ethics of new beginning would need to include an analysis of her discussion of "forgiving" (to deal with the irreversibility of the past) and "promising" (to deal with the unpredictability of the future). The critical question again, however, would be what Arendt thinks makes us responsible to forgive wrongs and keep promises other than our own preferences and cultural conditioning. See *The Human Condition*, 236–47. See also Donald Levine's discussion of Arendt's vision of forgiveness and promises in "The Promise of Ethiopia: Public Action, Civic Forgiveness, Creative Power," in *Interpreting Ethiopia*, 337–47.

bordering on antagonism toward the latter in her work,[102] this passage reads like an appeal to human *nature* or *creatureliness*, something given to us by God and to which we are accountable. The suppressed logic seems to run: (1) humans are the kinds of creatures we are in our plural natality, in which we participate in the speech and action that initiates and manifests the unique creatures that we are; (2) to violate this is to violate humanity itself; (3) humans *should* be the kinds of creatures we are, that is, it is fundamentally *good* for us to be who we are beyond our willing and nilling; therefore, (4) this violation is *wrong*, that is, against some real standard and thus *not right*.

But this seems to transgress Arendt's own logic seen earlier: (1) we have become the emancipated masters of nature; (2) there is no external or absolute Creator to whom we may appeal; (3) we no longer believe in "natural laws"; and thus (4) mankind must make its own beginning, whether this initiative leads to the Hell of the concentration camp or a glorious space of appearances in which men may present themselves in all of their newness and virtue.[103] Unless Arendt is willing to acknowledge that human beings have a normative nature (for example, their natality and plurality), which is given and guaranteed by a Creator beyond human willfulness and thus calls for human *responsiveness and obedience* rather than self-creation, it is hard to see how her "right" is really a *right* and not merely a manmade *invention*, as Nietzsche claimed, which can be respected or undone according to human will.[104]

On this point seems to hang Arendt's justification for calling "crimes against humanity" *crimes* and not just the unpleasant picture of birds of prey "bearing off little lambs," as Nietzsche insisted. We voice Arendt's own critique of the French Revolution's elevation of man as his self-creator and sovereign: "It is by no means certain whether this is possible"—or wise or desirable.[105] Arendt's estimation of the human capacity, to say nothing of our wisdom and warrant, for initiating new beginnings—seemingly unencumbered by the past and the kinds of creatures we have become—appears overoptimistic, unrealistic, and dangerous. It is unclear how she can overcome Nietzsche's "problem of morality."

---

102. See OT, 588, and HC, 10n2. See also Hannah Arendt, *Lectures on Kant's Political Philosophy*, ed. Ronald Beiner (Chicago: University of Chicago Press, 1992), 58–59.

103. See HC, chapter 5, "Action."

104. This raises the question, which Arendt addresses but never seems to answer in *On Revolution*, of whether revolutions implicitly subvert and invalidate themselves by definition and thus lead to perpetual revolution or anarchy. See R, 10–11 and 184, and "What Is Authority?," 502: "[Revolutions] seem to be the only salvation which this Roman-Western tradition has provided for emergencies. . . . To live in a political realm with neither authority nor the concomitant awareness that the source of authority transcends power and those who are in power, means to be confronted anew, without the religious trust in a sacred beginning and without the protection of traditional and therefore self-evident standards of behavior, by the elementary problems of human living-together."

105. OT, 379.

Additionally, Arendt's concluding quotation of Paul's words "Do thyself no harm; for we are all here" in Acts 16:28 strikes the sober reader as misleading. Only a few paragraphs before, Arendt explicitly states that one of the requirements of mankind's "first consciously planned beginning" is "the bitter realization that nothing has been promised us, no Messianic Age . . . no paradise after death."[106] Of course, Arendt writes with intimate knowledge of the Shoah and is defiantly witnessing that it did not succeed in exterminating her people. This witness should never be belittled. But if there is no ultimate hope for the annihilated even left open for agnostic aspiration, it seems euphemistic to conclude that "we are all here."[107]

In the face of mankind's "first consciously planned beginning," Arendt's position—at least in *The Origins of Totalitarianism*—seems to loop back from the climactic apostolic declaration of solidarity and hope despite prison to the abysmal post-totalitarian confession with which she began: "This moment of anticipation is like the calm that settles after all hopes have died" in which life lacks "specific value" and meaninglessness is an "irresistible temptation." When faced with the moral-spiritual exercise of universal entry sketched earlier, it is unclear to me how Arendt would maintain her fundamental gratitude and *amor mundi* because in her position, we are *not* all here, and there is no redemption for the murdered and no vindication of their "rights." This seems to leave the murderer omnipotent over the murdered. Thus, we are left in the twilight "unguided by any traditions"[108] about how to lay our civilizational foundation and restart our moral future at the precipice of "the problem of beginning."[109]

Is Arendt's "anonymous chance to perform something passionate and brave and austere . . . into man's chronicle"—a chance available only to the vast minority of privileged human beings and realizable by even fewer[110]—robust and adequate enough to sustain gratitude and *amor mundi*, much less a moral

---

106. OT, 627.

107. In R, 222, Arendt writes that "what saves the affairs of mortal men from the inherent futility is nothing but this incessant talk about them," that is, remembrance. But it is hard to see how this has any saving significance for the vast majority of the forgotten, those damned to double futility in life and in death with no memory left to earth.

108. LM, 1:12.

109. See LM, 2:209 (before in R, 205). In her later thought, for example, "Some Questions of Moral Philosophy" (1965–1966) and LM (1971–1975), Arendt develops a criterion of morality constituted by the integration of the self with itself as "two-in-one" (see Plato, *Republic*, Book IV, 443c). That is, if I commit a murder and can no longer live with myself as a murderer (that is, someone whose fellowship I find atrocious), then this is a clear sign that what I have done is morally wrong. The problem is that I do not see how Arendt's position can address the case of criminals who *can* live with themselves and indeed find their identity affirmed and strengthened by their criminal acts. See Seyla Benhabib, "Judgment and the Moral Foundations of Politics in Arendt's Thought," *Political Theory* 16, no. 1 (February 1998): 29–51.

110. Arendt herself acknowledged this point but did not address its ethical implications. See HC, 324.

orientation of love for others within the trial of universal entry, especially in light of her analysis of the descent into the mass annihilation and dehumanization of totalitarian hell that turned humans into the "homeless . . . stateless . . . rightless . . . scum of the earth" in "a world which everywhere seems to have come to an end"?[111]

In my judgment, Arendt's ethics of new beginning does not give us the resources we need to sustain these convictions and to answer Nietzsche's announcement of nihilism and call for the new philosopher of the will to power. The problem of morality persists.

Glover: Never Such Innocence Again, Self-Creation, and a Deliberate New Beginning for Morality

In some ways, Jonathan Glover's agenda in *Humanity: A Moral History of the 20th Century* is similar to Arendt's in *The Origins of Totalitarianism*.[112] For our purposes, his book can serve as a historical prologue and primer to the moral-spiritual exercise of universal entry, helping us with our "imaginative difficulty in making real to ourselves huge numbers of deaths and ruined lives."[113]

Glover painstakingly documents and analyzes "our history of cruelty and violence" in the twentieth century marked by "the worst ever man-made catastrophes." According to Glover's research, war killed over a hundred people *every hour* throughout the twentieth century, almost one person every thirty seconds! Thus, Glover spends hundreds of pages examining numerous cases of this devastating, horrific violence, from My Lai to the Rwandan genocide, from Nazi Germany to Soviet Russia. For Glover, this horrific historical heritage is "what we need to overcome if we are to move to a more peaceful world."[114] Thus, Glover's book slowly marches toward an urgent call for a new "start" based on "man-made moral traditions," a summons to "starting inter-group morality" before the tribalistic killing of the twentieth century totally engulfs humanity.[115]

As Arendt indicated, the ethical challenge for Glover is that he thinks most of Western society no longer believes in any objectively real moral law that can ground and guide our new beginning—our new morality. While "in Europe at the start of the twentieth century most people accepted the authority of morality," Glover underscores that today we struggle "to find good reasons for thinking that [the moral law] exists and that it has any claim on

---

111. OT, 341, 616.
112. Glover, *Humanity*. Henceforth cited as Glover.
113. Glover, xiv.
114. Glover, ix.
115. Glover, 410.

us."[116] Like Arendt, Glover directly connects this shift to "the collapse of the authority of religion and decline in belief in God." In short, for Glover, we have undergone a fundamental rupture in our experience and understanding of moral reality, which has left us dangerously disoriented and adrift: "Because of this history, it is (or should be) hard for thinking about ethics to carry on just as before."[117] With sobering finality, Glover entitles *Humanity*'s first chapter "Never Such Innocence Again."

Unsurprisingly, Glover confronts Nietzsche as his primary opponent on the level of ethical theory. Chapter 2 is entitled "Nietzsche's Challenge" and chapter 7 "Answering Nietzsche." In important ways, Glover's own position is deeply Nietzschean: he is calling humanity to make its own new beginning based on its own wisdom and power. That is, he sees the moral life, at least in part, as a process of self-creation based on our own values, which we decide and define for ourselves, left as we are with an "ethics without the moral law" (the title of part 1).[118]

But Glover is explicitly and emphatically aware of the problems of this essentially anarchic Nietzschean position. He writes,

> But some of us drawn to these ideas [of creating ourselves according to our own values] may feel aghast at where they took Nietzsche. Struggle, egoism, dominance, slavery, the majority having no right to existence, peoples that are failures, hardness, the festival of cruelty, the replacement of compassion for the weak by their destruction. If such a world is really the result of Nietzsche's thought, it seems a nightmare.[119]

Part 6 of Glover's book is chillingly titled "The Will to Create Mankind Anew: The Nazi Experiment." Glover is clearly worried about the unfettered human will and its drive for power.

Glover's response is to argue that Nietzsche's version of self-creation driven by the will to power is not the only option. He writes,

> These chilling Nietzschean conclusions do not follow from his premises about the value of self-creation and the absence of an external moral law. People's projects of self-creation may be guided by quite different values from his. Some of us do not want to be all dominance and assertion. We are free to reject any predetermined pattern, whether laid down by God or by Nietzsche. To value self-creation is not necessarily to think that it is the only object of life, which has to override everything else.[120]

---

116. Glover, 1.
117. Glover, 2.
118. See Glover, 14.
119. Glover, 17.
120. Glover, 17.

The fundamental problem for Glover's position appears in the words "may be" and "want." From mere description, there is no denial that "people's projects of self-creation *may be* guided by quite different values from [Nietzsche's]" based on what they happen to "want." But Glover is seemingly incapable of explaining *why* our "projects of self-creation" *ought* to be "guided by quite different values" and "wants," and why others' "projects of self-creation" *ought not* to be guided by these Nietzschean values and wants, other than this being what we ourselves happen to prefer and are willing to fight for, which was precisely Nietzsche's point.

Here we remain entirely within the grip of Nietzsche's argument: (1) there is nothing inherently real or binding about morality; (2) morality is our human invention; and (3) those who are strongest invent the morality that prevails and defines "reality." But none of these inventions, fundamentally speaking, is qualitatively "better" or "worse" than another; they remain "beyond good and evil." Indeed, they are *all* expressions of the will to power, whether in "sickened" or "noble" form.

Thus, Glover remains trapped in Nietzsche's simple but devastating question: *"Whose will to power is morality?"* In the context of this question, "people's projects of self-creation *may be* guided by quite different values" based on what they "want." Or they may *not* be based on *other* wants. But there is nothing beyond the competing, combating human will to adjudicate by which values "self-creation" *ought* and *ought not* to be "guided." As Nietzsche pointed out, "justification" and "obligation" are no longer part of the picture.

Glover's counter-argument throughout *Humanity* is rooted in a kind of human moral psychology and amounts to the claim that this is not actually the (entire) situation. Instead, Glover thinks that human self-creation is contextualized within and marked by certain "limits" and "moral resources," what we might characterize as a kind of British "sense theory" of morality, which we saw Nietzsche ridicule earlier in *Twilight of the Idols* as a Christian hangover.

First, against "amoralism," Glover discusses the role of "self-interest." He writes, "It is often in our own interest to behave well to other people. Society usually works to reinforce this. Rational self-interest will lead to a good deal of 'reciprocal altruism.'"[121] Glover sees self-interest cooperating with basic "social pressures and conventional moral rules" that can "shift the balance away from selfishness."[122] But here again we seem to remain solidly with Nietzsche: "morality" is about self-interest and self-assertion, even if a more placid and pacific version.

Second, Glover turns to discuss basic "moral resources," which he glosses as "certain human needs and psychological tendencies which work against

---

121. Glover, 18.
122. Glover, 20.

narrowly selfish behavior." These are needs and tendencies that "make it natural for people to display self-restraint, and to respect and care for others."[123]
Glover does not spend any time unpacking what he means by "natural," but
this concept seems to be extremely important and do most of the work in his
moral psychology and implicit ethics of new beginning.

The first "moral resource" that Glover discusses is our own sense of "moral
identity." For example, when we witness cruelty, we may experience "revul-
sion" and "contempt," the instinctive sense that this is not who we want to
be or the kind of behavior we want to accept. Conversely, when we witness
generosity, we may feel "respect or admiration." Glover states, "Many people
have their own, often very un-Nietzschean projects of self-creation. We have
a conception of what we are like, and of the kind of person we want to be,
which may limit what we are prepared to do to others."[124] Note again the importance of the words "we want," which raises MacIntyre's question, *Whose
Justice? Which Rationality?*[125]

Glover here repeats Arendt's argument from Socrates that if we would not
like to live with and be friends with (share "identity" with) a murderer, seeing
them as an unworthy person, then we should not commit murder because for
the rest of our lives we would be forced to live with someone we dislike, and
thus our identity would be fractured and divided against itself.[126] As already
stated, Glover's argument is explicitly (and seemingly exclusively) psychological, describing possible states of being and their motivation but not really
any moral normativity or obligation, though he does impressionistically describe "a moral charge when it is not a matter of style or personality, but is of
deeper character."[127] If one's "moral identity" revolts against certain things,
then for the sake of one's own wholeness one should oppose (or at least not
engage) in such things. (A few pages later, Glover acknowledges and rightly
worries that this sense of "moral identity" can become deeply tribalistic,
something we will see more explicitly with Lear below.[128])

Glover turns next to discuss what he calls "the human responses," which
also function as restraints on human selfishness. The first is the "tendency"
to approach people "with certain kinds of respect," perhaps because one sees
some "dignity" or "status" in them. Maybe they are members of a particular
community for which one has regard, or perhaps one extends respect simply

123. Glover, 22.
124. Glover, 22.
125. See Alasdair MacIntyre, *Whose Justice? Which Rationality* (Notre Dame, IN: University of
Notre Dame Press, 1989).
126. Glover, 27f.
127. Glover, 26.
128. Glover, 28. I worry that Jonathan Lear in his *Radial Hope: Ethics in the Face of Cultural
Devastation* (Cambridge, MA: Harvard University Press, 2006) falls into this trap or at least does not
articulate a clear way out of it. Henceforth cited as Lear.

because they are human. The other "response" that Glover discusses is "sympathy," which he glosses as "caring about the miseries and the happiness of others, and perhaps feeling a degree of identification with them."[129] Our lives are "entangled" with one another and we feel a "pull" that "destabilizes" self-interest to the point of caring for the suffering of strangers through sympathy, what Glover describes as "a need to reach out to others in pain."[130] For Glover, "ethics, being bound up with people, cannot escape soft-edged psychology," which amounts to "all dispositions and tendencies rather than hard universal laws," though he refers to Kant frequently throughout his book.[131]

These "human responses" of respect and sympathy together provide some "psychological backing" to the social pressures and moral conventions that limit Nietzschean values as we seek to make a new beginning without the moral law.[132] Moving beyond the implicit selfishness of "self-interest" as a "restraint," Glover states, "Human responses are the core of the humanity which contrasts with inhumanity"—a "humanity" that is sometimes a fact in the best cases but can always remain an "aspiration" or ideal toward which to strive as a higher way of life in other cases.

Glover's argument demands great admiration for its honesty, simplicity, modesty, and rootedness in empirical experience and evidence. Ours is a species with a "grim origin." We "won a dominant position on earth partly by using intelligence to devise methods of killing at a distance. And the packs of hunters who survived were often those who were best at killing other humans who were members of rival packs." For Glover, we are "still here" because we were better at killing others in our deep history, and we saw this violence erupt on an unprecedented scale and intensity via modern technology throughout the twentieth century. Given our historical heritage, Glover avers that "the prospects of reviving belief in a moral law are dim."[133]

For Glover, these are the two remaining options: "Morality could be abandoned, or it can be re-created." In the latter option, morality "may survive in a more defensible form when seen to be a human creation," which was essentially Nietzsche's position, though he did not care about constructing a "defensible form." For Glover, "We can shape it consciously to serve people's needs and interests, and to reflect the things we most care about."[134]

In short, then, Glover thinks that humanity can do differently and do better than it did in the twentieth century. And he sees this rooted in pragmatic self-interest and deeper psychological tendencies in the human species to seek

---

129. Glover, 22.
130. Glover, 24.
131. Glover, 37–38.
132. Glover, 23.
133. Glover, 40.
134. Glover, 41. Glover restates this position on the last pages of his book (409–10).

personal wholeness, to respect others, and to extend sympathy for sufferers, which should avert us to selfish violence. Somewhat similarly to Arendt, Glover's argument seems to be deeply, if ambiguously, dependent on some notion of human "nature": these are the kinds of creatures we are (at our best at least), and thus these are the kinds of creatures we should be. As a result, we should construct social values and political institutions "without external support" that will reinforce and defend "a move to a more peaceful world" as we attempt to "re-create" a morality "rooted in human needs and human values" against barbarism.[135] For Glover, the situation is urgent and demands immediate initiative: "If we do not start on man-made moral traditions, there will be a gap. Particularly in the relations between groups, amoralism may start to seem the natural state. And, once this happens, the idea of starting inter-group morality may come to seem utopian."[136]

The fundamental problem I see in Glover's position is that he never actually "answers" Nietzsche at all but plays into his problem of morality, despite Glover's ambiguous sense of human "nature" rooted and manifest in human psychology. Glover states that he and others do not "like" Nietzsche's position and thus that he "wants" to develop state machinery and public opinion to overcome it. But he never argues for why Nietzsche's position was wrong or even evil. Nor does he point out that making morality a human "invention" or "creation" means that Nietzsche's position is equally valid and that the moral life becomes a radical struggle for survival and success, which descriptively could seem accurate. After all, Glover's entire book is an overwhelming archive of evidence demonstrating that disrespect and brutality are just as "natural"—seemingly *more natural*—to the human species than "the human responses," and that "moral identity" is a deeply relative and not infrequently devastating motivation. If Glover's argument is merely based on "the grain of human nature" and experience, it seems that violence would be just as original and justifiable as other "human responses."[137] We must ask on what basis one human "creation" could possibly be superior to or more justified than another as we face Arendt's "problem of beginning" and attempt to "re-start" morality.

Glover's argument, then, points back to Nietzsche's, even as it opposes Nietzsche's particular moral preferences. Nietzsche too was an "inventor" of "morality," seeing the "new philosopher" as the "commander and legislator" for "new values." But Nietzsche had the added, albeit ironic, virtue of more explicitly admitting the amorality of his position. In the end, Glover plays into Nietzsche's hands: he does not "like" something, he wants to

---

135. Glover, ix, 406.
136. Glover, 410.
137. Glover, 409.

"overcome" it, and thus he names it various things like "disaster." But he does not acknowledge that he is waging a passive aggressive war of his own will to power, in which his "humanity" is on identical (a)moral footing with Nietzsche's "new philosopher" and his "great birds of prey."

Rather than a new beginning, then, Glover's psychology-based ethics as "human creation" seems more like *a restatement* of Nietzsche's "problem of morality," which, in light of the horrifying and overwhelming evidence of Glover's research on the twentieth century, leaves us stranded in Arendt's dystopian time "after all hopes have died" with its loss of value and meaninglessness.

A compelling argument that it is good to exist and that life in the world with others should be loved, and thus a sustainable motivation to embrace a responsible life of universal entry beyond the drive for power and survival, is lacking. From this perspective, Glover's opening statement takes on a more sinister, perhaps even nihilistic finality: "Never Such Innocence Again."

Lear: The Fate Worse than Death, the Crow Poet, and the New Crow Subjectivity

Jonathan Lear's study of the Crow Indian tribe's "cultural devastation" after being conquered and relocated to the reservation by the U.S. government addresses the same problem that we have been tracing through Nietzsche, Arendt, and Glover: the ethics of making a new beginning after devastation, what Lear names "ethics in the face of cultural devastation."[138]

To oversimplify Lear's complex analysis, the Crow's way of life—their way of being *Crow*, of being specific kinds of *persons*—was essentially constituted by hunting, making war against other tribes, and "planting coupsticks" on the open plain, which amounted to successfully planting one's spear in front of one's enemy in their territory as a display of one's bravery. These constitutive practices were what organized, energized, and made all of Crow life meaningful, valuable, and thus worthwhile—*Crow* life. Lear goes so far as to say that these activities were what made a Crow woman's cooking and child-rearing what it was: action teleologically oriented toward the successful achievement of hunting, warring, and planting coups.

Lear uses this ontological analysis of Crow life to interpret the deep meaning of Chief Plenty Coup's searching statement, "After this [relocation to the reservation], nothing happened." On the reservation, the constitutive Crow practices of hunting, warring, and planting coup sticks became impossible to perform, and thus the Crow people—Crow being or Crowness—came to an end. After being restricted to the reservation by the U.S. government, no more

---

138. Lear.

Crow events happened, and thus for the Crow, "nothing happened" at all. Crow history, Crow temporality, Crow being-in-the-world was "devastated."

In terms of personal identity, Lear describes this condition as "the fate worse than death" itself. The reason why life on the reservation was "the fate worse than death" is because it was no longer possible to die *as* a Crow and thus for death itself to have any intrinsic *Crow* meaning. The "cultural devastation" of the Crow way of life was in essence the destruction of what made life meaningful and worth caring about to begin with, whether that meant victory in battle, a brave death, or, especially for the women, a life and eventually a death devoted to serving and strengthening the *telos* of victory (or at least bravery in defeat) through activities like cooking and raising children.

If Lear is right, then, in his interpretation of Chief Plenty Coup's statement ("After this, nothing happened"), and thus if he is right that the move to the reservation was essentially the worst possible fate for the Crow ("the fate worse than death"), what could be done? Does the Crow story and other societies and civilizations in similar situations (one thinks of the modern state of Israel in the background of Lear's book) simply end in annihilation, even if their "life" goes on within the reservation? Or can a new beginning be made? This is the central question at the core of Lear's book, and his answer bears significant resemblance to what we have seen in Nietzsche, Arendt, and Glover, though I argue with a distinctively (and disturbingly) tribalistic core, which Glover worried about, as we have seen earlier.

Lear writes, "Although there were traditional chiefs when the Crow moved onto the reservation, over time it became unclear what a chief was supposed to do." Yes, they were meant to "lead," but Crow *leadership* outside the tribe's ontology-constituting activities of hunting and battle was no longer intelligible. Thus the question is raised, "What counts as real leadership now?" The problem is that the "criteria" for recognizing *Crow leadership*— legitimate Crow *beginners* to chart the course of their future—"are no longer viable," and thus it is "unclear on what basis new chiefs should be chosen" who could lead and make a new beginning for Crow life.[139] Lear summarizes:

> This, I think, shows the peculiar challenge that faces anyone whose civilization is under pressure. For if one is straining to live, and to help others, in a worthwhile way, the question can no longer be, say, "How shall I, as a Crow, go on?" but "What shall it be for me to go on *as a Crow*?" And one is forced to address this question at a time when it is no longer clear how one could possibly answer it.[140]

---

139. Lear, 45–46.
140. Lear, 47–48. See also 104: "The aim is to establish what *we* might legitimately hope at a time when the sense of purpose and meaning that has been bequeathed to us by our culture has collapsed."

Lear is clear that the aim of his interpretation is not "to foreclose on human hopefulness."[141] But he is trying to wrestle soberly with the reality that a co-herent, comprehensive way of life seemingly collapsed and came to an end.

In order to make a new beginning, Lear argues, "what would be required . . . would be a new Crow poet." He defines such a poet as "one who could take up the Crow past and—rather than use it for nostalgia or ersatz mimesis—project it into vibrant new ways for the Crow to live and be." Such a poet is someone who is "a creative maker of meaningful space." Against cynicism or despair, Lear insists, "no one is in a position to rule out that possibility."[142]

Lear's proposal here of a "new Crow poet" sounds exciting and hopeful. But it strikes this reader as profoundly problematic and perhaps a little dis-honest, and not a little reminiscent of Nietzsche's "new philosopher." Earlier in *Radical Hope*, Lear goes to great lengths to argue and demonstrate that the *Crow* way of life—their *being*—was constituted by hunting, battle, and planting coup sticks. Lear did not make any attempt to justify why this way of life may have been worthwhile or right to begin with; his interpretation was functional in nature: it was a way of life that made them *them* and gave them a sense of meaning and value, even if it revolved around trying to displace and destroy others. The point was that it worked and that it had come to an end, such that the Crow had been overtaken by a fate worse than death. As we have seen, "After that, nothing happened."

But now Lear seems to go soft and implicitly back-peddle with language of "new ways for the Crow to live and be" through "a creative maker of mean-ingful space." In this context, it seems possible—without stating how or with what justification—that the Crow can be Crow again *without* hunting, battle, and planting coup sticks. For all of the optimism and intelligence of Lear's analysis, this reader is led to sense that a sleight of hand has taken place: after the "devastation" of what made being a Crow a Crow, now the Crows through a "new poet" can be *Crow again* through activities that had never been part of their identity or constitutive way of life. It might make sense if Lear sim-ply argues that the Crow way of life was destroyed and abandoned and that the "Crow" people simply decided to become something else by making up a new way of life (perhaps a "conversion"), however much it might refer to their (dead) past. But to call this new "Crow life" *Crow* seems to renege on the center of his opening argument, which made the case of the Crow so grave and also so universally important.

But there is also a second problem. As noted, Lear never comments on *why* we should look at a life of hunting, raiding, and planting coup sticks—a life at the center of which is the attempt to take the lives and lands of others—as

141. Lear, 51.
142. Lear, 52.

worthwhile in the first place and thus why we should interpret its end as a "devastation" and not a deliverance. Moreover and more importantly, Lear does not provide any argument for why the new "Crow" way of life is itself ethically justified or justifiable. Yes, it may get launched, it may "work," and it may provide a teleological system of "meaning" for a certain group of people and their identity, at least until it is devastated and needs to be restarted again by yet another "new poet." But especially in light of its proximity to competing comprehensive interpretations of a morally worthwhile life, in each of which one is called to fully devote one's entire being to this way of life and thus to be utterly reduced to nothing by its devastation, providing some rigorous argument for *why* this new way of life should be taken seriously would seem to be a reasonable and responsible demand. How do we know that might is not simply making *right*, that practice is not substituting for *principle*, and that something's "working" (success) is not making it *worthwhile* (sacred)? How do we know that the "new Crow poet's" new morality is not simply a new tribalism, in which the lives and lands of others have no status or only arbitrary status and thus remain vulnerable to attack and devastation?

All of this, however unintentionally and ironically, would seem to open the door to the position of Nietzsche's new philosopher and the Nazi experiment of self-creation, amounting to an even weaker response than Arendt or Glover, because it seems to be founded primarily on group identity.

Lear does not seem to provide an answer to this question, and it is not clear that his (largely Aristotelian) moral philosophy can. Thus, it remains unclear if Lear and his "radical hope," in the book by that title at least, have remotely come to grips with Nietzsche's uncovering of "the problem of morality."[143] To be sure, Lear acknowledges that Chief Plenty Coup served as a "witness" of the "collapse of the Crow's future." Lear also rejects "all sorts of empty ways of going on 'as a Crow,'"[144] so he is not saying that just *any* innovation can count as a new, genuinely Crow beginning. Moreover, he writes,

> Such a witness manifests a new and intensified form of Crow subjectivity: he takes on the responsibility of declaring whether the ideals around which he has shaped his life are any longer livable. That is, he is willing to speak for the health and viability of the old ways of constituting oneself as a subject. But this can be done in the hope of clearing the ground for the creation of new forms of Crow subjectivity. There is reason to think that Plenty Coups told his story

---

143. See Jonathan Lear, *Open Minded: Working Out the Logic of the Soul* (Cambridge, MA: Harvard University Press, 1998), chapter 8, "Testing the Limits: The Place of Tragedy in Aristotle's Ethics." I am grateful to Charles Mathewes for this reference.

144. Lear, 52.

to preserve it; and he did so in the hope of a future in which things—Crow things—might start to happen again.[145]

But here again we are reminded of Nietzsche's earlier statement that man is "condemned to invention" and that the "new philosopher" would also be the "commander and legislator" of "new values" for his own great tribe.

What remains crucially unclear is how Lear's "new forms of Crow subjectivity" declared by the "new Crow poet"—or any new beginning for human life—can be distinguished from Nietzsche's will to power beyond good and evil in which Nietzsche's parable remains valid: "That lambs dislike great birds of prey does not seem strange: only it gives no ground for reproaching these birds of prey for bearing off little lambs."[146] This gruesome parable would seem to apply to the Crow's own devastation via the U.S. government's subjugation and their relocation to the reservation. Indeed, in light of an original past constituted by war and raiding, why would the "declaration" of "new forms" that serve the domination of Nietzsche's "birds of prey" in the Crow context not count as "a future in which things—Crow things—might start to happen again"—a new beginning that, in this case, would amount to a second coming of devastation for others, "after which nothing happened" *for them*? One worries that Lear's book falls prey to what we saw Nietzsche called "impure thinking," which, however unintentionally, "overlooks other men" in order to sustain itself.

In Lear's ethics of new beginning, more than in the previous two positions, an argument is lacking for goodness, love-worthiness, and thus a morality with the scope of universal entry. The problem of morality persists with greater intensity and greater danger for others.

SUMMARY: THE PERSISTENCE OF NIETZSCHE'S PROBLEM OF MORALITY

We saw earlier that Nietzsche forecasted a catastrophe of nihilism building on the horizon of the West, which he believed called for the making of a new beginning marked by the creation of new values. For Nietzsche, these new values were "beyond good and evil" and corresponded instead to the successful execution of the will to power, through which the weak and unworthy would be eliminated and the strong and noble would triumph. Such a new beginning would require "a sovereign disposition, great inventiveness, heroic purposiveness, noble being-for-oneself" free of any justification or right except the

---

145. Lear, 52. Here we are reminded of Arendt's claim that "salvation" comes through remembering and telling one's story, but Lear also does not address the fate of those lost to memory.

146. GM, I, §13.

willpower to affirm and assert this future. For Nietzsche, then, serious moral reflection *does* destroy itself, but this is not because the world is "evil" per se. Instead, the world is morally *empty*, and thus what remains is the open field in which the "new philosopher" can rise up above the slavishness of the mass and the endless anarchy—beginninglessness and lawlessness—of reality to display his greatness through the power of his will.

In the pages that followed, I tried to unpack and critically analyze the ethics of new beginning in Hannah Arendt, Jonathan Glover, and Jonathan Lear. In each case, I argued that their respective positions are unable to demonstrate why their proposals for our new beginning are justified and distinguishable from the novelty of the new philosopher's will to power. Moreover, given their extremely sobering accounts of human devastation and evil, their estimates of autonomous human wisdom and power to make a new beginning appear overoptimistic and potentially dangerous. Third, none of their positions has resources to offer the hope of a new beginning for the most brutally devastated and annihilated. Thus, injustice and evil appear to be just as original, authoritative, and ultimate as justice and goodness. The ethics of new beginning remains the sovereign, tragic work of human self-creation.

Within these strictly immanent perspectives, to anticipate a line from Bonhoeffer, "the wheel of history can no longer be rolled back."[147] And thus it remains unclear what justifies and energizes love for the world and life with others over against self-preservation, Stoic indifference, or nihilistic hatred beyond one's own personality, preference, or suppressed Christian principle. Universal entry survives at best as a heroic ideal, which may likely radicalize despair, and Nietzsche's "impure thinking" persists as a seemingly irresistible temptation in the face of such despair.

Overall, then, Nietzsche's (anti-)ethics of new beginning stands out as the most forceful option. And his gruesome parable remains insufficiently answered: "That lambs dislike great birds of prey does not seem strange: only it gives no ground for reproaching these birds of prey for bearing off little lambs." We may not *like* the great birds of prey, we may not *want* them to exist, we may even set up laws to criminalize them and war against them to the point of exterminating them, but in the beginning and end, all of us are playing the same anarchic game as they are, whether we register this as "invention" or "devastation." Thus, William Schweiker's "work of reconstruction," which we noted at the beginning of this chapter, remains and thus rightly confronts us as "the central business of contemporary moral theorists" as we live in a time of "constant revolution."[148]

---

147. *Ethics* (6:144).

148. For a critical interpretation of morality as "the path of invention," which broadly describes the three thinkers discussed in this chapter, see Michael Walzer, *Interpretation and Social Criticism*

A NEW START WITH BONHOEFFER

In the three chapters that follow, I will attempt to reconstruct Bonhoeffer's ethics of new beginning as a critical response and comprehensive alternative to Nietzsche's problem of morality and the inadequate new beginnings of Arendt, Glover, and Lear. My argument will be that Bonhoeffer presents us with a coherent, compelling vision that is able to defend the convictions that it is good to exist, that life in the world with others is worthy of love, and that these convictions should serve as our grounding, guiding orientation to reality within the demanding scope of universal entry.

In chapter 3, I will examine Bonhoeffer's interpretation of the human *incapacity* to make new beginnings in light of Bonhoeffer's basic interpretation of ruptures in our human nature and historical tradition. Here we will find that Bonhoeffer's estimation of our powers of beginning is far more critical and minimal than the earlier options. In fact, Bonhoeffer rejects any notion of self-creation, which challenges some contemporary preferences and expectations but also allows him to defend a normative account of morality and human responsibility.

In chapter 4, I will reconstruct Bonhoeffer's understanding of God's *justification* and *guidance* for human initiative as we seek a new beginning for our lives and moral order. This question of normativity is all the more important given Bonhoeffer's critique of the autonomous creature's self-creation and ensnarement in arbitrariness, which leads to what he calls the "murderous law of never-ending beginnings."

In chapter 5, I will elucidate six *practices* of new beginning in Bonhoeffer's thought, which I will set within his fundamental understanding of what "newness" actually means ("a new life in being there for others"), his vision of a counter-Nietzschean "radical revaluation" of values, and the importance of disciplined practice in human moral renewal.

In the conclusion and "Begin Anew," I will summarize my argument and discuss how Bonhoeffer provides the hopeful, challenging resources we need for the ethics of new beginning vis-à-vis the problem of the absence of God and human devastation in our world today.

Thus, I turn now to look at Bonhoeffer's evaluation of our capacities: Are we capable of making a new beginning for ourselves?

(Cambridge, MA: Harvard University Press, 1987), chapter 1. See also Charles Taylor, *Modern Social Imaginaries* (Durham, NC: Duke University Press, 2004), 96.

Chapter Three

"A Rift Irreparable through Human Initiative"

Devastation and the Human (In)Capacity to Make a New Beginning in Bonhoeffer's Thought

In this chapter I investigate Dietrich Bonhoeffer's interpretation of our capacity for making new beginnings. This question probes the heart of our condition as moral agents. As we shall see, Bonhoeffer interprets our drive for self-creation and thus to position ourselves as beginners to be a dangerous illusion, standing at the origin of much of the devastation in our nature and history.

I will take my lead primarily from Bonhoeffer's 1933 monograph *Creation and Fall: A Theological Exposition of Genesis 1–3*, which was originally given as a lecture course at the University of Berlin in the Winter of 1932–1933.[1] Strikingly, it was during this time (January 30) that Hitler became Chancellor and promised a new beginning for Germany.[2] In order to answer this question about our capacity for making new beginnings, I must first examine two fundamental ruptures that make the question so explicit, important, and problematic for Bonhoeffer.

The first rupture is ontological, taking place in the core of human nature and devastating the moral essence of humanity.[3] For Bonhoeffer, in the wake of this rupture, human nature is now marked by sin,[4] evil,[5] and death.[6] Bon-

---

1. For the limited literature on *Creation and Fall* and Bonhoeffer's creation theology, see the bibliography.

2. As I pointed out in the introduction, Hitler published an editorial already in 1925 for *Völkischer Beobachter* titled "The New Beginning." See chapter 4, notes 33 and 34 for more examples of this language in Nazi Germany.

3. "Meditation on Christmas" from December 1939 (15:530): "Human nature is the epitome of all human possibilities together."

4. See *Sanctorum Communio* (1:117), *Act and Being* (2:136), "Notes on the Concept of 'Sin'" from January 9, 1936 (15:345), and *Ethics* (6:157).

5. See Student Notes from Lecture Course "Review and Discussion of New Publications in Systematic Theology" from the winter semester of 1932–1933 (12:201): "Evil is not wanting to be dependent on others and not wanting to be there for others. Evil is the desire to be good on one's own."

6. Student notes from Bonhoeffer's outline on "Funeral Homilies" from 1936–1937 (14:740): "Death is not nonbeing . . . death is rather nondivine existence." Also *Sanctorum Communio* (1:285).

hoeffer often refers to this rupture within human nature in terms of our being "torn" or "fallen from the origin," which for Bonhoeffer is God's absolutely free and generous act of creating the world and human creatures "in the beginning" out of nothing. Having been "torn" from this founding beginning, it is no surprise that Bonhoeffer presents us with a deeply critical, dark analysis of the human person before God and with others in the world, even as he relentlessly affirms the goodness and love-worthiness of existence as God's gift, which remains always first and fundamental.[7]

The second rupture is historical but clearly not disconnected from Bonhoeffer's analysis of ruptured human nature after the beginning. As Bonhoeffer interpreted his times following World War I and in the shadows of World War II, he saw an era in European civilization, not unlike Nietzsche and Arendt, marked by an increasing "repudiation" of Christ's "form" and a perilous embrace of nihilism.[8] More particularly, Bonhoeffer thought that Christianity in its current form was cloaked in funeral garlands and coming to an end. In such a disordered time, Bonhoeffer saw a "spirit of annihilation" or "creative nothingness" overtaking his society and driving it toward destruction.[9] Given Bonhoeffer's interpretation of history, in which Christ's coming reveals the "origin, essence, and goal" of history, this rupture in Europe's historically Christian self-understanding could only prove disastrous. Without Christ, especially in view of Bonhoeffer's interpretation of fallen human nature, history becomes directionless and society becomes vulnerable to arbitrariness, lawlessness, claims to absolute power, and horrific violence.

Bonhoeffer's analysis of these two fundamental ruptures—ontological and historical, "after the beginning" and "here and now"—enables us to understand the importance and urgency of the question of the human capacity to make new beginnings. In essence, the question of new beginnings is the question of what grounds we have for hope in the present and future, both as singular persons and as a wider sociohistorical human community.

But Bonhoeffer's vision of rupture is precisely what makes him so deeply suspicious and critical of our capacity to make new beginnings for ourselves. Indeed, for Bonhoeffer, these basic ruptures help us to see that our quest to make new beginnings for ourselves is deeply ambiguous and sometimes devastating. Indeed, Bonhoeffer goes so far as to argue that our drive to make beginnings by and for ourselves—to make ourselves the founding origin and go first—is satanic and at the root of what ruptures the nature and history of humanity.

---

7. See *Ethics* (6:53).

8. As we shall see again in various places, Bonhoeffer thought the critique and challenge to Christianity was internally good for Christianity because it drove Christianity to confront its idolatries and perversions.

9. *Ethics* (6:122–23).

Paradoxically, then, we shall see that for Bonhoeffer the first and most fundamental step toward making a new beginning is the confession of our "fall from the origin," the acknowledgment of our incapacity to begin for ourselves now "in the middle," and thus the giving of our beginnings back to God. This is the first and fundamental cost for making a genuinely *new* beginning. Thereafter, humans are invited to assume the position of *followers* or those who come "after" the new beginning of Christ.

The discussion in this chapter, then, will point us toward our next chapter, which is concerned with the question of what justifies and provides guidance for the initiation of a new beginning in light of Bonhoeffer's deeply critical evaluation of human nature and society.

"TORN FROM THE ORIGIN": BONHOEFFER'S INTERPRETATION OF RUPTURED HUMAN NATURE

The Beginning

For Bonhoeffer, it is utterly fundamental that the Bible begins "In the beginning." According to Bonhoeffer, "The place where the Bible begins is one where our own most impassioned waves of thinking" continually gravitate but are also "thrown back upon themselves, and lose their strength in spray and foam."[10] The reason why is because Bonhoeffer thinks "the desire to ask after the beginning is the innermost passion of our thinking." The beginning "is what in the end imparts reality to every genuine question we ask."[11] Whenever we ask where we are coming from, what our lives might mean, and thus why they matter and how we should live, we are asking after the beginning. We are attempting to get to the roots of things, the ground and guide that give life and value to ourselves and reality. The beginning "is what in the end imparts reality to every genuine question we ask."[12]

But this is simultaneously the reason why our thinking faces its most radical limit in the beginning. According to Bonhoeffer, "we cannot speak of the beginning." Indeed, "Where the beginning begins, there our thinking stops."[13] Bonhoeffer argues that we cannot escape asking about the beginning if our life is to have a sense of ground and direction, and yet "we can never ask

---

10. *Creation and Fall* (3:25).

11. *Creation and Fall* (3:25).

12. Thus, Elshtain, *Who Are We?*, 22, is not exactly right when she claims the beginning for Bonhoeffer "is not, in any case, interesting theologically."

13. This sentence seems to allude to Kierkegaard's statement, "Faith begins precisely where thought stops." See *Fear and Trembling*, ed. and trans. Howard V. Hong and Edna H. Hong (Princeton, NJ: Princeton University Press, 1983), 53.

about it."[14] Why does the beginning show us to be so powerless, and what are the implications?

Bonhoeffer answers that the beginning by definition is "infinite" and "endless." Whenever we arrive at it, we can always go deeper and ask another question—Mann's "'again' and 'farther.'"[15] When we have concluded our regressive interrogation and reached our presumed "beginning," then we have most manifestly defeated ourselves and find ourselves inevitably grasping for what lies "behind" it for something prior and more fundamental.[16]

Ironically, then, thinking, as it dives after the beginning, is what simultaneously unveils the beginning's urgent importance and apparent impossibility. Thinking is what drives us to answer the question "why?," and yet "thinking can never answer its own last question why, because an answer to this would produce yet another why." In fact, Bonhoeffer interprets this very question "why?" as the first sign of "beginningless thinking," what he calls "the thinking of fallen humankind," which is trapped in an endless "circle." As we search for our beginning, we find that we "think in a circle. But we also feel and will in a circle. We exist in a circle."[17] In our finitude, Bonhoeffer judges that "the beginning is everywhere" but "for that very reason there is no beginning at all."[18]

This circular situation of human thinking, willing, and feeling exposes our entrapment in an irony bordering on perversity.[19] Human thinking most desperately wants to grasp the beginning because this is the ground and guide—the "why"[20]—for reality's and the self's meaning. And yet the beginning is what thinking resists most fiercely because it is also the boundary and end—the *limit*—of autonomous but contingent human thought and action.[21]

---

14. *Creation and Fall* (3:25). For the important Kantian background to this discussion, see *The Critique of Pure Reason*, Preface (Avii) and "The Antinomy of Pure Reason" (B447, A445/B473, A448/B476).

15. See Mann, *Joseph and His Brothers*, 3. Strikingly, the first volume of *Joseph and His Brothers* was published in 1933, the same year Bonhoeffer lectured on Genesis 1–3.

16. See Seminar Paper "The Theology of Crisis and Its Attitude toward Philosophy and Science" from the winter of 1930–1931 (10:475): "Cosmology may come to the assumption of a last ground of the world and may call that 'God,' all we can say in the name of Christian theology is that this God is not the God of revelation and not the creator."

17. This appears to be an allusion to Nietzsche's *Thus Spoke Zarathustra*, "Concerning the Virtuous," Pt. 2, §5. See "Concerning the Christian Idea of God" published in *The Journal of Religion* in 1932 (10:452): "Thinking does violence to reality, pulling it into the circle of the ego, taking away from it its original 'objectivity.'"

18. *Creation and Fall* (3:26).

19. Note Bonhoeffer's later comment on the "perversity" of the devil in his untitled Bible Study on Temptation from June 1938 (15:390): "The devil must deny that he is a creature of God in order to assert his own independence; thus he must deny his origin in order to be himself, which is an explicit perversity."

20. See Bonhoeffer's essay "On Karl Heim's *Glaube und Denken*" published in 1932 (12:254).

21. See "Theological Anthropology" given at the University of Berlin in the winter of 1932 (12:216) and "Lectures on Christology" during the summer of 1933 (12:305): "Transcendence is the boundary of the being that has been given to me." Note that already in *Sanctorum Communion*,

Caught in this "circulous vitiosus," Bonhoeffer writes, "thinking pounds itself to pieces on the beginning" precisely because "thinking wants to reach back to the beginning and yet never can want it."[22] As the self searches for its sources and seeks to claim its own ground, it is confronted by this contradiction in its core, this dividedness marked by obsessive desire and defiant aversion.

Idealism's Option

Here the self finds a solution, which Bonhoeffer sees embodied in Hegel's idealism and its attempt to "secure a beginning," a solution with similarities to the positions of Nietzsche, Arendt, Glover, and Lear.[23] The self can posit itself as its own beginning, seize the position of beginner, and "immediately" start with itself and its own reasons. Bonhoeffer calls this "the bold and violent action of enthroning reason in the place of God," which is, in fact, "but a systematic despair of its own beginning, indeed of any beginning."[24] For Bonhoeffer, this action is "bold and violent" because it implicitly acts out of the will to power's assertion of itself, the sheer postulation of the self's own primacy in self-consciousness.[25] But it amounts to "a systematic despair" for Bonhoeffer because it knows itself to be but an ungrounded fabrication, a raging wave that crashes against a boundary that it cannot overcome and wash into itself, which remains inaccessible and unknown.[26]

Bonhoeffer pairs "the doctrine of the primal state" with "eschatology," that is, the doctrine of the end or limit (1:58).

22. *Creation and Fall* (3:27).

23. See *Dietrich Bonhoeffers Hegel-Seminar 1933: Nach den Aufzeichnungen von Ferenc Lehel* (International Bonhoeffer Forum 8), ed. Ilse Tödt (Munich: Chr. Kaiser, 1988). For an interpretation of Bonhoeffer's reading of Hegel, see Charles Marsh, "Human Community and Divine Presence: Bonhoetter's Theological Critique of Hegel," *Scottish Journal of Theology* (Winter 1992). See also Friederike Barth, *Die Wirklichkeit des Guten: Dietrich Bonhoeffers "Ethik" and ihr philosophischer Hintergrund* (Tubingen: Mohr Siebeck, 2011), 44–80. For Hegel on "the beginning," see *Hegel's Science of Logic*, 67–78, and *Lectures on the Philosophy of Religion*, 113. To my knowledge, Plato, *Republic*, Book VII (533c) is the first to speak about "securing" (βεβαιώσηται) "the beginning" (τὴν ἀρχὴν) through "thinking" (διάνοια).

24. On idealism and "immediacy," see *Sanctorum Communio* (1:60), "Theological Anthropology" given at the University of Berlin in the winter of 1932 (12:216), and "Concerning the Christian Idea of God" published in 1932 (10:452).

25. For Bonhoeffer's definition of the will, see *Sanctorum Communio* (1:70, 72, 151). Note that Bonhoeffer sees the will as originating in the encounter with another person, and thus there is something inherently contradictory ("absurd") when the will is used fundamentally for itself. See *Act and Being* (2:1102).

26. It appears that Bonhoeffer is almost identically following Kierkegaard's critique of Hegel. See David Kangas, *Kierkegaard's Instant: On Beginnings* (Bloomington, IN: Indiana University Press, 2007), x, and Kierkegaard, *The Sickness unto Death*, 68. On Bonhoeffer's reception of Kierkegaard, see Barth, *Die Wirklichkeit des Guten*, 96–138.

The result is fundamental and far-reaching: "Human hatred of the unknown beginning." For Bonhoeffer, this hatred is precisely the manifestation of the fall of humanity, which exposes the spiritual rupture in the core of our existential and moral reality before God as creatures rebelling against our creatureliness. Unlike the animals, the human creature has the distinction and burden of "know[ing] itself to be totally deprived of its own self-determination, because it comes from the beginning and is moving toward the end without knowing what that means." But in this distinctive dispossession of ourselves and the claiming exposure of our own contingency in our reflexive consciousness, humans "hate the beginning and rise up in pride against it."[27]

This hatred of the beginning marks the fundamental break in human ontology for Bonhoeffer, the smashing of the human person's original integrity as a thinking, feeling, willing creature, which now finds itself in fragments "in the middle." Thus, the world becomes something to be overcome, mastered, and remade according to man's "bold and violent" beginning.

That Other

For Bonhoeffer, there are only two options for learning about "the beginning," only two voices that can speak concerning it. The first is "the evil one," the one who lies from the beginning and makes the lie its beginning, asserting its baseless sovereignty:

> I am the beginning, and you, O humankind, are the beginning. You were with me from the beginning. I have made you what you are, and with me your end is done away [*aufgehoben*[28]]. . . . Believe me, the liar from the beginning: lie, and you will be in the beginning and will be lord of the truth. Discover your beginning yourself.[29]

This, as we have seen, is the "bold and violent" idealist that "enthrones" itself through reason and force of will. This is the project of self-creation. Its "satanic" maxim is direct: "Discover your beginning yourself." Its promise of helping to overcome one's "end" is ultimately murderous.

The second witness Bonhoeffer names is "that other." "That other" is the God of the beginning, who is authorized to speak about the beginning because "no one can speak of the beginning but the one who was in the beginning." On this principle of originary presence, Bonhoeffer claims that "the Bible begins with the free confirmation, attestation, and revelation of God by God.

---

27. *Creation and Fall* (3:28).
28. Or "overcome" or almost "fulfilled."
29. *Creation and Fall* (3:28–29).

In the beginning God created."[30] Bonhoeffer's point is the following: If "that other," who is not me and not mine but *other*, was "in the beginning," then this one has the right and freedom to speak to me about what I cannot know by myself, namely, the beginning.

But this also means that the ego will not have the capacity or legitimacy to check this other's report, to verify and authorize its foundation from "behind" as sovereign master.[31] Instead, "the mystery remains a mystery," and the sheer fact of existence remains a miraculous gift: "that heaven and earth are there, that the miracle has come to pass, deserves all wonder."[32]

Quite provocatively, Bonhoeffer pauses here and makes explicit that even the first line of the Bible—"In the beginning, God created"—could itself be yet another fabrication of humanity, a religious "idol" that we set up out of "need" and "anxiety."[33] He writes, "In the beginning, God—that is just your lie, which is not better but even more cowardly than the lie of the evil one." (I will return to this passage in the conclusion.) The implicit question here is this: What finite creature could possibly claim to speak on their own ground about "God," who creates "in the beginning"? Such an attempt would be pure idolatry, anxiety, and self-deception looking for a stopgap masked as ultimate piety. Bonhoeffer asks, "And are we not all that person—we who out of the faintheartedness of our own lives, with their lack of a beginning and an end, cry out to a god who is but our own ego?"[34]

The stakes could not be any higher or more all-encompassing in where the Bible begins and where human thought crashes. Either God speaks about the beginning with "the free confirmation, attestation, and revelation of God by God" or such God-talk and drive for the beginning is pure violence and idolatry, what Bonhoeffer calls "an illusion produced by the faint-hearted imagination of a person who is unable to live in the middle with pride or with resignation."[35] These are the alternatives: human violence, resignation, or God's revelation.

---

30. *Creation and Fall* (3:29).

31. See Bonhoeffer's seminar paper "The Theology of Crisis and Its Attitude toward Philosophy and Science" from the winter of 1930–1931 (10:467). Note Arendt, *The Origins of Totalitarianism*, 604: "A theology which is not based on revelation as a given reality but treats God as an idea would be as mad as a zoology which is no longer sure of the physical, tangible existence of animals."

32. *Creation and Fall* (3:36). Note that for Bonhoeffer this "mystery" is not a "problem" but a source of wonder and dignity whose foundation is love. On "mystery" and modernity, see Sermon on 1 Corinthians 2:7–10 from May 27, 1934 (13:360). See Ernst Feil, *The Theology of Dietrich Bonhoeffer*, trans. Martin Rumscheidt (Philadelphia, PA: Fortress Press 1985), 5–6 and 27–28. Also Andreas Pangritz, "Mystery and Commandment in Leo Baeck's and Dietrich Bonhoeffer's Thinking," *European Judaism: A Journal for the New Europe* (Autumn 1997): 44–57. Compare Augustine, *City of God*, XII.15.

33. *Creation and Fall* (3:29).

34. *Creation and Fall* (3:30).

35. *Creation and Fall* (3:29).

Clearly, Bonhoeffer himself is convinced that the first words of the Bible are precisely the "revelation of God by God," by which "God alone tells us that God is in the beginning . . . by no other means than through this word."[36] And it is this divine revelation of the Bible that unveils humanity's hatred of "the unknown beginning" to be so devastating for human nature.

Originary Other-Love

In Bonhoeffer's "theological exposition," Genesis 1 reveals the Creator God who acts in the beginning out of absolute freedom to give life to what is not God as an initiative of self-giving love.[37] God begins in order to give life to beloved creatures, which are not merely churned out of God's being seeking itself by negation (as in Hegelianism[38]) but singular persons that are genuinely new, other, and free as finite creatures in the creator's image.[39] Thus, "this quite unrepeatable, unique, free event in the beginning" has nothing to do with the categories of "causality" for Bonhoeffer, which remain within the mechanistic domain of necessary reasons that can be traced back and captured by the human mind.[40]

For Bonhoeffer interpreting Genesis 1, *the beginning* is this miraculous *event*, which is not mediated by any law or principle that human beings could use to get "behind" and control God.[41] The Creator's act of beginning is "unconditioned" and mediated by *nothing* except the freedom of God without any other expla-

36. *Creation and Fall* (3:29–30). See "Confirmation Instruction Plan" from October 1936 (14:797).

37. *Creation and Fall* (3:41).

38. *Creation and Fall* (3:41). "God does not enter into what is created as its substance." See "Lectures on Christology" from summer 1933 (12:339): "The leitmotif of Israelite thinking is the preservation of the distance between Creator and creature."

39. This is the origin of Bonhoeffer's positive view of freedom, in which freedom is fundamentally "freedom for" (affirmative and relational) rather than "freedom from" (negative and individualistic). See *Act and Being* (2:112–13); *Creation and Fall* (3:63: "Being free means 'being-free-for-the-other'"); Sermon on John 8:32 from July 24, 1932 (11:470: "Being free means nothing else but being in love."); "Thoughts on William Paton's Book *The Church and the New Order*" from September 1941 (16:532). See Ann L. Nickson, *Bonhoeffer on Freedom: Courageously Grasping Reality*, Ashgate New Critical Thinking in Religion, Theology, and Biblical Studies (London: Ashgate, 2002).

40. *Creation and Fall* (3:32, 43). On Bonhoeffer's critical understanding of causality, see his course paper for Reinhold Niebuhr "The Character and Ethical Consequences of Religious Determinism" from 1930–1931 (10:441); "The Theology of Crisis and Its Attitude to Philosophy and Science" (10:475); Bonhoeffer's draft of "The Bethel Confession" from August 1933 (12:383–85).

41. See Bonhoeffer's Homiletical Exercise on Mark 4:26–29 from 1935 (14:368): "The miraculous: by God *alone automate* [on its own initiative]." Note *Discipleship* (4:189). See Ingolf Dalferth, "The Idea of Transcendence," in *The Axial Age and Its Consequences*, ed. Hans Joas and Robert Bellah (Cambridge, MA: Belknap Press of Harvard University Press, 2012), 170ff.: "[The event] is different from its symbolizations because it precedes and transcends them in a principal way: it is not a result of acts of symbolization, rather it is that without which these acts of symbolization would not be possible."

nation. The beginning is a gratuitous gift and act of omnipotence, which can only be received. Thus, there is no "link" between the Creator and the creation whatsoever other than God's word. And thus the world itself and the human self within it are groundless by definition, surrounded on both sides by an insuperable nothingness that cannot provide autonomous foundation or ownership: "The world exists in the midst of nothing, which means in the beginning."[42]

Crucially for Bonhoeffer, this radical divine act of unconditioned freedom was an act of gratuitous *grace*. It was an initiative of hospitality and generosity to give life to what by itself is nothing. Bonhoeffer calls this "the wholly new, the strange, inconceivable work of God's dominion and love," in which the one who "has no being of its own . . . receives its own being from God and praises God's being by its own being."[43]

As such, in the beginning, "the Creator denies [the Creator's own self], in that this grants form to what is created and grants to it its own being or existence before the Creator." Creation is thus at once what dispossesses the self of self-sufficient autonomy because I cannot claim even my self as my own right or possession (I am a *creature*), and it is also what gives reality and legitimacy to the self because it is given freely with genuine otherness from God (I *am* a creature). Bonhoeffer summarizes this fundamental, unrepeatable act of divine grace in this way: "Thereby the Creator enormously increases the power of the creation by giving to creation its own being as that which has form."[44]

In this paradoxical form, creation exists over against God in a new way, and in existing over against God "it wholly belongs to God."[45] Creation here is the fundamental event of newness, of initiating what has never been before, of God seemingly exceeding God's self by freely creating and affirming other, rational, willing creatures, who then make new beginnings. This, as mediated by Christ, is the fundament of Bonhoeffer's moral imagination, the key "precedent" for moral action, which will be freshly revealed and refounded in Christ's self-giving love on the cross later in the midst of history: divine generosity or "being there for others." Bonhoeffer names this "God's dominion and love."[46]

---

42. *Creation and Fall* (3:34).

43. *Creation and Fall* (3:36). See Schweiker, *Theological Ethics and Global Dynamics*, 106: "The moral meaning of faith in God as creator is that what is other than God, non-divine, fleeting, fragile, and finite, bears immeasurable worth."

44. Although he does not refer to Bonhoeffer, J. Richard Middleton, *The Liberating Image: The Imago Dei in Genesis 1* (Grand Rapids, MI: Brazos Press, 2005), 294–95, shows that Bonhoeffer's interpretation of Genesis 1 is historically-critically sound: the Creator "enhances [humans'] power and agency." Contrast this statement with Machiavelli, *The Prince*, 11: "We can draw a general rule which never fails or only rarely: the man who makes another powerful ruins himself." God is the opposite of the human hunger for power because God is originary Giver.

45. *Creation and Fall* (3:39). Note Kierkegaard in *Journals and Papers*, Vol. 2, 2:1251 / Pap. VII A 181.

46. *Creation and Fall* (3:36).

The Revolt

It is from this vantage point that we can better understand just how devastating and catastrophic the rupture of being "torn away from the beginning" is for human ontology in Bonhoeffer's thought.[47] Having been created in God's "dominion and love" out of nothing, to be "torn" away from God is to be cast out into what Bonhoeffer pictures as the breaking waves of existence, which momentarily crash and foam and then dissolve into nothingness.[48] Later in *Creation and Fall*, likely borrowing from Nietzsche's parable of "The Madman," Bonhoeffer uses the image of a meteor "dropping blindly into infinite space" to capture this ontological alienation.[49]

Here we need to give a more detailed sketch of the specific moral and existential implications of this fallout from "the beginning" in Bonhoeffer's ethics of new beginning. These dimensions are not chronologically or causally linked per se. But the following discussion indicates how Bonhoeffer interprets the mutually compromising and devastating dimensions of human nature, which he ultimately traces back to the last dimension we will explore, pride or the drive for self-creation to be "like God."

This summary and the following section will be crucial in helping us understand (1) why Bonhoeffer simultaneously thinks a new beginning is so important for humanity and (2) why he is so critical of and ultimately rejects the human capacity to make this new beginning for ourselves.

Anxiety

First, Bonhoeffer begins by describing the thinking, willing, feeling human person as divided from the beginning and restlessly searching for a new beginning. This reveals that the fallen person's being has become wracked with a deep though often suppressed *anxiety* [*Angst*].[50] Thus, for Bonhoeffer, the self's basic orientation toward the world and others, as well as God, is not neutral or innocently waiting to be attuned by a voluntary mood in the world. When we pay attention, we are always already anxious and uneasy in our own skin and the cosmos.

And this is because Bonhoeffer thinks "being in the middle causes anxiety," a kind of claustrophobia or vertigo.[51] As we have seen, "Humankind knows itself to be totally deprived of its own self-determination, because it comes from the beginning and is moving toward the end without knowing

---

47. *Creation and Fall* (3:37).
48. *Creation and Fall* (3:43).
49. *Creation and Fall* (3:120).
50. For further discussion of anxiety, see *Act and Being* (2:148), Sermon on Romans 11:6 from March 11, 1928 (10:481), *Discipleship* (4:173).
51. *Creation and Fall* (3:29).

what that means,"[52] stretched as we are between birth and death over which we have no power. The core of our anxiety, then, is that we are consciously aware of this contingency in the sources of who we are and our temporal constitution between past and future. Rather than "the middle" feeling like an open house, the fallen creature experiences its medial world as a place of dividedness, dis-ease, being exposed and pulled between two known unknowns on both sides of itself, which hold the possible answer to where it might be coming from and where it might be going, if anywhere. We are those "who feel anxiety before the spurious nothingness, before the beginning without a beginning and the end without an end."[53]

Most basically, then, Bonhoeffer describes human creatures as "unreconciled persons," persons whose "characteristic feature" is "restlessness." And Bonhoeffer links this to "why we are so worried, self-centered, unfriendly, distrustful, why we are untruthful and cowardly, why we are lonely, and why we are guilty." This anxiety in the middle between birth and death is "our secret."[54]

Obsessive Desire

Second, in the midst of our dividedness, Bonhoeffer sees the human person as driven with "obsessive desire" [*Sucht*].[55] In the middle between the beginning and the end, we crave to consume and to possess what we can. We feel pleasure and some security in the exercise of our will and the assertion of ourselves on others and our environment. This control makes us feel real, powerful, and thus less helpless. (This is likely the point from which Bonhoeffer would interpret Nietzsche's "will to power" while ultimately diagnosing it as a sign of our estrangement from "the beginning.")

In this condition of consumeristic desire, our love becomes confused, and we begin to see boundaries and otherness as limits to ourselves that must be overcome and absorbed. Bonhoeffer writes, "[The human] no longer sees the limit that the other person constitutes as grace but as . . . God's hatred, God's begrudging. This means that the human being no longer regards the other person with love."[56] Instead, the other person gets reduced to "the world of things" and God becomes "a religious object."[57] In the greedy desire of fallen human nature, the alterity that the other, divine or human, embodies comes

---

52. *Creation and Fall* (3:28).

53. *Creation and Fall* (3:36).

54. Sermon on 2 Corinthians 5:20 from October 22, 1933 (13:325).

55. *Creation and Fall* (3:101, 123).

56. *Creation and Fall* (3:122). See letter to Eberhard Bethge on March 19, 1944 (8:325): "Here I'm surrounded almost entirely by people clinging to their desires, so that they're not there for anyone else; they don't listen anymore, and aren't able to love their neighbor."

57. *Act and Being* (2:136).

to be seen as a diminishment of my fullness, a limit to my property, and thus an exception to my sovereignty. In order to *be* and be *content*, I must make mine—including the other person.[58] Thus, my desire must violate boundaries.

Bonhoeffer claims that this obsessive desire "thereby denies and destroys the creaturely nature of the other person." Rather than seeing the other person's creatureliness as the sacred endowment of God, which cannot be possessed by any other creature, the other person becomes part of my project, an instrument in my agenda, a "tool," as Nietzsche pointed out. And Bonhoeffer, at least in *Creation and Fall*, thinks this desiring consumerism "finds its primordial expression in sexuality." Bonhoeffer is certainly not saying that sexuality and the desire for sex are inherently sinful or dirty; sexuality too is the gift of God. But in the midst of sexual desire, Bonhoeffer discovers a particularly visceral manifestation of this dizzying, driving need to transgress the limits of the other person and possess for my self. He calls this an "extreme lack of respect for things-as-they-are" over against my self and aims.[59] Bonhoeffer summarizes, "Sexuality has torn the community of love completely to pieces, so that it has turned into an obsessive desire that affirms itself and denies the other as God's creature."[60] (Although Bonhoeffer does not offer it here, this would likely be his starting point for theological reflection on rape.)

Ultimately, this obsessive desire is perverse even to itself and further reveals the dividedness of humanity within itself. Bonhoeffer calls this "self-will" an "obsessive but powerless will for unity in a divided world." But such self-will cannot experience "unity" because "in losing his or her limit a human being has finally lost the other person," which amounts to "affirming oneself to the point of self-destruction."[61] This interpretation of "self-destruction" rests on Bonhoeffer's understanding of sociality as fundamental to human nature.[62] When I have alienated or destroyed others in my quest to enlarge my self and my "will for unity," I have made it impossible to be my self because humans are created for loving community with others. Enforced togetherness ironically leads to loneliness.

---

58. Note that Bonhoeffer is indirectly opposing Heidegger's idea that "mineness" or "always-being-my-own-being" [*Jemeinigkeit*] is somehow most fundamental to Dasein. See *Being and Time*, §9. In many ways, The Arcade Fire's 2017 album *Everything Now* is making this same point: our drive for "infinite content" and "everything now" leads to a hungry consumption of the other and deep loneliness.

59. *Creation and Fall* (3:123).

60. *Creation and Fall* (3:101). Bonhoeffer is alluding to his definition of "community" in *Sanctorum Communio* (1:60): "Community is the real bond of love between I and I."

61. *Creation and Fall* (3:123).

62. *Sanctorum Communio* (1:33): "Human spirit generally according to God's primal order of creation is possible and real only in sociality." *Sanctorum Communio* (1:78–79): "This net of sociality into which people are woven is prior to any will for community."

Thus, the basic structure we saw earlier repeats itself on the interpersonal level: when the beginning is captured, it is destroyed and yet another beginning is sought "behind" the beginning into the dark abyss of time. Likewise, when another thing or person is consumed and desire is seemingly sated, another thing or person is sought to satisfy my "limitless" "eroticism." But by consuming and destroying the integrity of otherness, I have destroyed that which I desire and the possibility of unity.[63] I am left by myself.

In this way the world, at least from the subject's point of view, becomes graceless or what Bonhoeffer names "this profound destruction of the original human condition,"[64] which was created in God's "dominion and love" for life together.

Loneliness

In anxiety and desire, Bonhoeffer sees human nature as wracked with intense loneliness and estrangement. He writes, "[the human] glorifies itself only in order to lie its way out of the dreadful loneliness [*grauenvolle Einsamkeit*] of a solitude in which no voice echoes to its own."[65] As we have just seen, when the otherness of the other person is dis-graced and denied by consumeristic desire vexed by anxiety, desire itself becomes a factory of loneliness, and thus the more intensely I desire in this manner, the more wildly alone and lonely I feel in the depths of my being. Thus, the quest for my satisfaction becomes the abyss of my discontent.

Bonhoeffer sees this ontological condition of being "torn from the origin" manifesting itself in the conditions of his society. As a twenty year old in one of his earliest sermons in 1926, Bonhoeffer observed,

A searching, an anxious groping and questioning for divine things permeates our own age. A great loneliness has come upon our age, the kind of loneliness found only in a godforsaken age. The enormous distress of isolation and homelessness has come upon the colossal, wild activity of countless masses of people in the midst of our big cities.[66]

Much later in his life, Bonhoeffer made a similar comment that sheds further light on this condition:

---

63. See also *Creation and Fall* (3:101, 123) and "The Nature of the Church" from spring of 1932 (11:293). For Bonhoeffer's distinction between "love" and "desire/eroticism," see "Lecture on Catechesis" from late 1935 (14:548), "Lecture on Pastoral Care" from 1935–1936 (14:568), *Discipleship* (4:125), *Life Together* (5:39), and "Lecture on Pastoral Counseling" from March 1938 (15:311), *Ethics* (6:188). The crucial distinction is always between a love that is oriented toward the other versus a love that is oriented toward oneself.
64. *Creation and Fall* (3:101).
65. *Creation and Fall* (3:142).
66. Sermon on Matthew 28:20 from April 15, 1928 (10:491).

Nothing can make a human being so conscious of the reality of powers opposed
to God in our lives as this loneliness, this helplessness, this fog spreading over
everything, this sense that there is no way out, and this raving impulse to get
oneself out of this hell of hopelessness.[67]

These passages illuminate the radical spiritual loneliness verging on hopelessness that Bonhoeffer sees inherent in the human creature's anxiety and
desire. If God the Beginner is by definition transcendent and not our creature,
then such consumeristic desire is intrinsically godless. It literally has no place
for God in its world, and thus even traces of longing for God to satisfy the
human's needs will be pathological and godless—idolatrous. And thus we are
not only humanly lonely in the depths of our being but also spiritually lonely,
and these lonelinesses, intimately linked for Bonhoeffer, lead to a "hell of
hopelessness" surging with "colossal, wild activity."

Much later in his *Ethics*, which in many ways is a rearticulation of basic
claims laid out in *Creation and Fall*, Bonhoeffer calls this loneliness "the
price of disunion from the origin," in which we exist as "god-against-
God."[68] Later still, in his uncompleted drama written in Tegel Prison,
Bonhoeffer suggestively has his main character Christoph say, "I only lose
my mind when I'm alone."[69] For Bonhoeffer, then, in the depths of our
moral nature, we are alone when we are alienated from our beginning in
God and others. In our anxious self-deifying desire, we become lonely and
lose ourselves. According to Bonhoeffer, "this sort of feeling undermines
every desire to live."[70]

Shame

In *Creation and Fall*, Bonhoeffer analyzes "shame" (*Scham*) as an expression
of "the fact that we no longer accept the other as God's gift but instead are
consumed with obsessive desire for the other."[71] But shame simultaneously
expresses the reverse of this situation, in which I realize that I am also the
object of the other's obsessive desire: "The other person too is no longer content to belong to me but desires to get something from me."[72] Shame, it would
seem, is attached to a deep intuition of the way that we mutually cheapen or

---

67. Sermon on Matthew 8:23–27 from January 15, 1933 (12:455).
68. *Ethics* (6:302).
69. From Scene 2 of Bonhoeffer's untitled prison drama (7:38). Remember that Arendt saw loneliness and the feeling of superfluousness as important factors in the origins of totalitarian. See *The
Origins of Totalitarianism*, 611–12. Compare Bonhoeffer's lecture on "The Right to Self-Assertion"
from February 4, 1932 (11:246) and "Lecture on Pastoral Care" from February 1936 (14:587).
70. Letter to Maria von Wedemeyer on March 24, 1943 (16:394).
71. *Creation and Fall* (3:101, 123).
72. *Creation and Fall* (3:101).

sham one another by instrumentalizing the world and reducing others to tools for our purposes.[73]

In this perverse "new thing"—this "innermost rupture in the community" between human and human that twists the "new thing" of God's creative gift[74]—Bonhoeffer sees humanity as "compelled to give unwilling witness to the fallen state of the ashamed."[75] That is, in the shame we feel in the way we instrumentalize and devalue one another, we find ourselves indirectly pointing to our original nakedness, which Bonhoeffer defines as "the essence of unity, of not being torn apart, of being for the other, of respect for what is given, of acknowledging the rights of the other as my limit and as a creature."[76] In the midst of our desire, we ironically cover and conceal ourselves before the desiring gaze of the other. And this for Bonhoeffer is an ontological-moral trace of something we have lost, which is particularly manifest in the complexity of human sexuality. Bonhoeffer later summarized this interpretation of fallen human nature in his *Ethics*:

> With God and others no longer serving as a protection and covering for them, human beings find themselves exposed. Shame appears. Shame is the irrepressible memory of disunion from their origin [*Ursprung*]. It is the pain of this disunion, and the helpless desire to reverse it. Human beings are ashamed because they have lost something that is part of their original nature and their wholeness. . . . There is something forced about enduring the gaze of another.[77]

This interpretation of shame as a basic ontological condition of fallen human nature has crucial hermeneutical implications in Bonhoeffer's thought. If it is the case that the world is now veiled and that humans, consciously or subliminally, hide and conceal themselves from one another, then Bonhoeffer—like so many other analysts of human nature—is right to emphasize our opacity to ourselves and to others, even as we live with a nagging intuition that something original to us has been lost, manifest in the most intimate dimension of our lives: our intercourse with others.[78] For Bonhoeffer, humanity lives surrounded by "a pale shadow" that secretly unveils a "yearning for its origin" even as it exacerbates our lostness.[79]

---

73. See Brian Gregor, "Shame and the Other: Bonhoeffer and Levinas on Human Dignity and Ethical Responsibility," in *Ontology and Ethics: Bonhoeffer and Contemporary Scholarship*, ed. Adam C. Clark and Michael G. Mawson (Eugene, OR: Pickwick Publishers, 2013), 72–85.

74. *Sanctorum Communio* (1:133).

75. *Creation and Fall* (3:124).

76. *Creation and Fall* (3:124).

77. *Ethics* (6:303–4).

78. See Clifford Green, "Two Bonhoeffers on Psychoanalysis," in *A Bonhoeffer Legacy*, ed. A. J. Klassen (Grand Rapids, MI: Eerdmans, 1981), 58–75, and Clifford Green, *Bonhoeffer: A Theology of Sociality* (Grand Rapids, MI: Eerdmans, 1999), 110.

79. See Sermon on Matthew 5:8 from August 12, 1928 (10:512).

Hatred, Violence, and Death

The human creature in its shameful estrangement from its origin "hates grace"[80] and experiences "hatred of the unknown beginning."[81] Hatred for Bonhoeffer is an extremely important (im)moral emotion that illuminates a fundamental orientation of humanity toward the world in its lostness. Inside of us, despite—or manifest within—our obsessive desire, there is the will to reject, condemn, and destroy existence, to express our sovereignty over others by devastating.[82] We think of the infant that finds pleasure in destroying what it has made.

Bonhoeffer imagines the original human creature angrily asking the Creator, "Why did you bring forth an imperfect creation?"[83] Full of self-justified hatred for the world in its contingent finitude and pain, we seek "a better god, a different god," which is our own selves rather than the weak Creator we despise as inadequate.[84] According to Bonhoeffer,

> Humanity has got what it wants; it has itself become the creator, source of life, fountainhead of the knowledge of good and evil. It is alone by itself, it lives out of its own resources, it no longer needs any others, it is the lord of its own world, even though that does mean now that it is the solitary lord and despot of its own mute, violated, silenced, dead, ego-world [*Ichwelt*].[85]

In such a world of our own making—"condemned to live without life"—Bonhoeffer sees the person and community locked in "a continuing, renewed rebellion against this existence [*Dasein*]," a "quarrel with life, a grasping at the life that would put an end to *this* life, that would be the new life."[86]

Paradoxically, then, in our hatred of this life and our lust for "the new life" as self-initiated creators, Bonhoeffer argues, "This life is precisely life on the way to death, and thus itself is death." Imprisoned within itself and despising boundaries, the human can only "hanker" after itself: "When Adam seeks God, when Adam seeks life, Adam seeks only Adam."[87] Thus, humanity's desire—our self-desire—"plunges . . . into an infinite thirst . . . an unquenchable, an eternal thirst," which for Bonhoeffer "is essentially a thirst

---

80. *Creation and Fall* (3:123).
81. *Creation and Fall* (3:28).
82. See Nietzsche, *On the Genealogy of Morals*, III, §1: "[The will] will rather will *nothingness* than *not* will."
83. *Creation and Fall* (3:129).
84. *Creation and Fall.* See also "Draft for a Catechism" published in 1932 (11:264) and Sermon on 2 Chronicles 20:12 on May 8, 1932 (11:435–36).
85. *Creation and Fall* (3:142).
86. *Creation and Fall* (3:143).
87. See Sermon on 1 Corinthians 13:4–7 from October 21, 1934 (13:382) on the "fiendishly distorted" love that appears to be oriented toward the other but is merely a form of self-love.

for death." Wanting to live and yet despising life, the creature estranged from its beginning hates existence and "wants death, wants to die."[88]

Thus, in answer to the question, "Why does Cain murder?," Bonhoeffer answers, "Out of hatred toward God."[89] In Genesis 4's account of the primal fratricide, Bonhoeffer sees a profound description of man's "destruction of life." In our drive for the new, we find ourselves in "a desperate raging"[90] that wills to uncreate creation: "That is why Adam's thirst for life is perverse."[91] And thus Adam's son Cain murders his brother, unraveling the implications of a dis-graced creation. This is striking analysis vis-à-vis the rise of Hitler and his proclamation of "new realities."

In *Discipleship*, Bonhoeffer later describes this perversity in human nature inclined toward violence in this way:

> Those who create their own god and their own world, those who allow their own desire to become their god, must inevitably hate other human beings who stand in their way and impede their designs. Strife, hatred, envy, murder, all have the same source: they spring from our own selfish desire.[92]

Later still in his prison poem titled "The Past," which meditates on the structures of time and the apparent loss of life to the past, Bonhoeffer describes this possessing mood again:

> My eyes and soul grow angry;
> I hate what I see,
> hate what moves me,
> hate everything alive and beautiful
> that would requite me for my loss.
> I want my life, I demand my own life
> back again:
> my past,
> you![93]

Here the past is pictured as a source of endless frustration and anger because it embodies the temporality in which the self is constantly being dispossessed by time. When I discover that I am incapable of this stability and ownership

---

88. *Creation and Fall* (3:141). Compare Sigmund Freud's "death drive" in *Civilization and Its Discontents*, trans. Joan Riviere (New York: Doubleday, 1958), chapters VI–VIII.

89. *Creation and Fall* (3:145). See Sermon on Revelation 2:4–5, 7 from November 6, 1932 (12:442): "They knew the reason why the world is evil, namely, hatred toward God and toward one's neighbor, the human love only for oneself."

90. *Creation and Fall* (3:144).

91. *Creation and Fall* (3:143).

92. *Discipleship* (4:264).

93. Poem titled "The Past" from early June 1944 (92:250).

by something so intimate and integral to me, time itself, I am tempted to "hate what I see, hate what moves me, hate everything alive and beautiful." The horizon of temporality in the present is dis-graced, and I hate "you."

Similarly, in his *Ethics*, Bonhoeffer writes,

> Radicalism always arises from a conscious or unconscious hatred of what exists. Christian radicalism, whether it would flee the world or improve it, comes from the hatred of creation. The radical cannot forgive God for having created what is. . . . On both sides . . . it is refusal to believe in God's creation.[94]

The "radical"—the one driven to grasp the roots of things to remake them—discovers within his self "the hatred of creation." Indeed, as Bonhoeffer said of Cain, the forefather of the builders of cities and civilization, the radical hates God for creating the world, for having chosen finite otherness in all of its fragility and interdependence rather than leaving vacuous nothingness or making autonomous gods. This, for Bonhoeffer, is the essence of nihilism.[95] And such nihilism easily gives way to "nothingness as God":

> No one knows its goal or its measure. Its rule is absolute. It is a creative nothingness that blows its anti-God breath into all that exists, creates the illusion of waking it to new life, and at the same time sucks out its true essence until it soon disintegrates into an empty husk and is discarded. Life, history, family, people, language, faith—the list could go on forever because nothingness spares nothing—all fall victim to nothingness.[96]

Indeed, Bonhoeffer believed that the "illusion of waking [existence] to new life" could grow so violent that "the end of all history" becomes "the murdered son of God" on the cross.[97] Torn from "the beginning that it wants and cannot want," this is ultimately what "the bold and violent action of enthroning reason in the place of God" looks like in Bonhoeffer's analysis of human nature: the murder of God and the human capacity for mass violence and genocide.[98]

From this perspective, Bonhoeffer thinks that "there can be . . . nothing more disturbing or agitating for human beings than to hear someone speak of the beginning as though it were not the totally ineffable, inexpressibly dark beyond of our own blind existence." When someone speaks of our *Anfang*, "People will fall upon such a person; they will call such a person the chief of

---

94. *Ethics* (6:155).
95. *Ethics* (6:123). See "Meditation on Psalm 119" from 1939–1940 (15:519) and Fyodor Dostoevsky, *Notes from Underground / The Double*, trans. Jessie Coulson (New York: Penguin, 1972), 123.
96. *Ethics* (6:128).
97. *Ethics* (3:145). See Sermon on 1 Corinthians 15:17 from April 8, 1928 (10:487).
98. *Creation and Fall* (3:27).

liars, or else indeed the savior; and they will kill that person when they hear what he says."[99] For such a person accepts and attests to the finite, limited nature of human life and the miracle of the beginning beyond human reach— to being a *creature*—in the world between the beginning and the end. Such a witness stands as the enemy to the human quest for self-creation and limitless power and as such must be eliminated.

A decade later, in the ruins of Hitler's promise of a new beginning, Bonhoeffer questioned from prison, "Why is it that we have hitherto thought with so little sobriety about the temptability and frailty of human beings?"[100]

Pride: To Be Sicut Deus

For Bonhoeffer, the mysterious root of humanity's estrangement from its beginning in God's gracious gift is "pride," the desire to be the Creator himself or what Bonhoeffer frequently glosses as the drive to be *sicut deus* ("like God").[101] At the core of this pride is the liar's promise: "Lie, and you will be in the beginning and will be lord of the truth. Discover your beginning yourself." Resenting its medial position after the beginning, the autonomous ego "hate[s] the beginning and rise[s] up in pride against it."[102]

Bonhoeffer offers several descriptions and glosses on this pride and self-idolatry across his corpus that are worth quoting here:

> The root of all sin is pride, *superbia*. I want to be for myself; I have a right to be myself, a right to my hatred and my desires, my life and my death . . . it is precisely in their wickedness that human beings want to be like God.[103]

> Flesh is everything within me that seeks to live from its own power and follows its own desire and its own will. Flesh is self-love and pride. . . . Flesh is hatred toward God.[104]

> Haughtiness before God is the root of all disobedience, of all violence, of all thoughtlessness. Haughtiness is the source of all rebellion, of all tumult, of all destruction.[105]

In *Creation and Fall*, Bonhoeffer uses several similar images and motifs to describe this fundamental pride or drive "to be for myself": "theft" against

---

99. *Creation and Fall* (3:28).
100. Essay "After Ten Years" from Christmas 1942 (8:44–45).
101. See *Creation and Fall* (3:111–14, 140–43); "Notes on the Concept of 'Sin'" (15:345); *Discipleship* (4:281); *Ethics* (6:277); "Outline for a Book" from August 1944 (8:503). Note the great similarity with Augustine's position in *City of God*, XIV, 3–4 and 13.
102. *Creation and Fall* (3:28).
103. *Life Together* (5:110). See Bonhoeffer's "Lectures on Pastoral Care" from 1936 (14:593).
104. Lecture on "Confirmation Instruction Plan" likely from October 1936 (14:793).
105. Untitled "Meditation on Psalm 119" from 1939–1940 (15:526).

God's generosity,[106] "tearing" away from God and others,[107] and the drive to get "behind" or "underneath" God and so to assume the position of the Beginner.[108]

A crucial description of pride that runs throughout Bonhoeffer's entire corpus is the distinction between "love" as "service" and "love" as the desire for "rulership."[109] Whereas God's founding act of creation—God's unconditioned beginning—is an act of self-denying, loving service for others, Bonhoeffer understands human pride as the drive to rule over what is other and thus to make a possession of the self and all reality. Thus, pride produces godlessness, in which the Creator is "pushed out" and the "ego-world" attempts to encompass everything within its reason and will. Love gives; pride takes. Love receives; pride forces.

For Bonhoeffer, such pride, with its attempt to be a "better god" in the place of God, is the root of "original sin" and the fundamental revolt that tears and estranges us from our beginning with others. It corrupts our nature with anxiety, consumeristic desire, loneliness, shame, anger, hate, violence, and ultimately murder. Ultimately, the I must be All, and this means that everything other must be absorbed or annihilated.

Hermeneutical Twilight and the Ambiguity of Moral Knowledge (Conscience)

Bonhoeffer's analysis of human nature estranged from its beginning has fundamental implications for his estimation of the capacities and reliability of human reason, hermeneutics, and conscience.[110]

---

106. *Creation and Fall* (3:54, 67, 89, 101, 110, 112, 117, 120, 123, 137, 145); Sermon on John 8:32 from July 24, 1932 (11:470); Lecture on the Catalogue of Vices from 1937 (14:730).

107. *Creation and Fall* (3:37, 54, 60, 115, 120, 122, 138); *Act and Being* (2:137, 161); Lecture on "The Anthropological Question in Contemporary Philosophy and Theology" from July 31, 1930 (10:402–3, 405); "The Nature of the Church" (11:293); Sermon on Psalm 63:3 from October 4, 1931 (11:403); "Lecture on Catechesis" from January 1936 (14:547); *Discipleship* (4:218); "After Ten Years" (8:39).

108. *Creation and Fall* (3:31, 32, 69, 106, 108, 110, 111, 113, 116, 120, 140); *Act and Being* (2:61); "The History of Twentieth-Century Systematic Theology" from winter 1931–1932 (11:231); "Lectures on Christology" from summer 1933 (12:304); lecture fragment on the "Doctrine of the Holy Spirit" from late 1936 (14:484); *Discipleship* (4:82); "Meditation on Psalm 119" (15:497); *Ethics* (6:249).

109. *Creation and Fall* (3:66, 117); *Discipleship* (4:230, 240, 264); *Sanctorum Communio* (1:60, 63, 97, 141, 177, 265); "Draft for a Catechism" published in 1932 (11:265); "The Nature of the Church" from summer 1932 (11:332); Letter to Wolfgang Staemmler on June 27, 1936 (14:196); essay on "The Confessing Church and the Ecumenical Movement" from August 1935 (14:411); Homiletical Exercise on Revelation 22:1–5 from 1935–1937 (14:771); lecture on "Congregational Development and Church Discipline in the New Testament" from March 1937 (14:819); *Life Together* (5:106); lecture outline on "Theology and the Congregation" from 1940 (16:495); *Ethics* (6:404).

110. For Bonhoeffer's understanding of the faculty of reason, see *Ethics* (6:174, 374). See Christiane Tietz-Steiding, *Bonhoeffers Kritik der verkrümmten Vernunft. Eine erkenntnistheoretische Untersuchung* (Tübingen: Mohr Sibeck, 1999), and Heinz Eduard Tödt, "Conscience in Dietrich

For example, Bonhoeffer writes that fallen humanity has been cast from "the unambiguous immediacy of its speech and its praise of the Creator into the ambiguity of utter strangeness and enigma." With our rational and linguistic faculties exiled from the clarity and integrity that God gives creation, Bonhoeffer says that "the trees and the animals" point to "incomprehensibility and arbitrariness," which often strike us as "grotesque." In our "state of disruption," we inhabit "this extraordinary twilight,"[111] and "psychologically we remain opaque to ourselves."[112] Bonhoeffer goes so far as to say that "human beings have lost their creaturely nature; this has been corrupted by their being sicut deus. The whole created world is now covered in a veil; it is silent and lacking explanation, opaque and enigmatic."[113]

For Bonhoeffer, there is one more crucial implication of this description of human ontology "torn from the beginning." Bonhoeffer argues that our very awareness of a distinction between "good and evil" is a sign of our condition "in the middle." That is, in the beginning, creation was *universally* and *exclusively good*, such that a duality between "good" and something otherwise would have made no sense and been incomprehensible to human creatures who lived in the grace of God's beginning. In the beginning, creation and human existence were truly "beyond good and evil."[114]

What this means is that "conscience" [*Gewissen*], rather than being a reliable guide to moral knowledge for Bonhoeffer, is rather the internalization of our "precipitous plunge" away from God and goodness. Bonhoeffer writes, "This flight, Adam's hiding away from God, we call conscience. Before the fall there was no conscience."[115] After the fall, in the voice of conscience, Bonhoeffer hears the human playing the ventriloquist of God, giving judgment to itself in the attempt to "evade God's judgment" by the evaluation of "a god who is but our own ego."[116] He summarizes,

> Conscience is not the voice of God within sinful human beings; instead it is precisely their defense against this voice. Yet precisely as a defense against this

---

Bonhoeffer's Ethical Theory and Practice," in *Bonhoeffer's Ethics: Old Europe and New Frontiers* (Kampen, The Netherlands: Kok Pharos Publishing House, 1991), 46–58.

111. *Creation and Fall* (3:134–35).

112. *Act and Being* (2:142).

113. *Creation and Fall* (3:126). See diary from New York in June 1939 (15:228–29): "It is remarkable how I am never quite clear about the motives for any of my decisions. . . . In the last resort one acts from a level which remains hidden from us." For the argument that this traditionally Christian position on the fall is not obscurantist but rather a catalyst for the scientific revolution, see Peter Harrison, *The Fall of Man and the Foundations of Science* (Cambridge: Cambridge University Press, 2007).

114. *Creation and Fall* (3:87). See *Ethics* (6:300).

115. *Creation and Fall* (3:128).

116. *Creation and Fall* (3:30). Bonhoeffer here is quite close to Nietzsche in *Beyond Good and Evil*, §291.

voice, conscience still points to it, in spite of all that human beings know and want.[117]

At best, then, like Bonhoeffer's analysis of shame, conscience is a treacherous trace or reminder that who and how we are now "in the middle" is not who and how we were meant to be "in the beginning." Much more than a help or inner guide, conscience presents us with an ambiguous *temptation* of confusing our voice with God's, of replacing God's call, "Adam, where are you?," with religious self-reassurances like the following: "Confess who you are, do not lose yourself in religious despair, be yourself." As a result, Bonhoeffer claims that God must "slay" human conscience amid "the ambiguous twilight of creation."[118]

Here we see again the depths of Bonhoeffer's critique of human self-deception. In the same way that he insisted that the statement "In the beginning, God created" could be an idolatrous lie to satisfy one's religious needs, so the rational faculties of the autonomous human are not seen as a reliable source of moral knowledge but rather a temptation that must be crucified and resurrected by the Creator.[119] In a sermon from prison, Bonhoeffer makes his position plain: "The world is ruled by forces against which reason can do nothing." This, Bonhoeffer judged, should lead to a more "sober" approach to who we are and our moral judgment.[120]

Four Additional Complexities

Before turning briefly to Bonhoeffer's analysis of historical rupture, four further complexities must be added to the picture of ontological rupture presented earlier that, again, help us understand why a new beginning is both so urgent and so problematic for Bonhoeffer.

First, if the brevity of the foregoing analysis risked a schematic abstractness, we must remember that this analysis was deeply personal and rooted in the real world for Bonhoeffer. It is worth quoting a moving passage at length that beautifully exhibits Bonhoeffer's sensitivity to human suffering and moral struggle "fallen from its origin":

> In the midst of glorious creation, we see a paralyzed child being pushed in a wheelchair. For those who still have a heart that has not become completely numb toward their neighbor, it becomes clear at that very moment that here

---

117. *Creation and Fall* (3:128). See *Act and Being* (2:138) and *Ethics* (6:276).

118. *Creation and Fall* (3:129).

119. Note that Bonhoeffer thinks conscience can be renewed after Christ's new beginning. See *Ethics* (6:278).

120. "Thoughts on the Day of the Baptism of Dietrich Wilhelm Rüdiger Bethge" from May 1944 (8:388).

something in our world is not right, that the world in which this image of torment and sorrow is possible is not the original creation of God. Here something that denies God has broken into the world. The world has fallen away from its origin; destructive powers have won power in it. . . . Every sickness prompts me to look into the depths of the world's sin and of my personal Godlessness. . . . Not only my body, my nerves, my mind is sick but my entire being, my heart is sick, sick from unbelief, from anxiety, from the godlessness of my life. And which healthy person does not also suffer from this most hidden and simultaneously most uncanny illness?[121]

These views of human nature are not meant to express a cold or detached condemnation of "others." To the contrary, Bonhoeffer is calling for an honest and care-full facing of the human brokenness that we all share, which shaped how Bonhoeffer viewed human weakness, disability, and sickness.

Second, Bonhoeffer also sees this originary rupture as having cosmic, world-encompassing implications, as this passage indicates. Still in *Creation and Fall*, Bonhoeffer writes, "God, the brother and sister, and the earth belong together. . . . The world is changed and destroyed in that human beings in their dividedness can no longer live with God, with one another, and with nature."[122] This is an area still needing comprehensive interpretation in Bonhoeffer's corpus, but we simply note here that Bonhoeffer sees sin as having transhuman, planetary implications.[123]

Third, as the quote also indicates, Bonhoeffer's relentless analysis and critique of our moral ontology does *not* imply any rejection of humanity or creation whatsoever. To the contrary, Bonhoeffer argues that creaturely life is God's gift and fundamentally good. This conviction is what drives him to take our condition so seriously and why Bonhoeffer thinks moral phenomena like "shame" and "conscience" are so important to analyze as faint traces back to our beginning. Bonhoeffer's love for the world is most fundamentally the reason why he is so passionately concerned with the problem of making a new beginning and thus why he so critically diagnoses our present condition.

Finally, with regard to the origin of evil and revolt against God in human nature, Bonhoeffer uniformly insists on "the incomprehensibility of this

---

121. Essay on "The Best Physician" from January 1941 (16:499–501).

122. *Creation and Fall* (3:67, 135).

123. In a letter to Walter Dreß on September 1, 1928, Bonhoeffer wrote, "I'm sure God also loves animals" (10:137). See Steven C. van den Heuvel, *Bonhoeffer's Christocentric Theology and Fundamental Debates in Environmental Ethics* (Eugene, OR: Pickwick, 2017); Terra Schwerin Rowe, *Toward a Better Worldliness: Ecology, Economy, and the Protestant Tradition* (Minneapolis, MN: Fortress Press, 2017), 157–68; and Larry Rasmussen, "Bonhoeffer: Ecological Theologian," in *Bonhoeffer and Interpretive Theory: Essays on Methods and Understanding*, ed. Peter Frick (Frankfurt am Main: Peter Lang, 2013), 251–68.

deed" and sets as his task only "to make clear its incomprehensibility."[124] This follows directly from Bonhoeffer's statement in his dissertation *Sanctorum Communio*: "Sin in every case is unfathomable, inexcusable defiance of God, arising from free will . . . the deed itself is something completely new, born of freedom and psychologically inexplicable"—a kind of human act of anticreation analogous to God's act of creation.[125]

For our purposes, let us simply note that in the same way Bonhoeffer sees pathologies of the Fall in our attempt to get back "behind" God's unconditioned beginning of creation and thereby to locate ourselves "in the beginning," so Bonhoeffer thinks the attempt to fully understand the roots of evil in ourselves is ultimately a reduplication of this irrational pride that will never be satisfied.[126] Part of what makes evil so wicked and rupturing is that it is incomprehensible and only leaves what Hannah Arendt called "holes of oblivion" in its wake.[127] While there is a certain affinity with fideism here, Bonhoeffer refuses to capitulate to "the bold and violent action of enthroning reason in the place of God" with its "systematic despair of the beginning."

"HERITAGE AND DECAY": BONHOEFFER'S ANALYSIS OF HISTORICAL RUPTURE IN EUROPEAN SOCIETY

The Thunderstorm

If Bonhoeffer pictured ruptured human nature "in the middle" as an ocean of waves crashing into spray and foam, he described his moment in history as "the black cloud and bright lightning flash of the thunderstorm":

> Seldom has a generation been as uninterested as ours in any kind of ethical theory or program. . . . This does not come from any ethical indifference in our times, but rather the reverse, from the pressure of a reality filled with concrete, ethical problems such as we have never had before in the history of the West. In a time when there were firm orders of life that permitted at most the small, usually undiscovered, sins of human weakness, when the criminal was abnormal

---

124. *Creation and Fall* (3:95). Also 3:104, 112, 117; Lecture on "The Anthropological Question in Contemporary Philosophy and Theology" from July 31, 1930 (10:404); Bible Study on "Temptation" from 1938 (15:390).

125. *Sanctorum Communio* (1:117).

126. See Stephen Mulhall, *Philosophical Myths of the Fall* (Princeton, NJ: Princeton University Press, 2005), 15.

127. See Albini Christian, *Il Male: Risvegliare L'umano in Hannah Arendt e Dietrich Bonhoeffer* (Cengia VR, Italy: Gabrielli Editori, 2016); Charles T. Mathewes, "A Tale of Two Judgments: Bonhoeffer and Arendt on Evil, Understanding, and Limits, and the Limits of Understanding Evil," in *The Journal of Religion* 80, no. 3 (July 2000), 375–404; and Insole, *Kant and the Creation of Freedom*, 133–34.

and removed from society under its outraged or pitying gaze, then the ethical as a theoretical problem could be interesting. Today we have villains and saints again, in full public view. The gray on gray of a sultry, rainy day turned into the black cloud and bright lightning flash of the thunderstorm.[128]

In fact, across Bonhoeffer's entire corpus, a growing storm system can be tracked that erupts into thunder and lightning as Nazism swept through Germany, which Bonhoeffer saw as shattering the historical identity and moral tradition of Western society similarly to Arendt and Glover.

Already in 1933, the year Hitler's Chancellorship began, Bonhoeffer wrote on the final page of *Creation and Fall,*

> It is with Cain that history begins, the history of death. Adam, the one who is preserved for death and consumed with thirst for *life*, begets Cain, the *murderer*. The new thing about Cain, the son of Adam, is that as sicut deus he himself lays violent hands on human life.[129]

In the same way that Cain's "history of death" and "violent hands" originated in Adam's ruptured relationship with God's generous beginning, so Bonhoeffer understands the "thunderstorm" of his historical moment as the result of a fundamental rupture in Western civilization's history as it grasped for "the new."

The Form of Christ, the Unity of the West

Despite writing that "it is with Cain that history begins," Bonhoeffer is equally emphatic throughout his work that with Jesus of Nazareth a more fundamental new beginning commenced in history. Indeed, as we will see in greater detail in chapter 4, Bonhoeffer understands Christ as humanity's "vicarious representative," which means that what happened to Christ "for us" and "in our place" also becomes true of humanity. Thus, Christ is the event and embodiment of our new beginning in the midst of history, the fulfillment of Isaiah's prophecy:

> "Do not remember the former things or consider the things of old. I am about to do a new thing" (Isa. 43:18–19). The new is the real end of the old; the new, however, is Christ. . . . The church speaks within the old world about the new world. And because it is surer of the new world than of anything else, it sees the old world only in the light of the new world.[130]

---

128. *Ethics* (6:76). See Sermon on Luke 12:35–40 from November 1931 (11:414).
129. *Creation and Fall* (3:145). Here Bonhoeffer is developing a claim from *Sanctorum Communio* (1:63).
130. *Creation and Fall* (3:21).

This new vision of the old world for Bonhoeffer serves as the basis of the claim that the coming of Christ two millennia ago was the beginning of "the new world" in the midst of human history, which initiated the renewal of God's act of creation and a new commencement for humanity sourced in eternity.[131]

It is precisely the newness of Christ's incarnate bisection of history—Christ's "new world" that exposes and claims the "old world"—that Bonhoeffer thinks makes *history* truly *historical* with a distinct past and future, giving it a narrative *form* and *heritage* or plot, which has constituted Western civilization's way of telling time.[132] Indeed, it is Christ himself who enables us to understand ourselves as "being in the middle" between the beginning of creation and the new beginning of the resurrection.

For Bonhoeffer, then, Christ's "form" is now meant to provide the normative paradigm and plot for human personhood and community across time, against seeing history circling in eternal recurrence like Nietzsche[133] or randomly flailing with no direction at all until dissolving into death.[134] This emplotment is why Bonhoeffer calls Christ "the origin, essence, and goal of history," without whom history remains meaningless and timeless—the grey on grey of a building thunderstorm.[135] Rather than a racial or ethnocentric or even regionalist notion, the interpretation of Christ's coming as the decisive event for history's emplotment is the basis of Bonhoeffer's statement that "the form of Christ is the unity of the Western peoples and . . . therefore none of these peoples can exist by itself or even be thought to so exist" because Christ is "the human for others."[136]

---

131. See "The Nature of the Church" (11:294): "The cross is the *dividing line between old and new humanity*." See Siedentop, *Inventing the Individual*, especially 332, 353, 360.

132. This position goes back to Bonhoeffer's earliest writings. See Bonhoeffer's diary from 1924 (9:105); "What Is Paul's View on Earthly Suffering?" (10:386); and *Sanctorum Communio* (1:94). See Michael DeJonge, "Bonhoeffer's Concept of the West," in *Bonhoeffer and Politics* (Frankfurt: Peter Lang, 2011), and Hans-Dirk van Hoogstraten, "Europe as Heritage: Christian Occident," in *Bonhoeffer's Ethics: Old Europe and New Frontiers* (Kampen, The Netherlands: Kok Pharos Publishing House, 1991), 97–111. Hannah Arendt also offers striking insights on Christ's "turning-point" for history. See *The Life of the Mind*, 2:18, 29.

133. See "Exercises in Pastoral Epistles" fragment from 1938 (15:324).

134. See the lecture on "Jesus Christ and the Essence of Christianity" from December 11, 1928 (10:345).

135. Bonhoeffer does not employ the concept of "axiality" as Karl Jaspers would in his 1949 *Ursprung und Ziel der Geschichte*. But his notion of Christ as the decisive dividing line between the past and future in Western history is very close to Jaspers's idea. See Hans Joas, "The Axial Age Debate as Religious Discourse," in *The Axial Age and Its Consequences*, eds. Robert Bellah and Hans Joas (Cambridge, MA: Belknap Press of Harvard University Press, 2012), 10.

136. *Ethics* (6:101). Lest it seem like Bonhoeffer is simplistically privileging "the West" over "the rest," see his comments on India in a letter to Julie Bonhoeffer on May 22, 1934 (13:152): "Christianity did in fact come from the East originally, but it has become so westernized and so permeated by civilized thought that, as we can now see, it is almost lost to us." Bonhoeffer planned to go to India and study under Gandhi, though the war prevented this.

"The Great Dying Out of Christianity" and "Western Godlessness"

This interpretation of Christ and history enables us to appreciate the gravity of Bonhoeffer's diagnosis of what was taking place in European society in his lifetime, as we noted earlier with Nietzsche and Arendt. In short, Bonhoeffer's entire corpus reveals that he believed Christianity was coming to an end in Europe, at least in its existing form,[137] and that, with it, the foundation of Europe's historical identity and moral order was collapsing into a destructive nihilism in which crucial limits were being lost and human life, especially for the weak and vulnerable, was radically endangered.

Already in his doctoral dissertation *Sanctorum Communio* (1927), Bonhoeffer had judged the church as appearing "profoundly impoverished and helpless" and being "in the gravest internal danger." He observed that "the masses have turned their back on her" and "the bourgeoisie's attachment to the church is threadbare."[138]

A year later, Bonhoeffer's analysis had become more severe:

> Events of recent decades have plunged us into an unprecedented crisis characterized by unclear political ideology as well as by complete helplessness in the face of pedagogical, ethical, and religious questions. The rug—or let us say the bourgeois parquet floor—has been ruthlessly pulled out from under our feet, and we must now search for a bit of *earth* on which to stand.[139] . . . All of us who still feel bound to the church in one way or another, and still feel responsible for addressing questions of morality—we are ourselves still in crisis, still searching, still perplexed. Who among us dares to answer unequivocally the question about the meaning of Europe's contemporary fate? [. . .] Our own age is getting out of joint. The vital force of our people, of Europe, seems broken. The hideous face of decadence, of immorality, of cynicism, of depravity grins at us from every corner and every crevice.[140]

Speaking of "a hitherto unprecedented revolution in morals," Bonhoeffer thought that "it would be difficult to find a period in history" that had "experienced as radical a change in . . . literature as has the period between 1910 and approximately 1925."[141] Swirling with such change, Bonhoeffer described his age as permeated by "a searching, an anxious groping and questioning

---

137. Letter to Karl-Friedrich Bonhoeffer on January 13, 1934 (13:81): "I am becoming more convinced every day that in the West Christianity is approaching its end—at least in its present form and its present interpretation." It's worth pointing out that this statement comes almost a decade before his prison writings, which some have wrongly seen as marking a massive shift in Bonhoeffer's thought.

138. *Sanctorum Communio* (1:23, 270, 272).

139. This seems to be an allusion to Nietzsche in *Twilight of the Idols*, IX:5, quoted in chapter 2.

140. Lecture "The Tragedy of the Prophetic and Its Lasting Meaning" from November 13, 1928 (10:326, 341).

141. Lecture "Basic Questions of a Christian Ethic" from February 1929 (10:360).

for divine things," "a kind of loneliness found only in a godforsaken age" pulsing with "the enormous distress of isolation and homelessness."[142] This led Bonhoeffer to ask the searching question, "Is there still something like the soul in an age such as ours, an age of machines, of economic competition, of the dominance of sports and fashion; is this nothing more than a cherished childhood memory, like so much else?" In his context recovering from war and in the midst of economic depression, Bonhoeffer thought, "It just sounds so strange and peculiar amid the confusion and loud voices extolling themselves, this little word 'soul.'"[143]

His own soul very much disturbed by the grinding poverty and unemployment of post-WWI Germany, Bonhoeffer wrote in a letter that "the misery is frightful, and the most terrible thing of all is the hopelessness of the situation." He went on to say, "We know how much we need the church, especially during the next winter, but what is its message and who will listen to it? It is awful to be almost damned to inactivity!"[144] Writing to his friend Erwin Sutz a few months later in 1931, Bonhoeffer continued to reflect on "the unprecedented situation of our public life here in Germany" and confessed:

> It really looks unbelievably serious. There apparently is really no one in Germany who has even the slightest overview of things. But in general everyone has a strong feeling that very great changes in the course of world history are before us. . . . Seven million unemployed, that means fifteen or twenty million people hungry. I don't know how Germany and how each individual can live through that. Intelligent people in the field of economics have told me that things look as if we are being pushed at an enormous speed toward a destination no one knows or could prevent. But will our church survive *another* catastrophe?[145] Will it not reach the end of its existence then, if we do not change immediately, speak and live completely differently? But how? Next Wednesday is a meeting of all Berlin pastors to discuss the winter problems; let's see what kind of problems there are! I fear bad things from this meeting. But no one knows how to do it better. And in times like these! What good is a person's theology? In a couple of weeks the work will start. The *omina* are strange.[146]

---

142. Sermon on Matthew 28:20 from April 15, 1928 (10:491).
143. Sermon on Psalm 62:2 from July 15, 1928 (10:500).
144. Letter to Paul Lehmann on August 23, 1931 (11:42–43).
145. The first "catastrophe," which Bonhoeffer would later endorse, seems to have been the separation of church and state in the Weimar Republic.
146. Letter to Erwin Sutz on October 8, 1931 (11:50). On December 19, 1930, Bonhoeffer to Max Diestel of American Christianity, "One big question continually attracting my attention . . . is whether one here really can still speak about Christianity, and where the criterion for such might be found" (10:266).

These are remarkable questions from a theologian and pastor. Having broached the possibility of the church "reach[ing] the end of its existence" in Germany amid social crisis and asking, "What good is a person's theology?," he wrote more intensely in another letter several days later to Helmut Rößler: "The great dying out of Christianity seems to be here. Is our time over?"[147]

Bonhoeffer confided in Sutz again almost a year later and groaned, "The situation here really looks desperate. . . . It may be that the day after tomorrow everything turns into chaos, and not because something great and new appears on the horizon, but simply because something rotten breaks down completely."[148] Bonhoeffer's essays, sermons, letters, addresses, and books relentlessly continued after the rise of Hitler to analyze and sound the warning siren against this "rotten" storm system rumbling with "the pressure of a reality filled with concrete, ethical problems such as we have never had before in the history of the West." With "the great dying out of Christianity," Bonhoeffer saw his society "at the very edge of the abyss of . . . complete moral chaos in the lives of nations."[149] Rejecting "pious illusion," Bonhoeffer insisted that "the world, if it is honest, can say nothing other than: 'the church is dead,' that the world can view our actions here as nothing other than the preparation for the funeral."[150] Without exaggeration and with disturbing contemporary resonance, Bonhoeffer spoke boldly:

> Things are coming to a crisis more horribly than ever before—*millions of starving people* whose wishes have been put off or unfulfilled, desperate people who have nothing to lose but their lives and who with their lives lose nothing—*humiliated and degraded nations*, who are not able to recover from their dishonor—*political extremes against political extremes, fanaticized against fanaticized*, false gods against false gods—and behind all this, a world bristling with weapons as never before, a world that is feverishly mobilizing for war, in order to guarantee peace through armaments, a world whose false gods have become the word "security," *securité*—a word without sacrifice, full of distrust and suspicion, because it still feels the terrors of the past in its bones.[151]

Sensing the coming catastrophe that Nietzsche presaged and Arendt described in retrospect, Bonhoeffer indicted his church and society (in that order) as "a house of cards blown away in a whirlwind," in which the so-called Protestant churches' singing of "A Mighty Fortress Is Our God" was nothing more than

---

147. Letter to Helmut Rößler on October 18, 1931 (11:55).
148. Letter to Erwin Sutz on May 17, 1932 (11:122).
149. "Report on a Conference of the World Alliance in Cambridge" from September 1931 (11:166) and "Welcoming Address" in Ciernohorské Kúpele from July 1932 (373–74). See "On the Theological Foundation of the Work of the World Alliance" from July 26, 1932 (11:358): "And now we only notice in the middle of the lake that the ice upon which we stand is cracking."
150. Untitled address at the International Youth Conference in Gland on August 29, 1932 (11:375).
151. Untitled address at the International Youth Conference in Gland on August 29, 1932 (11:378).

the self-deceiving "courage" of a child whistling "out of pure terror" in the darkness.[152]

In his *Ethics* manuscript "Heritage and Decay," Bonhoeffer lays out his most focused and sustained analysis of the rupture he believed was ripping through his age and civilization. Harkening back to the "creative nothingness" he saw unleashed in human nature's rupture from its beginning in *Creation and Fall*,[153] he concluded:

> Having lost its unity that was created by the form of Jesus Christ, the West is confronted by nothingness. Uncontrolled powers clash with each other. Everything that exists is threatened with annihilation. This is not just one crisis among others, but a conflict of ultimate seriousness. The Western world senses the uniqueness of this moment in which it stands and throws itself into the arms of nothingness. . . . It is again a specifically Western nothingness: a nothingness that is rebellious, violent, anti-God, and antihuman. Breaking away from all that is established, it is the utmost manifestation of all the forces opposed to God. It is nothingness as God; no one knows its goal or its measure. Its rule is absolute. It is a creative nothingness that blows its anti-God breath into all that exists, creates the illusion of waking it to new life, and at the same time sucks out its true essence until it soon disintegrates into an empty husk and is discarded. Life, history, family, people, language, faith—the list could go on forever because nothingness spares nothing—all fall victim to nothingness.[154]

For Bonhoeffer, living amid the totalitarian violence of Hitler's Germany, this description of lost unity and the onslaught of "nothingness" cuts to the core of "the unique situation of our time" and its "actual decay."[155] Rather than a conservative, alarmist pessimism, Bonhoeffer—much like Nietzsche but a generation later in the midst of Nazism—thought this "catastrophe" was the most objective appraisal of what was taking place in Western civilization. At the end of the road of the French Revolution, which Bonhoeffer calls "the new intellectual unity of the West," and its rejection of the self-revealed God with its "desire for absolute freedom," similar to Arendt's analysis in *Origins*, combined with the increasing idolization of technological power and totalitarian force, "lies nihilism" and a "spirit of annihilation." The anxious and obsessive "deifying" of humanity, such that man's creaturely limits and worldly finitude can no longer be loved as God's gifts amid life with others but rather must be overcome as

---

152. Untitled address at the International Youth Conference in Gland on August 29, 1932 (11:378). See also *Ethics* (6:392).

153. *Creation and Fall* (3:33).

154. *Ethics* (6:127). This passage is strikingly reminiscent of Nietzsche's *The Will to Power*, Preface, §2 but without the idea of necessity.

155. *Ethics* (6:132).

obstacles to the fulfillment of an infinite desire, can only result in radical violence.[156]

For Bonhoeffer, the stakes could not be more fundamental or far-reaching. In a sermon from 1934, he declared, "a human life is only meaningful and worthwhile to the extent that it has love in it" and, negatively, "a life is nothing, is meaningless and worthless, when it is without love."[157] (Recall his earlier statement in *Creation and Fall* but now in this historical-political context: "[The human] no longer sees the limit that the other person constitutes as grace. . . . This means that the human being no longer regards the other person with love."[158]) As Bonhoeffer put it later from prison, "When we lack the courage once again to establish a genuine sense of boundaries between human beings and personally to fight for them, we perish in an anarchy of human values" and "chaos is at the door."[159] This catastrophe in the core of human community is what Bonhoeffer saw unfolding in his time and its drive for "new life," while the "form of Christ" was abandoned as the unifying plot for human life and society and the church remained largely silent or supportive of Nazism.

Bonhoeffer names this chaos "Western godlessness," which is "hopelessly godless" and "emphatically Christian" precisely because in its very rejection of the Christian God it cannot rid itself of its originally religious drive and devotion. Such "godlessness" thus becomes another form of fanaticism. With bitter irony, "the new human being" forged in the "factory of new humanity" is confronted with "a strange repetition of the biblical fall": "what is created turns against its creator," and the promise of newness devolves into disorder and annihilation. The result of this anxiety, desire, loneliness, anger, and pride surging in society was that "human beings destroy themselves" as the violent hand of Cain continues to (de)form history.[160]

In this situation, Bonhoeffer thought that, at least on the level of popular culture and Christianity, "the question about a historical heritage," which could provide a sense of meaning and direction for moral memory and imagination, and thus a convicted moral realism for responsible ethical agency within certain basic limits, had been "snuffed out." Having lost the "form of Christ," historical identity and a certain moral time consciousness or normative historical emplotment had been lost: "There is no future and no past." What remained was "only the present moment rescued from nothingness and the desire to grasp the next moment. Already yesterday's concerns

---

156. *Ethics* (6:122). See "Exposition on the First Table of the Ten Words of God" from June or July 1944 (16:638):
157. Sermon on 1 Corinthians 13:1–3 from October 14, 1934 (13:377).
158. *Creation and Fall* (3:122).
159. Essay "After Ten Years" from Christmas 1942 (8:47).
160. *Ethics* (6:122–23).

are consigned to forgetfulness and tomorrow's are too far away to obligate us today."[161] History loses its energizing direction and binding responsibility vis-à-vis the abandoned "form of Christ," and thus it becomes vulnerable to the violent (de)construction of arbitrary will and the "spirit of annihilation."

It was this experience and analysis of the spiritual and moral devastation of Western civilization that fueled Bonhoeffer's prison meditations and drove him to wrestle with fundamental, cascading questions about the foundations of moral order and the future of Christianity, to which we will return in chapter 4 and the conclusion:

> Have there ever been people in history who in their time, like us, had so little ground under their feet, people to whom every possible alternative open to them at the time appeared equally unbearable, senseless, and contrary to life?[162]
>
> What is Christianity, or who is Christ actually for us today? . . . We are approaching a completely religionless age; people as they are now simply cannot be religious anymore. . . . The foundations are being pulled out from under all that "Christianity" has previously meant for us, and the only people among whom we might end up in terms of "religion" are "the last of the knights" or a few intellectually dishonest people. Are these supposed to be the chosen few? . . . What does a church, a congregation, a sermon, a liturgy, a Christian life, mean in a religionless world? How do we talk about God—without religion, that is, without the temporally conditioned presuppositions of metaphysics, of inner life, and so on? How do we speak (or perhaps we can no longer even "speak" the way we used to) in a "worldly" way about "God"? How do we go about being "religionless-worldly" Christians, how can we be *ek-klesia*, those who are called out, without understanding ourselves religiously as privileged, but instead seeing ourselves as belonging wholly to the world? Christ would then no longer be the object of religion, but something else entirely, truly lord of the world. But what does that mean? In a religionless situation, what do ritual and prayer mean? Is this where the "arcane discipline," or the difference . . . between the penultimate and the ultimate, have their significance?[163]

CONCLUSION: THE STATUS OF OUR MORAL AGENCY, HISTORICAL IDENTITY, AND REJECTION OF SELF-CREATION

In this chapter, I have attempted to unpack Dietrich Bonhoeffer's understanding of two fundamental ruptures that provide the context in which we

---

161. *Ethics* (6:128).
162. "After Ten Years" from Christmas 1942 (8:38). Bonhoeffer repeatedly used the metaphor of "ground under one's feet" throughout his writings.
163. Letter to Eberhard Bethge on April 30, 1944 (8:361–65).

can appreciate the explicit importance and problem of the human capacity to make new beginnings in his thought. This discussion focused on the kinds of creatures Bonhoeffer thinks we are and thus the status of our moral agency, as well as "when" Bonhoeffer thinks we are and thus the status of our moral tradition in history.

The first rupture took place in human nature itself, through which humanity was "torn" from its origin in God's generous act "in the beginning" and subjected to existential and moral corruption "in the middle" until death. We analyzed this ontological rupture in terms of anxiety, obsessive desire, loneliness, shame, hatred, violence, and death, all of which Bonhoeffer roots in human pride or the desire to be "like God," which "hates the beginning."

Bonhoeffer saw the second rupture unfolding in the contemporary cultural-political reality of European society, in which "the form of Christ" that had provided "the unity of the West" and thus the norm and energy of its moral tradition was being rejected and replaced by a void in which "there is no future and no past." We analyzed this societal rupture in terms of "the great dying out of Christianity," the rejection of limits amid human desperation, and a growing "spirit of annihilation" amid "Western godlessness," which Bonhoeffer insightfully recognized was producing a devastating moral "chaos."[164]

These ruptures not only allow us to appreciate the urgent importance of a new beginning in Bonhoeffer's thought (*We need to begin again!*). They also enable us to understand the fundamental problem (*We are not capable of making a new beginning for ourselves!*). Throughout we saw that Bonhoeffer rejected the idea of "self-creation." Thus, in Bonhoeffer's critical evaluation, if we are left to ourselves and our own initiatives and traditions, humans find themselves in a hopeless situation. We are not qualified to be our own beginners; we are unreliable and make false starts, which sometimes lead to devastation.

A passage from Bonhoeffer's early lecture "Jesus Christ and the Essence of Christianity" provides a helpful summary of his view:

Christianity is neither congenial to culture nor does it have faith in progress. It has peered too deeply into the two deepest realities of life. The trembling fear of death and guilt has seized Christianity too powerfully. The seriousness of having to die and of having to bear guilt—this universal human fate is too frightening to allow any hope in solutions deriving from human initiative. Christians see a terrible rift running through the world, a rift that is utterly irreparable through recourse to any human initiative; and they see this rift—thus the tragedy of their lives—still or even for the first time in its full scope precisely at the heights of human initiative, that is, in culture itself. Greek sensibility understands nothing of such things.[165]

---

164. *Ethics* (6:122–23).
165. Delivered on December 11, 1928 (10:355).

It is precisely this "recourse" to "human initiative" that Bonhoeffer sees as the satanic temptation that cuts to the roots of our rupture from God, others, and ourselves. The way backward and forward—into our deep past and future—is blocked by "a terrible rift running through the world," both in ourselves and in our tradition, which when humans try to overcome it on their own end up intensifying it. Paradoxically, Bonhoeffer thinks this rupture becomes manifest "for the first time in its full scope precisely at the heights of human initiative," a judgment he made before the rise of Nazism.

To summarize, then:

First and most fundamentally, without the revelation of God, human creatures do not know what our beginning is, where we are coming from, where we are going, and thus how we are meant to live—what Bonhoeffer calls our "why" or "what in the end imparts reality to every genuine question we ask." The beginning remains inaccessible to our attempts at comprehension and control now "in the middle" marked by a "terrible rift," which is manifested in our moral dividedness in ourselves and our alienation from the heritage that made history meaningful and valuable rather than something to be conquered, condemned, or overcome. For Bonhoeffer, the human creature is "totally deprived of its own self-determination, because it comes from the beginning and is moving toward the end without knowing what that means." And thus we find and lose ourselves amid an "anarchy of human values."

As such, second, all our attempts to make beginnings for our and by ourselves—to assume the posture of beginner and self-creation—amount to satanic lies that unravel into idolatry, violence, and systematic despair. For Bonhoeffer, *"The denial of the origin belongs to the essence of the tempter,"*[166] and this is all that human initiatives can produce with their autonomous wisdom and power: denials of the origin, which act without a beginning and expose themselves to the temptation of self-invalidating anarchy. This is what Bonhoeffer will call "the murderous law of never-ending beginnings," as we will see in chapter 4.

Of course, Bonhoeffer recognizes that we may postulate and attempt to fabricate and enforce all sorts of beginnings, what he called the "bold and violent action" of "idealism" and "radicalism," which often end up constructing "factories of new humanity" like Hitler did. But these commencements are undercut by their own arbitrariness and origin in the will to power's self-assertion "torn" from their origin. They are only "justified" on their own strength and thus vulnerable to the overthrow of the stronger, which for Bonhoeffer is always death itself—often inflicted at the hands of Cain's children. Ironically, then, such "new beginnings" are really traumatized and trauma-

---

166. Untitled Notes on the Concept of Temptation (15:347) and untitled Bible Study on Temptation from June 1938 (15:391, 399).

tizing repetitions and reinforcements of the *old* way of the "mute, violated, silenced, dead, ego-world" in its estrangement from the beginning. Rather than sources of hope, "the heights of human initiative" all too often become abysmal sources of despair.

Bonhoeffer's analysis of human nature, combined with his analysis of Christianity's funeral in early twentieth-century Germany, convinced him that if there is to be a new beginning for humanity that can renew the goodness of the world and our love as moral agents, it must come from God, from the first Beginner. Paradoxically, the way in which human creatures may begin to hope to begin again is to relinquish our powers of initiative and to take the risk of allowing God to go first, trusting that then—*after* God's beginning, the work of "that other"—"justice, truth, science, art, culture, humanity, freedom, and patriotism, after long wanderings, find their way back to their origin."[167]

For Bonhoeffer, then, any further, adequate discussion of the ethics of new beginning must take into account the morally devastated condition of human nature and the fundamentally ruptured nature of our moral-historical self-understanding. Without facing these problems directly, our accounts of who we are, where we are, and what we are capable of as beginners—for good and evil—are simply too naïve, dishonest, unramified, and misleading.[168] We will have an incomplete and inadequately critical appraisal of our qualification and reliability to serve as beginners for ourselves and others.

This is the initial claim and cost of Bonhoeffer's ethics of new beginning: we must relinquish our status as primary beginners to follow after "that other."

This, in turn, provides the context in which we must wrestle with the problem of the next chapter. How can a new beginning for humanity and history be justified, guided, and energized in Bonhoeffer's thought since his belief in "God's dominion and love" will not allow a retreat into passivity or resignation to the triumph of nihilism?

---

167. *Ethics* (6:132).
168. See "Notes on the Concept of Sin" from January 1936 (15:345): "Because the essence of sin is to obtain praise for oneself and to judge over good and evil, sin can never recognize its own sinfulness."

Chapter Four

"Only with God Is There a New Way, a New Beginning"

Justification and Guidance for New Beginning in Bonhoeffer's Thought

Precisely those who act in the freedom of their very own responsibility see their action as both flowing into and springing from God's guidance. Free action as it determines history recognizes itself ultimately as being God's action, the purest activity as passivity. Only in this perspective is it possible to speak now of good in history. . . . This is because everything real is summed up in Christ, who, by definition, is the origin of any and all action that is in accord with reality.

It is not Christ who has to justify himself before the world by acknowledging the values of justice, truth, and freedom. Instead, it is these values that find themselves in need of justification, and their justification is Jesus Christ alone.[1]

—Dietrich Bonhoeffer

In chapter 3, I argued that Bonhoeffer is deeply critical of and ultimately rejects the human capacity to make new beginnings for ourselves. For Bonhoeffer, we are creatures for whom there is a devastating rupture with our beginning.

We are devastated in our moral nature "in the middle," having been "torn" from the beginning of God's act of creation through our pride. With our "bold and violent action" to enthrone or "initiate" ourselves in the beginning, we have become estranged from ourselves and others, including "that other" God. Bonhoeffer goes so far as to claim, "Human beings have lost their creaturely nature."[2] Here self-creation is not an option.

Moreover, Bonhoeffer believes that we are ruptured in our history, having "repudiated" the "form of Christ" that provided "the unity of the West"

---

1. *Ethics* (6:226, 231, 345).
2. *Creation and Fall* (3:126).

as a historical heritage constituted by an absolute reference point beyond mythology, eternal recurrence, and randomness.[3] In this state of historical repudiation and rupture, Bonhoeffer sees a "spirit of annihilation" at work that promises "the new," including a "new humanity," but that only results in confusion, violation of limits, and the devastation of God's good creation. In such a situation, "Human beings destroy themselves."[4] While people today regularly refer to "the right side of history," Bonhoeffer would be suspicious of our claim to moral clarity and question what justifies us to divide history in this way. The implication is that we are too morally disoriented to make a new beginning for ourselves in history.

Taken together, in both human moral ontology and historical self-understanding, Bonhoeffer diagnoses "a terrible rift running through the world" that is "utterly irreparable through recourse to any human initiative."[5] Thus, Bonhoeffer interprets the primal maxim "Discover your beginning yourself" as the satanic counsel of despair that rips humanity to pieces and initiates a storming "history of death" wrenched and written by "violent hands."[6]

If Bonhoeffer is right that this is the basic state of human moral ontology and history, then the question must be asked how any new beginning could be justified at all. How could we possibly distinguish between (1) a trustworthy, legitimate new beginning in which we should rightfully hope, actively participate, and perhaps even risk our lives and (2) yet another act of arbitrary self-assertion and violence that only manifests and intensifies illusion, idolatry, and death?

That is the question this chapter seeks to address in Bonhoeffer's work. In it, I will argue that Bonhoeffer fundamentally believes that God must be welcomed to go first—both in God's free act of creation, God's commanding word, and God's incarnating presence through Christ in history—and that humans are called to "follow after" (*nachfolgen*[7]) God's founding leadership and initiating action.[8] That is, humans are called to begin by returning the gift of their beginnings to God and freely assuming a penultimate, posterior position of moral agency.

On this path, "the beginning" is both lost and found, relinquished and regiven. On one hand, the human drive for primacy must be abandoned. But

3. *Ethics* (6:132).
4. *Ethics* (6:122–23).
5. "Jesus Christ and the Essence of Christianity" from December 11, 1928 (10:355).
6. *Creation and Fall* (3:28–29).
7. For a study of this important concept in Bonhoeffer's thought, see Florian Schmitz, *"Nachfolge": zur Theologie Dietrich Bonhoeffers* (Göttingen: Vandenhoeck & Ruprecht, 2013), especially chapter 4. See also Brian Gregor, "Following-After and Becoming Human: A Study of Bonhoeffer and Kierkegaard," in *Becoming Human, Being Human: Dietrich Bonhoeffer and Social Thought*, ed. Jens Zimmermann and Brian Gregory (Eugene, OR: Wipf and Stock, 2010).
8. See *Sanctorum Communio* (1:139).

in so doing, Bonhoeffer thinks we discover a better, more original beginning that is God's initiative, after which *all of us* may follow as finite and beloved creatures. It is here in God's beginning that we discover "liberation from the murderous law of never-ending beginnings."

For this study, we will take our lead from Bonhoeffer's 1934 sermon in London "Beginning with Christ," move to his 1939–1940 exposition of Psalm 119 developed during his illegal work with the underground collective pastorates, and then turn to some discussions in his *Ethics* and *Letters and Papers from Prison*, in which Bonhoeffer makes explicit that Christ's command and way of life are constituted by "being there for others." For Bonhoeffer, this "being there for others" or *Stellvertretung* is the ultimate ground of reality in creation, and it is the new initiative of God in history through which humans may also find a new beginning, both now and in what he calls "the new world of the resurrection," after devastating moral devastation.[9]

"BEGINNING WITH CHRIST" (1934)

After Bonhoeffer finished giving his lectures on *Creation and Fall* at the University of Berlin and Hitler had begun entrenching his power as Chancellor of Germany in 1933, Bonhoeffer did not abandon the topic of beginnings, which had been so fundamental to his course and public discourse in that fateful winter. A year later, now serving as the pastor of two German congregations in London to get some distance and disappointed with his church's silence in the face of Hitler, Bonhoeffer chose to entitle his New Year's sermon on January 1, 1934, "Beginning with Christ"—a title of subtle protest and defiance to Hitler's promise to make a new beginning for Germany.[10]

Bonhoeffer takes as his text Luke 9:57–62, in which Jesus calls out to various men, "Follow me," and they reply, "Let me first."[11] Bonhoeffer begins his sermon by quoting the widely known maxim "The road to hell is paved with good intentions."[12] Here the "good intention" is the assumption that human agents essentially know how they should begin and what they should do. For Bonhoeffer, "such a person thinks that a good intention is enough for a new beginning," supposing that "one can make a new start entirely on

---

9. For Bonhoeffer's interpretation of the resurrection, see the discussion in chapter 5.

10. See Bethge, *Dietrich Bonhoeffer*, 275. We could also look earlier at Bonhoeffer's sermon on May 20, 1926, in which he addresses the question, "How can we begin, we ask ourselves, to work toward becoming a wealthy, carefree, happy, respected nation once again?" and warns against the "idols" of "family, folk, nation, church, club, and . . . the growth of our own 'personality,'" which distract us from "God's will" (9:473), the only true source of a new beginning, quoting Acts 5:38–39.

11. For another exposition of this text, see *Discipleship* (4:61ff).

12. "Beginning with Christ" (13:347).

one's own, whenever one wants to."[13] As we have seen, for Bonhoeffer such an assumption and thus the response of "Let me first" to Jesus's call "Follow me" amounts to "an evil illusion" that would prove historically disastrous. It is the prime marker of alienation from God, others, and even oneself.[14] Thus, the call of Christ is lost by assuming that one already knows how to begin on one's own.

This claim connects back to Bonhoeffer's critique of conscience that we saw in *Creation and Fall*, in which Bonhoeffer argued that "conscience" is all too often the human creature's subtle attempt to maintain one's own primacy and substitute one's own voice for the voice of God. In this case, the "good intention" is precisely the human attempt to be good on one's own terms and for one's self-justification. But what goes disguised in this religious exercise of moral arbitration is the human's unwillingness to expose itself to someone *other* than itself, to the free voice of God who speaks from beyond and before what Bonhoeffer calls the human ego's "I-world." This is the background to Bonhoeffer's potentially confusing claim that knowledge of "good and evil" and, with it, a self-justifying "morality" is itself an effect of sin.

Bonhoeffer's New Year's rejection of "good intentions" to make a "new beginning" in which the human agent says "Let me first" also stretches forward to a similar argument that stands at the head of Bonhoeffer's first *Ethics* manuscript titled "Christ, Reality, and Good." There Bonhoeffer writes that "those who wish even to focus on the problem of a Christian ethic" find themselves "faced with an outrageous demand." From the very start, "they must give up as inappropriate to the topic the very two questions that led them to deal with the ethical problem: 'How can I be good?' and 'How can I do something good?'"

For Bonhoeffer, to begin with these questions—tacit good intentions— "presupposes a decision about ultimate reality, that is, a decision of faith."[15] When we begin with ourselves and our own preestablished questions, however obviously good they may appear to us, Bonhoeffer sees us making an implicit "decision" that reveals our interpretation of fundamental reality and thus where we place our most basic "faith," which often remains suppressed and unthought: we ourselves are primary, ultimately real and worthy of trust, and thus able to ask the guiding questions, which will set the trajectory for what follows. But this is precisely the "old world" whose way leads to the devastating ruptures of pride, violence, and death "in the middle."[16]

---

13. "Beginning with Christ" (13:348).
14. "Beginning with Christ" (13:347).
15. *Ethics* (6:47). See *Sanctorum Communio* (1:277), in which Bonhoeffer defines a "reality" as that which is "established by God, and fundamentally 'prior' to all experience."
16. *Ethics* (6:356).

Thus, Bonhoeffer argues that if we are truly interested in "the problem of a Christian ethic," then we "must ask the wholly other, completely different question: what is the will of God?"[17] That is, "If it turns out . . . that these realities, myself and the world, are themselves imbedded in a wholly other ultimate reality, namely the reality of God the Creator, Reconciler, and Redeemer," then this means that "the ethical problem takes on a whole new aspect."[18] In this case, what will be of first importance—what deserves and claims the beginning—will not be my questions and initiatives ("Let me first") but "God's self-witness, God's revelation,"[19] what Bonhoeffer named "the free confirmation, attestation, and revelation of God by God" in *Creation and Fall*.[20] Bonhoeffer calls this conscious awareness that "the ultimate reality is revelation" the "turning point, the pivot, of all perception of reality as such." In revelation, "the ultimate, or final, reality discloses itself to be at the same time the first reality, God as the first and last, the Alpha and Omega," without whom we are torn apart in "separation from both origin and goal."[21]

Returning to Bonhoeffer's 1934 sermon "Beginning with Christ," we can now better understand the logic of Bonhoeffer's fundamental claim at the beginning of the New Year as he served his congregation and reflected on the "new realities" ripping through his church and society:

> It is God alone who makes a new beginning with a person, when God is pleased to do so, and not the human being who undertakes to do it with God. So a new beginning is not something one can do for oneself. One can only pray for it to happen. As long as people rely only on themselves and try to live that way, that is still the old way, the same way as in the past. Only with God is there a new way, a new beginning. . . . But we can pray only when we have realized that there is something we cannot do for ourselves, that we have reached our limit, that someone else must be the one to begin.[22]

Rather than a resentful misanthropy or pessimistic passivity, Bonhoeffer's claim here expresses the wonder and liberation that the finite self is not the totality of reality vis-à-vis the "the solitary lord and despot of its own mute, violated, silenced, dead, ego-world" from chapter 3.[23] The self is not the only one who wills and begins. Instead, the finite human creature is "imbedded

---

17. *Ethics* (6:47).
18. *Ethics* (6:48).
19. *Ethics* (6:48).
20. *Creation and Fall* (3:29).
21. *Creation and Fall* (6:48–49). In *Ethics*, recognizing our "penultimacy" vis-à-vis the "ultimate" is isomorphic to recognizing our "medial" condition vis-à-vis the "origin" in *Creation and Fall*. On Bonhoeffer's (likely Barthian) language of "origin and goal," see Bethge, *Dietrich Bonhoeffer*, 75–76.
22. "Beginning with Christ" (13:348). For the same logic, see "The Reconstruction of Jerusalem according to Ezra and Nehemiah" from April 21, 1936 (14:917).
23. *Creation and Fall* (3:142).

in a wholly other ultimate reality" that enables the immanent world of consciousness to take on "a whole new aspect." Rather than beginnings being self-made and reducible to one's willpower—whether creation itself, New Year's resolutions, or larger new beginnings in society and politics—these mysteries when rightly understood point us to the discovery of a divine otherness that both precedes and empowers our finitude, grounding and guiding us in the middle between birth and the future, and thus also judging our presumption and will to power.

Thus, Bonhoeffer's blunt declaration "someone else must be the one to begin" is not simply a defeat or abdication. It is the opening to a larger, more complex, more fundamental horizon in which I hear the call "Follow me," which initiates and dignifies my freedom, liberates it from "arbitrariness" and "violence," and reconnects me to my mysterious origins.[24] For Bonhoeffer, then, the costly claim of God's beginning on the primacy and autonomy of human beginners is great, but its promise is greater and good: "So a new beginning is not something one can do for oneself. . . . Only with God is there a new way, a new beginning."

This is the source of Bonhoeffer's confidence and urgency in his preaching amid the building totalitarian "thunderstorm" we traced in chapter 3: "Christ calls you to a new beginning—take your chance, just because it is he! Now, today, because Christ is moving on—go with him, answer his call, now!" Rather than being trapped in the paralysis or violence of trying to "secure" our beginning, Bonhoeffer admonishes the community, "Leave your fear, worry, and guilt behind. Look up at the one who has given you a new beginning."[25] In light of what was coming, Bonhoeffer's urgency was not extreme.

Both the freeing newness and the radical challenge of being *given*—rather than *making*—a new beginning from "that other" should not be overlooked or underestimated. As we saw in *Creation and Fall*, Bonhoeffer thinks that it is precisely humanity's posture of "being for the other, of respect for what is given, of acknowledging the rights of the other as my limit"[26] that has been devastated in the self's fall and the West's repudiation of Christ as lord of history. And thus, as we have seen earlier in his *Ethics*, to be open to being *given* a new beginning from beyond oneself in Christ represents a transformative encounter with "a wholly other ultimate reality" in which "the ethical problem takes on a whole new aspect."[27] Being *given* a new beginning points to the dialectical tension of the self as God's generous gift but thus also the self's dispossession

24. Note Bonhoeffer's early distinctions between "force" and "domination" within a logic of mechanism versus "command" and "freedom"/"obedience" within a logic of community in *Sanctorum Communio* (1:92). See *Ethics* on the relationship between freedom and obedience united in responsibility (6:287).
25. "Beginning with Christ" (13:349).
26. *Creation and Fall* (3:124).
27. *Ethics* (6:48).

as private property with its obsessive desire, pride, and violence. To be made open to the reception of this new beginning of God after having been "torn from the origin" and "hating grace" thus opens to the mystery of predestination, of God's priority and primacy, throughout Bonhoeffer's theology.[28]

But what I wish to emphasize is that for Bonhoeffer the mystery of being *given* a new beginning is not servitude or something to be resented but rather the fundamental event of generosity and liberation, which restores our capacity for action and calls us to follow after God's founding act of creation "to greatly increase the power" of his new creatures.

In light of the unfamiliarity and fragility of humans "looking up to one who has given [us] a new beginning" due to our habituated orientation that says "Let me first," Bonhoeffer concludes his sermon with a final challenge to our "good intentions": "Let our new beginning with Christ be followed by a story of going with Christ. What that means is beginning each day with him. That is what matters."[29] This practical admonition of daily exercise in Christological beginning points ahead to our next chapter, in which Bonhoeffer will emphasize the importance of daily disciplined practice in following after the way of Christ's new beginning.

MEDITATIONS ON PSALM 119 (1939–1940)

Over the course of the next year, Bonhoeffer himself discerned Christ's call to a momentous new beginning. In mid-April 1935 he returned from London to Germany to serve as the founding director of the Finkenwalde Preachers' Seminary.[30] Finkenwalde and other similar seminaries were established to independently train pastors for ministry in the Confessing Church, which had broken away from the Nazified Reich Church. Only two years into this new endeavor, these seminaries were banned by an edict from Heinrich Himmler. A month later, the Gestapo shut down Finkenwalde, and twenty-seven former students were arrested.

Rather than acquiescing to the demands of the Third Reich, Bonhoeffer made contacts with the political resistance against Hitler in February 1938. This connection would eventually lead to his involvement in the conspiracy against Hitler, which would ultimately lead to his death.[31] Bonhoeffer then

---

28. See *Sanctorum Communio* (1:164ff.) for an early discussion of predestination as both an individual and sociological concept. See also Sermon on Psalm 58 from July 11, 1937 (14:966)
29. "Beginning with Christ" (13:349).
30. See the "Introduction" to Dietrich Bonhoeffer Works Volume 14, "What Was Finkenwalde?"
31. See Marsh, *Strange Glory*, 287, and Bethge, *Dietrich Bonhoeffer*, 515: "It may have been during this period [1936, when his right to teach was revoked] that Bonhoeffer's thoughts first turned to the possibility of political action."

decided to make yet another new beginning and served in the illegal, underground "collective pastorates," in which dissident pastors continued to be
trained for Christian service.[32]

By September 3, 1939—two days after Germany's invasion of Poland—
Britain and France had declared war on Germany. A month later, on October 6, Hitler proclaimed his "offer of peace" to the Western world if only
it would recognize the "new realities" he had unleashed on Europe, which
must be understood in the context of his larger new beginning agenda. As
Hitler himself declared, "Those who see in National Socialism nothing more
than a political movement know scarcely anything of it. It is more even than
a religion: it is the will to create mankind anew."[33] Soon before this, in April
1939, to honor Hitler's fiftieth birthday, the theological journal *Junge Kirche*
published this statement:

> The *Führer*, powerfully fighting his way through old worlds, seeing with his
> mind's eye what is new and compelling its realizations, is named on those few
> pages of world history that are reserved for the initiators of a new epoch. . . . The
> figure of the *Führer* has brought a new obligation for the church too.[34]

It was around this time that Bonhoeffer embraced an unanticipated new beginning and threw in his lot with the resistance.

With Bonhoeffer's personal and political contexts centered on crucial
decisions and soaring declarations of "the will to create mankind anew" in
"a new epoch," we should not be surprised that he again turned explicitly to
reflect on the issue of new beginnings in his study and teaching. At the start
of his work in Berlin some fifteen years before, Bonhoeffer had already
written that

> the real study of *theologia sacra* begins when, in the midst of questioning and
> seeking, human beings encounter the cross; when they recognize the endpoint of
> their own passions in the suffering of God at the hands of humankind, and real-
> ize that their entire vitality stands in judgment. . . . One should, in such times of
> confusion, go back to the very beginning, to our sources to the true Bible, to the

---

32. Bonhoeffer was clearly aware that his activities, even before the collective pastorates, were
breaking the Fifth Decree for Implementing the Law for Protecting the German Evangelical Church
(1935), which forbade the Confessing Church from providing theological education. See letter to
Philipp Cromwell from early 1936 (14:147) and letter to Karl-Friedrich Bonhoeffer on November 29,
1937 (14:320). For Bonhoeffer's theological analysis of justified law breaking, see chapter 5.

33. Quoted in Glover, *Humanity*, 315. In 1933, Hitler argued that the German Christians represented "the new" in German Christianity. See Doris L. Bergen, *Twisted Cross: The German Christian
Movement in the Third Reich* (Chapel Hill, NC: University of North Carolina Press, 1996), 10. In the
same year, the popular German Christian minister Reinhold Krause called for "a dramatically new,
all-encompassing German people's church" (Bergen, *Twisted Cross*, 103).

34. Quoted in Bethge, *Dietrich Bonhoeffer*, 648.

true Luther. One should keep on, ever more undaunted and joyfully, becoming a theologian ἀληθεύοντες δὲ ἐν ἀγάπῃ [speaking the truth in love—Eph. 4:15].[35]

And this is precisely what Bonhoeffer did afresh in the winter of 1939–1940 with its unprecedented promises of newness and the realities of escalating violence, suffering, and total war.

Bonhoeffer turned to expound theologically on Psalm 119, which, according to Bethge, Bonhoeffer judged to be "the climax of his theological life."[36] In this extensive, untitled "meditation," Bonhoeffer unpacks and develops similar themes that we have found already in *Creation and Fall* and "Beginning with Christ," which help us to explicate further Bonhoeffer's understanding of the theological justification, guidance, and energy for new beginnings.

Bonhoeffer begins,

> Whoever speaks this way ["Happy are those who . . . walk in the law of the Lord"] presumes that the beginning has already occurred. He points out that the life with God consists not only and not essentially of always new beginnings. Therefore, the psalmist calls it a change, a walking in God's law. Thus he confirms the beginning that has occurred, accepts it as valid, does not want to go back behind it. Because God's beginning with us has already occurred, our life with God is a path being walked within God's law.[37]

With this introduction, Bonhoeffer harkens back to a fundamental claim that he made in *Creation and Fall*.

For Bonhoeffer, the drive to get "back behind" God's fundamental act of creation "in the beginning," which founds the "law" for our "path," is the first sign of ultimately murderous pride. This pride cannot accept a transcendent other who precedes and gives life to my finite self as free grace ("love") and who, as such, stands as an absolute limit to my autonomous comprehension and control ("dominion"). Such a person has no "faith" for what is beyond the self but must rather possess the origin in its self.

But the psalmist is different. He has undergone a fundamental "change" and thus he "walks in God's law." By doing so, he "confirms the beginning that has already occurred," celebrating the call to follow in God's path marked out by God's law. Rather than grasping for "always new beginnings," this life is energized with continuity and commitment, an acceptance of "what

---

35. "What Should a Student of Theology Do Today?" from November 1933 (12:433, 435). See also the examination paper "What Is Paul's View on Earthly Suffering?" from July 5, 1930 (10:386).

36. Bethge, *Dietrich Bonhoeffer*, 667.

37. "Meditation on Psalm 119" (15:496–97). What Bonhoeffer says here about following the law after the beginning mirrors his vision of Christian education. See "Lecture on Catechesis" from late 1935 (14:537): "Christian education begins where all other education ceases: What is essential *has already happened.*"

is valid" that is freed from second guessing and starting over again and again. This is the way of true "happiness" against Hitler's promises.

Reminding us of the waves that "crash and spray" into nothing from *Creation and Fall*, Bonhoeffer is unambiguous:

> To wait for a new beginning, day after day, thinking that one has found it count-less times only to declare it lost in the evening: this is the complete destruction of faith in that God who set the beginning once through his forgiving and renew-ing word in Jesus Christ.[38]

To the contrary of this restless cycle, the human who "walks" after God's law is the one who freely "confirms" God's free beginning before the self and thereby discovers "liberation" from what Bonhoeffer profoundly names "the murderous law of never-ending beginnings." By allowing God to go first in creation and again in Christ, the "Herculean" cycle of self-assertion, violence, and deadly (permanent?) revolution is overcome, or rather *preceded and pre-empted*, once and for all. In this way, we are "allowed to be actually on the way," and God's law guards and guides us "as by a good angel."[39]

Bonhoeffer continues, "God has set the beginning; this is the joyful cer-tainty of faith. . . . From that very thing I have been freed; the beginning, God's beginning, lies behind me once and for all."[40] Put in the context of *Creation and Fall*, we might rephrase this statement: "I was not the one who created myself. God has set the beginning. From that very thing I have been freed; the beginning, God's beginning, lies behind me once and for all."

Thus, Bonhoeffer defines the "church" as the community of people who know themselves and address one another as those "who *have already been* granted a new beginning and who walk together on the path that begins with God finding those who are his."[41] Rather than making its own beginning like Hitler and the German Christians, the authentic church is the community of posterior people, those who recognize and celebrate their penultimacy/penarchy "after" God. For this community on such a path there is "only one danger," and that is precisely the obsessive desire "to step back behind this beginning," a temptation, as we saw in chapter 3, that hates "grace" and dis-graces our origin by mutating it into an object to be captured and controlled

---

38. "Meditation on Psalm 119" (15:497). In the German, it is easier to see that Bonhoeffer is play-ing on the sense of "law" (*Gesetz*) and God's act of "setting" (*setzen*) "the beginning."

39. *Ethics* (6:385).

40. "Meditation on Psalm 119" (15:497). This is Bonhoeffer's fundamental, theological position vis-à-vis the problem that Arendt thematized in *On Revolution*, 184, about lawless lawmaking.

41. "Meditation on Psalm 119" (15:497). This passage on "those who are his" again explicitly raises the (ethical) problem of "predestination." Bonhoeffer's thought seems to move confidently in a universalistic trajectory, while not minimizing the gravity of human agency and responsibility. See chapter 5, note 247.

by and for ourselves. This, again, is the drive to be "in the beginning" rather than in the middle of God's initiative.

On this basis, Bonhoeffer makes an important, indeed founding, move, which he frequently names "the *petitio principii*" throughout his writings. He argues that the question of the beginning should be relinquished and its answer accepted as established, once and for all. The ones who have freely accepted the grace of being creatures of God in the world of creation should understand themselves "as people who have been placed on the path and now cannot do otherwise."[42] In this way, rather than being "worn down" and "killed" by the endless struggle for a "new beginning," these people cease their "revolt" and are buoyantly "borne" and "sheltered" by the gracious, claiming beginning God has made in creation and Christ.

Analogously, rather than seeking to nail down a fixed "moral doctrine" or timeless "norm" or "ideal" in the anxiety of the middle, these people will look to a "historical event" through which "God has already begun life with us."[43] The key is not endless thinking, as in idealism's option, which Bonhoeffer pictured as crashing waves foaming into nothingness or a maddened circle consuming itself. The key is a personal response to concrete historical events through which the beginning action of God occurs, namely, creation at the mysterious origin of the universe, the coming of Christ in the midst of history, and, as we shall see shortly, our encounter with our neighbors, strangers, and enemies. "Christ was not an idea but rather an event,"[44] and that event lays claim on us and guides us.[45]

Crucially, then, Bonhoeffer claims that for those who have chosen to follow after the path of God's gracious beginning, the "command of God" does not present itself as an enslaving necessity but as "the law for life."[46] Freed from "the agony of their own beginnings," those who follow after God's beginning in God's commands are truly "happy," and their own beginnings and initiatives are now reunited with the freedom of God to give life and love for what is not God but what is irreducibly other: finite creation. Here the anxious, nihilistic allergy against divine and human otherness is healed. Bonhoeffer writes, "Happy are those because they have overcome all the internal divisions that arise from the discrepancy between their own beginnings and the beginning by God," such that they are now "complete, whole, undivided,

---

42. "Meditation on Psalm 119" (15:498). Note the similarity with Nelson Mandela's self-understanding in *Long Walk to Freedom: The Autobiography of Nelson Mandela* (New York: Little, Brown and Company, 1995), 95.

43. "Meditation on Psalm 119" (15:499). See sermon on Psalm 42 at Zingst on June 2, 1935 (14:847).

44. See *Ethics* (6:228): "Good is the action that is in accordance with the reality of Jesus Christ."

45. "Lectures on Christology" (12:336).

46. "Meditation on Psalm 119" (15:499).

unassailable."[47] In this way, humans reunite their will with the will of God by which God created all things "in the beginning." Thus, paradoxically, the act of obedience to God's law, which would appear initially as a relinquishment and loss, is for Bonhoeffer the ultimate act of liberation and freedom, indeed an "increase of power" whereby we rediscover the infinitely generous gift giving of God to be with and for genuine others.[48]

This is the ground of Bonhoeffer's fundamentally world-affirming theology, which binds together freedom and love in the beginning and ever after on the path of history and the vocation of human agency. He writes that Christians should not "want to be more spiritual than God himself" and thereby devalue or reject the world through enthusiastic asceticism.[49] To the contrary, the ones who give thanks to the Creator have discovered "the fullness of the world's gifts that God bestows on those who live in his laws."[50] Rejecting the instrumentalization of life, Bonhoeffer insists, "Life is God's goal with us. If it becomes a means to an end, then a contradiction enters life that makes it a torment. Then the goal, the good, is sought in the hereafter, and that can be acquired only by the negation of life."[51] Such an anticreational, often religiously escapist instrumentalism only leads to humans who become "haters and despisers of life and lovers and devotees of ideas."[52]

To the contrary, gratitude for the gifts of God in God's beginning for the world and ourselves is the source of "the satisfied heart" that can experience "joy."[53] Gratitude doesn't instrumentalize the world; it celebrates and serves it. Indeed, this is the antidote to the nihilism—"the radical repudiation of value, meaning, desirability" in which "'why?' finds no answer"—that we encountered in chapter 1 with Nietzsche. Here we discover the foundations for Bonhoeffer's later claim in his *Ethics* manuscript "Natural Life" that embodied, worldly life "never revolves around being a means to an end, but is fulfilled by its intrinsic claim to joy" "understood as a pure gift of God."[54]

For Bonhoeffer, then, legitimate human freedom borne of God's beginning is essentially *following after* or *walking with* God on God's path:

> God's ways are the ways that he has treaded before us and that we are to walk with him now. God does not allow us to walk a path that he has not walked

47. "Meditation on Psalm 119" (15:500).
48. See Sermon on James 1:21–25 from summer of 1926 (9:497).
49. Bonhoeffer critiques the desire to be "even more spiritual than God" again in his *Prayerbook of the Bible* (5:168).
50. "Meditation on Psalm 119" (15:501).
51. See the *Ethics* manuscript "Natural Life" (6:179).
52. "Meditation on Psalm 119" (15:519). Here Bonhoeffer is clearly responding to Nietzsche's critique of Christian nihilism.
53. "Meditation on Psalm 119" (15:501, 515). On gratitude, see chapter 5.
54. *Ethics* (6: 188, 180).

before and on which he would not precede us. It is the way cleared by God and protected by God on which he calls us.[55]

Bonhoeffer is not saying that God micromanages our lives like an overweening parent or obsessively controls our future like a tyrannical overlord. Bonhoeffer's point is that God does not call humans to walk any path—including the open path of the future, suffering, and death—that God has not first willingly accepted and undergone for us and thence with us.[56] God has embraced the responsibility to *precede* us, to serve as our "Precedent."[57] Thus, the core of what it means to be fully human as worldly creatures is "not a timeless idea but an action of God and of the human being in history" in which "to know the way, to be on the right path, never alleviates responsibility and guilt" but "renders them more severe" as we follow God's leading initiative.[58]

All of this implies what Bonhoeffer immediately makes explicit: "The one who commands, not the commandments, is the focus. We are encountered by a You, not an It, an idea, in the commandments."[59] To see the "commandments" as essentially impersonal principles or ideas would reveal that we are still trapped in the "old way"—"the world of things" dominated by an object-constituting ego—in which a voluntary beginning is rejected and morality is essentially a form of self-justification and self-possession (the "I-world") rather than a way of life that is originarily with and for others. To the contrary, God remains *You*, the one who addresses us in God's own transcendence, which we cannot penetrate but that can, nevertheless, speak to us and guide our embodied agency.[60] Here again we see the offense and gift of God's beginning, God's path-making primacy.

Bonhoeffer's theological personalism has important ethical implications.[61] He writes, "I look at God's commandments when I base my decisions neither on other people nor even on my own thoughts or experiences, but rather when I ask ever anew, even if contrary to my pious thoughts and experiences, for what

---

55. "Meditation on Psalm 119" (15:504).
56. See *Sanctorum Communio* (1:242), *Discipleship* (4:937), and letter to Ernst Wolf on September 13, 1942 (16:359).
57. Bethge defines Bonhoeffer's understanding of theology as "a knowledge that seeks to follow God where God has already preceded us." See Bethge, *Dietrich Bonhoeffer*, 867.
58. "Meditation on Psalm 119" (15:504).
59. "Meditation on Psalm 119" (15:505).
60. See Sermon on Matthew 28:20 from April 15, 1928 (10:494).
61. For Bonhoeffer's discussion of the *"Christian-ethical concept of person,"* see *Sanctorum Communio* (1:34, 59, 1:44ff., especially 148). See also DeJonge, *Bonhoeffer's Theological Formation*, vii; Mark S. Brocker, "The Community of God, Jesus Christ, and Responsibility: The Responsible Person and the Responsible Community in the Ethics of Dietrich Bonhoeffer" (PhD Diss., University of Chicago, 1996), chapter 2 ("Christian Concept of the Person"); and Barth, *Die Wirklichkeit des Guten*, 195–230, in which Barth discusses the importance of personhood in Bonhoeffer's thought, his reception of "dialogical personalism," and his interaction with Grisebach

God commands me."[62] This means that the posture of the ethical life is one of fundamental openness, alertness, and readiness to be surprised and called out of my self "ever anew" in the midst of the world, which can sometimes offend my piety and upset my emotions.[63] The posture of the ethical life is a kind of welcome and responsiveness to "that other"—a life of obedience or hearing.

This vision of ethics as human action that follows the unpredictable beginning of God's creation and commands in Christ is fundamentally a form of self-transcendence. It is a way of life in which what it means to be a self is to live in responsible or response-able relationship with and for others, beginning with God but never ending with God and always extending to every other "impenetrable You."[64] Thus, like Jesus's call "Follow me" to the men who said, "Let me first," Bonhoeffer argues, "First, we need to unlearn completely saying: 'I want,' before God teaches us through the Holy Spirit to say it new and correctly."[65] Here we begin to see the radical *newness* of the moral life as Bonhoeffer envisions it.

It is worth emphasizing again that, rather than a form of mutilation or resentful denial contra Nietzsche, Bonhoeffer sees this retraining of desire as the revelation of grace in which life in its intrinsic value can be newly affirmed, opened, and enlarged:

> Thus the circle is completed. God's grace stood at the beginning; it makes our beginning so that we may be freed from our own beginnings. Grace put us on the way, and it is grace that we call upon, step-by-step. . . . I ask for life, as the servant asks his master. Life is a benefaction from God. Life is not a means to an end but is fulfillment in itself. God created us so that we may live; he reconciled us and redeemed us so that we may live. He does not want to see the triumph of ideas over a devastated field of corpses. Ideas exist for the sake of life, not life for the sake of ideas.[66]

At a time when Hitler, with his "will to create mankind anew," was declaring "new realities" to the world and being celebrated by Christians as "the initiator of a new epoch," Bonhoeffer's vision of life "freed from our own beginnings" by a "grace that puts us on the way" was subversive and powerful. With great sobriety, Bonhoeffer realized that the human drive for beginning was governed

---

62. "Meditation on Psalm 119" (15:507). See *Sanctorum Communio* (1:238) and *Ethics* (6:396).

63. *Life Together* (5:89). For a full discussion of this posture and practice, see chapter 5.

64. See Hans Joas, *Do We Need Religion? On the Experience of Self-Transcendence* (Boulder; London: Paradigm Publishers, 2008), 7, and Ingolf Dalferth, "The Idea of Transcendence," in *The Axial Age and Its Consequences*, ed. Hans Joas and Robert Bellah (Cambridge, MA: Belknap Press of Harvard University Press, 2012), 168.

65. On the Holy Spirit, see "The Nature of the Church" from summer 1932 (11:306) and Sermon on 2 Corinthians 5:10 from November 19, 1933 (13:329): "For each person, therefore, there is only one essential question in life: what position do you take toward this Spirit?"

66. "Meditation on Psalm 119" (15:511, 519).

by a "murderous law" that would lead to "the triumph of ideas over a devastated field of corpses" unless God's grace stands at our beginning. Bonhoeffer was calling for a radical reorientation.

CLARIFICATIONS

Here we should pause briefly and ask some critical questions to clarify what Bonhoeffer is saying as we move deeper into his ethics and thus the justification and guidance we need for new beginning.

The Hermeneutics of Divine Revelation

First, how are we able to recognize God's "word" and "command" about which Bonhoeffer speaks so confidently? What are the hermeneutics of divine revelation by which we can differentiate God's communication from our own and others' persistent idolatries and fantasies?[67] This question is especially urgent given Bonhoeffer's critique of the unreliability of autonomous human reason and conscience, which we saw in the previous chapter.[68]

Bonhoeffer's answer is direct and provocative: "I must close the eyes of my senses when I want to see what God shows me. God blinds me when he wants to let me see his word. He opens the eyes of the blind. Now I see what I would not have recognized otherwise, namely, that God's law is full of wonders."[69] This is a challenging claim about the heteronomous nature of revelation and the "wonders" of God's law. But it follows directly from Bonhoeffer's preceding claim about the personality of God as "You" and not "It." In the same way that we cannot derive or divine the thoughts of other people unless they pass beyond themselves in language, address us with their word, and we actually listen to them, so Bonhoeffer believes that revelation and its reception are entirely contingent and dependent on God actually speaking to us.[70]

Bonhoeffer is insistent to defend God from becoming an impersonal principle or moralistic rule. Bonhoeffer sees both as reducing God to a tool,

---

67. On the necessity of revelation, see *Sanctorum Communio* (1:141) and "The Theology of Crisis" from 1930–1931 (especially 10:465).

68. See Ernst Feil, *The Theology of Dietrich Bonhoeffer*, trans. Martin Rumscheidt (Philadelphia, PA: Fortress Press 1985), chapter 2, and Ralf K. Wüstenberg and Jens Zimmermann, eds., *God Speaks to Us: Dietrich Bonhoeffer's Biblical Hermeneutics* (Frankfurt am Main: Peter Lang GmbH, Internationaler Verlag der Wissenschaften, 2013).

69. "Meditation on Psalm 119" (15:520). See Bonhoeffer's paper "Can One Distinguish between a Historical and a Pneumatological Interpretation of Scripture?" from the summer of 1925 (9:290–91).

70. See "Lectures on Christology" (12:309); *Act and Being* (2:81); "Confirmation Instruction Plan" from early 1938 (14:787): *"How can you recognize God's will?. . . Only if God actually speaks his commandment to me can I know it."*

which we pick up at will, wield for our own purposes, and then leave behind unchanged, unaddressed, and unclaimed in "[our] deepest essence."[71] God, like human persons (or, Bonhoeffer would argue, human persons like God), cannot be fully intuited, anticipated, exhausted, or substituted in thought but must be listened to and waited on "wide awake and attentive."[72]

For Bonhoeffer, then, "God speaks just as specifically to us [as to Abraham or Moses], or God does not speak at all."[73] Otherwise, "God" remains merely "my own divine *Doppelgänger*," and faith is shown to be yet another godless human enterprise, what Bonhoeffer understands by "religion."[74] Bonhoeffer insists on an epistemic reversal: "The object must become subject."[75]

Of course, Bonhoeffer is not naïvely unaware that this is a fundamental and non-self-evident claim with all-encompassing implications for ethics, the understanding of the self, and all of reality. But he is even more emphatic that God—the one who is in the beginning, indeed, Christ who *is* "the beginning"—cannot be proved (or disproved) but must be waited on and listened to if we are to know anything of God based on his fundamentally personalistic conception of God. He writes,

> It is perhaps too obvious to mention, that as a consequence of this notion of revelation the question of grounds for belief in God is superfluous because it involves a contradiction. For what better ground does one need and is possible than God's word itself? Any theology that is ashamed of this *petitio principii* cannot escape being ashamed of Him who gives it whatever meaning it possesses.[76]

Bonhoeffer's point is that there is no "ground" deeper than God, no "hinterland" before God, who is by definition without ground but Godself. Referring to God's freedom to self-reveal and speak as "the epitome of an act ex nihilo" or "eternal beginning," Bonhoeffer insists that "God is always the One who is to come; that is God's transcendence. One can only have God by expecting God."[77] Thus, revelation requires *waiting on transcendence* much

---

71. Letter to Rüdiger Schleicher from April 8, 1936 (14:168): "Either I determine the place where I want to find God, or I let him determine the place where he wants to be found. If it is I who says where God is to be found, then I will always find a God there who in some manner corresponds to me, is pleasing to me, who is commensurate with my own nature." See "Lectures on Christology" (12:303).

72. Address on Luke 12:35ff from November 22, 1926 (9:505).

73. *Ethics* (6:379). See *Life Together* (5:156), in which Bonhoeffer uses the analogy of a child learning language by being spoken to by her parent.

74. Letter to Rüdiger Schleicher on April 8, 1936 (14:169).

75. "Can One Distinguish between a Historical and a Pneumatological Interpretation of Scripture?" from the summer of 1925 (9:291).

76. Seminar paper on "The Theology of Crisis and Its Attitude toward Philosophy and Science" from 1930–1931 (10:467).

77. Lecture course on "The History of Twentieth-Century Systematic Theology" from winter of 1931–1932 (11:230). Also (11:229). See *Act and Being* (2:81).

more than rationalistic apologetics, what Bonhoeffer calls *nachdenken*, the epistemic parallel of *Nachfolge* or following-after, which means "to think after."[78] Thinking after the beginning—a hermeneutics of revelation—is truly a *Nachdenke*, a thinking-after:

> God must be the One who says, "I am the absolute beginning." We know about God only when God is the One who speaks. . . . We should begin with God's own beginning set for us. Nobody knows that in advance; we must each receive it as told us; God's word is the absolute *petitio principii*.[79] *Deus dixit*—to accept this is the beginning of all genuine theological thinking, to allow space for the freedom of the living God.[80]

Bonhoeffer makes these larger points in a different way in his earlier "Lectures on Christology" at the University of Berlin in the summer semester of 1933. There Bonhoeffer argued that if we are asking *how* God is able to reveal himself, we have already started off by asking the wrong question and remain "chained to our own authority" with our "*cor curvum in se.*"[81] For the question of "how" assumes a kind of mechanistic or technological process, by which, if we could only figure out the intermediating links, we could actually derive and fabricate the "result" or "product" in advance. This would not be a *revelation* in time at all but merely "this object X fit into the classification that I already have at hand."[82]

Thus, Bonhoeffer argues that we must ask *who* the God is who reveals himself to us, a question that begins by acknowledging that God is not a puzzling problem to be unraveled but a *You*—a personal subject—to be listened to or ignored, obeyed or disobeyed. Unlike the "immanent" question, "The question of 'who' expresses the otherness of the other."[83] Thus, Bonhoeffer boldly argues that the starting language of theology is actually *silence*: "In proclaiming Christ, the church falls on its knees in silence before the inexpressible, the *arreton*. To speak of Christ is to be silent, and to be silent about Christ is

---

78. Lecture course "The History of Twentieth-Century Systematic Theology" from winter of 1931–1932 (11:235): "To know is to acknowledge, to think [is to] reflect [Nachdenken]." See chapter 5 on the practice of prayer and discernment.

79. Compare Levinas, *Totality and Infinity*, 305.

80. "The History of Twentieth-Century Systematic Theology" (11:230). Especially in his earlier work, which tends to give more attention to epistemology, Bonhoeffer referred often to the "petitio principii," the principle "like can be understood only by like" and "finitum (in)capax infiniti." See Jens Zimmermann, "Finitum Capax Infiniti or the Presencing of Christ: A Response to Stephen Plant and Robert Steiner," in *God's Speaks to Us: Dietrich Bonhoeffer's Biblical Hermeneutics*, ed. Ralf Wüstenberg and Jens Zimmerman (Frankfurt: Peter Lang, 2013), 85–98.

81. "Lectures on Christology" (12:303).

82. "Lectures on Christology" (12:301). See Sermon on John 8:32 from July 24, 1932 (11:470): "You thought you could make the truth, create it, proclaim it—but with that you presumed to be God and failed in it. You crucified the truth."

83. "Lectures on Christology" (12:303).

to speak. That is obedient affirmation of God's revelation, which takes place through the Word."[84] Here religious "good intentions" to "go first" and speak for God, rather than allowing space for God to speak and thinking-after, can be among the most dangerous and misleading.

It is important to emphasize here that Bonhoeffer does not think believers should be "ashamed" but rather ennobled and inspired by this fundamental mystery and freedom of God's revelation that brings us to silence. He wrote early in his career, "The lack of mystery in our modern life means decay and impoverishment for us. A human life is of worth to the extent that it keeps its respect for mystery."[85] Bonhoeffer, who always deeply loved and paid attention to children, compared this "honoring of mystery" to the keeping alive of "some of the child we used to be," like the invisible roots of a tree hidden in the darkness of the soil that keep the tree strong and fruitful. And Bonhoeffer thought God's revelation was no exception, even if "that is what we do not want to hear" but rather "want to get to the bottom of this mystery to calculate and explain it." Likely referring to Nietzsche's critique of "mummifying" philosophy,[86] Bonhoeffer argues that the drive to "dissect" God's revelation only "succeeds in killing the life in it." To the contrary: "The mystery remains a mystery. It eludes our grasp."

Even so, Bonhoeffer is clear that "mystery" does not simply mean "not knowing something." For Bonhoeffer, "knowledge does not dispel the mystery but only deepens it." Perhaps equally offensive to unbeliever and believer alike, Bonhoeffer concludes, "all our thinking about God must serve only to make us see how completely beyond us and how *mysterious* God is." Thus, we must always remember, "Every dogma of the church only points to the mystery of God."[87] Here we see that Bonhoeffer's insistence on the primacy of revelation, which could have appeared as a dangerous dogmatism potentially leading to religious extremism, is actually a call for profound humility, religious self-critique, and a willingness to radically enlarge the scope of our listening for God beyond the boundaries of our established assumptions and customs.

I am not aware of a place where Bonhoeffer makes this claim explicitly, but an important implication of his hermeneutics of divine revelation seems to be

---

84. "Lectures on Christology" (12:300). Silence is a rich and repeated topic in Bonhoeffer's writings. See Fritz de Lange, *Waiting for the Word: Dietrich Bonhoeffer on Speaking about God*, trans. Martin N. Walton (Grand Rapids, MI: Eerdmans, 2000), especially chapters 1 and 4. Note Augustine, *On Christian Teaching*, trans. R. P. H. Green (New York: Oxford University Press, 1997), I, 13, 10: "God is unspeakable," and Gustavo Gutiérrez, *On Job: God-Talk and the Suffering of the Innocent*, trans. Matthew J. O'Connell (Maryknoll, NY: Orbis Books, 1987), xiv: "Silence, the time of quiet, is [the] first act and the necessary mediation for the time of speaking about the Lord or doing theo-logy, which is second act."

85. Sermon on 1 Corinthians 2:7–10 from May 27, 1934 (13:361).

86. Nietzsche, *Twilight of the Idols*, §1, "'Reason' in Philosophy."

87. Sermon on 1 Corinthians 2:7–10 from May 27, 1934 (13:361).

thus. If Christians are willing to allow themselves this much openness for the free self-communication of God, then Christians should be the most committed defenders of others' rights to do the same in *their* religious life. What could be perceived as Bonhoeffer's "fideism," when rightly interpreted, should lead to a principle of nonviolence and religious freedom in which we acknowledge our lack of sovereign certainty (*we are not in the beginning*) and thus the faith-based nature of all religious claims (*we all come after*), which serves as a foundation for the public sphere (*we all share a similar situation of faith*).[88] Rather than a warrant for the status quo or fundamentalist self-assertion, Bonhoeffer's view of revelation is a principle of reform, renewal, and dialogue.

For Bonhoeffer, then, the question of recognizing God's communication and command is essentially an *ethical-spiritual* problem, which he calls "obedient affirmation." Its heart is in dynamic relations between persons, the freedom of human responsiveness, and thus the risk of error and rebellion. It is *not* primarily an *epistemological-procedural* problem, which can be figured out in advance, locked down, and used for one's own advantage.[89] Revoicing themes from earlier, Bonhoeffer writes, "The only task of my theological thinking must be to make room for the transcendent personality of God in every sentence," a posture of hospitality in which the other is freely welcomed and given time and space "to be their self" in my place.[90]

This call "to make room for the transcendent personality of God" is the basis of Bonhoeffer's claim concerning divine recognition:

To recognize Christ means to recognize and do his will for us and with us; it means to love God and the brethren (John 4:7–8; 4:20). It is the blessedness of the father when he recognizes the son as son, and it is the blessedness of the son when he recognizes the father as father. This mutual recognition is love and community.[91]

For Bonhoeffer, the truly fundamental "problem" of revelation is not epistemic method but obedient action.[92] The basic question is not "conception" and "comprehension" but "mutual recognition" or "love and community."[93]

---

88. See Taylor, *Modern Social Imaginaries*, chapter 6 and chapter 13.
89. For Bonhoeffer's critical account of the rise of modern hermeneutics with Descartes, Kant, Fichte, and Hegel, see *Sanctorum Communio* (1:40ff). Note *Act and Being* (2:31): "The concept of revelation must . . . yield an epistemology of its own." See also his early essays "Concerning the Christian Idea of God" and "The Theology of Crisis" in Volume 10.
90. "Concerning the Christian Idea of God" from 1932 (10:455). See also "The Nature of the Church" from 1932 (11:278); "On the Theological Foundation of the Work of the World Alliance" from July 1932 (11:367); and letter to Ruth Roberta Stahlberg from March 23, 1940 (16:37).
91. Sermon on John 10:11–16 from January, 1940 (15:550).
92. Dogmatic Exercise on "Theological Anthropology" from late 1932 (12:226): "Obedience means to belong to a person in that you listen to his or her words. Obedience means belonging in the form of hearing."
93. See Bonhoeffer's early claim in his Sermon on Luke 17:7–10 on October 18, 1925 (9:453–54): "God should be acknowledged and believed in, not understood and proved." Also Sermon on John

As we have seen already in *Creation and Fall*, to begin with the assumption that God cannot speak for himself is predicated on a certain grace-hating or dis-gracing refusal to "make room" for what precedes and surpasses us,[94] which revelation reverses by being welcomed.

Of course, as we have also seen in *Creation and Fall*, Bonhoeffer is keenly attuned to the human propensity for illusion and idolatry. Thus, he provocatively insisted that even the words "In the beginning, God created" could be the ultimate lie born of human insecurity and lust for power over reality. Indeed, in his *Ethics*, he wrote that "a larger part" of even "traditional Christian ethical thought stands like a Colossus obstructing our way" for this very reason.[95] The point, then, is not that Bonhoeffer's hermeneutics of divine revelation—of God's own beginning and initiative to communicate Godself—makes us uncritical and gullible but that it calls for an intensified readiness and responsiveness for the voice of an other beyond our egocentric conjuring and construction: *"Perfect understanding is perfect love . . .* in order even to be able to see something, we need to love it."[96]

In summary, then, God must speak in order for revelation to be possible and thus for God's command to be recognizable and thus for our new beginnings to be justified and guided. If God does not speak, there is no word: "God must be the One who says, 'I am the absolute beginning.'" Rather than a "feeble, tamed horse" (what Bonhoeffer calls "usable Christianity"), Christ is a "fiery stallion" who makes challenging demands on our freedom as creatures.[97] Thus, returning directly to his meditation on Psalm 119 and the metaphor of epistemic "blindness," Bonhoeffer concludes,

> Each day it is new prayer, when we open our eyes in the morning and when we close them at night, that God may give us illuminated eyes of the heart, eyes wide open when the day wants to deceive our natural eyes and when night dupes us with bad dreams, eyes opened and enlightened, filled at all times with the wonders of God's law. We must emulate the blind Bartimaeus.[98]

8:32 from July 24, 1932 (11:464): "But Christ came into the world not so that we should understand him but so that we should cling to him." Also Sermon on 1 Corinthians 13:8–12 from October 28, 1934 (13:387): *"Perfect understanding is perfect love . . .* in order even to be able to see something, we need to love it. . . . Knowing without loving is . . . a childish attempt to become master of the world in a sneaking way."

94. *Creation and Fall* (3:29).

95. *Ethics* (6:55).

96. Sermon on 1 Corinthians 13:8–12 from October 28, 1934 (13:387). Compare Emmanuel Levinas, "Is Ontology Fundamental?," in *Emmanuel Levinas: Basic Philosophical Writings*, ed. Adriaan T. Peperzak, Simon Critchley, and Robert Bernasconi (Bloomington, IN: Indiana University Press, 1996), 4: "To think is no longer to contemplate but to commit oneself, to be engulfed by what one thinks, to be involved."

97. Lecture on "Contemporizing the New Testament" from August 23, 1935 (14:414).

98. "Meditation on Psalm 119" (15:520).

The Will and Command of God

Second and much more briefly, what does Bonhoeffer see as the basic content of the revealed "command" or "will of God," which provides the fundamental justification ("the path") for his ethics of new beginning?[99] Getting greater clarity on this question will enable us to move toward an interpretation of other important claims in Bonhoeffer's work.

Throughout his corpus, Bonhoeffer's understanding of the will and command of God is consistent and unambiguous: love for God and love for our neighbors. We can isolate several key formulations:

> *Love for our neighbor is our will to embrace God's will for the other person*; God's will for the other person is defined for us in the unrestricted command to surrender our self-centered will to our neighbor, which neither means to love the other instead of God, nor to love God in the other, but to put the other in our own place and to love the neighbor instead of ourselves. . . . Love gives itself up to the other unrestrictedly, seeking nothing for itself. But to surrender oneself to the other means obeying God; it is based on surrender to God's will. *God's love, therefore, is at the same time self-surrender and will for community.*[100]

> If I still am not familiar enough with that will [of God], I can get the answer from Jesus: Go home and love your brothers and sisters, your wife, your children, your parents, and your friends. Get along with your neighbor, help those who need help, give what you have to those who do not have; be peace-loving and compassionate, be pure of thought and word; live in the world.[101]

> To be illuminated by Christ means to love God above all things and your neighbor as yourself. That alone can be called "living."[102]

> Following Christ means very simply, Go and do likewise—do as the Lord himself did. The question of whether God actually commanded *us* to do these things is the serpent's question.[103]

> Jesus gives the disciples a simple rule, by which even the most simpleminded can evaluate whether their dealings with others are right or wrong: they need

---

99. *Ethics* (6:378): "*The commandment is the sole authorization of ethical discourse.* The commandment of God is the total and concrete claim of human beings by the merciful and holy God in Jesus Christ. . . . God's commandment is God's speech to human beings." For one of Bonhoeffer's earliest detailed discussions of God's command, see "On the Theological Foundation of the Work of the World Alliance" from July 26, 1932 (11:356–69). See Lisa Dahill, "Probing the Will of God: Bonhoeffer and Discernment," in *Dialog* 41, no. 1 (Spring 2002): 42–49.

100. *Sanctorum Communio* (1:171, 173), echoed in "After Ten Years" from Christmas of 1942 (8:45).

101. Sermon on 1 John 2:17 from August 26, 1928 (10:520).

102. Baptism sermon on Ephesians 5:14 from October 1932 (11:475).

103. Essay on "What Is Church?" from January 1933 (12:262).

only reverse the I and the You in the relationship. They need only put themselves in the other's place and the other in their own. "Do unto others as you
would have them do unto you." . . . [Love of God and neighbor] is the only
aspect in which the command was unambiguous.[104]

> The [good] action's norm is not a universal principle, but the concrete neighbor,
> as given to me by God. . . . God and neighbor, as we encounter them in Jesus
> Christ, are not only the limits of responsible action . . . but they are also its
> origin. Irresponsible action is defined by its disregard for these limits of God
> and neighbor. . . . This is precisely why [responsible life] can be sustained by
> an ultimate joy and confidence, knowing that in its origin, essence, and goal it
> is sheltered in Christ.[105]

What these passages symphonically make plain is that for Bonhoeffer—from
his doctoral dissertation to his *Ethics*—the basic, unambiguous content of the
personal command of God is love for others, including the natural phenomena
of creation, the human neighbor, and the divine other. It is this command of
love that grounds and must guide human initiative. This is both "the origin"
and "limit" of responsible action, which Bonhoeffer thinks is "unambiguous"
in Christian revelation.

And for Bonhoeffer, this command follows from the way or "precedent"
of God in creation as we have seen in *Creation and Fall*. There Bonhoeffer
describes God's creation of the world as an event of generous gift giving, an
act of "self-denial" through the intentional increase of the other's power by
giving them independent existence, which enables love and mutual belonging
in community.[106] Here we see on display Bonhoeffer's principle that "creation
and the law are the two great inviolable statutes of God that belong indis-
solubly together, since the same God has given them (Ps. 19)."[107] Creation is
the divine act of neighbor-love, and the ethical life follows on this originary
path through history.

But as these passages already make clear, Bonhoeffer's understanding of
creation and law also leads into and comes out of Bonhoeffer's fundamental
understanding of the person and work of *Jesus Christ*, which he sums up with
the concept "vicarious representative action." Unpacking *Stellvertretung* will
enable us to understand with further depth and complexity how Bonhoeffer

---

104. *Discipleship* (4:174, 203).
105. *Ethics* (6:221, 269). For the repeated phrase "origin, essence, and goal," see *Ethics* (6:49,
69–70, 226, 251, 253, 259–60, 268–70, 402).
106. *Creation and Fall* (3:39).
107. "Meditation on Psalm 119" (15:507). See "Review and Discussion of New Publications in
Systematic Theology" from winter 1932–1933 (12:194): "Creation and revelation [in Jesus Christ]
must never be played against each other."

understands the justification and guidance of new beginning as humans follow after the way of God in the grace of creation and Christ.

Stellvertretung: "One for the Other"

As we saw in chapter 3, Bonhoeffer thinks, "Human beings have lost their creaturely nature."[108] That is, the basic problem confronting humanity is not merely our inadequate knowledge or immoral behavior. In Bonhoeffer's searching analysis, we are ruptured and devastated in the very depths of our humanness, having been cut off from our origin in God, to the point that "human beings destroy themselves."[109] If this is the case—and thus if our reception of God's self-revelation and our obedience to God's commands will always be fallible, imperfect, and sometimes diabolical—what could possibly justify a new beginning for creatures in this devastated condition and provide genuine guidance and hope?

Bonhoeffer's answer is found in what he calls *Stellvertretung* or "vicarious representative action." This is Christ's action in which he freely and intentionally gives his life for us in our place.[110] To repeat, Bonhoeffer's thought powerfully emphasized the integrity and singularity of individual persons, starting mysteriously with God. Part of what Bonhoeffer found so distressing, destructive, and ultimately "godless" about Nazism and its ideology was the mass movements and anonymous crowds glued together by collective loneliness, desperation, and the loss of personal identity. Nonetheless, this recognition of singular human personhood did not prevent Bonhoeffer from also emphasizing the reality of "human nature," in which each person participates and to which each person contributes. Bonhoeffer defined this as "the epitome of all human possibilities together."[111]

This notion is the basis of Bonhoeffer's fundamental claim that Christ himself, by taking on human nature with his incarnation and "vicarious representative action,"[112] is the beginning of the "new humanity" in which the old

---

108. *Creation and Fall* (3:126).

109. *Ethics* (6:122–23).

110. The concept of *Stellvertretung* is constitutive for Bonhoeffer's understanding of responsibility. See William Schweiker, *Responsibility and Christian Ethics* (New York: Cambridge University Press, 1995), 57. For systematic interpretations, see Brocker, "The Community of God, Jesus Christ, and Responsibility"; Paul George Nielson, "The Concepts of Responsibility and Vocation in the Theological Ethics of Dietrich Bonhoeffer" (PhD Diss., University of Chicago, 1998); Vivienne Blackburn, *Dietrich Bonhoeffer and Simone Weil: A Study in Christian Responsiveness* (Bern: Peter Lang AG, European Academic Publishers, 2004); Barth, *Die Wirklichkeit des Guten*), 230–315; and Clark Elliston, *Dietrich Bonhoeffer and the Ethical Self: Christology, Ethics, and Formation* (Minneapolis, MN: Fortress Press, 2016).

111. "Theological Letter on Christmas" from December 1939 (15:530).

112. "Theological Letter on Christmas": "In the birth of Jesus Christ, God took on [*annehmen*] humanity, not just a single human being."

rule of sin and death is overthrown and replaced with Christ's own life and form, sourced in his "eternal beginning."

Bonhoeffer unpacked this grounding principle explicitly already in his doctoral dissertation *Sanctorum Communio*, which is worth quoting at length:

> Since death as the wages of sin (Rom. 6:23) first constitutes *history*, so *life that abides in love* breaks the continuity of the historical process—not empirically, but objectively. Death can still completely separate past and future for our eyes, but not for the life that abides in the love of Christ. *This is why the principle of vicarious representative action* can become fundamental for the church-community of God in and through Christ. Not "solidarity," which is never possible between Christ and human beings, but vicarious representative action is the life-principle of the new humanity. True, I know myself to be in a guilty solidarity with the other person, but my service to the other person springs from the life-principle of vicarious representative action . . .
>
> Because . . . the entire new humanity is established in reality in Jesus Christ, *he represents the whole history of humanity in his historical life.* Christ's history is marked by the fact that in it humanity-in-Adam is transformed into humanity-in-Christ. As the human body of Jesus Christ became the resurrection body, so the corpus Adae became the corpus Christi.[113]

Several claims in this dense passage need to be drawn out.

First, Bonhoeffer is emphatic that fallen human creatures do not have "solidarity" with Christ, whose life of "love breaks the continuity of the historical process." Such an orientation for Bonhoeffer would be nothing new at all but rather show us to be still trapped in the same situation of saying, "Let me first" with our "good intentions." We cannot save ourselves or autonomously attach ourselves to God.

Second, rather than "solidarity," *Stellvertretung* is Christ's willing initiative to *stand in our place on our behalf,* to be our representative and thus to take everything we had coming to us and to give us all that he is as our own.[114] In working note 86 for his *Ethics*, Bonhoeffer captured this idea in its simplest form: "*Principle of vicarious representative action*: one for the other—fights, works, administers, studies, prays."[115] By taking on human nature itself in all of its "totality" and "possibilities," Christ reveals himself to be "one for the other," "that other" who is for us from the creation of the world and now at the turning point of history.

---

113. *Santorum Communio* (1:146), emphases original. Bonhoeffer repeated this argument in various places, for example, "Lecture on Homiletics" from 1936 (14:510); *Discipleship* (4:213–14 and 4:283); *Ethics* (6:403).

114. Bonhoeffer's logic here is deeply Pauline. See 2 Corinthians 8:9.

115. *Ethics* (6:388–89).

Third, for Bonhoeffer this means that Christ is the *founder* of a "new community," indeed, precisely a "new humanity" that is *constituted* by being gracefully welcomed and included "in Christ." The old ruptured "humanity-in-Adam" is now "transformed into humanity-in-Christ." As the founder of a new community under a new constitution, Christ is also its Lord, the one who decides and determines the "rule" by which this community will be governed and guided, which for Bonhoeffer is nothing other than the "life-principle" of Christ's own life of living on behalf of others, what Bonhoeffer simply calls "service" or the command of neighbor-love as we have seen earlier.[116] This is why I have been referring to God's action in creation and Christ as the "precedent"—what comes before, governs, and guides the moral life—in Bonhoeffer's ethics of new beginning.

Indeed, what manifests Christ's life to be *new* for Bonhoeffer is precisely his way of life *for others* in love, which "breaks the continuity of the historical process." In his 1932 lecture course on "The Nature of the Church," Bonhoeffer insisted, "Adam stands not in the place of the other but rather in his own. Christ stands in the place of humanity!" As we have seen in chapter 3, the fundamental problem with humanity—with "Adam"—is that we insist on being for ourselves, standing our ground, coercing and even killing in order to control, consume, and comprehend what is beyond ourselves. But Christ is someone completely new, indeed, the newness that is at the mysterious origin of the world, such that Bonhoeffer names Christ "the new" itself.[117] Christ was "one for the other," was "the Christ precisely in being there completely for the world and not for himself."[118] This is fundamentally new—the essence of the new—in Bonhoeffer's analysis of humanity. In short, Christ undid Adam's damning precedent by doing what Adam could not do by himself: "stand in the place of the other" to welcome the other as grace.

Here Bonhoeffer interprets Christ as acting as our "vicarious representative" in four specific ways: first, Christ took on and dignified our creatureliness in the mystery of the Incarnation; second, Christ entered into the community of Israel and fulfilled the law on our behalf (a dangerous idea in the context of Nazi anti-Semitism); third, on the cross, Christ suffers and dies in our place; and fourth, in the resurrection, "Christ is risen for us all."[119]

Thus, with Christ as the Lord, brother, and energizing spirit of the new community, Bonhoeffer can summarize: "As such a one, who he is, Christ is

---

116. See the chapter 5 for a discussion of the practice of service in Bonhoeffer's thought.

117. See *Creation and Fall* (3:22) and sermon on Revelation 2:1–7 from Finkenwalde on October 25, 1936 (14:955).

118. *Ethics* (6:404).

119. "The Nature of the Church" (11:296ff). This is repeatedly the structure for how Bonhoeffer talks about Christ throughout his works, most notably in his *Ethics*. For a further discussion of the resurrection, see chapter 5.

the new humanity. Christ is simultaneously the foundation and beginner and fulfiller of the church."[120] Christ is the new beginning, who welcomes us to follow after his pioneering way and share in his community by embracing our humanity.

Throughout his career, Bonhoeffer never tired of expounding this "life-principle," which he saw as the foundation of the "new humanity" in Christ as our "Lord" and "brother" and thus the heart of God's new beginning for community after the destruction of human nature in the Fall. In a 1935 sermon, Bonhoeffer simply called this way of life Christ's "strange glory"—that the Creator and Lord of the universe would take up the posture of the suffering servant on behalf of revolting enemies and share his life in community with them. At Finkenwalde, Bonhoeffer expounded with intensified feeling:

> On the cross . . . the Christ bears the burden of his brother. He risks his soul for that of his brother, and thus in bearing the cross does vicarious representation [*Stellvertretung*] come about by the power of that which the body of Christ already bore for us.[121]

By the time that Bonhoeffer began work on his monumental *Ethics* and wrote his letters from prison, the concept—indeed, the historical *event*—of *Stellvertretung* was the cornerstone of Bonhoeffer's understanding of God's gift and call into a new beginning by Christ, which exceeds human power but welcomes and empowers all persons in their singularity and relationality with others.

In what is likely the final manuscript draft for his *Ethics* titled "Concrete Commandment and the Divine Mandates," Bonhoeffer further developed the sociological implications of this life-principle: the very meaning of the church community is that "there are human beings who stand vicariously in the place [*stellvertretend dastehen*] of all other human beings, of the whole world." As this community "gathers around the divine word," a "body in its own right" has been constituted that is "separate from the worldly orders." Thus, *Stellvertretung* constitutes a "dual relationship" for the community of Christ:

> The Christian community stands in the place in which the whole world should stand. In this respect it serves the world as vicarious representative; it is there for the world's sake. On the other hand, the place where the church-community stands is the place where the world fulfills its own destiny; the church-community is the "new creation," the "new creature," the goal of God's ways on earth. In this dual vicarious representation, the church-community is in complete com-

---

120. "The Nature of the Church" (11:301).
121. Student notes on lecture section on Service to God and Service to One Another from early 1936 (14:476).

munity with its Lord; it follows in discipleship [*Nachfolge*] the one who was the Christ precisely in being there completely for the world and not for himself.[122]

Here Bonhoeffer articulates a vision of robust community that is antitribalistic in its essence and universal in its scope, without also being imperial or colonial. The very identity of Christ himself, who is the founder and form (we might say "president") of the community—indeed, what Bonhoeffer claims makes Christ *Christ*—is "precisely in being there completely for the world and not for himself." Bonhoeffer soon intensified this claim in his book outline from prison: "Jesus only 'is there for others.' Jesus' 'being-for-others' is the experience of transcendence!"[123] Here Jesus is defined simply as "the human being for others."[124] Thus, like Christ, Christ's new community finds its new beginning in following after (*Nachfolge*) Christ in this self-giving way of life for others and the world.

Thus, the church is created as a community whose paradoxical identity is not to be for itself but rather to be a community that is "there for the world's sake." This means that the church, insofar as it bears witness to and participates in Christ's life for others, is for Bonhoeffer the very presence of salvation in the old creation "in the place of all other human beings." The church is "the new creation," whose essence is a moral transformation of the old "I-world" constituted by conquest and consumerism into this "strange glory" of self-sacrifice and service.

This cluster of claims must be understood as the fundamental ground for Bonhoeffer's repeated declarations that (1) the Nazified Reich Church was no "church" at all and (2) "there is no salvation outside the church," which for Bonhoeffer was represented in Germany, at least initially, by the Confessing Church.[125] Rather than a new religious tribalism or parochialism, Bonhoeffer's revoicing of Cyprian's ancient statement in the midst of the Third Reich was an insurrectionary declaration of spiritual revolt and moral responsibility: *there is no salvation outside of the community that freely gives itself for others, including its enemies, in the way of Christ's suffering love.*[126] For Bonhoeffer,

---

122. *Ethics* (6:403–4).

123. On transcendence, see "Lectures on Christology" (12:300–301); Catechetical Exam on Matthew 8:5–13 from November 10, 1927 (9:558–59); sermon on Psalm 62:2 from Barcelona on July 15, 1928 (10:502ff.); sermon on Isaiah 9:6–7 from Christmas 1940 (16:611, 613–15); untitled prison drama from Christmas 1943 (7:48); letter to Maria von Wedemeyer on December 24, 1943 (92:143); "Exposition on the First Table of the Ten Words of God" from June or July 1944 (16:641); letter to Bethge on April 30, 1944 (8:367).

124. "Outline for a Book" from early August 1944 (8:501).

125. See "On the Question of Church Communion" from April 1936 (14:675). Note Bonhoeffer's clarification (14:688): "The reference has been merely to the true, abiding church of Christ, which has 'always' viewed its own faith as necessary for salvation."

126. This is the key for understanding emphatic statements like the one in Sermon on 1 Corinthians 12:26–27 on July 29, 1928 (10:510) about the necessity of the church for salvation and renewal.

all other soteriologies—all other regimes promising a new humanity, a new creation, a new beginning—were idolatrous delusions that could only lead to destruction and death. (Remember from chapter 3 that Bonhoeffer calls "security" a "false god" representing "a word without sacrifice, full of distrust and suspicion."[127])

This, furthermore, was the ground for Bonhoeffer's confession that as a faithful Christian he had to pray for the defeat of his nation for the sake of the victory of Christian civilization, in which others could be respected, protected, and loved.[128] This was because Germany had become the antithesis of a community for others. Thus, however surprisingly for the secular reader, Bonhoeffer understood his theology of revelation and theological ethics of new beginning as the most radical and compelling defense for liberal society in which all individuals, especially the weak, the vulnerable, and the oppressed, are recognized as having intrinsic worth and the right to freedom and justice, to the point of abandoning and rejecting German nationalism.

For Bonhoeffer, this way of life for others in the form of Christ was the very essence of what it meant to be human and what it meant to be Christian, two ways of talking about the renewal of one's original nature as God's creation in the beginning. In his *Ethics*, he wrote, "To live as a human being before God, in the light of God's becoming human, can only mean to be there not for oneself, but for God and for other human beings."[129] Later from prison, paying the price for his own service to others under oppression and annihilation and his resistance to Hitler's "new realities," Bonhoeffer's mind was defiantly unchanged:

Being a Christian does not mean being religious in a certain way, making oneself into something or other (a sinner, penitent, or saint) according to some method or other. Instead it means being human, not a certain type of human being, but the human being Christ created in us. It is not a religious act that makes someone a Christian, but rather sharing in God's suffering in the worldly life. That is "*metanoia*," not thinking first of one's own needs, questions, sins, and fears but allowing oneself to be pulled into walking the path that Jesus walks, the messianic event, in which Isa. 53 is now being fulfilled![130]

The Divine Mandates: "In Search of the Origin"

In Bonhoeffer's ethics, the elements providing the justification for new beginning traced in this chapter—the creating initiative of God, the personal

---

127. Untitled address at the International Youth Conference in Gland on August 29, 1932 (11:375).
128. See Bethge, *Dietrich Bonhoeffer*, 744, who quotes Bonhoeffer as saying, "I pray for the defeat of my country, for I think that is the only possibility of paying for all the suffering that my country has caused in the world."
129. *Ethics* (6:400).
130. Letter to Bethge on July 16, 1944 (8:480).

call and command of God, and the vicarious representative action of God in Christ and Christ's new community—come together in Bonhoeffer's notion of the "divine mandates."[131] In his *Ethics* manuscript "The Concrete Commandment and the Divine Mandates," Bonhoeffer defines a mandate as "the concrete divine commission grounded in the revelation of Christ and the testimony of Scripture; it is the authorization and legitimization to declare a particular divine commandment, the conferring of divine authority on an earthly institution."

But a mandate is not only a "divine commission" that follows from a "particular divine commandment" that endows an "earthly institution" with "authority." A mandate is to be understood simultaneously as God's act of commandeering and forming a certain earthly domain for God's special purpose: "The bearer of the mandate acts as a vicarious representative, as a stand-in for the one who issued the commission."[132] That is, in receiving the commission and command of God, the earthly institutions that have been mandated by God according to Bonhoeffer are meant to act as "vicarious representatives" of God, which have no intrinsic or autonomous authority of their own but rather serve God by serving the life of the world. The important nuance here is not a move back to "Christendom" (see discussion shortly) but the theological claim that all earthly power is fundamentally derivative, limited, and subject to criticism. Human institutions have no absolute claim to inherent sovereignty, and thus they are constituted by accountability and moral responsibility. Institutions here are not purely constructed and functional in nature but both can claim a moral authority and be claimed by moral accountability.

According to Bonhoeffer, there are four mandates, all of which find their unity in God's command in Scripture: "the church, marriage and family, culture, and government." In each case, Bonhoeffer is emphatic that "divine authorizing, legitimizing, and sanctioning" is the "sole foundation" of these mandates.[133] This means that the mandates are not grounded in "human

---

131. See William Warren Butler, "A Comparison of the Ethics of Emil Brunner and Dietrich Bonhoeffer: With Special Attention to the Orders of Creation and the Mandates" (PhD Diss., Emory University, 1970). For a recent interpretation, see Robin Lovin, "The Mandates in an Age of Globalization," in *Ontology and Ethics: Bonhoeffer and Contemporary Scholarship*, ed. Adam C. Clark and Michael G. Mawson (Eugene, OR: Pickwick Publishers, 2013), 19–31. See also Barth, *Die Wirklichkeit des Guten*, 350–59. It is worth noting that Bonhoeffer turned to the "mandates" as an alternative to the "orders of creation," which were being used by Nazified theologians (for example, Paul Althaus and Emanuel Hirsch) as a perverse justification for racism, nationalism, and war. See Robert Ericksen, *Theologians under Hitler: Gerhard Kittel, Paul Althaus, and Emanuel Hirsch* (New Haven, CT: Yale University Press, 1985). Note Bonhoeffer's early critique of this phraseology in "On the Theological Foundation of the Work of the World Alliance" in 1932, judging that it must be "waived" and replaced by "orders of preservation" oriented toward Christ's "new creation" (11:362–64).
132. *Ethics* (6:389).
133. *Ethics* (6:388).

favoritism," "institutional-bureaucratic thinking," or "earthly power relations," which Bonhoeffer thinks derive from "the dark forces of destruction,
of negation, of doubt, and of rebellion" and lead to "the deepest hostility,
mistrust, deception, envy," and "terror."[134] (The crucial background to which
Bonhoeffer is alluding is the notion of "orders of creation," which German
theologians were using to defend the Nazi ideas of racial superiority and
war.[135]) None of the mandates can ever legitimately devolve into tribalism
or mere self-preservation; again, they have a moral core and accountability.

Writing in the midst of World War II, Bonhoeffer confesses, "the fact that
an authentic order instituted from above" is "possible at all" must manifest
itself "as what it actually is, a miracle." Particularly in a time of such incredible devastation, the mandates flow out of and are recognizable by faith in
the exact way that we have seen with revelation earlier.[136] Even in the midst
of total war and mass annihilation, the "miracle" of "an authentic order instituted from above" remains a source of critique, guidance, and hope.

As divine commandments meant to embody the new principle of *Stellvertretung* for practical institutional reality in the world, it is not surprising that
Bonhoeffer sees the mandates as being complexly related to one another,
serving one another, and also limiting one another. He writes, "Only in their
being-with-one-another [*Miteinander*], for-one-another [*Füreinander*], and
over-against-one-another [*Gegeneinander*] do the divine mandates of church,
marriage and family, culture, and government communicate the commandment of God as it is revealed in Jesus Christ."[137] Without this *with-* and
for-one-another, Bonhoeffer says that the claim to any divine authorization
collapses. Thus, Bonhoeffer envisions these "mandates" as being triply limited: by the God who initiates and authorizes them, by the other mandates in
reflexive interaction, and by the constituency whom the mandates are meant
to serve.[138] (It is worth noting here again that what could be misinterpreted as
a religious dogmatism teetering toward fundamentalism flows into a robust
argument for a plurality of mutually limiting and serving powers in a society
constituted by moral responsibility for others.)

Much more could be said about the mandates in Bonhoeffer's thought,
but what is important here for our purposes is the way in which Bonhoeffer
understands the mandate of the church as mediating with its witness the rule
of Christ for the world, which itself reveals the *origin* and thereby sustains

134. *Ethics* (6:390–91).
135. See note 131 in this chapter.
136. *Ethics* (6:392). See the essay "'Personal' and 'Objective' Ethics" likely from the summer
of 1942 (16:549) for a compact explanation of Bonhoeffer's comprehensive understanding of the
mandates.
137. *Ethics* (6:393).
138. *Ethics* (6:394).

the normative *justification* of the family, cultural life, and government in Bonhoeffer's thought. Bonhoeffer writes,

> The lordship of Jesus Christ is not a foreign rule. . . . It is the lordship of the one through whom and toward whom all created being exists, indeed the one in whom all created being finds its origin, essence, and goal.[139] Jesus Christ does not impose a foreign law on created being, but neither does Christ permit created being to have any autonomy apart from Christ's commandment. . . . The commandment of Jesus Christ does not establish the rule of the church over government, nor the rule of government over family, nor of culture over government and church, or whatever other relationship of dominance might be conceivable here.[140] . . . Only through this liberation, which springs from the proclaimed rule of Christ [*Christusherrschaft*], can the divine mandates be properly with-one-another, for-one-another, and against-one-another.[141]

Here Bonhoeffer is clear that the specific mandate of the church does not re-institute some Christendom-style theocracy in which all of life is subservient to the institution of the church.[142] To the contrary, Bonhoeffer believes that the witness of the church to the lordship of Jesus Christ liberates all of the mandates from the "arbitrariness" and willfulness in which they all too easily become isolated from one another or seek to dominate over one another, keeping in mind the "murderous law of never-ending beginnings."[143] By proclaiming the rule of Christ—the "human being for others"—the church serves as a community *in* the world and *for* the world precisely by reintroducing all of "created being" to its "origin, essence, and goal" and thus the fulfillment of "its own law." (The complexity of this view will not allow for a simplistic binary between "autonomy" and "heteronomy.") Only in relation to their origin—to that generous source that acts out of unconditioned freedom for the flourishing of others—can human institutional life be rightly ordered *with*, *for*, and *against* one another (that is, in mutually limiting relationality).

Torn from this origin in Christ, Bonhoeffer sees these mandates as collapsing into "pseudo-worldliness" in which "the world ceases to be worldly"

---

139. See "'Personal' and 'Objective' Ethics" from summer of 1942 (?) (16:547–51). Bonhoeffer rejected the notion of "orders of creation" for this Christocentric notion of "orders" or "mandates" because of the way Nazified theology abused the former as a justification for racism and violence by claiming that the German race/nation was a distinct creation of God from the beginning that should be kept pure. See note 131 in this chapter.

140. See "On the Question of Church Communion" from April 1936 (14:660–61) for a discussion of the "boundaries and scope of the church" meant to limit the church from encroaching on other mandates, which he saw "Catholicism, Orthodoxy, and Pietism" doing.

141. *Ethics* (6:402).

142. See *Ethics* (6:361) and letter to Bethge on July 16, 1944 (8:478).

143. See his essay "State and Church" from April 1941 (16:502–28) and "Lectures on Christology" (12:326).

through its "unquenchable desire for its own deification."[144] One mandate by itself makes itself a god, attempts to trump the others, and ends up rehearsing "the murderous law of never-ending beginnings" marked by nihilism and "violent hands."

As we saw in chapter 3, this is precisely the catastrophe that Bonhoeffer saw ripping through and devastating Europe. With the "form of Christ" having been "repudiated" as the "unity of the West," Bonhoeffer found himself in an anarchic time threatened by a "war of total annihilation in which everything that serves one's own cause, even crime, is justified."[145] Bonhoeffer saw the West "sliding" into "a specifically Western godlessness" and "creative nothingness" that is "rebellious, violent, anti-God, and antihuman," promising "new life" but leaving behind the "field of corpses" he attacked in his meditation on Psalm 119: "Its rule is absolute. . . . Life, history, family, people, language, faith—the list could go on forever because nothingness spares nothing—all fall victim to nothingness."[146]

In this situation of nihilistic decay and violence on the brink of total war in which the created finitude of worldly life was rejected, perhaps we can better appreciate the resoluteness and urgency with which Bonhoeffer insisted upon the special mandate of the church to proclaim the rule of Christ, which includes and reopens "the sphere of freedom" to all people and the other mandates.[147] By "sticking to its calling" and "preaching the risen Jesus Christ," Bonhoeffer thought the church could "deal a deadly blow to the spirit of annihilation." Indeed, in a time surging with desire for absolute freedom and arbitrary power, Bonhoeffer believed,

> All the elements of order that still remain seek to be near the church. Justice, truth, science, art, culture, humanity, freedom, and patriotism, after long wanderings, find their way back to their origin. The more the church holds to its central message, the more effective it is. Its suffering is infinitely more dangerous to the spirit of destruction than the political power that it may still retain.[148]

That is, as a community called in word and deed to bear witness to the form of Christ, whose life was freely given "with and for others" and had up until now constituted the "unity of the West," Bonhoeffer saw the church as a prophetic institution that, if itself transformed, could lead a devastated civi-

---

144. *Ethics* (6:401). William Schweiker has helpfully pointed out how very Protestant Bonhoeffer's perspective is here, seeing society as "interacting powers" rather than a hierarchical order.

145. *Ethics* (6:110).

146. *Ethics* (6:128).

147. See letter to Renate and Eberhard Bethge on January 23, 1944 (8:268), in which Bonhoeffer discusses why Christians should be able to make music, practice friendship, and pursue education even in the darkest times because of their faith.

148. *Ethics* (6:132). See 6:345.

lization (including family, education, culture, and government) back to the originary sources and values of human flourishing in Christ after they had become "homeless" and lost their justification in "arbitrariness."[149]

It is from within this complex vision of Christ as the "origin, essence, and goal" of such a mutually limiting and strengthening network of "mandates" that Bonhoeffer could write,

It is not Christ who has to justify himself before the world by acknowledging the values of justice, truth, and freedom. Instead, it is these values that find themselves in need of justification, and their justification is Jesus Christ alone. It is not a "Christian culture" that still has to make the name of Jesus Christ acceptable to the world; instead, the crucified Christ has become the refuge, justification, protection, and claim for these higher values and their defenders who have been made to suffer.[150]

Religionless Christianity

If this is the case—if the church is called by God to attack the "spirit of annihilation" with its witness to God's free initiative, concrete commands, vicarious representative action, and mandates through which "a miracle of a new awakening of faith" becomes possible[151]—how are we to make sense of Bonhoeffer's scathing criticism of the churches and his announcement of "religionless Christianity" in his famous prison writings, whose genealogy we traced in chapter 3? Did Bonhoeffer's prison experience lead him to move beyond or even abandon the theological position we have been reconstructing in the earlier pages?[152]

The most plausible interpretation, on the contrary, is that Bonhoeffer's prison experience actually led him to intensify and even radicalize the basic claims we have been tracing throughout his corpus, in which case the basic structure of his thought is marked by a profound continuity.[153] In his "Outline

---

149. As we saw already in chapter 3 and will see again in the next section and next chapter, Bonhoeffer thought the church had basically failed in this calling, and thus he thought its fundamental posture should be one of repentance and confession of its sin. See *Ethics* (6:140) and chapter 5.

150. *Ethics* (6:226, 231, 345).

151. *Ethics* (6:131).

152. For an analysis of the "death of God" in Bonhoeffer's thought, see the conclusion.

153. Bonhoeffer's critical comments must be taken with full seriousness. But Bonhoeffer himself interprets his work and contextualizes these claims within consistent affirmations of the continuity of his life and work. Bonhoeffer confirms as much in his letter to Eberhard Bethge dated July 21, 1944, in the midst of their theological correspondence (8:486), in which Bonhoeffer acknowledges "the dangers" of his book *Discipleship* (mainly its emphasis on "a saintly life") but concludes, "I still stand by it." For passages in which Bonhoeffer discusses shifts in his life and thought, see his journal entry on March 13, 1928, criticizing Barth's dogmatic approach (10:76); letter on February 23, 1930, on transitioning out of academia (10:205); letter on January 27, 1936, to Elizabeth Zinn on discovering the Bible, prayer, the call to the church, and pacifism, which "changed and transformed my life to this very day" and before which "I was not yet a Christian but rather in an utterly wild and uncontrolled

for a Book" dated to August 1944, Bonhoeffer writes, deepening what we have seen already in *Ethics*, about "the arts [and] the sciences in search of their origin." But he concludes the paragraph by writing the following: "Decisive: Church defending itself. No risk taking for others."[154] Earlier in another meditation, Bonhoeffer had recorded, "Our church has been fighting during these years only for its self-preservation, as if that were an end in itself. It has become incapable of bringing the word of reconciliation and redemption to humankind and to the world."[155] Based on what we have seen in the previous section, this means that the church was no longer acting as a "mandate" but as an idolatrous institution without justification in danger of falling prey to the arbitrary "spirit of annihilation."

The implications for Bonhoeffer's ethics of new beginning cannot be overestimated or exaggerated: a "church" in which there is "no risk taking for others" is precisely a *Christless* church, which is still ruptured from the Creator. It is no "church" at all (*ekklesia* or "called out") and thus no guiding community into the new beginning of God's way for the world.[156] And thus witness to the life-giving, life-justifying origin is cut off from "the arts and sciences," which then become "homeless."[157]

---

fashion my own master" (14:134); letter to Bethge on June 25, 1942 (16:329: "But I sense how an opposition to all that is 'religious' is growing in me. . . . None of these are new thoughts and insights at all. Because I believe that I am on the verge of some kind of breakthrough I am letting things take their own course and do not resist"); letter to Max Diestel on November 5, 1942 (16:367: "I realize that I am indebted to you for the decisive initiatives in my external, professional, and personal life. . . . It was perhaps one single telephone call—namely, in December 1927—that set my entire thinking on a track from which it has not yet deviated and never will"); letter to Bethge on November 26, 1943 (8:199: "What has taken place in the past seven and a half months has left us both unchanged in the essentials"); letter to Bethge on April 22, 1944 (8:357: "You mustn't indulge in any illusions about me. I've certainly learned a great deal, but I don't think I have changed very much. There are people who change, and many who can hardly change at all. I don't think I have ever changed much, except at the time of my first impressions abroad, and under the first conscious influence of Papa's personality. It was then that a turning from the phraseological to the real ensued. . . . Neither of us has really experienced a break in his life. . . . Continuity with one's own past is actually a great gift"); letter to Bethge on June 8, 1944 (8:430: "My view, however [against Bultmann], is that the full content, including the 'mythological' concepts, must remain"). See Eberhard Bethge, "Turning Points in Bonhoeffer's Life and Thought," in *Bonhoeffer in a World Come of Age*, ed. Peter Vorkink (Philadelphia, PA: Fortress Press, 1968), 31–102; Carl Friedrich von Weizsäcker, "Thoughts of a Non-Theologian on Dietrich Bonhoeffer's Theological Development," *Ecumenical Review* 29, no. 2 (April 1976): 156–73; and Richard Weikart, "So Many Bonhoeffers," *Trinity Journal* 32 NS (2011): 69–81. I find the latter a poor interpretation of Bonhoeffer.

154. "Outline for a Book" from August 1944 (8:500).

155. "Thoughts on the Day of the Baptism of Dietrich Wilhelm Rüdiger Bethge" from May 1944 (8:389).

156. See Brigitte Kahl, "Church for Others: Bonhoeffer, Paul, and the Critique of Empire," in *Interpreting Bonhoeffer: Historical Perspectives, Emerging Issues*, ed. Clifford Green and Guy Carter (Minneapolis, MN: Fortress Press, 2013), 169–80. See Bethge, *Dietrich Bonhoeffer*, 505: "There were those who, like Bonhoeffer, had become ministers not in order to rescue what still survived; their only hope for a mission of truth in the Germany of that era rested in a church without privileges."

157. Already in London in 1934–1935, Bonhoeffer was criticizing "a church-not-worthy-to-be-church" (13:189), and before that in his address on the World Alliance in 1932, Bonhoeffer called for

Indeed, this is precisely what Bonhoeffer understands by the term "religion," used pejoratively as a social structure or metaphysical superstructure that exists to preserve and privilege itself by turning God into a tool at its disposal for its purposes, rather than freely risking itself as a "vicarious representative" for the world in the form of Christ.[158] Here we see the depths of Bonhoeffer's analysis of the ambiguity of religion and religious speech, including the ambiguity of Christian religion and its claim to be "the church."[159] A "Christian church" in which there is "no risk taking for others"—even if it uses the Bible and speaks a "religious" language to justify itself—is itself the most disastrous and truly diabolical instance of the man who said, "Let me first" in response to Jesus's call, "Follow me!" A church in which "justice, truth, science, art, culture, humanity, freedom, and patriotism" cannot "find their way back to their origin" in the self-giving beginning of God in Christ "with and for others" is a human fabrication. It has fallen for the deceiver's temptation, "Discover your beginning yourself!" and thereby—even in the best of its "good intentions"—walked the road toward hell that destroys creation and falls into the "murderous law of never-ending beginnings." Such a church has fallen prey to "usable Christianity."[160]

In the very next paragraph of his "Outline," Bonhoeffer asks the most fundamental question that a Christian theologian can ask: "Who is God?" Bonhoeffer's answer is telling, and it takes us into the core of Bonhoeffer's ethics of new beginning. He responds, "Not primarily a general belief in God's omnipotence, and so on," which as mere intellectual assent to articles of doctrine would amount to "just a prolongation of a piece of the world."[161] *Who is God?* Bonhoeffer answers, "encounter with Jesus Christ." But who

---

"a protest against every form of church that does not honor the question of the truth above all." As we will see in chapter 5, one of these acts of "risk" for others in the church for Bonhoeffer was the open confession of its own sin and failure. See *Ethics* (6:142).

158. In *Sanctorum Communio* (1:59–60), Bonhoeffer can speak positively of "religion." But already in *Act and Being*, Bonhoeffer begins to use the term "religion" with negative connotations, and thereafter seemingly only critiques and condemns "religion" as the human's idolatrous attempt to reach or replace God as an "object" or "possession." See Benkt-Erik Benktson, *Christus und die Religion: Der Religionsbegriff bei Barth, Bonhoeffer und Schleiermacher* (Stuttgart: Valver, 1967); von Weizsäcker, "Thoughts of a Non-Theologian on Dietrich Bonhoeffer's Theological Development," 156–73, especially169ff.; Feil, *The Theology of Dietrich Bonhoeffer*, 160ff.; Bethge, *Dietrich Bonhoeffer*, 871ff.; Tom Greggs, *Theology Against Religion: Constructive Dialogues with Bonhoeffer and Barth* (London: T & T Clark, 2011).

159. For a longer discussion of this point, see the conclusion. Bethge, *Dietrich Bonhoeffer*, 876, is right in his claim that "Bonhoeffer's life consisted of a constant fight to overcome the dangerously privileged character of the Christian religion."

160. Strikingly, Bethge documents in his *Dietrich Bonhoeffer*, 887, that Bonhoeffer's final prison writings "did not give a completed ecclesiology that we could hold on to, but left this, of all things, entirely open." Bethge claims that Bonhoeffer's ecclesiology "ended with unsettled questions. At the end Bonhoeffer arrived at a state that was highly critical of the church. His ecclesiology seemed entirely absorbed within the *theologia crucis.*"

161. "Outline for a Book" (8:501).

is *Jesus Christ*? Jesus is the "reversal of all human experience," precisely because "Jesus only 'is there for others.'" Jesus—"the human being for others! therefore the Crucified One"—is the one who can only be reached and, indeed, the one who only has being in "being-for-others," which Bonhoeffer names "the experience of transcendence." He insists boldly,

> Only through this liberation from self, through this "being-for-others" unto death do omnipotence, omniscience, and omnipresence come into being. Faith is participating in this being of Jesus. (Becoming human, cross, resurrection.) Our relationship to God is no "religious" relationship to some highest, most powerful, and best being imaginable—that is no genuine transcendence. Instead, our relationship to God is a new life in "being there for others," through participation in the being of Jesus. The transcendent is not the infinite, unattainable task, but the neighbor within reach in any given situation. God in human form![162]

Let us be clear. When Bonhoeffer writes that "our relationship to God is a new life in 'being there for others,'" this life is *new* precisely because it is *there for others*, which means that the boundaries of my closed "ego-world" have been transcended and what exceeds my categories and control, namely God and my neighbor, encounter me as for the first time in bonds of welcome and service (that is, the rediscovery of alterity as grace). What I thought could be taken for granted in my horizon or instrumentalized for my purposes or even destroyed by my power—God and my neighbor—are now met in a totally new way, and thus I myself in this encounter become new. In this "liberation from self," even to the point of risking my own self in death, "a new life" is revealed and a new beginning commences through my life with neighbors, which follows in the way of God's action and command "in the beginning" to increase power and give grace.

Far from a transformation or abandonment of Bonhoeffer's pre-prison theology, then, when Bonhoeffer summarizes his position by saying that "the church is church only when it is there for others" and that it "must participate in the worldly tasks of life in the community, not by dominating" but by itself embodying "what a life with Christ is, what it means 'to be there for others,'"[163] this must be interpreted as the intensification and clarification of the core of Bonhoeffer's entire theology and ethics of new beginning from his earliest sermons and dissertation onward. His analysis of the problems of "nihilism" and "Western godlessness" had grown more severe, his interpretation of history more complex, and his view of the needed response more radical ("as a first step the church must give away all its property to those in

---

162. "Outline for a Book" (8:501).
163. "Outline for a Book" (8:503).

need"). But the core of his thought, which led him to these precise insights, remained consistent and clear.

This type of "religionless" or "worldly" Christianity, which could "confront the vices of hubris, the worship of power, envy, and illusionism"[164] and proclaim the rule of Christ's resurrection in and for the world, remained for Bonhoeffer the mandate of God and the simultaneous way of "new life" and "return to the origin." In this "path," Christ could be recognized afresh as "the refuge, justification, protection, and claim" for "the higher values," which had been devastated in Western civilization and "useable Christianity" by their "repudiation" of Christ's vicarious "form."[165]

CONCLUSION

In this chapter, I have attempted to reconstruct Bonhoeffer's theological ethics of new beginning. In particular, I have been interested in the way Bonhoeffer was able to discriminate between a justified new beginning and an arbitrary act of randomness or violence by finite will.

For Bonhoeffer, a new beginning after devastation in human nature and human history must commence with the initiative of God the Creator, Redeemer, and Reconciler. This means, paradoxically, that the first step of a new beginning for humanity must be the renunciation of the orientation that says, "Let me first" for obedience to the call of Jesus who says, "Follow me." Having "begun with Christ," Bonhoeffer envisions the truly human life as an unceasing responsiveness to the self-revealed command of God in Christ, which is concretized in the command of love for others, divine and human, which frees us from the "murderous law of never-ending beginnings."

Next, we probed into Bonhoeffer's understanding of Christ's initiative to stand in our place on our behalf, *Stellvertretung* or the new "life-principle" of "one for the other." As our representative, Christ himself becomes the historical incarnation of God's law and breaks the power of death, which had ruptured human nature, in order to create a "new humanity."

We then looked at Bonhoeffer's understanding of "the divine mandates" (that is, marriage and family, church, culture, and government) and how they concretize the command of God and the form of vicarious representative action for institutional life in the world. In particular, we looked at Bonhoeffer's understanding of the mandate of the church, through which the ultimate justification for the life of the world in Christ the Creator is revealed and thus through which the world is called to return to its life-giving origin. Following

---

164. "Outline for a Book" (8:503).
165. *Ethics* (6:345).

after this origin, limited power, accountability, and the positive vocation of moral responsibility for the flourishing of life are rediscovered.

Finally, we made the case that Bonhoeffer's prison writings, rather than abandoning or substantially altering this theology, actually intensify Bonhoeffer's fundamental understanding of "new life" and "new beginning" as freely "being there for others" even to the point of death. It is precisely this principle of the priority of the other person rooted in love that Bonhoeffer uses as the measure for his critique of idolatrous religion and secular nihilism, which say, "Let me first" and have at their core "no risk taking for others."

All throughout this chapter and particularly in the last section, we have seen that Bonhoeffer believes that the most important element of the ethics of new beginning is not primarily lining up one's intellectual ideas and religious beliefs. Indeed, Bonhoeffer emphasized how "good intentions," "ethical questions," "conscience," and sometimes even Scripture itself can actually be distractions or defenses against the call of God into a transformative way of life with and for others.[166] This is why Bonhoeffer could claim that "a larger part" of even "traditional Christian ethical thought stands like a Colossus obstructing our way" as he faced the catastrophic new beginning of Nazi totalitarianism.

Thus, in chapter 5, we will turn to Bonhoeffer's understanding of the *practices* of new beginning in the midst of concrete life with others, which spring from God's beginning and bear witness to radical hope for individuals, society, and the world of creation.

---

166. Sermon on John 3:16–21 from February 20, 1940 (15:560).

Chapter Five

"The Dawning of the New World, the New Order"

Practices of New Beginning in Bonhoeffer's Thought

THE BEGINNING:
"A NEW LIFE IN BEING THERE FOR OTHERS"

In chapters 3 and 4, perhaps our central discovery in Bonhoeffer's ethics of new beginning has been that the "new beginning" is not something that we can autonomously make for ourselves, whether as individuals or in society. The "new" most fundamentally is *the other person*, starting with God and extending to all people. And thus a new beginning is fundamentally becoming open to welcome and respond to others in all of their transcendent distance and nearness, joy and pain.[1] However strange to our minds, the "new beginning" is not something that we can make or that is within the self's power to commence.

Indeed, Bonhoeffer worries deeply that the mindset that thinks we can make our beginnings for ourselves is still very much a reflection of the "old world" and its sometimes murderous self-entrapment. The "new" is fundamentally found in the other person and thus in the self finding ears for her voice, eyes for her face, space for her presence, responsiveness to her initiative, and concern and sacrifice for her suffering in love.[2] As Bonhoeffer wrote in *Creation and Fall*, Christ—"the human being for others"—"is the begin-

---

1. For Bonhoeffer's understanding of "transcendence," the core of which is the otherness of the other person and his or her freedom to address and respond to me rather than being constituted and controlled by me, see chapter 4, note 123. For a brilliant discussion of various conceptions of transcendence, see Ingolf Dalferth, "The Idea of Transcendence," 146–88, 173: "The difference between 'old' and 'new' is visible only from the standpoint of the event [of the transcendent], not from the standpoint of the self."

2. See Gustavo Gutiérrez, *A Theology of Liberation*, trans. Caridad Inda and John Eagleson (Maryknoll, NY: Orbis Books, 1973), 307.

ning, the new, the end of our whole world."[3] And as Bonhoeffer proclaimed in a sermon from this period, "Jesus Christ, God himself, speaks to us from every human being; the other person, this enigmatic, impenetrable You, is God's claim on us; indeed, is the holy God in person whom we encounter."[4] This echoes in Bonhoeffer's later writing in *Life Together*: "I can never know in advance how God's image should appear in others. That image always takes on a completely new and unique form whose origin is found solely in God's free and sovereign act of creation."[5] The "new act," then, "is in fact the act of *love*, brought about by the Spirit, which is the very heart of community of spirit. I organize my relation to the other with a single end in mind, namely to fulfill God's will by loving the other."[6]

Thus, the new beginning is the mysterious start—*startle*, in fact[7]—that happens to the self when this recognition occurs, when the other person's life opens the self's world as grace and calls us out of ourselves in a new posture of love and responsibility toward people, creation, and God.[8] As Bonhoeffer observed in 1928, "A people whose members love one another—this is unprecedented, transcending all human experience."[9]

I believe this is the reason why Bonhoeffer repeatedly names Jesus himself "the new" and "the new beginning."[10] If Jesus is "the human being for others,"[11] then this means that Jesus is the one whose fundamental posture is not toward himself or for himself but with and for others, even to the point of standing in others' place on their behalf unto death, what Bonhoeffer calls *Stellvertretung*. Jesus begins and enters into our humanity in order to welcome those who are different and independent of him, including "enemies" who oppose him and seek to take his life. Jesus's beginning is grace

---

3. *Creation and Fall* (3:22).

4. Sermon on Matthew 28:20 from April 15, 1928 (10:492, 494–95). For a study of this claim in the thought of Martin Luther, who so deeply influenced Bonhoeffer, see Tuomo Mannermaa, *Two Kinds of Love: Martin Luther's Religious World*, trans. Kirsi I. Stjerna (Minneapolis, MN: Fortress Press, 2010), especially chapter 6.

5. *Life Together* (5:95).

6. *Sanctorum Communio* (1:262).

7. See Arendt, *The Human Condition*, 177: "This character of startling unexpectedness is inherent in all beginnings and in all origins."

8. See Sermon on John 8:32 from July 24, 1932 (11:470).

9. Sermon on 1 Corinthians 12:26–27 from July 29, 1928 (10:507, also 536). See Sermon on 1 Corinthians 12:27 from Barcelona on July 29, 1928 (10:507) and Wedding Sermon on John 13:34 from July 18, 1936 (14:937).

10. *Creation and Fall* (3:22). See also Sermon on Revelation 2:1–7 from October 25, 1936 (14:955–57); "Lecture on Pastoral Counseling" from March 1938 (15:309); Sermon on Luke 12:35–40 from November 29, 1931 (11:409); "Lectures on Christology" (12:327). Bonhoeffer is clearly following Paul (for example, Colossians 1:18) and early Christian thought (for example, *The Epistle to Diognetus*, in *The Apostolic Fathers*, Vol. 2, trans. Kirsopp Lake [Cambridge, MA: Harvard University Press, 1985], XI.4).

11. "Outline for a Book" (8:501). See Feil, *The Theology of Dietrich Bonhoeffer*, 92–95 ("The 'Being-for-Others' of Jesus").

for others, a gift given before the waves of our consciousness can crash and sweep it away.[12] This is revealed both in the mystery of creation, whereby the fundamental new beginning of reality is commenced by the power of Christ "to greatly increase the power of the creation," but also in the crucifixion and resurrection, where Christ willingly suffers and dies in our place, while in that very act defeating death with life in order to resurrect a "new humanity."

Moreover, as we have seen earlier, Bonhoeffer claims that the generosity of Jesus's new way of life is met anew in each of our encounters with others, if only we have the eyes to see. In one of his early sermons, Bonhoeffer declares,

> Jesus Christ is also in us every step we take, in every person we meet. . . . Jesus Christ, God himself, speaks to us from every human being; the other person, this enigmatic, impenetrable You, is God's claim on us; indeed, is the holy God in person whom we encounter. God's claim is made on us in the wanderer on the street, the beggar at the door, the sick person at the door of the church, though certainly no less in every person near to us, in every person with whom we are together day. "Just as you did it to one the least of these, you did it to me," Jesus says. I am for you, you are for me God's claim, God himself; in this recognition, our gaze opens to the fullness of the divine life in the world. Now life in the human community acquires its divine meaning. This community itself is one of the forms of God's revelation. God is with us long as there is community.[13]

Rather than being greedy or self-protective for his singular status, Jesus is the most generous self, who bestows sacred significance on every other, especially those in whom we least expect to find this "strange glory."[14] Here the "divine meaning" and "the fullness of the divine life" become manifest between us for the first time in the world that we share by God's grace in its inexhaustible newness.

From this basis, we should interpret Bonhoeffer's prison formulation as precise and essential to his entire theology: "Our relationship with God is 'a new life in being there for others.'"[15] The *newness* of the new life—what makes it "unprecedented" and "transcendent"—is found in our "being there

---

12. See *Ethics*, especially 6:231, 400, and 405. The implication for the church is this (6:405): "The church community does not struggle for itself; it does not speak for its own cause. . . . Instead, the church-community struggles and speaks and acts, precisely for others, for the world, for its enemies."

13. Sermon on Matthew 28:20 from April 15, 1928 (10:492, 494–95). This Christological vision of the other, often in the context of Christian confession but also in the encounter with the stranger and always connected with his notion of *Stellvertretung*, reaches back to the earliest foundations of Bonhoeffer's thought and stretches throughout his corpus.

14. See Matthew 25:31–46, a text to which Bonhoeffer repeatedly returned.

15. "Outline for a Book" (8:501). For a discussion of "being there for others," which appears to be a reference to Luther, see Walter Dreß, "Religiöses Denken und christliche Verkündigung in der Theologie Dietrich Bonhoeffer," in *Theologia Viatorum* 14 (1997–1998): 35–61; 60–61n6.

for others," rather than grasping after ourselves and our beginnings.[16] This newness starts with God, who precedes us and initiated "in the beginning" this self-transcendent, other-welcoming way of existing in love, and it infuses all of our relations with others initiated in love.

By implication, then, a life that is not essentially "there for others"—however "novel" or "innovative" it may appear to be, whether in personal style, society, technology, politics, or any other field—is still *old* for Bonhoeffer, old in the fatally aged sense of the "mute, violated, silenced, dead, I-world."[17] More precisely, a life that is not fundamentally "there for others" is a *godless* life, even if it is saturated in religious piety and cultural innovation, a life that finds itself trapped in "the murderous law of never-ending beginnings" and animated with the "spirit of annihilation."

Perhaps we should not be surprised, then, that the fundamental practices of "new beginning" that can be elucidated in Bonhoeffer's work are not so much techniques that we perform to shape ourselves, insert ourselves in the world, or assert ourselves on others. (Remember Bonhoeffer insists that we cannot claim by ourselves to have "solidarity" with God or to save ourselves, the epitome of the "old way.") These practices are not human "initiatives" per se. Thus, Bonhoeffer's practices of new beginning are quite different from philosophical practices of "self-creation," "self-cultivation," or "techniques of the self" following after Foucault and Hadot.[18] These practices are rather at their heart concerned with *welcoming, waiting upon, and responding to others*, which amounts to miraculous patience and openness, again beginning with God. Bonhoeffer calls this "paradoxically passive action" or "the purest activity as passivity."[19]

This paradoxical name for these practices does not indicate any acquiescence, hesitation, or sedated "passivity" in Bonhoeffer's ethics of new beginning, much less a resentful or disengaged indifference. As his family and his own life demonstrate, Bonhoeffer was not against scientific discovery, cultural innovation, and creative action, to the point of political resistance and tyrannicide. Marilynne Robinson rightly observes, "Evidence of discipline . . . is

---

16. Letter to Bethge on August 21, 1944 (8:515). See *Ethics* (6:400); letter to Bethge on August 14, 1944 (8:509); and "Thoughts on the Day of Baptism of Dietrich Wilhelm Rüdiger Bethge" from May 1944 (8:389).

17. *Creation and Fall* (3:142).

18. See Pierre Hadot, *Philosophy as a Way of Life: Spiritual Exercises from Socrates to Foucault*, ed. Arnold Davidson (New York: Wiley-Blackwell, 1995).

19. See *Ethics* (6:47, 226). See also "The Nature of the Church" (11:319) and Mother Teresa, *Come Be My Light: The Private Writings of the "Saint of Calcutta,"* ed. Brian Kolodiejchuk (New York: Doubleday, 2007), 200: "You begin well your mission life, by being first a patient." See Ingolf Dalferth, "The Idea of Transcendence," 152: "In being put into question by the other I become passively what I could never have become actively: the neighbor of my neighbor."

everywhere [in Bonhoeffer's life]."[20] Bonhoeffer lived an astonishingly active life and was ultimately executed for treason to the German state due to his activities working as a double agent amid the plot to assassinate Hitler and build international support for a transition to a new regime in Nazi Germany.

Nonetheless, if our prime temptation is to begin for ourselves, and if this temptation leads to the devastation in human nature and history we saw in chapter 3, and thus if what is truly "new" is *the other person* and the self's openness and care for others as grace, then Bonhoeffer's practices of new beginning were "paradoxically passive" practices centered on welcoming, waiting on, and responding to others, beginning with God, rather than projects in which the self is making its own beginning. Insofar as our initiatives participate in a life that is "there for others," then they too may participate in and be signs of responsible new beginnings, which are ultimately grounded, energized, and guided by God.

But Bonhoeffer is critically concerned that our "good intentions" and expressions "Let me first" are paving a way to hell marked by a "murderous law of never-ending beginnings," which can only be transformed through this fundamental posture of being with and for others, which emerges in the practices we will describe in this chapter. I do not see a simple or easy way to resolve the tension and paradox between the "passivity" and "activity" in such "practices." Bonhoeffer insisted that they be held together, and I believe this paradox must not be resolved but embraced and inhabited in a responsible ethics of new beginning that does justice to human finitude and freedom, the givenness of our beginnings and our capacity for voluntary initiative.[21]

BONHOEFFER'S RADICAL REVALUATION

Before we turn to discuss the practices of new beginning in Bonhoeffer's thought, one more piece of framework is needed. Throughout Bonhoeffer's writings, Bonhoeffer describes a "revaluation" that takes place in human life and morality when God goes before us and paves the path of our new beginning.[22] In this revaluation, the "old world"—what we assumed could be taken for granted as valueless and at best instrumental for our purposes—is

---

20. Marilynne Robinson, *The Death of Adam: Essays on Modern Thought* (London: Picador, 2005), 112.

21. For reflection on the relation of passion and action in human life more generally, see *Act and Being* (2:116) and "The Right to Self-Assertion," February 4, 1932 (11:253). Note David Brookes's article, "The Art of Presence" in *The New York Times* (January 20, 2014).

22. See Nietzsche, *Beyond Good and Evil*, §203. Note that both Eichmann and Goebbels spoke of the "revaluation of values." See Glover, *Humanity*, 356.

revealed to be the new way of God, and what we assumed to be most novel and valuable is often unmasked as empty and ephemeral.

In his very early Barcelona lecture "Jesus Christ and the Essence of Christianity" (1928), Bonhoeffer writes that Jesus's "turn" to children and "the morally and socially least of these, those viewed as less worthy" was "something totally unprecedented and new in world history, and in the person of Jesus it seems to constitute a break." Bonhoeffer argues that Plato opened his school for "philosophers" and "those who strive to live an ethical life." Similarly, Buddha "sought his following among ascetics." By contrast, "Jesus becomes the discoverer of the child" and the lover of the sinner.[23] In Jesus's ministry,

> All traditional values seem to topple, to be revalued. . . . Here the light of eternity falls upon that which is eternally disregarded, the eternally insignificant, the weak, ignoble, unknown, the least of these, the oppressed and despised; here that light radiates out over the houses of the prostitutes and tax collectors . . . here that light pours out from eternity upon the working, toiling, sinning masses. . . . Christianity preaches the infinite worth of that which is seemingly worthless and the infinite worthlessness of that which is seemingly so valued. What is weak shall become strong through God, and what dies shall live.[24]

From this perspective, it should be manifest that Bonhoeffer's practices of new beginning, when rightly understood, can never lead to a new self-righteousness, elitism, or exclusivism. To the contrary, their very core is this recognition of "the infinite worth of that which is seemingly worthless," which destroys exclusionary boundaries and devaluing measures.

Bonhoeffer attributes Jesus's radical "revaluation" to his "unprecedented idea of God," in which God "utterly transcends" and is "totally different" from "human thought and will," precisely because "God wants those who have nothing." God loves the nobody, the nothing, the nonentity. "This God," Bonhoeffer writes, "wants only one thing from people, namely that they be nothing before him, and demands nothing from people but that they make absolutely no claims." Paradoxically, then, it is "religion and morality" that hide "the germ of hubris," the "perspective of human initiative," in which we idolize our self-creation and have no ears for "a message about the eternally other"—in which we hate the grace of God's beginning.[25] Here Bonhoeffer

23. "Jesus Christ and the Essence of Christianity" from 1928 in Barcelona (10:350–51). Note Bonhoeffer's later interpretation of Christ's birth in a Sermon on Isaiah 9:6–7 from Christmas 1940 (16:611, 613): "That for which kings and statesmen, philosophers and artists, founders of religion and teachers of morals exert themselves in vain now takes place through a newborn child. . . . In the very lowliness and weakness of the child the authority over all the world has its origin."

24. "Jesus Christ and the Essence of Christianity" from 1928 in Barcelona (10:352, 354).

25. "Jesus Christ and the Essence of Christianity" (10:352).

calls "the Greek spirit" "the most severe enemy of Christianity" because the "Greek sensibility understands nothing of such things."[26]

Four years later, back in Berlin, in a sermon on Jesus's statement "The truth will make you free" (John 8:32), Bonhoeffer continues this meditation on re-valuation via what he sees as "perhaps the most revolutionary passage in the whole New Testament." Rather than addressing "the great political or scientific revolutionaries and their loyal followers," those we so often see as "the fighters for progress and knowledge,"[27] Bonhoeffer sees Jesus's proclamation as addressed to "the child," "the fool," and "the crucified one." This is what he calls "a strange assortment of people, of saviors of humanity, of revolutionaries."[28] After God's beginning, these are the kinds of people who have abandoned the "Greek" lie that "our action, our strength, our courage, our race, our moral-ity—in short, *we*, we will make ourselves free."[29] Bonhoeffer worries that the ones that we see as the real novelists, the innovators, the initiators of new begin-nings—perhaps thinking of Hitler and his "new realities"—are trapped in this oldest lie that ends up diminishing, excluding, and destroying others:

> You thought you could make the truth, create it, proclaim it—but with that you presumed to be God and failed in it. You crucified the truth. . . . You lived as if you were alone in the world. You found in yourself the source of truth which is only in God. And for that reason you hated the other people, who do the same. You found in yourself the center of the world, and precisely this was the lie. You considered your brother in the world to be the domain of your rule and did not see that all of you, you and they, live from God's truth. You wrenched yourself out of communion with God and your brother and believed you could live alone. You hated God and your brother, because they contradicted your truth. That was the lie; that is why you are a liar through and through. Your wanting to be alone, your hatred is the lie.[30]

By contrast, Jesus's "unprecedented idea of God" led to the elevation of the "least of these" and a moral universalism that dignified all people in bonds of self-giving community.

Thus, against the "lie" of autonomous self-creation, which we saw play-ing significant roles in the thinkers discussed in chapter 1 and Bonhoeffer's

---

26. "Jesus Christ and the Essence of Christianity" (10:355). Siedentop's book *Inventing the Indi-vidual* and his analysis of the moral order of the ancient family, city, and cosmos shows Bonhoeffer's claim to be historically accurate rather than sermonic hyperbole.

27. Sermon on John 8:32 from July 24, 1932 (11:465). Seidentop argues that even Stoic cosmo-politanism was originally imbued with self-exaltation and status inequality over others.

28. Sermon on John 8:32 from 1932 (11:467).

29. Sermon on John 8:32 from 1932 (11:468).

30. Sermon on John 8:32 from 1932 (11:470). See Nietzsche, *Twilight of the Idols*, §49, in which Nietzsche praises Goethe for having "created himself" and thus become an exemplar of "a spirit who has *become free*."

analysis of devastation in chapter 3, Bonhoeffer proclaims that true freedom does not mean "becoming great in the world," whether that be tied to our action, race, morality, or religion, but rather "becoming free from oneself, from the lie that I am the only one there, that I am the center of the world, from the hatred with which I scorn God's creation, free from oneself for others." For Bonhoeffer, in being given a "gaze" now able "to see the other person," God's truth "destroys our lie and creates truth. It destroys hatred and creates love" precisely because "God's truth is God's love, and God's love makes us free from ourselves for others." Indeed, Bonhoeffer asserts, "Being free means nothing else but being in love."[31] Here Bonhoeffer's theological "revaluation" utterly destroys any legitimate ground for racism, sexism, ableism, and other ideologies that exclude and annihilate others as beloved creatures of God.

Bonhoeffer then makes explicit what is implicit in this claim for human life, society, and morality: "The human being who loves because he has been made free by God's truth is the most revolutionary human being on earth. He is the overturning of all values; he is the explosive material in human society; he is the most dangerous human being." Rather than hypocritically elevating the Christian here to some exceptional "greatness," Bonhoeffer's point is that the Christian is someone who has recognized that "human beings are, in their deepest being, untruthful," and thus the Christian should be "ready at any time to let the light of truth fall upon him" out of love for others. He or she can see through the lie and actively oppose it, and thus becomes "revolutionary," "explosive," and "dangerous" to the order built on the lie. The result is that no one, especially the weak and vulnerable, can be overlooked, excluded, or subjected to oppression or violent death without protest.[32]

Two years later, in a London sermon, Bonhoeffer pressed further with this meditation on revaluation. There he argues, "Ultimately our whole attitude toward life, toward man and God depends on the answer" we give to the "all-important" question, "what is the meaning of physical or mental or moral weakness?"[33] Bonhoeffer lifts up "poor people, ill people, insane people—people who cannot help themselves but who have just to rely on other people

---

31. Sermon on John 8:32 from 1932 (11:471).
32. Note Sermon on Colossians 3:1–4 from June 19, 1932 (11:459).
33. Sermon on 2 Corinthians 12:9 from 1934 (13:401). Bonhoeffer's question should be compared with Hitler's view of weakness, quoted in Glover, *Humanity*, 337: "My pedagogy is hard. What is weak must be hammered away. In my fortresses of the Teutonic Order a young generation will grow up before which the world will tremble. I want the young to be violent, domineering, undismayed, cruel. The young must be all these things. They must be able to bear pain. There must be nothing weak or gentle about them." Note also Nietzsche, *The Antichrist*, §2: "The weak and ill-constituted shall perish: first principle of *our* philosophy. And one shall help them to do so. What is more harmful than any vice? Active sympathy for the ill-constituted and weak—Christianity."

for help, for love for, care." He tries to assume the "outlook on life" of "a cripple, a hopelessly ill man, a socially exploited man, a coloured man in a white society, an untouchable."[34] Rather than "a religion of slaves" driven by "inferiority complexes" (Nietzsche's critique), Bonhoeffer argues that Christianity "gave new meaning" to weakness and devalued people in opposition to "an aristocratic philosophy of life which glorified strength and power and violence as the ultimate ideals of humanity."[35] Weakness calls humanity to "love and help," to "care and reverence," not as an act of "condescension" but as "sharing God's own suffering and weakness in the world" on behalf of others. This, for Bonhoeffer, paradoxically reveals that "God is mighty where man is nothing."[36]

Bonhoeffer's conclusion is consistent and clear: "Christianity stands or falls with its revolutionary protest against violence, arbitrariness, and pride of power and with its apologia for the weak. . . . So Christianity means a devaluation of all human values and the establishment of a new order of values in the sight of Christ."[37] This, again, is the ethical ground for Bonhoeffer's claim in *Ethics* that "it is not a 'Christian culture' that still has to make the name of Jesus Christ acceptable to the world; instead, the crucified Christ has become the refuge, justification, protection, and claim for these higher values and their defenders who have been made to suffer."[38] For Bonhoeffer, Christianity "stands or falls with its revolutionary protest" in defense of Christ's "new order of values" in which the question of weakness is met with answers of love, presence, and service.

Bonhoeffer's meditations on Christianity's "revaluation" or "overturning" of the world's values could be traced throughout the remainder of his

---

34. Compare Bonhoeffer's statement with that of a prominent German Christian from the same period as recorded in Bergen, *Twisted Cross*, 40: "God created humans in his own image! All the miserable ones and cripples in the institutions do not fit. That is not order, but disorder." Bergen, *Twisted Cross*, 68, quotes a book of the German Christian Reich Bishop Müller, who wrote in 1939, "[Love for the German homeland and German people] hates everything soft and weak because it knows that all life can only then remain healthy and fit for life when everything antagonistic to life, the rotten and the indecent, is cleared out of the way and destroyed."

35. Sermon on 2 Corinthians 12:9 from London 1934 (13:402).

36. Sermon on 2 Corinthians 12:9 from London 1934 (13:404). Bonhoeffer's claim that this love does not amount to "condescension" but a life that is *with* others in addition to being "for" others ("reverence" and "sharing") is crucial in heading off legitimate worries from feminist and liberation theologians that Bonhoeffer's ethics here may fall into an unrecognized but pernicious paternalism. Bonhoeffer's ethic of responsibility certainly leads him to see those with greater privilege as having special responsibilities, but this does not lead to a view of superiority or paternalism that diminishes the integrity and agency of those in suffering or oppression. See his presentation on "The Inner Life of the German Evangelical Church" from August 5, 1936 (14:711) on the true power of God's willing embrace of suffering. See Barbara Hilkert Andolsen, "Agape in Feminist Ethics," in *Feminist Theological Ethics*, ed. Lois K. Daly (Louisville, LA: Westminster John Knox Press, 1994).

37. Sermon on 2 Corinthians 12:9 from London 1934 (13:402–3). See Sermon on Luke 16:19–31 from May 29, 1932 (11:445) and *Discipleship* (4:238): "Jesus Christ already has brought about an upheaval of the whole world by liberating both slave and free."

38. *Ethics* (6:226, 231, 345).

corpus. For example, in *Discipleship* Bonhoeffer writes that those Jesus blesses in his Beatitudes—those we see as "unworthy of living, superfluous to this earth"[39] like those who weep, make peace, the meek and persecuted—are truly "the noblest asset, the highest value the world possesses" without whom "the earth can no longer survive."[40] He summarizes that in the Christ "who made everything new," "everything was devalued which had value in the eyes of the people, and everything was called blessed which had no value."[41]

In his *Ethics*, Bonhoeffer writes that "not an ideal human, but human beings as they are; not an ideal world, but the real world"—"what we exert ourselves to grow beyond" and "leave behind"—is "for God the ground of unfathomable love." For Bonhoeffer, this revaluating love is rooted in "the conception and birth of Jesus Christ" on behalf of dying, sinful people.[42] Earthly, human life with its weakness and limits is embraced as valuable and worthy of love in Christ.

This takes us forward to Bonhoeffer's last writings and back to our opening claim about the meaning of "newness" and a "new beginning" in Bonhoeffer's thought, which serves as the ground, guide, and energy for his vision of practices of new beginning. In his prison outline for a book in which he intended to summarize his latest theologizing, Bonhoeffer wrote,

> Here there is a reversal of all human existence, in the very fact that Jesus only "is there for others." Only through this liberation from self, through this "being-there-for-others" unto death do omnipotence, omniscience, and omnipresence come into being. Faith is participating in this being of Jesus. (Becoming human, cross, resurrection.) Our relationship to God is no "religious" relationship to some highest, most powerful, and best being imaginable—that is no genuine transcendence. Instead, our relationship to God is a new life in "being there for others," through participating in the being of Jesus. The transcendent is not the infinite, unattainable task, but the neighbor within reach in any given situation. God in human form![43]

---

39. Bonhoeffer is almost certainly referring to the popular rhetoric of his time. In 1939, Hitler announced the "Euthanasia Program" that was intended to eliminate seventy thousand "lives unworthy of living." Quoted in Bergen, *Twisted Cross*, 40. See notes 33 and 34 in this chapter and Gerrens von Uwe, *Medizinisches Ethos und Theologische Ethik: Karl und Dietrich Bonhoeffer in der Auseinandersetzung um Zwangssterilisation und "Euthanasie" im Nationalsozialismus* (München: Oldenbourg, 1996)

40. *Discipleship* (4:110–11).

41. *Discipleship* (4:115). For other crucial passages, see *Discipleship* (4:105) and Sermon on Luke 1:46–55 from December 17, 1933 (13:343).

42. *Ethics* (6:84). Note in the previously cited sermon (13:344–45) that Bonhoeffer calls the birth of Jesus through the peasant Mary "the reversal of all things . . . to show us where and who God really is, and from this standpoint to judge all human desire for greatness, to devalue it and pull it down from its throne."

43. "Outline for a Book" from August 1944 (8:501).

At the climax of Bonhoeffer's theology, the other person—whether God or the neighbor—is "transcendent," and the life that is "there for" them is *new*. They face and address us from outside ourselves, calling for our love and service—*being there for them*—as the fundamental essence of "new life" after the lie we have told ourselves and the idol we have made of ourselves.[44] This way of "being there" represents nothing short of "a reversal of all human existence," which opens to "an experience of incomparable value" rooted in "the perspective of the outcasts, the suspects, the maltreated, the powerless, the oppressed and reviled, in short from the perspective of the suffering."[45]

Thus, from the beginning to the end of Bonhoeffer's corpus, we can trace the claim that Christian theological ethics requires a fundamental revaluation, a "new order of values." This "reversal" represents "the dawn of the new world" in which what we previously thought was "new" and of the utmost importance is now reduced to dated insignificance and what we thought was nothing—primarily the weak, the excluded, the suffering neighbor—is now revealed as most worthy of love and care, indeed, the manifestation of God and new life in the world.

Such a "radical revaluation" could only point toward becoming "free from oneself for others,"[46] to "this liberation from self, through this 'being-there-for-others,'" which amounts to "a new life" that is truly the most "explosive material in human society."[47] This is Christianity's "revolutionary protest." It is also the framework in which any discussion of Bonhoeffer's practices of new beginning must be situated.

PRACTICE IN BONHOEFFER'S THOUGHT: "THE HARDEST AND MOST SACRED WORK"

If Bonhoeffer was right that "the encounter with Jesus turned all human values upside down,"[48] then we should not be surprised that Bonhoeffer thought serious *practice* was fundamental to the new life following after God's new beginning in Christ. If who we are as people, not only as individuals in our thinking, willing, and feeling, but also in our religious, cultural, political, and global systems, has become so deeply attached to and governed by "strength

44. See "Outline for a Book" (8:503).

45. "After Ten Years" (8:52). William Schweiker has pointed out to me "how distant this all is to Heidegger's 'da-sein' and also Nietzsche. I am not a 'thrown-project being towards death' but the recipient of the other. This makes ethics philosophically basic despite [Bonhoeffer's] early criticism of 'ethics.'" I am grateful for this insight.

46. Sermon on John 8:32 from July 24, 1932 (11:471).

47. Sermon on John 8:32 from July 24, 1932 (11:471).

48. Letter to Bethge from June 30, 1944 (8:450–51).

and power and violence" as the "ultimate ideals of humanity,"[49] then the formation of what God has begun with us and for us in Christ will require strenuous, repeated effort and habituation. This is what Bonhoeffer called "*exercitia*," a disciplined response to God's gracious initiative.[50]

The need for this transformative training becomes especially clear when we step away from abstractions and think concretely about our compromised moral condition as we saw in chapter 3. This is even more the case when we focus loving attention like Bonhoeffer did on "poor people, ill people, insane people—people who cannot help themselves but who have just to rely on other people for help, for love for, care."[51] The challenge is intensified even further when we remember Bonhoeffer's context amid unprecedented genocide and our own contemporary realities of consumerism, extreme poverty, racism, sexual abuse, exclusion, religious fundamentalism, and horrific violence.

Despite being his best friend, Eberhard Bethge was mistaken when he wrote to Bonhoeffer in prison, "To put it plainly, the importance of the forms of Christian practice, Christian activities, and Christian 'devotion' is something that we are just beginning to pay attention to, despite all our relativizing and questioning."[52] Already in one of his earliest sermons from July 15, 1928, when he was still twenty-one, Bonhoeffer had proclaimed,

> Contact with God must be practiced; otherwise we can never find the right tone, the right word, the right language when God surprises us. We must learn the language of God, laboriously learn that language; we must work so that we, too, are able to speak with God. Prayer must also be practiced through serious work. Confusing religion with emotional daydreaming is a grievous, fateful error. Religion takes work, perhaps the hardest and certainly the most sacred work a person can undertake.[53]

From the beginning, Bonhoeffer fiercely opposed "emotional daydreaming" and considered spiritual practice "perhaps the hardest" and "certainly the most sacred work" for being human with others in the world.

In his 1932–1933 course on "Theological Anthropology," Bonhoeffer argued that

---

49. Sermon on Psalm 63:3 from October 4, 1931 (11:402).

50. *Discipleship* (4:158). See Lisa Dahill, *Reading from the Underside of Selfhood: Bonhoeffer and Spiritual Formation* (Eugene, OR: Pickwick Publications, 2009), chapter 3, and Albrecht Schödl, *"Unsere Augen sehen nach dir": Dietrich Bonhoeffer im Kontext einer aszetischen Theologie* (Leipzig: Evangelische Verlagsanstalt, 2006).

51. Sermon on 2 Corinthians 12:9 from London 1934 (13:402).

52. Letter to Bonhoeffer from January 9, 1944 (8:252). See Robinson, *The Death of Adam*, 112: "Evidence of discipline [in Bonhoeffer's life] . . . is everywhere."

53. Sermon on Psalm 62:2 from July 15, 1928 (10:503).

the *habitus* of Christian character distinguishes itself from that of individuality in that it is gained through practice. The practice that forms the Christian *habitus* must begin with [letting it find itself] in the penultimate. It is a practice of formed humans to look beyond themselves.[54]

That is, rather than spontaneously making of oneself whatever one wishes (what Bonhoeffer means here by "individuality" or what we might call "self-creation"), true Christian character is "gained" through the difficult labor of "practice." And this practice for Bonhoeffer is paradoxical: it is rooted in God and yet it "begins . . . in the penultimate," in worldly life as we know and live it now. Moreover, it forms who we are as persons and yet its true fruit is "to look beyond [ourselves]." Bonhoeffer elaborates on this paradox, stating that "Christian character . . . carries within it a basic element of neglecting itself" precisely because such practice is the antithesis of narcissistic self-obsession. It begins with the rejection of the lie that I can create the truth and initiate my own transformation. Rather, I confront "the knowledge of myself as sinner," as well as the "knowledge of my justification" through God's gracious initiative calling me out of myself for others. Thus, our "practice" is truly a *response to another*. In this way, Bonhoeffer writes that "character formation" is both "secondary" and "penultimate" but nonetheless "significant as practice."[55]

Similarly, in *Discipleship* (1937), Bonhoeffer teaches, "The life of a disciple requires the strict practice of austerity. The only purpose of such *exercitia* is to make disciples more willing and more joyous in following the designated path and doing the works required of them." This again points to the paradox of Bonhoeffer's "passive action": I must embrace "the strict practice of austerity" and "*exercitia*," but the goal is "following the designated path" set before me by another, Christ. Through such practice, Bonhoeffer believes that "the selfish and lethargic will," which on its own "resists being of service, is disciplined; the flesh is chastened and punished."[56]

Bonhoeffer believes that such practice also reminds the self of "the estrangement of my Christian life from the world." This is not again some kind of self-exaltation or spiritual separatism but a reminder of the strangeness and difficulty of this "revaluated" and thus *new* life. Bonhoeffer summarizes what is at stake in practice: "A life which remains without an ascetic discipline, which indulges in all the desires of the flesh as long as they are 'permitted' by

---

54. Lecture course on "Theological Anthropology" from winter 1932–1933 (12:231).

55. Lecture course on "Theological Anthropology" from winter 1932–1933 (12:232).

56. Note that by "flesh," like Paul, Bonhoeffer does *not* mean "the body" but the habituated and enslaving tendencies of the self toward selfishness to the exclusion or harm of others, starting with God. Thus, Bonhoeffer's language of "chastening" and "punishment" here should not be interpreted as some kind of disguised masochism but practical training to live with greater constancy in the way of love for God and others.

the justitia civilis, will find it difficult to enter the service of Christ. Satiated flesh is unwilling to pray and is unfit for self-sacrificing service."[57] Here we see again that the core of practice is a readiness for alterity, a waiting on transcendence, whether that takes the form of "prayer" to God or "self-sacrificing service" for the neighbor. As Bonhoeffer wrote in *Life Together* (1938), "Every act of self-discipline by a Christian is also a service to the community."[58]

For all followers of the new way of God in love and service, Bonhoeffer insisted that we must not "misunderstand Christian freedom as complete lack of law." To the contrary, "only the one who is willing to obey can be seized by faith."[59] Here Bonhoeffer alludes to his paradoxical maxim from *Discipleship*, "*only the believers obey*, and *only the obedient believe*,"[60] by which he intended to head off any possibility that his starting conviction about the primacy of *God's* action could result in "cheap grace" that aborts the beginning of a genuinely changed life ("costly grace"), thereby justifying the status quo.[61]

Later in 1940, in a reflection on the Lord's Supper for a monthly newsletter for dissident pastors, Bonhoeffer wrote similarly, "Proper thoughts only come from proper practice."[62] For Bonhoeffer, the life of the mind—what he called *nachdenken* or "thinking-after" God's beginning—is formed and trained through spiritual practice and the movement of the body, which connects back to what we saw in the last chapter concerning Bonhoeffer's epistemology and hermeneutics of revelation.

Bonhoeffer's conviction about the basic importance of practice for renewing human character, thinking, and culture did not change in his final writings. For example, in one of his final manuscripts for his *Ethics*, Bonhoeffer lamented the condition of the Protestant church with regard to spiritual discipline: "Very widespread among Protestants is an inability even to understand the significance of disciplined practices such as spiritual exercises, asceticism, meditation, and contemplation."[63] This statement comes just before Bonhoeffer's critique of "a frightening confusion" and "arrogance" in

---

57. *Discipleship* (4:158). Note, however, Bonhoeffer's opposition to perfectionism (4:270): "The aim of church discipline is not to create a community of those who are perfect. Its sole aim is to build up a community of those who truly live under God's forgiving mercy."

58. *Life Together* (5:92).

59. "Meditation on Psalm 119" (15:517).

60. *Discipleship* (4:63). See Florian Schmitz, "Only the Believers Obey, and Only the Obedient Believe: Notes on Dietrich Bonhoeffer's Biblical Hermeneutics with Reference to Discipleship," in *God Speaks to Us: Dietrich Bonhoeffer's Biblical Hermeneutics*, ed. Ralf K. Wüstenberg and Jens Zimmermann (Frankfurt: Peter Lang, 2013), 169–86.

61. *Discipleship* (4:62): "The first step puts the follower into the situation of being able to believe. If people do not follow, then they remain behind, then they do not learn to believe. Those called must get out of their situations, in which they cannot believe, into a situation in which faith can begin."

62. "*On the Lord's Supper*: A Guide to the Study of Article 7 of the Lutheran Formula of Concord" from 1940 (15:538).

63. *Ethics* (6:407).

the church vis-à-vis culture and politics, including the oath of loyalty to Hitler and conscientious objection.

Earlier in his manuscript titled "Ultimate and Penultimate Things," Bonhoeffer continued to dwell in the tension of divine initiative and human *exerticia*, insisting on the positive and negative implications of human action. He wrote, "The condition in which grace meets us is not irrelevant, even though it is always only by grace that grace comes to us." Stated in reverse, Bonhoeffer thought that "we can make it hard for ourselves and others to come to faith" by the way we live and the "condition" that we form in and around ourselves. (This reminds us of the challenge to "make room" for God seen in chapter 4 vis-à-vis revelation.) So the beginning of God in no way "excludes the task of preparing the way."[64] To the contrary, "It is . . . a commission of immeasurable responsibility given to all who know about the coming of Jesus Christ."[65]

But lest we misunderstand and so unduly relax the paradoxical tension of his position, Bonhoeffer is equally clear in his *Ethics* manuscript "Ethics as Formation" about what this practical formation is intended to cultivate: "Formation occurs only by being drawn into the form of Jesus Christ, by *being conformed to the unique form of the one who became human, was crucified, and is risen.*" Jesus is the one who freely drew near and willingly gave his life with and for others, for sinners and enemies. And as such, "Christ remains the only one who forms; Christian people do not form the world with their ideas. Rather, Christ forms human beings to a form the same as Christ's own."[66] This is Bonhoeffer's rejection of any Christendom-nostalgic "enthusiasm" and Christian manipulation.

Finally, in his prison sermon for the wedding of his niece Renate and his friend Eberhard Bethge (May 15, 1943), Bonhoeffer again meditated on the reality of human fallenness and the great importance of spiritual practice for beginning a new life together. He asked, "But how can both of them [husband and wife] as fallible human beings live in the community of Christ and do their part unless they each constantly pray and receive forgiveness, unless each helps the other to live as a Christian?" Even for his most trusted friend and partner in theological education and pastoral training, Bonhoeffer answered, "Here very much depends on the right beginning and daily practice."[67]

---

64. In fact, Bonhoeffer was contemplating titling what became his *Ethics* as *Preparing the Way*. See *Ethics* (6:166–67), which follows Bonhoeffer's position in *Creation and Fall*, "Beginning with Christ," and his "Meditation on Psalm 119."

65. *Ethics* (6:162).

66. *Ethics* (6:93).

67. "After Ten Years" (8:87).

Having briefly surveyed the importance of spiritual practice throughout Bonhoeffer's writings, within the orienting framework of Bonhoeffer's revolutionary "revaluation," the task of the remainder of this chapter is to provide a description of some spiritual practices that Bonhoeffer identified as especially crucial for beginning anew—for living a life that welcomes, waits on, and responds to God and others in love. These descriptions are not intended to be exhaustive; there are important practices that will be left unaddressed due to space (for example, the Eucharist and Bible reading).[68] Neither are these practices exactly sequential in order, though we should note their mutually implicative and empowering nature when seen as a coherent whole.

What is most important to notice in each case and overall remains this: if the heart of a new beginning for Bonhoeffer is found in human persons becoming open to others and embracing "a new life in being there for others"—including both "that other" God and "the neighbor within reach"—then more than practices of personal initiative, these are practices of opening, receptivity, and responsibility with and for others, which intentionally and explicitly challenge the human drive to begin for ourselves, regardless of our "good intentions." These are practices for unlearning the lie of the first deceiver to "discover your beginning yourself" and a path for growing into the "liberation from self" that accompanies the "new life in being there for others." This is the way of welcome and waiting on transcendence.[69]

BONHOEFFER'S PRACTICES OF NEW BEGINNING

Baptism

Bonhoeffer consistently refers to baptism as the "beginning" or "birth" of the newly human life and one of the "forms of the first reality of creation in this aeon" energized with "creative origins."[70] Importantly for Bonhoeffer, the primary form of baptism is *infant* baptism, and thus it is literally an event that takes place in community before and beyond the willpower of the person being baptized: "Christian education begins where all other education ceases: What is essential *has already happened.*"[71] In a sermon preached in Berlin in

---

68. On Bible reading, see Letter to Bethge from June 25, 1942 (16:329) and Letter to Bethge from March 19, 1944 (8:326).

69. For a short summary of these practices and their implications, see "Begin Again."

70. See "Co-Report on the 'Reflection on the Question of Baptism' in Reference to the Question of Infant Baptism" from 1942 (16:561): "On the Theological Foundation of the Work of the World Alliance" from July 26, 1932 (11:361); letter to Bethge from February 12, 1944 (8:295). For the ancient Christian roots of this view, see Helen Rhee, ed., *Wealth and Poverty in Early Christianity* (Minneapolis, MN: Fortress Press, 2017), xviii–xix.

71. Lectures on "Catechesis" from 1935–1936 (14:537–544): "Hence the child must from the very outset be confronted with the aggravation of the unqualified elective action of the *gratia praeveniens.*

1932, Bonhoeffer proclaimed, "this first encounter [with the ancient church of Christ in baptism] is an event that reaches far beyond all our wishes and actions, an event of a completely different order, an event originating not from human beings but from God."[72]

As such, the sacramental practice of baptism mirrors the event of creation, through which God initiates a beginning that precedes us and we cannot remember or access by ourselves but which serves as the condition for the possibility of our life and agency. "Baptism is God's action with regard to the child, the greatest gift."[73] The gift, which we cannot choose, gives us to ourselves and energizes and ennobles our lives.

Thus, in *Discipleship*, Bonhoeffer calls baptism "a paradoxically passive action," corresponding to our natural birth, which is "something that is given to us, something that we suffer." Baptism is "suffering Christ's call." Through baptism, "we become Christ's possession," and this shift in the self's ownership "implies a *break*. Christ invades the realm of Satan and lays hold of those who belong to him, thereby creating his church-community." What this means for Bonhoeffer is that "past and present are thus torn asunder. The old has passed away, everything has become new" by Christ's power.[74] Baptism liberates us from the "mute, dead ego-world" of the old Adam.

Bonhoeffer emphasizes that this fundamental "break" that takes place in baptism, infant or otherwise, "does not come about by our breaking our chains out of an unquenchable thirst to see our life and all things ordered in a new and free way." In this mentality, baptism would be reductively rendered just another technology of self-creation whereby we attempt to renew ourselves for our own aims. To the contrary, baptism "deprives" me of "my immediate relationship to the given realities of the world" because Christ is now the "mediator and Lord who has stepped in between me and the world." (Here we must remember Bonhoeffer's understanding of *Stellvertretung* discussed in chapter 4). Baptism, then, is quite literally a citizenship-changing event of being born into a new community, which means that the baptized "no longer belong to the world" and thus are no longer "subject to it." Instead, "They belong to Christ alone, and relate to the world only through Christ."[75]

This preempts the church's inclination to run after young people in an undignified fashion." For helpful comments on Bonhoeffer's view of infant baptism, see Bethge, *Dietrich Bonhoeffer*, 707–8.

72. Baptism sermon on Ephesians 5:14 from October 1932 (11:473). Here I am reminded of Hans-Georg Gadamer's claim in *Truth and Method*, second revised edition (New York: Continuum, 1989), xxviii, that the world that makes our hermeneutical consciousness possible "happens to us over and above our wanting and choosing." We might say that baptism is the constitution for the hermeneutics of the new world of the resurrection.

73. "Baptismal Homilies" from 1936–1937 (14:737).

74. *Discipleship* (4:207).

75. "Co-Report on the 'Reflection on the Question of Baptism' in Reference to the Question of Infant Baptism" (16:556).

This claim implies something utterly fundamental for Bonhoeffer's under-standing of selfhood and ethics. Most basically, baptism is a symbol of the self's *death* (passing under the water) and, only after death, does it represent the self's new birth or resurrection (rising out of the water). Part of the mad-dening desperation of the sinful condition of the self subject to the world, as we saw in chapter 3, is that death is precisely what the self needs most in order to start over, and yet suicide is not a solution to the self's alienation but only the most terminal symptom of its despair. In sin, death becomes a perverse fixation that wells up in "a thirst for death"[76] and all too easily gives way to a "spirit of annihilation" that risks destroying any possibility of a new beginning.[77]

This desperate condition of the self is why Bonhoeffer speaks paradoxically of baptism as "the grace-filled death," which is "the rule of the cross under which Jesus places his disciples."[78] In baptism, "the break with the world is ab-solute": "we die in Christ alone." In baptism, we receive "a gift of grace which we can never create for ourselves," which is the judgment of God on our sins and out of which "rises the new self which has died to the world and to sin." As such, this "gracious death" is "not the final, angry rejection of the creature by its creator but rather the gracious acceptance of the creature by its creator."

For Bonhoeffer, then, baptism is the only fundamental response to the death drive.[79] There is no other, less radical way to begin anew for Bon-hoeffer. We need this radical end at the start of our new beginning: *death*. Bonhoeffer writes, "Those who become Christ's own must come under his cross. They must suffer and die with him." This is at once Christ's "rule" and Christ's "gift" for the fallen self, the offense and gratuity of *Nachfolge* and *Nachdenke* with Christ.[80]

Thus, as we saw in chapter 4, baptism is the founding event in the person's history that should, in principle, mark the end of our pathological drive to grasp our origin like waves crashing against the beach. Bonhoeffer writes, "To wait for a new beginning, day after day, thinking that one has found it countless times only to declare it lost in the evening: this is the complete de-struction of faith in that God who set the beginning once through his forgiv-ing and renewing word in Jesus Christ, that is, in my baptism, in my rebirth, in my conversion."[81] The unrepeatable event of baptism is the miraculous gift of God that gives the executed and newborn creature "freedom from the

---

76. *Creation and Fall* (3:143).
77. *Ethics* (6:122–23).
78. *Discipleship* (4:208). See *Ethics* (6:251).
79. See Freud, *Civilization and Its Discontents*, VI.
80. See Bonhoeffer's lecture notes for his "Confirmation Instruction Plan" likely from 1936 (14:812).
81. "Meditation on Psalm 119" (15:497).

murderous law of never-ending beginnings."[82] After baptism, we can walk forward confidently and without second guessing this new life in being there for others.

Here we can appreciate why Bonhoeffer sees "baptism" and "discipleship" as essentially identical concepts and callings: baptism is the beginning of learning to follow after Christ and his life-giving command, whose heart is love for the neighbor.[83] Through baptism, the believer's sins are forgiven, and the person becomes "the house in which the Holy Spirit dwells," who is the personal presence of Christ with us that "gives us true understanding of Christ's nature and will."[84]

In summary, then, for Bonhoeffer, baptism is the founding event of "a new start in life."[85] It marks the end of a life "ruled by one's own will and desire" and "the recognition that there must be a superior will above our own will, and superior power above our own power," namely, Christ. And this means, quite simply, that "there is no room left for selfishness and egoism." Instead, after baptism, we live in the world by "God's own word and promise to be with [us], to love [us], to forgive [us] all sins, to help [us] in every need, to sanctify [our] life, to make [us] holy and innocent, to make [us] a child of God." Indeed, for Bonhoeffer, baptism is precisely "the call to the human being into childhood, a call that can be understood only eschatologically" because it is a past event that plots the direction of our future whereby "the whole of [our] past life acquires seriousness and temporal continuity" in faith, hope, and love rooted in Christ's resurrection.[86] (Here Bonhoeffer applies on the level of the self what he argued on the level of history in his *Ethics*: Christ's coming initiates and makes possible "temporal continuity" rather than endless circularity or chaos.)

Before moving forward, we must underscore that baptism for Bonhoeffer is not reducible to a religious ritual of merely private significance. Baptism is the death of the fallen descendant of Cain whose "violent hands" began the "history of death" by the murder of the brother.[87] If baptism is this fundamental event of death and new beginning in the self, we should not be surprised that Bonhoeffer drew radical social and political implications from it.

For example, in his critical essay on Protestant Christianity in America titled "Protestantism without Reformation," Bonhoeffer wrote that, properly understood and practiced, "Baptism . . . would have called into question the legitimacy of slavery and brought undeniable privileges and rights to the

---

82. "Meditation on Psalm 119" (15:497). See *Discipleship* (4:258).
83. *Discipleship* (4:207) and Baptism sermon on Ephesians 5:14 from October 1932 (11:475).
84. *Discipleship* (4:209).
85. Baptismal Homily on Joshua 24:15 from June 1934 (13:364).
86. *Act and Being* (2:159).
87. *Creation and Fall* (3:145).

Negroes."[88] In the new rule and community established by Christ's beginning, the Christian perpetuation of racism and slavery should have been unthinkable and abominable.[89] In the waters of baptism, all persons are equally under God's judgment and equally welcomed into God's new life of grace and goodness. Here devaluing customs and ideologies of inequality, exclusion, and violence are nullified and must be washed away.

This claim directly contradicted the popular German Christian ideology of Bonhoeffer's day that insisted, "They say that everyone is equal before God. But baptism never made a Jew into a German, nor did it ever straighten a crooked, hooked nose. . . . We want a Christianity that is true to our race."[90] Bonhoeffer's point was still more radical: baptism does not make a "Jew" into a "German." Baptism recognizes and renews the fact that *both* "Jews" and "Germans" *and everyone else* are *humans*, creatures and children of God, who are welcomed into a new beginning of love and service for all people.[91]

Here we can more concretely appreciate what Bonhoeffer meant when he wrote, "The human being who loves because he has been made free by God's truth is the most revolutionary human being on earth. He is the overturning of all values; he is the explosive material in human society; he is the most dangerous human being."[92] For Bonhoeffer, baptism should have made atrocities like American slavery and the German Holocaust unimaginable abominations for a "Christian" people called to follow the Christ who stands as a "refuge" to our "highest values." Those who took their baptism seriously should have seen their baptism as a divine enlistment to oppose and resist these horrors.

Baptism, then, as the self's "grace-filled death" and "resurrection," is the first practice in the new beginning of following after Christ with and for others.

---

88. "Protestantism without Reformation" from August 1939 (15:457).

89. See Josiah Ulysses Young III, *No Difference in Fare: Dietrich Bonhoeffer and the Problem of Racism* (Grand Rapids, MI: Eerdmans, 1998), and Williams, *Bonhoeffer's Black Jesus.* On December 1, 1930, Bonhoeffer wrote to his parents from Philadelphia, "In Washington I lived completely among the Negroes and through the students was able to become acquainted with all the leading figures of the Negro movement, was in their homes, and had extraordinarily interesting discussions with them. . . . The conditions [of segregation] are really rather unbelievable. Not just separate railway cars, tramways, and buses . . . when I wanted to eat in a small restaurant with a Negro, I was refused service" (10:258). On December 30, 1930, Bonhoeffer wrote to Max Diestel, "In general, I'm increasingly discovering greater religious power and originality with Negroes" (10:266). See 10:269, 293, 315 ("the 'black Christ'"), 321 ("the real face of America").

90. Excerpt from a pastor's speech at a well-attended German Christian meeting in February 1934 as recorded in Bergen, *Twisted Cross*, 22. Note also p. 30: "Through baptism, a Negro who lived in Germany would by no means become a German. It is the same for a Jew." See the section on "Baptism" in *Twisted Cross*, 85ff., especially 86: "In a system based on distinctions of blood . . . baptism must be denied any efficacy."

91. See "The Church and the Jewish Question" from June 1933 (12:370): "Where Jew and German together stand under God's Word is church; it will be proven whether or not the church is still church."

92. Sermon on John 8:32 (11:471).

Prayer, Intercession, and Discernment

With prayer, we come upon a trinity of interconnected practices that run like a bright line throughout Bonhoeffer's entire corpus: (1) prayer and intercession; (2) repentance, confession, and forgiveness of sin; and (3) sacrificial service.

Already in his doctoral dissertation *Sanctorum Communio* (1927, 1930), Bonhoeffer wrote the following outline of these three practices, which he summarized as "actions of love":

> This being-for-each-other must now be actualized through acts of love. *Three great, positive possibilities of acting for each other* in the community of saints present themselves: *self-renouncing, active work for the neighbor; intercessory prayer; and, finally, the mutual forgiveness of sins* in God's name. All of these involve giving up the self "for" my neighbor's benefit, with the readiness to do and bear everything in the neighbor's place, indeed, if necessary, to sacrifice myself, standing as a *substitute* for my neighbor. Even if a purely vicarious action is rarely actualized, it is intended in every genuine act of love.[93]

For Bonhoeffer, each of these practices was (1) an "act of love," (2) "for each other," (3) "in the community of saints," which thus (4) embody the willingness to "give up the self for my neighbor's benefit" and "the readiness to do and bear everything in the neighbor's place" to the point of self-sacrifice. The line from this first formulation to Bonhoeffer's prison formulation of "a new life in being there for others" is direct and unmistakable.

A year later, in a sermon from Barcelona on July 29, 1928, Bonhoeffer added this further commentary, emphasizing the almost mystical Christological significance of these self-giving practices:

> You can and should become a Christ to me and I to you. Our congregations have forgotten what insuperable [strength] emanates from confession and the forgiveness of sins, in which one not only helps the other in . . . distress, nor merely prays for forgiveness of that person's sins, but redeems, reconciles that person by acting in Christ's stead, by becoming Christ for that other person. Sacrifice, intercession, and the forgiveness of sins are the miraculous powers of the Christian church-community; all three can be summed up in the one word "love," the love God showed us, or "becoming Christ for the other person" [Luther].[94]

A great deal could be written about Bonhoeffer's understanding and practice of the "miraculous power" of prayer whose essence is "love." But let us note these important elements before looking at the other practices.

---

93. *Sanctorum Communio* (1:184).
94. Sermon from Barcelona on July 29, 1928 (10:508–9). On this important phrase, see Ulrik Becker Nissen, "Being Christ for the Other," *Studia Theologica* 64, no. 2 (December 2010): 177–98.

Prayer

First, prayer for Bonhoeffer is most basically openness and listening for God. Any genuine new beginning must begin with prayer, which is meant to ground and guide our lives with and for others. It is a practice of waiting on transcendence.

As we saw in chapter 4, Bonhoeffer insisted, "It is God alone who makes a new beginning with a person, when God is pleased to do so, and not the human being who undertakes to do it with God."[95] The clear implication is that "a new beginning is not something one can do for oneself." But this challenge to the human inclination "Let me first" is not the end of the story for Bonhoeffer, leading to fatalistic piety and complicity with the current state of things. Bonhoeffer continues, "One can only *pray* for it to happen." And "we can pray only when we have realized that there is something we cannot do for ourselves, that we have reached our limit, that someone else must be the one to begin."[96]

Thus, prayer for Bonhoeffer is a practice that is inseparable from an explicit recognition of our finitude as creatures, combined with an active hospitality to God's presence and initiative. In the same way that Bonhoeffer called baptism "a paradoxically passive action," prayer takes the initiative to let God go first. Prayer actively waits on God. It is a practice of self-transcendence and listening that is ready for encounter and calling from "that other" God, who initiates our lives with others. Prayer is the time when "that other" comes to mind and goes before us.

Ironically quoting Nietzsche, Bonhoeffer calls prayer "a 'waiting for God to draw near.'"[97] Thus, Bonhoeffer writes in *Life Together*, "Prayer means nothing else but the readiness to appropriate the Word, and what is more, to let it speak to me in my personal situation, in my particular tasks, decisions, sins, and temptations."[98] Prayer is a radical act of opening the self and becoming vulnerable before the one totally beyond our self-seeking attempts at comprehension and control. As such, prayer as listening is a fundamental interruption in the ordinary orientation of the self, which reorients our work, decision-making, and moral struggle.

Unsurprisingly, then, as we have seen earlier, Bonhoeffer did not think prayer was easy. To the contrary, he believed that "we must learn the language of God, laboriously learn that language; we must work so that we,

---

95. "Beginning with Christ," Sermon on Luke 9:57–62 from January 1, 1934 (13:348).
96. "Beginning with Christ" (emphasis added). See also the parallel statement in "The Reconstruction of Jerusalem" from April 1936 (14:917).
97. *Sanctorum Communio* (1:186).
98. *Life Together* (5:89). Bonhoeffer held prayer and Scripture reading closely together, again related to his worry about human arbitrariness. See *Life Together* (5:70) and "The Holy Spirit according to Luther " from February 1926 (9:357).

too, are able to speak with God." For Bonhoeffer prayer is the antithesis to "emotional daydreaming," which remains trapped in the self's narcissism. It is rather "the most sacred work a person can undertake."[99]

Strikingly, then, Bonhoeffer attributed the "very reason things look so frightening around us" to a neglect or abandonment of genuine prayer throughout society.[100] "Our age has little room at all for prayer," Bonhoeffer observed. "Prayer has become alien to us." "And yet one thing is certain: the Christian cause lives or dies . . . with prayer." When we stop listening for God, the wellsprings of our beginnings are cut off, and we lose guidance and energy for works of love.

In "an age of machines, of economic competition, of the dominance of sports and fashion,"[101] perhaps this closure of "room" for prayer should not surprise us because for Bonhoeffer such a fundamental openness toward God begins in *silence* and *self-surrender*: "Being silent before God means yielding to God the right to have the first and last word concerning us, and means accepting that word whatever it may be, for all eternity."[102] In his Christology lectures, as we saw in chapter 4, Bonhoeffer elaborated further on the primacy of silence in prayer before God as opposed to a "mystagogical" mindlessness that only amounts to "prattle":

> The silence of the church is silence before the Word. In proclaiming Christ, the church falls on its knees in silence before the inexpressible, the *arreton*. To speak of Christ is to be silent, and to be silent about Christ is to speak. That is obedient affirmation of God's revelation, which takes place through the Word. The church's speech through silence is the right way to proclaim Christ. *Siope prospuneistho to arreton* [Let the inexpressible be honored with silence] (Cyril). To pray is to keep silent and at the same time to cry out, before God in both cases, in the light of God's Word.[103]

Prayer renounces the sovereign position of the knower and controller. Prayer's silent, obedient listening and waiting is thus, again, essentially a counter-cultural practice in self-transcendence before the presence of the other person, here the incarnate Christ. As in the Lord's Prayer, we "leave [ourselves] completely aside for a moment" and "we first learn to say: your name, your kingdom, your will. You first, and again you. Your name and not

---

99. Sermon on Psalm 62:2 from July 15, 1928 (10:503).

100. Sermon for the Second Theological Examination on 1 Thessalonians 5:16–18 from July 20, 1930 (10:576). See "Guide to Daily Meditation" from May 22, 1936 (14:935): "Basically, the backdrop to all our problems and helplessness is our own trouble with prayer; for too long many of us simply had no real help or guidance."

101. Sermon on Psalm 62:2 from July 15, 1928 (10:500).

102. Sermon on Psalm 62:2 from July 15, 1928 (10:502).

103. "Lectures on Christology" (12:300–301). On silence in Bonhoeffer's thought, see chapter 4, note 84.

mine, your will and not mine."[104] Here narcissism, our addiction to noise, and our protests of "Let me first" are renounced and retrained in silence, waiting, listening, and responding to God. Thus, our discussion in chapter 4 about discerning and following the "will" and "command" of God would be incomprehensible without it being rooted in Bonhoeffer's practice of prayer.[105]

In this way, in all places, at all times, with all people, God is given the freedom to begin and go first, to be heard and followed as we wait attuned in readiness. Just like Bonhoeffer conceptually identified "baptism" and "discipleship," so he writes, "'Pray' and 'follow' go hand in hand—there cannot be one without the other. Praying confidently and following readily: there's a full life for you . . . if we follow Christ, our future, too, can be nothing but good."[106]

Intercession

Second, prayer for Bonhoeffer is equally constitutive for and concerned with our relationships with *human* others, what Bonhoeffer calls "intercession." We find a helpful summary in his doctoral dissertation *Sanctorum Communio*:

> In intercession the nature of Christian love again proves to be work "with," "for," and ultimately "in place of" our neighbor, thereby drawing the neighbor deeper and deeper into the church-community. Thus, when one person intercedes in the name of Christ on behalf of the other, the whole church-community—which actually means "Christ existing as church-community" . . . participates in that person's prayer.[107]

In the same way that prayer before God is a practical, unceasing posture of readiness and responsiveness to God, prayer is just as much for Bonhoeffer a practical, unceasing posture of openness and service *for one's neighbors*, in which we relinquish our priority and self-assertion out of love for the other person and their needs.[108] Intercession requires this attunement to the other, this concern and mindfulness for their concerns and needs, which enlarges and enriches community.

---

104. Catechesis in the Second Theological Examination on the Fifth Petition of the Lord's Prayer from June 29, 1930 (10:560).

105. See Sermon on Psalm 62:2 from July 15, 1928 (10:500) and "Can One Distinguish between a Historical and a Pneumatological Interpretation of Scripture, and How Does Dogmatics Relate to This Question?" from summer 1925 (9:298).

106. Letter to Maria von Wedemeyer from April 23, 1944 (92:223).

107. *Sanctorum Communio* (1:188).

108. See James Cone, *God of the Oppressed*, revised edition (Maryknoll, NY: Orbis, 1997), 133: "[Prayer] is the beginning of the Christian practice of liberation."

Bonhoeffer writes in *Life Together*, "Just as our love for God begins with listening to God's Word, the beginning of love for other Christians is learning to listen to them." Here Bonhoeffer is extremely specific: if our "time is too precious to spend listening," we "will never really have time for God and others but only for [ourselves] and for [our] own words and plans." Thus, Bonhoeffer concludes, "the *first* service one owes to others," and as such the beginning of prayer, "involves listening to them."[109] Thus, "intercession" is primarily a practice of listening to others and then bringing them before God in love and faith.

Bonhoeffer's listening interpretation of intercession as "work 'with,' 'for,' and ultimately 'in the place of' our neighbor" had radical implications for his understanding of human life and beginning. Bonhoeffer writes that in such prayer, "A third person is drawn into my solitary relation with God, or rather, in intercession I step into the other's place and my prayer, even though it remains my own, is nonetheless prayed out of the other's affliction and need." Rather than a private religious piety, through prayer, "I really enter into the other, into the other's sin and affliction; I am afflicted by the other person's sins and weaknesses."[110] Thus, intercessory prayer is the practice in which the self is opened and the other comes to mind and claims my responsibility. I learn to reflect on the complexity of their lives, to put myself in their situations, and to bring them before God in love. Thus, prayer as Bonhoeffer envisions it should make forgetfulness of others impossible. As I live a life of intercession, "a third person"—the other, my neighbor—"is drawn into my solitary relation with God," and I willingly embrace "the other's affliction and need" as I practice the presence of God without ceasing.

The implication of the practice of intercession is that I as a singular self no longer live for myself or even only for God. Here Bonhoeffer alerts us that a simplistically "theocentric" spirituality is dangerous if it forgets others. The intercessory self is no longer private property. The person that prays is a self for the other, a person that no longer occupies its own place but opens itself as a shared space of welcome and care for the other person in their greatest weakness, failure, and devastation. In such prayer, Bonhoeffer says that the "sins of the unknown sailor . . . afflict me no less than those of my closest friend," for in my prayer I recognize my own sin and failure and that Christ's life was given for every sinner, including those who are distant and strange to me. Here we see that Bonhoeffer's vision of prayer opens up and empowers the moral horizon of universal entry discussed in chapter 1.

Thus, in the same way that Bonhoeffer thought that baptism should have transformed white Americans' relationships with slaves and African Americans

---

109. *Life Together* (5:98).
110. *Sanctorum Communio* (1:186).

in general, so too prayer should implicitly universalize both our recognition of human fallenness and our recognition of God's forgiveness and love for other people beyond boundaries of kinship or nationality. He writes, "In intercessory prayer the face that may have been strange and intolerable to me is transformed into the face of one for whom Christ died, the face of a pardoned sinner." He continues,

> The fact that the church-community should and can see every person, whether powerful or despised, as in need of God's grace makes it completely *free and fearless* in its encounter with people and takes away any contempt for human-kind and all hatred. Because I am to "pray for all people," I therefore cannot despise or hate any person; otherwise my prayer is a lie.[111]

When we recognize that we are commanded to pray for *all people*, the notion of privileging special statuses and hating those that others despise becomes contradictory and must be renounced. Prayer rules out privilege and hatred and retrains them in love through the most ordinary and ongoing practice of the Christ follower's new life. When I pray, the "strange and intolerable" face becomes the face of my brother or sister, the face of another sinner who is welcomed into Christ's outreach and embrace. Thus "fear" and "contempt" in our interpersonal and wider relations should be overcome as we pray and intercede for others. We become "free and fearless" in our "encounter with people."

In such a posture of self-giving prayer, Bonhoeffer does not hesitate to say that "we can become a Christ to our neighbor." Bonhoeffer does not mean that a human agent replaces Christ. But he does mean that, "if God does the final work," such a posture of forgiveness and love toward other people in prayer "can redeem another, in the power of the church."[112] For this forgiveness is precisely the form of Christ himself, that is, "the vicarious representative love of Christ on the cross," who cried out for his murderers, "Forgive them, for they know not what they do."[113] And such a form of life demolishes "ethical self-confidence," in which we might delude ourselves into thinking that we are righteous and self-sufficient. It generates "infinite gratitude," not only for God but also for brothers and sisters who also pray for us and tolerate our failures.[114]

---

111. "The Letter to Timothy. Chapter 1" from summer 1938 (15:328). See *Life Together* (5:90): "[In prayer] I can no longer condemn or hate other Christians for whom I pray, no matter how much trouble they cause me. . . . That is a blessed discovery for the Christian who is beginning to offer intercessory prayer for others. As far as we are concerned, there is no dislike, no personal tension, no disunity or strife, that cannot be overcome by intercessory prayer."
112. *Sanctorum Communio* (1:188).
113. See "The Nature of the Church" from July 1932 (11:322–26): "[In intercession] I really stand in the place of the other."
114. "The Nature of the Church" from July 1932.

But Bonhoeffer pushes further in his interpretation of intercession as the human practice of the form of Christ. Following Paul's precedent in Romans 9:3 ("I could wish that I myself were cursed and cut off from Christ for the sake of my people"), Bonhoeffer writes,

> Paul seeks to win for the people he loves community with God that he loves above all else, and he curses himself out of community with God and from his people to the place of damnation, where they are, precisely because he truly loves both community with God and his people, which means, because he is obedient to the command that we should unreservedly surrender ourselves to the neighbor.[115]

This, for Bonhoeffer, should be the extent of our love in our life of intercessory prayer: the willingness to give our salvation up for the salvation of the other.[116] And rather than this willingness to sacrifice one's own community with God for the neighbor being an expression of "weakness" or even "disobedience," Bonhoeffer claims that by this very posture "[we] remain where [we] wish God to ban [us] from, namely in the most intimate communion with God." This is because this intercessory, vicarious representative action—even to the point of one's own damnation—is what "constitutes the most complete obedience" to God's new beginning in Christ and the cross.

Indeed, Bonhoeffer believes that it is precisely this kind of radical, prayerful self-sacrifice that proves the unprecedented quality of our love to begin with. This "love ultimately does not seek community, but wants to affirm the 'other' as such," and thus, without intending so, "the less it seeks, the more certainly it finds."[117] Rather than "loving" others to get something from them, this intercessory love is willing to lose itself for others. It "affirms the 'other' as such." From this perspective, Bonhoeffer writes, "Community is constituted by the complete self-forgetfulness of love. I and You face each other no longer essentially in a demanding but in a giving way, revealing [our] hearts that have been conquered by God's will."[118] Intercession is the foundation for this transfigured gaze and life together.

This self-giving personhood in intercession for the other is the basis of Bonhoeffer's call for enemy love because "love" here is not predicated on what we can get for ourselves and thus the desert or usefulness of the other

---

115. *Sanctorum Communio* (1:185).

116. Here Bonhoeffer is a counter example to Camus's indictment of Christians in his *Notebooks*: "So many men are deprived of grace. How can one live without grace? One has to try it and do what Christianity never did: be concerned with the damned." Quoted in Patricia Munhall et al., *The Emergence of Man into the 21st Century* (Sudbury, MA: Jones and Bartlett Publishers, 2002), 401.

117. Munhall et al. *The Emergence of Man into the 21st Century.* See *Life Together* (5:42, 44).

118. *Sanctorum Communio* (1:190). Bonhoeffer continues this reflection on personhood as self-giving in *Act and Being* (2:128): "The person 'is' only in the act of self-giving. Yet, the person 'is' free from the one to whom it gives itself."

person but the calling of Christ to give and serve even when this care is not deserved or repaid.[119] Thus, the enemy is just as worthy of intercession and concern as the others for whom we intercede.

In summary, then, the practice of intercessory prayer is in essence "individuals organizing themselves to realize the divine will for others, to serve the realization of God's rule in the church community." It is for this reason that Bonhoeffer thought "common prayer" should be emphasized equally with personal prayer, whereby the community embraces an active posture of being "with," "for," and even "in the place of" its neighbors, as well as its enemies, in love. Here we appreciate with greater depth Bonhoeffer's critical comment that "prayer has become alien to us, and for that very reason things look so frightening around us."[120] According to Bonhoeffer, following Luther, "the devil is more afraid of a thatched roof under which a congregation prays, than of a magnificent cathedral in which many masses are said."[121]

Discernment for Theology and Daily Beginnings

In his prison correspondence with Eberhard Bethge, Bonhoeffer intensely wrestled with the reality of the church's failure to bear witness to and live this kind of genuinely prayerful life "for others" in the midst of the Holocaust. In a letter to Bethge attached to his "Outline for a Book," Bonhoeffer confessed to his friend, "the church must get out of its stagnation" and "get back out into the fresh air of intellectual discourse with the world," even if this required "[risking] saying controversial things."[122] Having seen earlier how Bonhoeffer understands prayer as fundamentally orienting the self toward God and the neighbor in a posture of listening responsiveness and service, we should not be surprised that Bonhoeffer wrote Bethge, "Prayer . . . alone allows us to begin and do this kind of work."[123] For Bonhoeffer, prophetic, subversive, and *truthful* theology could only be initiated and articulated in a life of prayer following after the crucified Christ.[124]

---

119. See *Life Together* (5:43). Bonhoeffer indignantly asks Christians (15:467), "Or do we think that God would love us more than our enemies? Do we think that we of all people are the favorite children of God?" Bonhoeffer's own act of joining the resistance and opposing Hitler should make clear that this ethical perspective does not directly or indirectly condone or demand a wife in a situation of abuse to simply "give herself" to her husband if that means continuing to accept his abuse. We will see later that part of Bonhoeffer's vision of "service" includes active "resistance," which could include self-defense in certain circumstances. But this worry should be noted and taken extremely seriously.

120. Wedding sermon on 1 Thessalonians 5:16–18 from April 15, 1936 (10:576).

121. *Sanctorum Communio* (1:188).

122. Letter to Bethge from August 1944 (8:498).

123. Letter to Bethge from August 1944 (8:499). See also Letter to Hildegard Lämmerhirdt from July 1934 (13:185), "Second Letter from Finkenwalde" from November 29, 1935 (14:124), and "Meditation on Christmas" from December 1939 (15:528): "*Theologia sacra*—it originates in prayerful kneeling before the mystery of the divine child in the stable."

124. See "Morning blessing. Devotion" from summer 1935 (14:866).

This claim was particularly acute for Bonhoeffer vis-à-vis the horrific violence and devastation of his time, in which "we are being thrown back all the way to the beginnings of our understanding." In such a time of devastating moral and spiritual rupture, the language of Christian theology— "reconciliation and redemption," "rebirth and Holy Spirit, love for one's enemies, cross and resurrection," "to live in Christ and follow Christ"—had become "so difficult and remote that we hardly dare speak of it anymore." Still, Bonhoeffer remained convinced that "in these words and actions handed down to us, we sense something totally new and revolutionary," which would ultimately come to voice in "a new language, perhaps quite nonreligious language, but liberating and redeeming like Jesus's language, so that people will be alarmed and yet overcome by its claiming that God makes peace with humankind and that God's kingdom is drawing near."[125] In order to prepare for that kind of thinking and witness, Bonhoeffer's call was practical and demanding: "We can be Christians today in only two ways, through prayer and in doing justice among human beings. All Christian thinking, talking, and organizing must be born anew out of prayer and action."[126]

Finally, it is important to emphasize that Bonhoeffer understood prayer as the literal new beginning of one's life each morning and thus the energizing context for one's work throughout the day. He taught his dissident students at Finkenwalde in 1935:

Each new morning is a new beginning for our lives. . . . God created day and night that we might not wander around without limits but rather might already see our goal, namely, evening, lying before us in the morning. Just as the ancient sun rises daily anew, so also is God's eternal mercy new every morning (Lam. 3:23). Being able to grasp God's ancient faithfulness anew each morning, being able to begin a new life with God daily in the midst of one's present life with God, that is the gift God gives us with each new morning.[127]

---

125. Once again, this prison theology was nothing new for Bonhoeffer. See "On the Theological Foundation of the Work of the World Alliance" from July 26, 1932: "Whenever the church of Christ in its history has come to a new understanding of its nature, it has brought forth a new theology commensurate with this self-understanding. A change in the church's self-understanding proves itself to be genuine when it brings forth a theology" (11:356).

126. "Thoughts on the Day of Baptism of Dietrich Wilhelm Rüdiger Bethge" from May 1944 (8:389–90). Here as elsewhere Bonhoeffer's most mature thinking reflects his earliest convictions. See *Act and Being* (2:217) and "The Inner Life of the German Evangelical Church" from August 5, 1936 (14:716). In Bonhoeffer's August 8, 1934, letter to Bishop Ammundsen (13:179), in which Bonhoeffer resolutely wrote, "an immediate decision confronts us: National Socialist *or* Christian," he continued, "However hard and difficult it may be for us all, we have got to face it and go through with it, without trying to be diplomatic, but speaking frankly and as Christians. And we shall discover the way by praying together."

127. "Morning blessing. Devotion" (14:864). Also "Guide to Daily Meditation" from May 1936 (14:933).

Beginning with prayer, we "grasp God's ancient faithfulness anew each morning." Thus, we receive direction and energy to do God's will in new circumstances and tasks.

Bonhoeffer repeated this call "to begin a new life with God daily in the midst of one's present life" through prayer several times in diverse contexts in the remainder of his scholarship and ministry, which makes clear that this practice had special importance and power in Bonhoeffer's theological ethics. He thought that beginning our day in prayer could help overcome "temptations," "the weakness and discouragement in our work, the disorder and lack of discipline in our thinking and dealings with other people."[128] As he wrote to Eberhard Bethge in 1941, in such an "unsettled" time, a "firm morning prayer time" must not be neglected. Prayer "clarifies what one is to do and say throughout the day," and with prayer "one becomes 'self-directed' in daily decisions."[129]

So, for Bonhoeffer, "the first word and the first thought" of the morning belong to God.[130] Recognizing our finitude and the gift of being alive, "we begin a new life with God daily." This repeated new beginning in prayer each morning is "decisive" for our use of time, our energy and resilience, our approach to others, and our capacity to avoid self-deception. Rather than prayerfulness leading to a kind of infantile dependency and inactivity, Bonhoeffer thinks that prayer leads to being appropriately "self-directed" in the decisions of our lives. Our literal new beginning each day is to be made by opening ourselves to God, offering intercession for our neighbors, and gaining wisdom for redemptive communication and action in the world.

It is striking that on the final day of his life, Bonhoeffer himself continued this practice of new beginning:

> On the morning of that day between five and six o'clock the prisoners . . . were taken from their cells and the verdicts of the court martial read out to them. Through the half-open door in one room of the huts I saw Pastor Bonhoeffer, before taking off his prison garb, kneeling on the floor praying fervently to his God. I was most deeply moved by the way this unusually lovable man prayed, so devout and so certain that God heard his prayer. At the place of execution, he again said a short prayer and then climbed the steps to the gallows, brave and composed. His death ensued after a few seconds. In the almost fifty years that I worked as a doctor, I have hardly ever seen a man die so entirely submissive to the will of God.[131]

---

128. *Life Together* (5:76). See also (5:51).
129. Letter to Bethge from February 14, 1941 (16:153).
130. *Life Together* (5:51).
131. The testimony of a doctor from Flossenbürg prison camp, as quoted in Bethge, *Dietrich Bonhoeffer*, 927–28.

Repentance, Confession, and Forgiveness

Bonhoeffer's work repeatedly affirms that for a new life and a new beginning to be made, we must consistently face, acknowledge, and renounce our old life, confess our sin to God and others in the community of Christ, and receive forgiveness. This is the third practice of "giving up the self 'for' my neighbor's benefit" in Bonhoeffer's corpus.[132]

Repentance

In his prison letters, Bonhoeffer gives repentance its simplest and most penetrating gloss: he calls it "ultimate honesty."[133] For Bonhoeffer, the core of this ultimate honesty is the acknowledgment that we have lived godless lives and contributed to building a godless world. With our false beginnings in our thoughts, feelings, choices, and relationships with others, we have "pushed God out of the world" and "onto the cross." Rather than gratefully receiving the gift of creation and thus the gift of others, we have striven for ownership and possessiveness. Rather than recognizing our own finite creatureliness and humbly listening for God and following God's voice, we have attempted to divinize ourselves and grasped to be godlike in our autonomous initiatives. Rather than the truth, we have embraced and institutionalized the satanic lie and temptation that says, "Discover your beginning for yourself" and "Let me first." Rather than loving and serving our neighbor, we have used the other as our tool, idol, or enemy.

All of these habituated choices and practices, knowingly or not, have reduced our world, aggrandized ourselves, and made less space and time for the vastness and singularity of others, starting with God the creator and reaching down to the child, the sick, the weak, the sinner. In this way, our lives become more and more godless, even as we may become more and more religious in our appearances and associations. We have less and less hospitality and attentive openness for what is other than ourselves, what precedes ourselves, what calls for our care and service and thus calls us beyond ourselves. We come to have a more distorted and deceived interpretation of ourselves.

The wake of our beginnings is a life that murders God in Bonhoeffer's estimation; it is the life that puts Jesus on the cross. Thus, for a new beginning to be made, we must begin by repenting. We must embrace "ultimate honesty," even to the point of facing the reality that we have contributed to a world *etsi deus non daretur*—"as if there is no god"—to which God humbly consents and in which God shockingly suffers.[134]

---

132. *Sanctorum Communio* (1:184).
133. Letter to Bethge on July 16, 1944 (8:478).
134. For a further discussion of God being "pushed out of the world," see the conclusion.

As earlier, rather than being something that we do on our own by our own wisdom and power, Bonhoeffer sees repentance as an activity that starts with the other by grace.[135] Similar to prayer, Bonhoeffer consistently links and even identifies "repentance" with "listening," first to God and also to the neighbor.

In *Sanctorum Communio*, Bonhoeffer summarizes what we have just seen like this: "The transformation into a new community-of-God is possible only if the deficiency of the old is recognized."[136] Starting over is not possible until we recognize the failure of our old way and world. Bonhoeffer continues,

> To bring this about, Jesus calls to repentance, which means he reveals God's ultimate claim and subjects the human past and present to its reality. To recognize that we are guilty makes us solitary before God; we begin to recognize what has long been the case objectively, namely that we are in a state of [ethical] isolation.[137]

Here "repentance" is really "God's ultimate claim" in the "call" of Jesus, which leads to a clarified "objectivity" toward our past and our moral reality that makes us stand "solitary before God."

Bonhoeffer makes the same point more explicitly several years later, stating in a sermon from 1936, "The path of repentance and hope leads through hearing. Hearing is the key. The word alone is able to bring about repentance and hope."[138] Bonhoeffer says this directly after declaring, "Remember that first love; remember the beginnings—or better, the beginning, which is Jesus Christ himself; remember from what you have fallen! That is the basis of all reformation." The beginning of repentance is *hearing*, which exposes our fallenness, awakens us to Christ's beginning, and brings about "reformation."

We need to underscore the specific understanding Bonhoeffer has here of "repentance" or "ultimate honesty." Bonhoeffer is not calling for "soul-searching" or a "turn inward," a kind of private inventory of our virtues and vices in preparation for doing better, which all too easily falls into "the net of self-centered introspection."[139] Bonhoeffer is calling for an ultimate openness to God, to the one who precedes and exceeds our consciousness, comprehension, and control, our religiosity and idolatry, indeed, our conscience and its self-condemnation or self-justification. Rather than a further digging into the self, Bonhoeffer understands repentance as a reverse movement beyond the

---

135. See *Ethics* (6:135): "Therein lies the miracle."
136. *Sanctorum Communio* (1:148)
137. *Sanctorum Communio* (1:149).
138. Sermon on Revelation 2:1–7 from October 25, 1936 (14:957).
139. *Life Together* (5:88).

self in which we hear and respond to a call that lays claim to us, indeed, that reveals who we truly are beyond our wishing and self-representation.[140]

In a letter from July 18, 1935, to Leonard Hodgson, Bonhoeffer insisted, "Should not the message of Jesus Christ lead everyone of us, first of all, to repentance and thus command him to listen to the words of every brother in Christ, and perhaps submit his own opinion to the correction of his brother?"[141] This concentrated "listening" to "every brother" is what a life of repentance and "ultimate honesty" required for Bonhoeffer, equally operative within the church and its disputes as anywhere else: the willingness to hear the other person and correct our own views in response to them. This practice must also include willingly subjecting our religious "slogans" to the scrutiny of others. Indeed, as we have seen earlier, Bonhoeffer saw this posture of listening as "the very first and simplest act of love for one's neighbor."[142]

From his earliest papers, Bonhoeffer is clear that this kind of "repentance" is not a once-and-done event but a way of life for the follower of Christ. At the age of twenty, Bonhoeffer wrote, "Our work is daily repentance precisely because we are obedient to God." And such "daily repentance" is "the first and last thing that anyone who has become a doer of the word must do." Rather than our initiative or inward gaze, which is done once and left behind, Bonhoeffer admonishes, "God's claim and love has preceded [us]. Accept God's word, hear it and do it!"[143] And such daily practice leads to crucial new insight for our responsibility:

> This is the world in which I live, in which I sin by sowing hate and lovelessness day by day. This is the fruit of what I and my brothers have sown—and these people here . . . are my brothers, my brothers in sin, in hate and evil and love-lessness, my brothers in guilt. Whatever happens to them is meant for me too; they are only showing me God's finger pointed in anger, pointed at me as well. So let us repent and realize *our* guilt and not judge.[144]

Thus, repentance's ultimate honesty destroys self-righteousness, judgmental-ism toward others, and the externalization of responsibility. On the "dangerous ground" of repentance, our self-justifying judgment is called into question, and we become open to recognizing our share in the decay and destruction unfolding around us rather than scapegoating others. In repentance, we become "brothers in guilt."

---

140. See "The Concept of Confession from the Standpoint of the Concept of Truth" from 1933 (12:284) and Letter to Bethge from July 16, 1944 (8:480).

141. Letter to Leonard Hodgson from July 18, 1935 (14:71).

142. Lecture on "Pastoral Counseling" from March 1938 (15:309).

143. Sermon on James 1:21–25 from summer 1926 (9:497–99). Here Bonhoeffer links the call of repentance to God's call to Adam in the Garden: "Adam, where are you?"

144. Sermon from London in the summer of 1934 (13:369).

For Bonhoeffer, then, this "dangerous ground" of "ultimate honesty" before God and others is necessary for moving toward a genuinely new beginning. Bonhoeffer called this "a quiet journey, a strange and slow-moving journey, which leads through repentance to newness of life. But it is the only way that is God's way." Bonhoeffer prays, "Lord, lead your people to repentance, beginning with us!"[145]

Confession

But, similar to prayer moving toward intercession, Bonhoeffer does not stop with repentance as a personal practice. He insists throughout his work that the true fruit of repentance is the confession of sin to a brother or sister. Not only are we to acknowledge our guilt and privately take stock of it on our own before God, we are also called to name it and renounce it in the hearing of others.[146]

In *Life Together*, Bonhoeffer describes the confession of sin as a twofold "breakthrough" that liberates our lives in community:

> In confession there takes place a *breakthrough to community*. . . . Now one is allowed to be a sinner and still enjoy the grace of God. We can admit our sins and in this very act find community for the first time. . . . In confession there occurs a *breakthrough to the cross*. The root of all sin is pride, *superbia*. I want to be for myself; I have a right to be myself, a right to my hatred and my desires, my life and my death. The spirit and flesh of human beings are inflamed by pride, for it is precisely in their wickedness that human beings want to be like God. Confession in the presence of another believer is the most profound kind of humiliation. It hurts, makes one feel small; it deals a terrible blow to one's pride.[147]

First, then, in confession, we no longer hide, evade, or deny the truth about ourselves but come clean with others and thus enter into a new quality of community characterized by trust and embrace.[148]

In doing so, second, we cut the root of our sin, pride, whose deepest drive is "to be for [ourselves]" and to have a "right" to ourselves, including our hatreds and desires. Thus, our pride is "humiliated" and we experience the strange but wonderful liberation of becoming "small" and thus having room for others, who also confess their sin. This is the "new human being" who recognizes the social outcast and enemy as a moral equal to be respected and responded to in bonds of loves.

---

145. Sermon from London in the summer of 1934.

146. See "The Best Physician" from January 1941 (16:501); "The Space of the Church Proclamation and of Its Confession (14:813); and *Ethics* (6:396).

147. *Life Together* (5:110). See theses on "Personal Confession and Lord's Supper" from 1936 (14:593).

148. See "Homily for Personal Confession on Proverbs 28:13" from summer 1935 (14:862).

Later in a related seminary lecture, Bonhoeffer describes confession as both "simple" and "nevertheless penetrating the utmost depths of our lives." Here he admits that many people will see the confession of sin as "more difficult . . . than a dangerous operation."[149] He also acknowledges that such an act "may seem like a strange change of and solution to this question" of becoming new in the depths of our being. But he insists that such incredulity only distracts "those who have not yet experienced the healing of the whole person through confession and forgiveness." The vocalization of the confession of sin is like "a loud scream for everyone, the birth of a new world," announcing the self's abandonment of its own self-enclosed world and both boldly and humbly welcoming the help of the other.[150] In confession, we come out of ourselves. Thus, the free confession of sin to another marks the slow beginning of healing for the moral ruptures we discussed in chapter 3.

Forgiveness

Third, in response to my confession, Bonhoeffer teaches that the listening brother or sister "becomes Christ for me" and speaks Christ's promise of forgiveness in the hearing of my sin. He writes in *Life Together*,

> When [Christ gave his people authority to forgive sins], Christ made us into the community of faith, and in that community Christ made the other Christian to be grace for us. Now each stands in Christ's place. . . . Through Christ other Christians have become Christ for us in the power and authority of Christ's commandment. Other Christians stand before us as the sign of God's truth and grace. . . . When I go to another believer to confess, I am going to God.[151]

Earlier in his lecture course on "The Nature of the Church," Bonhoeffer said similarly that in the announcement of forgiveness, "God's truth takes place through the brother" and "ends all torture," whereby the other serves as God's vicarious representative on earth for the sinner in the form of Christ.[152]

Thus, when Bonhoeffer later wrote from prison that the essence of true repentance is "being pulled into the messianic event" of Christ's suffering for others, he was only intensifying this earlier theme of the brother or sister taking on the form of Christ, receiving confession, and proclaiming the forgiveness of God that obliterates all sin.[153] As he taught at Finkenwalde in his theses on "Personal Confession and Lord's Supper," "Each person becomes

---

149. "The Best Physician" (16:501).
150. Lecture course on "The Nature of the Church" from summer 1932 (11:326). See *Sanctorum Communio* (1:228).
151. *Life Together* (5:109).
152. Lecture course on "The Nature of the Church" from summer 1932 (11:326).
153. See *Discipleship* (4:88). Note letter to Bethge from February 12, 1944 (8:296), in which Bonhoeffer seems to deemphasize confession in prison.

Christ for the other."[154] The wider sociological and political implications of such a community for fighting intolerance and exclusion, as well as for strengthening trust and cooperation, should not be underestimated.[155]

In both receiving and proclaiming the forgiveness of Christ in Christ's role as the vicarious representative of God, Bonhoeffer believes that the human person experiences in community a "breakthrough to new life" in which "'Everything old has passed away'" and "'Everything has become new' (2 Cor. 5:17)."[156] This, again, confirms my argument at the beginning of this chapter about Bonhoeffer's understanding of "the new." In the community of confession and forgiveness,

> Christ has made a new beginning with us. As the first disciples left everything be-hind and followed Jesus' call, so in confession the Christian gives up everything and follows. Confession is following after [*Nachfolge*]. Life with Jesus Christ and the community of faith has begun. . . . In confession, Christians begin to renounce their sins. The power of sin is broken. From now on, the Christian gains one victory after another. What happened to us in baptism is given to us anew in confession. We are delivered from darkness into the rule of Jesus Christ.[157]

Thus, as we have seen with both baptism and prayer, Bonhoeffer identifies the practice of repentance, confession, and forgiveness with "discipleship" or "following after" (*Nachfolge*) Christ, who goes before humanity and makes a new beginning with us and for us. Rather than human agents beginning for themselves and thus literally taking the initiative, Christ calls us to follow after *his* initiative through the gift of forgiveness.

In the work of forgiveness, Bonhoeffer believes that "the last shackle of loneliness—hatred—is shattered and the community is established and created anew."[158] Paradoxically, the recognition of sin and its confession to a trusted brother or sister in community becomes an antidote to loneliness, the feeling of superfluousness, and hatred. Bonhoeffer goes so far as to argue that without the "miracle" of confession and forgiveness, "all previously existing community is shown to have been illusory, annulled, destroyed, and broken through" based on his understanding of human nature sketched in chapter 3.[159] Only through the

---

154. "Personal Confession and Lord's Supper" (14:747). See *Ethics* (6:395).

155. This is part of Larry Siedentop's argument in *Inventing the Individual*, particularly the rec-ognition of universal sinfulness and thus the need for universal confession and forgiveness, a kind of universal "care of souls" that promotes the individual and his or her importance above other social roles like the family, class, gender, caste, or race.

156. *Life Together* (5:112).

157. *Life Together* (5:112).

158. Essay on "Thy Kingdom Come! The Prayer of the Church-Community for God's Kingdom on Earth" from November 1932 (12:293).

159. See "Personal Confession (according to the Large Catechism)" (14:748) and "The Holy Spirit according to Luther" from February 1926 (9:350).

challenge of repentance, confession, and forgiveness is true community found for the first time. In it, human nature with its pride, obsessive desire, loneliness, and hatred begins to be renewed through daily practice with others.[160]

Nevertheless, as we have seen already in chapters 3 and 4, Bonhoeffer's view of the church as the community of repentance, confession, and forgiveness did not lead him to a dogmatic optimism or naïve blindness about the reality of the church. To the contrary, Bonhoeffer saw the church's failure to be precisely this kind of repentant, confessional, forgiving community as digging its grave and killing its credibility and voice in society. Even for the Confessing Church in its opposition to the Nazified Reich Church, Bonhoeffer insisted that it must make "first of all . . . a *confession of sin*" as the precondition for any "confession" of faith or theology to society. He interrogated, "Does the Confessing Church know that the confession of the fathers and the confession against the enemies of Jesus Christ attain credibility and authority only where a confession against oneself comes first, where the *damnamus* [we reject] is directed first of all against one's own front?"[161]

This "*damnamus*" "directed first of all against one's own front" is exactly what Bonhoeffer articulated years later in his *Ethics* manuscript "Guilt, Justification, and Renewal." Now in the midst of war, Bonhoeffer walks step by step through each of the Ten Commandments and confesses the failure of the church to obey God's Word on behalf of others. Concerning the command against murder, Bonhoeffer confesses,

> The church confesses that it has witnessed the arbitrary use of brutal force, the suffering in body and soul of countless innocent people, that it has witnessed oppression, hatred, and murder without raising its voice for the victims and without finding ways of rushing to help them. It has become guilty of the lives of the weakest and most defenseless brothers and sisters of Jesus Christ.[162]

Bonhoeffer concludes these ten confessions with this overarching confession of ecclesial failure to the point of "apostasy from Christ" in the face of societal evil:

> The church confesses itself guilty of violating all of the Ten Commandments. It confesses thereby its apostasy from Christ. It has not so borne witness to the

---

160. *Discipleship* (4:158). See lecture "On the Theological Foundation of the Work of the World Alliance" on July 26, 1932 (11:365): "The final and only enduring basis of any community of peace: the forgiveness of sins. The sole reason that Christians have a community of peace is because the one wishes to forgive the sins of the other." On the daily practice of repentance, see *Life Together* (5:103).

161. Essay on "The Confessing Church and the Ecumenical Movement" from August 1935 (14:407).

162. *Ethics* (6:139). The "defenseless brothers and sisters of Christ" is almost certainly a reference to Jews. See Bonhoeffer's prison poem "Night Voices" (8:467), in which Bonhoeffer continues this confession of the church's failure to confront evil.

truth of God in a way that leads all inquiry and science to recognize its origin in this truth. It has not so proclaimed the righteousness of God that all human justice must see there its own source and essence. It has not been able to make the loving care of God so credible that all human economic activity would be guided by it in its task. By falling silent the church became guilty for the loss of responsible action in society, courageous intervention, and the readiness to suffer for what is acknowledged as right. It is guilty of the government's falling away from Christ.[163]

With astonishing sobriety, rather than pointing fingers away from the church or trying to explain its failures, Bonhoeffer goes so far as to confess the guilt of the church for the confusion and corruption in contemporary science, justice, economic life, societal responsibility, and government. Bonhoeffer's self-directed "*damnamus*" takes up the guilt of a society producing the Holocaust and says, "We are responsible. Forgive us." This is the practice of "ultimate honesty" on the communal level, which rejects self-justification and scapegoating, without which Bonhoeffer thought a new beginning is impossible and always already trapped in the old.

For Bonhoeffer, such radical repentance, confession, and (request for) forgiveness starting in the church was the only path for renewal in Western society with its "repudiation" of the "form of Christ." He argues, "The justification of the West, which has fallen away from Christ, lies only in God's justification of the church, leading it into full confession of guilt and into the form of the cross. The renewal of the West lies completely in God's renewal of the church, which leads it into community with the resurrected and living Jesus Christ."[164] Analogously to the way that Christ stands as the redeeming vicarious representative before God for the church, so the church must willingly stand in the place of the West's sins before Christ and in its act of humble confession show the way back to Christ "the new beginning," who calls us into the "new life in being there for others."[165]

Rather than any kind of cheap optimism, Bonhoeffer admits that "here the claim to full atonement by the guilty for the past is renounced; here it is recognized that what is past can never be restored by human power, that the wheel of history can no longer be rolled back."[166] Human beings by themselves have no power to raise the dead or to redeem the evils that have been done, leaving individual lives and society in ruins. What Bonhoeffer does hope for through the confession of the church is that the guilt of the past in

---

163. *Ethics* (6:140). See Jennifer McBride, *The Church for the World: A Theology of Public Witness*, reprint edition (New York: Oxford University Press, 2014), especially chapter 5.

164. *Ethics* (6:142).

165. Thus, we can see again how dire Bonhoeffer's evaluation was in his "Outline for a Book" from prison in which he wrote of the church's "no risk-taking for others."

166. *Ethics* (6:144).

society can be "scarred over" with the restoration of basic "justice, order, and peace" and that "something like forgiveness," if only "a weak shadow of the forgiveness that Jesus Christ gives to believers," can be accomplished after arbitrariness, violence, and war have been recognized as self-destructive and wrong.[167]

Thus, in his brief manuscript on "Guilt, Justification, Renewal," Bonhoeffer seems to envision two interconnected, tensioned pathways or "speeds" for moving forward in church and society after devastating rupture: "For the church and for individual believers, there can only be a full break with guilt and a new beginning, through the gift of forgiveness of sin. But in the historical life of nations there can only be a slow process of healing."[168] This differentiation makes sense in light of Bonhoeffer's extremely demanding understanding of what forgiveness means and requires. For example, in a Finkenwalde sermon from 1935, Bonhoeffer makes clear that

> to forgive would mean having nothing but good thoughts about the person and *supporting* that person whenever we can. . . . To forgive seven times—genuinely to forgive, would mean making the best of the wrong that has been done to us, would mean repaying evil with good; it means accepting the other person as if that person had always been our dearest brother—no small feat. Indeed, what we tend to call forgiving and forgetting [is] Live and let live. But then genuinely forgiving, forgiving out of pure love, love that simply refuses to turn the other person loose and instead insists on supporting that person—that is certainly no small feat. . . . Forgiving has neither beginning nor end; it takes place daily, unceasingly, for ultimately it comes from God. This is what liberates us from forced relationships with others, for here we are liberated from ourselves; here we are permitted to surrender our own rights in order to help and serve others.[169]

In society with its painful "scarring over" and "slow process of healing" after devastation, only "something like forgiveness" can be called and hoped for in Bonhoeffer's modest estimation. But in the community of the church, whose life is Christ's own self-giving vicarious representative action, a "full break with the past" and "a new beginning through the gift of forgiveness" must be demanded, which starts from its own confession of sin and failure.[170] Bonhoeffer's judgment is unambiguous: "Without forgiveness, you cannot live as Christians."[171]

---

167. *Ethics*.
168. *Ethics* (6:142). See (6:142ff.).
169. Sermon on Matthew 18:21–35 from November 17, 1935 (14:896).
170. *Ethics* (6:142): "The church can let this happen to itself, or it will cease to be the church of Christ. Whoever stifles or spoils the church's confession of guilt is hopelessly guilty before Christ."
171. Wedding sermon on John 13:34 from July 18, 1936 (14:938). See sermon on Matthew 18:21–35 from Finkenwalde on November 17, 1935 (14:899).

Thus, we see again that, in the same way that the practices of baptism and prayer should break parochial preferences and prejudices, repentance, confession, and forgiveness should create the foundation of a new inclusive, egalitarian community constituted not only by an objective moral equality but also a call for active, mutual love and service to all. "God's edifice for eternity is forgiveness and overpowering divine love."[172]

Service, Resistance, and Suffering

Service

The fourth "act of love" and practice of new beginning, which flows from and fulfills the previous practices of "being there for others," is what Bonhoeffer names "self-renouncing, active work for the neighbor" or *service*. We can also link our discussion of service with Bonhoeffer's repeated emphasis on the power of suffering, as well as the possibility of political resistance. In *Sanctorum Communio*, Bonhoeffer wrote,

> It is apparent that in self-renouncing work for the neighbor I give up happiness. We are called to advocate vicariously [*Stellvertretendes Eintreten*] for the other in everyday matters, to give up possessions, honor, and even our whole lives. With the whole strength that we owe to the church-community we ought to work in it. The "strong" do not have their abilities for themselves, in order to consider themselves superior to the church-community; they have them "for the common good" (1 Cor. 12:7). Every material, intellectual, or spiritual gift fulfills its purpose only when used in the church-community. Love demands that we give up our own advantage. This may even include our community with God itself. Here we see the love that voluntarily seeks to submit itself to God's wrath on behalf of the other members of the community, which wishes God's wrath for itself in order that they may have community with God, which takes their place, as Christ took our place.[173]

Thus, service takes the form of a practical life of helpfulness for others. Rather than privileging our comfort and happiness, we enter into the needs and struggles of others. Rather than protecting our wealth and privilege, we learn to see our resources as gifts for others and practice generosity and sharing. Rather than seeing life as a competition in which others are ranked as more and less valuable/strong, our vision is transfigured to see life as community with others. Thus, in service, human life and love is revaluated through daily practice for "the common good."

---

172. Sermon on Psalm 127:1 from May 20, 1926 (9:474–75).

173. *Sanctorum Communio* (1:184). See lecture course on "The Nature of the Church" given at the University of Berlin in spring 1932 (11:322), in which Bonhoeffer rewords and expands this passage.

In a later sermon, Bonhoeffer called a people who live this way "the most powerful people in the world." Despite having risked happiness for others, this people's work finds its source in "a joyous heart," which responds to the "gift of God that transcends human strength" in the vicarious representative action of Jesus with us and for us.[174] Such a community is no longer afraid of and constrained by death but can freely give itself for others even to the point of sacrifice unto death because "the promise of the resurrection [is valid] here also."[175]

This, then, is the grounds on which Bonhoeffer repeatedly reinterprets "rule" in Christian imagination and community as "service." As the antithesis of control and coercion, service follows after God's own founding action in creation, when God makes a beginning to "greatly increase the power" of others.[176] Thus, we are reminded that for Bonhoeffer "freedom" and "creativity" are not primarily modes of self-expression—ways in which we exert and exhibit ourselves before others—but relational forms of "being there for others."

This early understanding of what it looks like to "begin with" and "follow after" Christ is surely what comes to voice afresh in Bonhoeffer's prison correspondence. For example, when Bonhoeffer writes his friend Eberhard and says, "we can be Christians today in only two ways, through prayer and in doing justice among human beings. All Christian thinking, talking, and organizing must be born anew out of prayer and action," Bonhoeffer is simply sharpening the implications of what he had always believed about "self-renouncing work for the neighbor," which he thought revealed something "new and revolutionary."[177]

The same is the case when Bonhoeffer writes later in the "Conclusions" of his "Outline for a Book" that "the church is church only when it is there for others. As a first step it must give away all its property to those in need. The clergy must live solely on the freewill offerings of the congregations and perhaps be engaged in some secular vocation."[178] By calling the church toward radical generosity and pastoral service "in some secular vocation," Bonhoeffer is again simply making good of and intensifying his earliest insights in *Sanctorum Communio* about the "call" of the vicarious Christ to "give up happiness" and "give up possessions" for others, especially the weak, out of a joyous heart.[179]

---

174. Sermon on 1 Corinthians 12:26–27 from July 29, 1928 (10:508).
175. "The Nature of the Church" from spring 1932 (11:322).
176. See *Creation and Fall* (3:66, 117).
177. "Thought on the Day of the Baptism of D. W. R. Bethge" (8:390).
178. "Outline for a Book" (8:503).
179. So we might say that even as "happiness" is given up, a higher joy is received, one that is constituted by its moral and spiritual quality rather than selfish stimulation and pleasure.

Political Resistance

Bonhoeffer's vision of a practical commitment to "self-renouncing work for
the neighbor," even to the point of sacrificing one's community with God as
the highest form of obedience to Christ, must be understood as the theological
ground for his later work as a double-agent with the German *Abwehr*, whose
ultimate aim was the assassination of Adolf Hitler, peaceful negotiations
with the foreign powers amid war, and the transition to a new government.[180]
Rather than an aberration or break from his earlier position, including his
fierce commitment to peace, Bonhoeffer's involvement within the political
resistance—which ultimately led to his arrest, conviction as an "enemy of
the state," and his execution[181]—must be interpreted as the application of
his practical commitment to service under extreme circumstances in which

---

180. It is important to realize that Bonhoeffer was a politically conscious person since his early
youth. For example, when he was thirteen, he wrote a letter to his parents on May 20, 1919, asking,
"What do you think of the terms of peace [to the First World War]? I hardly believe that one can
accept them in their present form . . . it might lead to a nationwide protest" (9:29). Three years later,
he was discussing "Erzberger's assassination" with his parents and wrote, "It is crazy that we don't
subscribe to the newspaper" (9:45). He also mentions that he himself bought one each day to stay
informed, despite the expense. On June 24, 1922, he wrote his sister Sabine about the assassination of Rathenau (Germany's foreign minister) and condemned "right-wing Bolshevik scoundrels"
(9:49). On July 7, 1922, he wrote to his parents about a "narrow-mindedly right-wing" man he met
on a train and sarcastically comments, "The only thing he had forgotten was his swastika" (9:50).
A year later, Bonhoeffer reports that he was "learning about the political situation from Vowärts,"
a social democratic newspaper (9:63), and later added, "I don't like being without a newspaper for
several days" (9:68). When Bonhoeffer was seventeen, he was a military volunteer as a rifleman for
two weeks (9:74). There are numerous references to politics throughout Bonhoeffer's letters. Thus I
find Helmut Rößler's claim in his letter to Bonhoeffer on February 22, 1931, simply false: "You, of
course, are 'unpolitical' by your very nature." Interestingly, Roßler continues, "This is not to say I
fail to recognize your own temptations," which seems to indicate that Bonhoeffer may have spoken
with him about getting directly involved with political action already in 1931 (10:283). See Christiane
Tietz and Jens Zimmermann, eds., *Bonhoeffer, Religion and Politics*, Fourth International Bonhoeffer Colloquium (Frankfurt: Peter Lang, 2012); Kirsten Busch Nielsen, Ralf Karolus Wüstenberg, and
Jens Zimmermann, eds., *Dem Rad in die Speichen fallen: das Politische in der Theologie Dietrich
Bonhoeffers* (Gütersloh: Gütersloher Verlag, 2013); and Clifford Green, "Pacifism and Tyrannicide:
Bonhoeffer's Christian Peace Ethic," *Studies in Christian Ethics* 18, no. 3 (December 2005): 31–47.

181. For the surviving official documents directly or indirectly related to Bonhoeffer's imprisonment and indictment, see DBWE Volume 16, items 224–39a. The indictment files against Bonhoeffer
are found in 16:435–45, which include a note that he was not a member of the Nazi Party (16:437)
and an indictment for "acts of subversion of military power" (16:445). In a later indictment from December 20, 1944, we read of Dietrich's brother Karl, "In 1943–1944 on German soil the defendants
Dr. [Karl] Bonhoeffer and Dr. Schleicher took part and agreed to cooperate in the operation to overthrow the National Socialist regime, through the elimination of the Führer by cowardly assassination
or by another act of violence that included the possibility of his death, and to end the war through
ignominious dealings with the enemies. . . . [They are] traitors to their country, [and] have thereby
placed themselves outside the community of the German people" (16:461). At the same time, Perels
confessed that he learned from "Pastor Dietrich Bonhoeffer" of "a plan . . . in military circles to alter
the existing political conditions by force" and "the goal was to rob the Führer forcibly of his ruling
power" (16:461). In the indictment against Constantin von Dietze on April 9, 1945, the record states,
"he and [Dietrich] Bonhoeffer reckoned with the possibility of a violent realization of the domestic
changes, which would establish the precondition for their ecclesial and economic-political plans,
and they also consented to this sort of violent solution" (16:467). Years before, on March 19, 1941,

neighbors were being violently devastated and murderously annihilated. Thus, Bonhoeffer's political resistance was consistent and simply followed through with the implications of his most basic convictions about service for others in need.[182]

Soon after his crucial 1932 address on the World Alliance, Bonhoeffer famously wrote in his 1933 essay "The Church and the Jewish Question,"

> The third possibility [of church action] is not just to bind up the wounds of the victims beneath the wheel but to seize the wheel itself. Such an action would be direct political action on the part of the church. This is only possible and called for if the church sees the state to be failing in its function of creating law and order, that is, if the church perceives that the state, without scruples, has created either too much or too little law and order. It must see in either eventuality a threat to the existence of the state and thus to its own existence as well. There would be

---

Bonhoeffer was banned from publishing due to "activity subverting the people" and "the deficiency in reliability" of his political loyalty (16:181).

182. Bonhoeffer's lecture "On the Theological Foundation of the Work of the World Alliance" in Czechoslovakia on July 26, 1932, is perhaps the earliest, most important public sketch of the theological framework that led to his political resistance to Hitler, including his willingness to participate in tyrannicide. Note especially 11:364–66, 369: "*Every order*—be it the oldest and holiest—*can be broken*—and must be, when it is locked within itself, hardened, and when it no longer permits the proclamation of the revelation. From this point, the church of Christ must judge the orders of the world . . . it must keep its eyes on this alone: which orders are most likely to stop this radical decline of the world in sin and death and will thereby be in a position to hold open the way for the gospel. . . . Wherever a community of peace endangers or suffocates truth and justice, the community of peace must be broken and the battle must be declared. . . . *Struggle* as possible action with respect to Christ becomes understandable . . . it can be an order of preservation for the future of Christ . . . struggle can protect the openness for the revelation in Christ better than external peace, in that it breaks the hardened, self-enclosed order . . . the state finds in the church a critical boundary of its possibilities and must therefore regard the church as a critic of its action." Thus, the church was called to a "venture and decision" based on "the absolute critical and radical commandment" of Christ for "truth and justice" (11:364). Note well: Bonhoeffer opposed modern "war" and said "we should not balk here at using the word 'pacifism'" because he thought modern war technology was "idolatrized" and would lead to "the certain self-destruction of both warring parties"—*not* because he thought the limited, strategic use of violent force as such was absolutely opposed to God's will in extreme situations (11:366). It was the unlimited, destructive use of force—"a very specific means of struggle forbidden today by God"—that Bonhoeffer opposed, not force itself. Thus, six months before Hitler became Germany's Chancellor, Bonhoeffer was already outlining the grounds for tyrannicide as a limited use of force to preserve truth and justice in obedience to Christ. See also Bonhoeffer's essay "What Is Church?" from January 1933 (12:265): "The church's preaching is of necessity 'political'. . . it is first of all the critical limit of all political actions." In "The Führer and the Individual in the Younger Generation" from February 1933 (12:279), Bonhoeffer critiques "the political-messianic idea of leader" (12:278) for creating a "misleader" (12:280) who fails to recognize their "penultimate"—not ultimate—authority (12:281). In his letter on September 11, 1934, to Erwin Sutz, Bonhoeffer had already decided it was pointless to try to reason with Hitler and that doing so would only empower Hitler to "convert" the church to his ideology (12:217–18). Stanley Hauerwas is badly wrong that Bonhoeffer was anything like a simple pacifist, but I agree with his statement in "Dietrich Bonhoeffer," in *The Blackwell Companion to Political Theology*, ed. Peter Scott and William Cavanaugh (Malden, MA: Blackwell Publishing, 2004), 136: "From the very beginning Bonhoeffer was attempting to develop a theological politics . . . the theological position Bonhoeffer took in those books [*Sanctorum Communio* and *Act and Being*] made the subsequent politics of his life and work inevitable."

too little if any one group of citizens is deprived of its rights. . . . [In that case] the state would find itself in the action of self-negation.[183]

Under extreme situations, the church must not sit silently. And for Bonhoeffer, such "direct political action" was always grounded in a commitment to "wounded victims" and rightless minority communities, whose abuse by the state revealed that the state's "law and order" was really a sham and "the action of self-negation."

Here we are crucially reminded of Bonhoeffer's understanding of the "divine mandates" and the vocation of government discussed in chapter 4. As a mandate of God, government cannot claim autonomous legitimacy and thus violent impunity. When it rules through either too little law (toward anarchy) or too much law (toward totalitarianism), it invalidates itself and opens the way for theologically justified resistance to restore the functioning of God's mandates for the flourishing of human life. We see this even more lucidly when we remember that Bonhoeffer understands a "mandate" as an institutional calling by God to embody Christ's vicarious representative action, especially for the weak and vulnerable. Thus, a government that oppresses and annihilates others can claim no divine legitimacy but has rather become antichrist in its essence. It has deauthorized itself in its "action of self-negation." Thus, political resistance on behalf of suffering neighbors becomes an act of obedience to God and merely the continuation of the "self-renouncing work" that should energize the Christian life from the beginning.

However insurrectionary, then, those who follow Christ's rule must obey "the critical nomos" against the state and its promise of "security" when it oversteps its limits. Bonhoeffer is unambiguous: "One cannot serve two gods, the cross and the German Reich."[184] Bonhoeffer sharpened this point in his August 8, 1934, letter to Bishop Ammundsen: "An immediate decision confronts us: National Socialist *or* Christian."[185] Thus, self-renouncing work grounds and guides an ethic of political resistance in situations of extreme state violence.

---

183. Essay on "The Church and the Jewish Question" from 1933 (12:365–66). Note Bonhoeffer's further qualification in *Discipleship* (4:93): "Not the caprice of a self-willed life, but Christ himself leads the disciple to such a break [with the naturally given situation]." Bonhoeffer repeats this passage later in his essay "'Personal' and 'Objective' Ethics" likely from summer 1942 (16:541f.): "Is the church merely to pick up the victims, or must the church take hold of the spokes of the wheel itself? . . . Thus there is a Christian responsibility for the worldly orders, and there are assertions within a Christian ethic that refer to this responsibility."

184. Lecture course on "Review and Discussion of New Publications in Systematic Theology" from winter 1932–1933 (12:209).

185. Letter to Bishop Ammundsen on August 8, 1934 (13: 191). See Bonhoeffer's statement on February 28, 1936, "From the Preachers' Seminary to the Provisional Administration of the German Evangelical Church" (14:143) critiquing blind obedience to Hitler's state of emergency.

Almost a decade later, in his *Ethics* manuscript "History and Good [2]," Bonhoeffer continued working through and articulating the implications of his thought:

> There are occasions when, in the course of historical life, the strict observance of the explicit law of a state, a corporation, a family, but also of a scientific discovery, entails a clash with the basic necessities of human life. In such cases, appropriate responsible action departs from the domain governed by laws and principles, from the normal and regular, and instead is confronted with the extraordinary situation of ultimate necessities that are beyond any possible regulation by law.[186]

It is imperative to note immediately that "such cases" of "responsible action" in "the extraordinary situation of ultimate necessities" did not amount to a free for all of arbitrary self-assertion for Bonhoeffer, which would amount to a collapse back into "the murderous law of never-ending beginnings" or "radicalism," Christian or otherwise.[187] In fact, he continues, "there is only one evil greater than force, namely, force as a principle, a law, a norm."[188]

Instead, when Bonhoeffer summarizes his position and writes, "the structure of responsible action involves both *willingness to become guilty* and *freedom*. . . . everyone who acts responsibly becomes guilty," we should think immediately of his earliest arguments about "following after" (*Nachfolge*) Christ's "vicarious representative action" (*Stellvertretung*), by which Christ takes on all the guilt of sinful humanity in our place and for our freedom. As vicarious representatives of Christ and his new beginning, we must vigilantly remain alert for the "occasions" in which "strict observance of the explicit law of the state" can no longer coexist with obedience to Christ and the "ultimate necessities" of self-giving service, even if this means becoming personally "guilty."

To repeat, the possibility of political resistance was simply the intensified application under extreme circumstances of Bonhoeffer's earliest calls for "self-renouncing work for the neighbor" to the point of "giving up happiness" and voluntarily sacrificing one's own salvation for others. Rather than saving himself, Christ took on the guilt of humanity to the point of his cry of dereliction, "My God, my God, why have you forsaken me?" Christians must be willing to enter into the same position of sacrifice and death for others by a resisting murderous government that would destroy them.

Thus, when Bonhoeffer says that everyone who acts "responsibly" becomes "guilty," he does not at all mean that we accede momentarily to violence per se. He means that we freely give ourselves on behalf of endangered neighbors,

---

186. *Ethics* (6:273).
187. See "Meditation on Psalm 119" from 1939–1940 (15:497) and *Ethics* (6:155).
188. *Ethics* (6:273).

even if this service requires specific actions that make us "guilty" before God (for example, lying as a double agent or participating in a larger plot whose aim is to kill a tyrant).[189] Rather than an "exceptional" instance of self-assertion, like Hitler's own suspension of law for dictatorial power with the "Enabling Act" of 1933, resistance is the ultimate form of self-sacrifice, which explicitly recognizes the "guilt" involved and yet willingly acts out of love for others under oppression and thus in disobedience to the state rather than the old quest for self-righteousness and self-justification.[190] (Ironically, quietism betrays far greater Pelagian tendencies with its quest for personal purity than principled political resistance as an act of obedience to God that trusts in God's gracious forgiveness.)

Thus, we are reminded again of Bonhoeffer's earlier words about "the human being who loves":

> He has been made free by God's truth [and] is the most revolutionary human being on earth. He is the overturning of all values; he is the explosive material in human society; he is the most dangerous human being.

This "dangerousness" is not because the Christian has embraced the "Greek" lie that "we will make ourselves free" or because we want to become "heroes." To the contrary, the Christ follower is "the most revolutionary human being on earth" because he or she has rejected this lie and its tendency to instrumentalize and destroy others for its purposes. Having begun with Christ's new life in being there for others, Christians have committed themselves to Christ's radical revaluation and thus cannot sit silently while others are harmed and murdered.[191] Thus, their "revolutionary protest for the weak" be-

---

189. It is striking to note that Bonhoeffer would sign off some of his sensitive letters with "Heil Hitler!" (for example, to Manfred Roeder on June 10, 1943, in 16:410), which was a blatant falsification of his tyrannicidal conviction. Bonhoeffer clearly lied to Roeder when he insisted that he was primarily "an academic theologian" and that he "remained strictly in compliance with my ban on speaking" (16:417). Bonhoeffer speaks of hiding his work in Military Intelligence with "the fiction that my activity was primarily on behalf of the church" (16:419). He also tries to make his theology seem purely quietistic, insisting that he unquestioningly obeyed the state out of "Christian conscience" based on Romans 13, which was clearly false (16:422). Bonhoeffer is referred to as an "agent" in the notes from the interrogation of Wilhelm Canaris (16:412). See Christine Schliesser, *Everyone Who Acts Responsibly Becomes Guilty: Bonhoeffer's Concept of Accepting Guilt* (Louisville, KY: Westminster John Knox Press, 2008). See also John de Gruchy, "Resistance, Democracy, and New Realities: Bonhoeffer's Political Witness Then and Now," paper presented at XI International Bonhoeffer Congress, Sigtuna, Sweden, June 27–July 1, 2012.

190. See "After Ten Years" (8:46) for a discussion of the so-called state of exception, especially vis-à-vis the political philosophy of Bonhoeffer's contemporary Carl Schmitt in his *Political Theology*. See Christian Strohm, *Theologische Ethik im Kampf gegen den Nationalsoziailsmus* (München: C. Kaiser, 1989), 36–39, and Petra Brown, "Bonhoeffer, Schmitt, and the State of Exception," *Pacifica: Australasian Theological Studies* 26, no. 3 (2013): 246–64.

191. Sermon on John 8:32 (11:471). See again "On the Theological Foundation of the Work of the World Alliance" (11:366): "[Struggle] can be an order of preservation for the future of Christ, toward the new creation."

comes "explosive" in totalistic contexts of extreme oppression and violence. Christians must say no to totalitarian politics and willingly resist it to the point of death for others.[192]

Suffering

Throughout his ethics, Bonhoeffer saw no contradiction between "responsible action in society, courageous intervention, and the readiness to suffer for what is acknowledged as right."[193] Indeed, the church's willingness to suffer with and for other suffering people is for Bonhoeffer perhaps the most powerful form of witness to the new beginning Christ has made.

As we have seen in chapter 4, Bonhoeffer believed that "all the elements of order that still remain seek to be near the church. Justice, truth, science, art, culture, humanity, freedom, and patriotism, after long wanderings, find their way back to their origin. The more the church holds to its central message, the more effective it is." But what may initially sound like a triumphalist ideology is in fact the opposite: "[The church's] suffering is infinitely more dangerous to the spirit of destruction than the political power that it may still retain."[194] Bonhoeffer thought the church was at its most powerful when it was most willing to give up its power and suffer with and for other suffering people in the form of Christ. And it was *this* practice of voluntary suffering that would point the way back to the "origin, essence, and goal" of the "higher values," which had become homeless in Western civilization after it repudiated the form of Christ.

Bonhoeffer's intense love for the world and his fierce rejection of all "false apocalypticism" should make clear that his emphasis on the willingness to suffer as a key practice in his ethics of new beginning does not conceal any hidden resentment or masochistic tendencies.[195] Rather, for selves and systems as devastated as Bonhoeffer thought they were, the "new life in being there for others" would undoubtedly provoke vigorous and sometimes violent opposition. Bonhoeffer was clearly serious when he called this life of following after

---

192. Bonhoeffer paid for his sacrificial resistance with his life and also his immediate legacy. Bethge documents that Bonhoeffer's church in Berlin-Brandenburg refused to acknowledge him as a "martyr" and made public announcements condemning the assassination attempts of July 20, 1944, "whatever the intention." A local pastor told the Bonhoeffer family they should protest streets being named after their son "because we don't want the names of our colleagues, who were killed for their faith, lumped together with political martyrs." See Bethge, *Dietrich Bonhoeffer*, 931.

193. *Ethics* (6:140).

194. *Ethics* (6:132). See the lecture on "The Right to Self-Assertion" from February 4, 1932 (11:257): "The church believes in all seriousness, in a time of the deepest ideological division, that it can and may stand there where ideologies reach their end and something new and ultimate begins."

195. Letter to Erwin Sutz on September 21, 1941 (16:220). For similar passages related to marriage and hope for the future, see letter to Gustav Seydel on June 23, 1942 (16:328); letter to Maria von Wedemeyer on January 17, 1943 (16:383); letter to Maria von Wedemeyer on August 9, 1943 (92:61–62); and wedding sermon for Renate and Eberhard Bethge on May 15, 1943 (8:82–84).

Christ's beginning "revolutionary" and "dangerous." He was equally serious
when he wrote in *Discipleship*,

> Those who enter into discipleship enter into Jesus' death. They turn their living
> into dying; such has been the case from the very beginning. The cross is not the
> terrible end of a pious, happy life. Instead, it stands at the beginning of com-
> munity with Jesus Christ. Whenever Christ calls us, his call leads us to death.[196]

The opposite of a resentful suicide mission, Bonhoeffer understood "following after" as a life rooted in the "grace-filled death" of baptism and thereafter
lived in service for others. Thus, from the very beginning, it is constituted
by the free embrace of ultimate sacrifices of comfort, safety, and life itself
when necessary, like Christ who willingly faced death as "the human being
for others."[197] This is, indeed, the founding call of Christ for the new life.
This was also the life to which Bonhoeffer committed himself in his return to
"the fate of Germany" from the safety of New York City in 1939, convinced
as he was that sharing in Germany's sufferings was the only legitimate way
that he could share in Germany's reconstruction and renewal after the war.[198]

In his *Ethics*, Bonhoeffer wrote about a "new recognition of the origin that
is awakened and bestowed through suffering, that is a flight to Christ resulting from persecution."[199] Whereas in strength and autonomy humans all too
easily fall prey to the lie of self-creation that powers self-preservation and
self-promotion, suffering and persecution have a hermeneutically clarifying
power that reminds humans of their limitations, dependency, and origin in
God.[200] Bonhoeffer continues this insight in a meditation from prison: "Not
only action but suffering, too, is a way to freedom. In suffering, liberation
consists in being allowed to let the matter out of one's own hands into the
hands of God." Suffering trains us to let go of our grasping for possession and
control without simply giving up.

In this perspective, Bonhoeffer makes a striking claim: "Death is the
epitome of human freedom. Whether the human deed is a matter of faith
depends on whether people understand their own suffering as a continuation

---

196. *Discipleship* (4:87). See Sermon for the Lector on Matthew 2:13–23 from January 1940
(15:492).

197. See "Meditation on Psalm 119" (15:407). Note Finkenwalde Circular Letter from December
1942 (16:378), in which he warns against "confusing ourselves with Christ."

198. See Letter from Paul Lehmann to Timothy Lehmann on July 17, 1939 (15:253). See Bonhoeffer's own reflections on his return in a letter to Bethge on December 22, 1943 (8:236) and again
months later (8:352). See also the notes for von Dohnanyi's interrogation on April 16, 1943 (16:407).

199. *Ethics* (6:345).

200. See "After Ten Years" (8:52): "Personal suffering is a more useful key, a more fruitful principle than personal happiness for exploring the meaning of the world in contemplation and action."
Note that Bonhoeffer immediately differentiates this insight from *ressentiment*. As often, Bonhoeffer
is reiterating a much earlier claim. See letter to Julie Bonhoeffer on August 20, 1933 (12:158).

of their action, as a consummation of freedom. I find this very important and very comforting."[201] Here the suffering that afflicts the agent is interpreted as "the continuation" of their agency, rather than the end or defeat of it. From this point of view, death does not result in the annihilation of freedom, as it must in a purely secular perspective, but rather increases "human freedom" through the resurrection (discussed shortly). Voluntarily suffering and dying for others, then, becomes the most perspicacious revelation and "consummation" of one's life—a paradoxical new beginning—rather than its end, a conviction Bonhoeffer named in his last words, as we shall see shortly.

Thus, as with baptism and each of the practices within the reality of the new beginning described earlier, Bonhoeffer does not understand action and suffering—being agent and patient, taking initiative and opening oneself to execution—as contradictory or incoherent but as complimentary. Already in *Creation and Fall*, Bonhoeffer had written, "The church . . . sees the beginning only in dying."[202] This fits into the larger framework of "paradoxically passive action" I discussed earlier.

It is also worth noting that Bonhoeffer thought the willingness to suffer was essential for distinguishing the true people of God founded in Christ from what he called "the church-political community," which will always opt for its own security and increased power rather than the "new life in being there for others" within the radical revaluation of Christ. In the midst of suffering, "we shall rediscover ourselves as individuals" and, in that way, "shall we discover what discipleship means" beyond the institutional edifice and inertia of the church. While Bonhoeffer rejects "a new kind of Christian heroism,"[203] which reduces down to a concealed narcissism, he sees suffering as an unavoidable differentiator between the life of true "following after" and the manufacture of a religious identity, which remains most fundamentally concerned with one's self and one's people rather than others, especially the poor, the oppressed, and the powerless.[204] Bonhoeffer insists that unless we are willing to follow Christ into suffering, we cannot claim to have ever genuinely *begun* with Christ at all. Our religion remains at best "good intentions," the (often sublimated) statement "Let me first" that still plunges toward hell. Disturbingly, Bonhoeffer judges, "this is precisely where we have all become so blind." Indeed, Bonhoeffer thought an "all too intact church" could be an

---

201. Notes II from Tegel Prison, July–August 1944 (8:493).
202. *Creation and Fall* (3:22).
203. As so often, Bonhoeffer's criticism and choice of words is likely related to popular rhetoric in his context. A German Christian flyer from 1935 read, "We want a kind of Christianity—with which one can do something in life, a Christianity of which our youth will say: that is alive, there is heroism there. That is not 'only' for old women, but for the life-affirming men of the Third Reich." See Bergen, *Twisted Cross*, 61.
204. Letter to George Bell on July 31, 1934 (13:189).

impediment to the true proclamation of Christ's new beginning in a suffering world.[205]

Perhaps unsurprisingly, Bonhoeffer's attention to the importance of suffering became more acute and emphatic throughout his imprisonment leading up to his execution. As we have seen already, Bonhoeffer passionately critiques the religious drive for a "deus ex machina" God who swoops in and obviates all the painful implications of this "new life in being there for others" amid a catastrophically fallen creation that had "pushed God out of the world." Against such an idol, Bonhoeffer famously insisted,

> Before God, and with God, we live without God. God consents to be pushed out of the world and onto the cross; God is weak and powerless in the world and in precisely this way, and only so, is at our side and helps. . . . Christ helps us not by virtue of his omnipotence but rather by virtue of his weakness and suffering [Matt. 8:17]. This is the crucial distinction between Christianity and all religions. Human religiosity directs people in need to the power of God in the world, God as deus ex machina. The Bible directs people toward the powerlessness and the suffering of God; only the suffering God can help. To this extent one many say that the previously described development toward the world's coming of age, which has cleared the way by eliminating a false notion of God, frees us to see the God of the Bible, who gains ground and power in the world by being powerless. . . . The human being is called upon to share in God's suffering at the hands of a godless world.[206]

As has been increasingly recognized, this is not a simplistic "death of God" theology but a demanding theology of the crucified but living Christ who calls humans to follow after him into self-sacrificial suffering with and for others in the midst of horrific violence, whether on a cross or in genocidal catastrophe.[207] Christ's death represents the clearest and most radical rejection of the "Greek lie" of self-creation. Thus, the practical way of life that follows after it is the only true "return to the origin," that path that points us to the miracle of the unconditioned love of God for finite creatures in the beginning "to greatly increase the power of God's creation." When Bonhoeffer identifies "being a Christian" with "allowing oneself to be pulled into walking the path that Jesus walks, the messianic event," which means "sharing in

205. Letter to George Bell on July 31, 1934: "There could be no greater catastrophe now than a church-not-worthy-to-be-church being followed by an arrogant, all too intact church. . . . For in the end, it is suffering alone that will overcome the world, lift up the cross, and make it visible. All this is not hope for a new kind of Christian heroism, but it is this alone that will create the ground on which one can stand and credibly proclaim Christ."

206. Letter to Bethge on July 16, 1944 (8:478). This theme was well established in Bonhoeffer's work prior to prison. See Sermon on 2 Corinthians 12:9 from London 1934 (13:404) and the letter to the Leibholz Family from May 21, 1942 (16:284).

207. For a more extended discussion of "God is dead" in Bonhoeffer's thought, see the conclusion.

the sufferings of God,"[208] he is pointing back to his earliest theology's call to "self-renouncing work for the neighbor," which takes up the form of Christ's "vicarious representative action."

This is the demanding, concrete content of the "new life" after the catastrophe of the self's crashing waves seek to sweep all things into itself. When born in love, "suffering, too, is a way to freedom."[209] Indeed, Bonhoeffer wrote proleptically in one of his earliest essays, quoting Luther, "What one begins in the name of God can be accomplished only through difficulty, earnest prayer, and much suffering."[210] Here we sense afresh Bonhoeffer's sobriety and seriousness when he called these practices of new beginning "the hardest and most sacred work a person can undertake." Suffering and death, as the "consummation" of a life of self-renouncing work, as well as political resistance in extreme situations, is quite literally "paradoxically passive action" on the way to freedom.

Gratitude

Bonhoeffer may have thought that an essential element of authentic service is the willingness to "give up happiness," but never did Bonhoeffer relinquish gratitude for others, for life, for God—"for small things, for the beginning."[211] Indeed, Bonhoeffer consistently and insistently wrote about gratitude as a fundamental practice of new beginning with others that follows and thinks after Christ's beginning.

Gratitude opens us to see and receive the gifts that surround us. In an early sermon, Bonhoeffer called "joyfulness . . . the basic attitude of Christian life before God," which is "based on gratitude for receiving all life and all goodness from God." In its simplest form, Bonhoeffer calls "gratitude . . . receptivity toward God," which "thus resembles faith."[212]

In this posture of thankful receptivity, life itself in the world and our relationships with others are transfigured as the gifts of God that call for thanksgiving. A few moments later, Bonhoeffer describes gratitude as the "powerful root that secures the life of the joyous Christian to God's foundation: *Give*

208. Letter to Bethge on July 16, 1944 (8:480).
209. Letter to Bethge on July 28, 1944 (8:493).
210. Seminar paper on "Luther's Feelings about His Work as Expressed in the Final Years of His Life Based on His Correspondence of 1540–1546" from summer 1925 (9:259).
211. Notes on the Concept of "Gratitude" from winter 1938–1939 (15:380). See "After Ten Years" (8:51): "Each new day is a miracle." Payne Best, a British prisoner of war who was with Bonhoeffer in Buchenwald and Flossenbürg in the final days of his life, recalled that Bonhoeffer "always seemed to diffuse an atmosphere of happiness, of joy in every smallest event in life, of deep gratitude for the mere fact that he was alive." See Bethge, *Dietrich Bonhoeffer*, 920.
212. Sermon for the Second Theological Examination on 1 Thessalonians 5:16–18 on July 20, 1930 (10:572).

thanks in all circumstances."[213] Precisely by giving thanks to God in *all* circumstances for all of God's gifts, "one finds the miraculous, Christian element," which goes beyond a pagan idolatry that only gives thanks for "beneficent gifts," which favor oneself. Such gratitude "makes us rich and gives us energy because it makes us receptive."[214] That is, in gratitude, "we make room for God" and "let him in completely," thereby blowing open the walls of "the solitary lord and despot" with "its own mute, violated, silenced, dead, I-world."[215] Gratitude enlarges the self's boundaries and opens our eyes to the wonders of the world that come from God, even if this challenges the self's aims and agendas. Indeed, all of reality is seen as gift and one's worldly gaze is fundamentally transfigured: "For the grateful everything is a gift, for they know that there are for them absolutely no deserved possessions. Therefore they do not differentiate between what is deserved and undeserved, between what is earned and what is received, because in their eyes even what is earned is received; even what is deserved is gift."

Thus, in the practice of gratitude, worldly life is dispossessed as potential private property to be conquered and controlled; it is, instead, the open horizon of God's generosity and hospitality. With its posture of receptivity and thanksgiving, Bonhoeffer believes that "gratitude is always a sign of humility," which renounces the attitude that says, "*mine* by right! Everything else is nothing; only I am something."[216] Moreover, the logic of a cutthroat meritocracy is relaxed, as we realize in gratitude that even our most basic conditions and capacities come to us as gifts. Even what we could perceive as "deserved" and "earned" is more radically undergirded by *gift*, which enables us to come home to the truly radical insight that "there are for [the grateful] no deserved possessions." Bonhoeffer sees no limits to gratitude in the world: "[Gratitude] encompasses all the gifts of the created world. It embraces even pain and suffering. It penetrates the deepest darkness until it has found within it the love of God in Jesus Christ."[217]

Bonhoeffer thought this gratitude was an essential element of renewed human community. In *Life Together*, he wrote,

---

213. Sermon for the Second Theological Examination on 1 Thessalonians 5:16–18 on July 20, 1930 (10:578).

214. See wedding sermon on 1 Thessalonians 5:16–18 from April 15, 1936 (14:916); Draft for a Worship Service on 2 Corinthians 2:14, 6:10 on February 25, 1939 (15:484); and Letter to Maria von Wedemeyer from January 2, 1944 (92:151).

215. *Creation and Fall* (3:142). This same approach is reflected in Bonhoeffer's view of "reformation" in a letter to Ruther Roberta Stahlberg from March 23, 1940 (16:36): "We are not the ones who reform the church, but we are indeed very capable of blocking the way if God has decided to renew it. For us it can only be a matter of making room, of creating space." See also "State and Church" probably from 1941 (16:526).

216. Homiletical Exercise on 2 Timothy Chapter 3 from 1938 (15:338).

217. Reflection "On Gratitude among Christians" from July 26, 1940 (16:490).

We enter into that life together with other Christians, not as those who make demands, but as those who thankfully receive. We thank God for what God has done for us. We thank God for giving us other Christians who live by God's call, forgiveness, and promise. We do not complain about what God does not give us; rather we are thankful for what God does give us daily.[218]

Gratitude retrains us from viewing others as vending machines and tools for ourselves. Instead, we see others as people who have received God's sacred call, forgiveness, and promise. Our basic relation subtly shifts from "making demands" to "giving thanks" for one another. Thus, we learn to complain less.

In his "Notes on the Concept of Gratitude," Bonhoeffer argues, "freedom finds its boundaries in the ability to give thanks."[219] Here gratitude becomes a crucial moral measure, a practical criterion for differentiating genuinely free, life-giving initiative from self-assertion in community.[220] The grateful beginner asks himself or herself, "If I do that, will the other be able to give thanks for it?" If the answer is negative, the action may be selfish and thus not truly following after Christ. Bonhoeffer enlarges on this insight in *Ethics*, where he describes "the denial, suspension, or destruction of natural rights and duties" as precisely an "attack at the roots" of the "gratitude that preserves the life we have received, and at the same time places this life in the service of the Creator."[221]

Thus, at its heart, Bonhoeffer sees gratitude as a basic receptivity and humility toward God and others, which transfigures our gaze, renews our community, renounces consumerism and judgmentalism, and orients our freedom for responsible action. In all of these ways, as the recognition of the generosity of God, gratitude is a way of life that has embraced God's personal call to *obedience*. Bonhoeffer questions, "How could someone for whom God's word is of no personal concern thank God? What kind of thanksgiving would it be that receives the gifts but refuses the obedience that is owed to the giver?"[222] Such "thanksgiving" without "obedience" only has room for "a friendly, impersonal destiny" or "my luck to which I do not feel any obligation," which are repudiations of the God of the beginning.

Here Bonhoeffer's view and practice of gratitude manifests a strikingly richer and more robust concept than Nietzsche's Yes-saying and Arendt's gratitude for givenness, in which there is no one to thank and thus no built-in notion of moral accountability and obedience. By contrast, Bonhoeffer

218. *Life Together* (5:36).
219. Notes on the Concept of "Gratitude" from winter 1938–1939 (15:382).
220. See also Notes on the Concept of "Gratitude" from winter 1938–1939: "That for which I can thank God is good. That for which I cannot thank God is evil."
221. *Ethics* (6:180).
222. "Meditation on Psalm 119" from 1939–1940 (15:508).

argues, "Gratitude to God that does not come from an obedient heart is hypocrisy and audacity. Only where the revealed word of God has overcome the heart that it wants to obey him, can the heart thank God for worldly and heavenly gifts."[223] As such, gratitude has a normative structure and becomes the fundamental moral orientation of the new life. In gratitude, we not only give thanks for the gift of all things, but we also recognize that these gifts point to a *Giver*, who has called us to follow in his way of service and sacrifice, the core of which is responsibility with and for others, which includes those who are distant, strange, and even hostile to ourselves.

Finally, Bonhoeffer sees gratitude as fundamental to the ordering of the self in time, especially the past and present in times of devastation. This view is repeated both before and during Bonhoeffer's imprisonment:

> In gratitude I attain the right relationship to my past; in gratitude what is past becomes fruitful for the present. Without gratitude my past sinks into darkness and enigma, into nothingness. In order not to lose my past, but rather to reclaim it completely, repentance must, however, also accompany gratitude. In gratitude and repentance my life is gathered into unity. . . . The word of God accuses me until I translate my thanks for gifts I have received into a sincere changing of my ways and into active love. But then the word of God bestows on me a free conscience to give thanks in the midst of a wicked and suffering world.[224]

Coupled with repentance, gratitude enables everything that is past and seemingly passed away to escape the oblivion of forgetfulness, denial, and the resentment that so easily wells up from this loss, which we saw earlier in chapter 3. Together, repentance and gratitude serve as a fundamental affirmation of life in time, in which the past, present, and future are "gathered into unity."[225] Rather than simply abandoning what has been or bitterly resenting the fact that it is no more or has changed, in gratitude "what is past becomes fruitful for the present."

As we remember our past and give thanks for its good gifts, we are also brought before the accusation of our failures and the wrongs we have committed. Thankfulness for the past is joined with confession and a renewed commitment to personal transformation in the present for the future. Thus, in prison Bonhoeffer wrote, "We must continually bathe all that is past in a solution of gratitude and penitence; then we shall gain and preserve it," being "profoundly, unselfishly grateful for God's gifts and regretful for the perverse way in which we so often vitiate them." Through gratitude combined with repentance, "we can look back on the past and draw on all its strength,"

---

223. "Meditation on Psalm 119" from 1939–1940 (15:508).
224. "On Gratitude among Christians" from July 26, 1940 (16:491).
225. Letter to Renate and Eberhard Bethge on December 24, 1943 (8:238).

knowing that "God's grace and God's forgiveness preside over all that is past."[226] Here the notion that "nothing is lost" is not a mantra of superstition or a polite euphemism in the face of horrific devastation but a confession of faith in God, which generates genuine gratitude between past and future but refuses to sugarcoat wrongs requiring confession.

Gratitude combined with repentance was Bonhoeffer's response to the crisis of his age, in which life in time was being reduced to "only the present moment rescued from nothingness and the desire to grasp the next moment." In such a consumeristic, violent amnesia, "already yesterday's concerns are consigned to forgetfulness and tomorrow's are too far away to obligate us today."[227] Bonhoeffer judged that "the loss of this 'moral memory'" was dangerously compromising, if not devastating, for basic human ties like "love, marriage, friendship, loyalty" and "good things" like "justice, truth, beauty" and "great achievement," all of which depend on "time and steadfastness."[228]

Against this "forgetfulness," as one gives thanks for the past in memory and receives forgiveness for one's sins, one "musters new hope and will to live."[229] In this Yes-saying to life, we are empowered to "look together with great trust into the future. For we have not only one another, but we all have and know the one who has given us this time and also holds our future in hand."[230] The one who lives in this spirit of gratitude has the power to "bless" the world, even in the midst of affliction, which means "laying one's hand on something and saying: Despite everything, you belong to God."[231]

Bonhoeffer's extraordinary strength and resilience in prison until his death must be attributed, at least in part, to his own daily new beginning of gratitude and thanksgiving, through which "life"—past, present, and future—"is gathered into unity," even in the ruins of war. In fact, Bonhoeffer himself denied that he had even truly suffered while in prison as he repeatedly emphasized his gratitude and affirmation for the gift of life even under the worst conditions.[232] Thus, gratitude was essential for Bonhoeffer himself as a challenging practice of new beginning within his ethics and personal discipline in prison amid war.

---

226. Undated letter to Maria von Wedemeyer in 1944 (92:229). See Letter to Bethge on November 18, 1943 (8:181); the poem "The Past" from June 1944 (8:421); and letter to Bethge on August 10, 1944 (8:505).

227. *Ethics* (6:128).

228. Letter to Bethge on February 1, 1944 (8:284). See also (8:385).

229. Letter to Bethge on November 26, 1943 (8:200).

230. Letter to Paula Bonhoeffer on December 28, 1940 (16:113).

231. Daily Text Meditation from June 7–8, 1944 (16:632).

232. See letters to Bethge on March 9, 1944 (8:322) and April 11, 1944 (8:352–53) on Bonhoeffer's decision to return to Germany, his lack of regret, and his deep gratitude even if his life were to end in prison.

In summary, gratitude is the "basic attitude of the Christian life." It is a thankful receptivity to God that opens the self, transfigures our gaze to see the gifts in all things, relaxes prideful meritocracy, renounces possessive consumerism, nourishes healthy community, hems in our freedom as agents, protects natural rights and duties, unifies our life in time, energizes us to say Yes to one another, strengthens our will to live, and ultimately redirects us again to God in obedience, the Giver of all gifts. Gratitude is the "wellspring of love for God and others." From prison, Bonhoeffer exclaims,

> What a profoundly transforming power gratitude can be—it is the Yes—this word so difficult and so marvelous, appearing so seldom among mortals—from which all this springs—may God from whom every Yes comes grant that we may speak this Yes always thus and always more and more to one another throughout our entire life.[233]

Witnessing the Resurrection

As radically hopeful and grateful as Bonhoeffer may have been, it would not be fully accurate to call him an "optimist." As we have already seen, Bonhoeffer stated that, vis-à-vis the historical and political devastation of his time, "here the claim to full atonement by the guilty for the past is renounced." Moreover, "here it is recognized that what is past can never be restored by human power, that the wheel of history can no longer be rolled back." At best, on the human level, the arbitrariness and violence of atrocity and total war must be "scarred over" through the restoration of basic "justice, order, and peace." Even then, however, only "something like" or "a weak shadow of" "intrahistorical forgiveness" might be possible. Bonhoeffer hated "noble lies," the things we say out of our sentimentality, wishful fantasies, and cowardice that are false but make us feel better and thus muddy language and confuse reality. And thus he speaks with a sober realism: "Here it is recognized that what is past can never be restored by human power."[234]

For Bonhoeffer, all of these practices would ultimately be powerless and hopeless without the final, practical promise of God to resurrect the dead, create a new world, and thus make a consummate new beginning in which God's founding intentions for all creation will be fully vindicated and re-

---

233. Letter to Maria von Wedemeyer on January 24, 1943 (16:387). See *Ethics* (6:91): "Within the risen Christ the new humanity is borne, the final, sovereign Yes of God to new human being." Also "On Gratitude among Christians" (16:491): "To be thankful means to say yes to all that God gives 'at all times and for everything' (Eph. 5:20)."
234. *Ethics* (6:144).

stored beyond death.[235] These are the stakes for Bonhoeffer when we embrace "ultimate honesty" and look at the world without blinders.

An entire study could be done on Bonhoeffer's understanding of the resurrection and its role in his ethics of new beginning. But the following elements are most important. Throughout, we should interpret the resurrection as *God's own* ultimate practice/promise of new beginning after human and historical devastation to which finite human creatures can *bear witness* by faith. This again is a "paradoxically passive action."

First, Bonhoeffer understands Christ's resurrection as the death of death itself and God's affirmation of embodied, finite life in the material world.[236] The resurrection is thus the ultimate rejection of spiritualizing escapism, in which the goal of life is to overcome the world and leave it behind for something higher and better, even as the resurrection is the ultimate promise of hope for new life beyond the world as we presently know it.

In *Sanctorum Communio*, Bonhoeffer writes, "In the resurrection of Jesus Christ his death is revealed as the death of death itself, and with this the boundary of history marked by death is abolished, the human body becomes resurrection-body, and the humanity-of-Adam has become the church of Christ." Seeing it as already but not yet, Bonhoeffer proclaims, "in the resurrection the heart of God has broken through sin and death."[237] Later in his address "Thy Kingdom Come: Prayer of the Church-Community," Bonhoeffer names the resurrection "the absolute miracle." In it, "the law of death is shattered; here the kingdom of God itself comes to us, in our world; here is God's declaration to the world, God's blessing, which annuls the curse."[238]

What this meant for Bonhoeffer was that *"the resurrection of Jesus Christ is God's Yes to the creature."*[239] The resurrection, isomorphic with the beginning of creation, is the ground of the claim that individuals have intrinsic value and ultimate worth that cannot be annulled by the violence of another or the inevitability of biological death. The report of the empty tomb in the Gospels demonstrates that "what takes place here is not the destruction of life in the body but its new creation." Rather than some "Christ-idea" that metaphorically "lives on" in the Christian community, the bodily resurrection of Christ is "God's Yes to the new creature in the midst of the old," which

---

235. Throughout Bonhoeffer's theology, the "beginning" and "end" are seen as isomorphic. See *Sanctorum Communio* (1:61). In his lectures on "The History of Twentieth-Century Systematic Theology" (11:239), he links "revelation," "prehistory," and "eschatology."

236. See *Creation and Fall* (3:79): "[Humanity] is the image of God not in spite of but precisely in its bodily nature. For in their bodily nature human beings are related to the earth and to other bodies; they are there for others and are dependent upon others."

237. *Sanctorum Communio* (1:151). See "Notes on Death" from 1938–1939 (15:372).

238. "Thy Kingdom Come!" (12:291). See *Ethics* (6:91). For Bonhoeffer's earliest mention of miracles, see his 1925 essay on Scripture interpretation (9:296).

239. Reflection on "Resurrection" from March 1940 (16:474).

testifies that "God has not given up on the Earth but has personally won it back."[240]

For Bonhoeffer the implication is clear: "Those who affirm the resurrection of Christ in faith can no longer flee the world, nor can they still be enslaved to the world, for within the old creation they have perceived the new creation of God."[241] Both enslavement to the old world and escapism from it are ruled out by the resurrection's affirmation of the body and the earth under God's new creation: "It is our earth that will be made new, the same earth on which the cross of Christ once stood. But it is a new earth; 'the former things shall not be remembered.' . . . We reject the false doctrine that would seek to tear the world of hope apart from our world, so that the first has nothing to do with the second. We see his as an attempt to escape."[242]

These earliest claims of Bonhoeffer's theology remain consistent through-out his *Ethics* and prison writings. In *Ethics*, he writes, "Jesus has risen as human; so he has given human beings the gift of resurrection. Thus human beings remain human, but in a new resurrected way that is completely un-like the old." If this is the case, then, "Eternal life, the new life, breaks ever more powerfully into earthly life and creates space for itself within it."[243] The power and promise of the resurrection begins now in the world.

Likewise in his writing from prison, Bonhoeffer articulated the same inter-pretation of the resurrection as an affirmation of "earthly life" and the worth of the individual: "What matters is not the beyond but this world, how it is created and preserved, is given laws, reconciled, and renewed. What is be-yond this world is meant, in the gospel, to be there *for* this world." For Bon-hoeffer, this did not result in "the anthropocentric sense of liberal, mystical, pietistic, ethical theology" but rather "the biblical sense" of God's incarnate action in history.[244]

The new beginning that Christ made in the resurrection, then, shatters death and offers the ultimate affirmation of life in the material world as God's gift. Here the structure of God's action "in the beginning" is repeated and vindicated as good: what is before and beyond finite life is *for* finite life and "radically increases its power." The first and final miracles are isomorphic, mutually interpreting and empowering.

Second, Bonhoeffer consistently understands Christ's resurrection as the climax of Christ's vicarious representative action through which Christ has recreated human nature itself and thus proleptically resurrected all individual persons. For example, in *Ethics*, Bonhoeffer writes, "In Jesus Christ, the one

240. Reflection on "Resurrection" from March 1940.
241. See Sermon on Psalm 42 from June 2, 1935 (14:847).
242. Draft of "The Bethel Confession" from August 1933 (12:423).
243. *Ethics* (6:158).
244. Letter to Bethge on May 5, 1944 (8:373).

who became human was crucified and is risen; humanity has become new. What happened to Christ has happened for all, for he was *the* human being. The new human being has been created."[245] Perhaps more explicitly unpacking the implications of this understanding of Christ's action in the resurrection as humanity's vicarious representative, Bonhoeffer writes from prison,

> What does that mean, "I will restore it all"? Nothing is lost; in Christ all things are taken up, preserved, albeit in transfigured form, transparent, clear, liberated from the torment of self-serving demands. . . . The doctrine originating in Eph. 1:10 of the restoration of all things, *anakephalaiosis—re-capitulatio* (Iranaeus), is a magnificent and consummately consoling thought.[246]

Here we see how Bonhoeffer's corpus dwells in the tension of affirming Christ's ultimate triumph while remaining shy of an explicit affirmation of universal salvation regardless of individual faith.[247] What is important for our purposes is that Bonhoeffer consistently taught that Christ's resurrection was the new creation of human nature itself, and this thought seemed to move him increasingly toward the understanding that, in Christ's action, all people would eventually be redeemed and healed in the new life of the resurrection.

Thus, third, Bonhoeffer repeatedly interprets the final resurrection of humanity as God's ultimate new beginning for creation and, indeed, the hermeneutical key for faith in the original beginning of creation itself. For example, in *Creation and Fall*, Bonhoeffer writes,

> The God of creation, of the utter beginning, is the God of the resurrection. The world exists from the beginning in the sign of the resurrection of Christ from the dead. Indeed it is because we know of the resurrection that we know of God's creation in the beginning, of God's creating out of nothing. The dead Jesus Christ of Good Friday and the resurrection *kurios* of Easter Sunday—that is creation out of nothing, creation from the beginning. . . . The one who is the beginning destroys the nothing, and in his resurrection creates the new creation.[248]

---

245. *Ethics* (6:91). This claim is rooted in *Sanctorum Communio* (1:136). See also "Theological Letter on Christmas" from 1939 (15:530): "In the birth of Jesus Christ, God took on [*annehmen*] humanity, not just a single human being."

246. Letter to Bethge on December 19, 1943 (8:229).

247. Though note the Homiletical Exercise on Revelation 22:1–5 from 1935–1937 (14:767–68): "[The fruits of the Spirit] will miraculously ripen and will—let us point out as an aside—also make the final nonbelievers healthy." See also Bonhoeffer's prison poem "Christians and Heathens" from July 8, 1944 (8:461): "God goes to all people in their need . . . and forgives them both [Christians and heathens]." On this question, see Joseph McGarry, "Dietrich Bonhoeffer and *Apocatastasis*: A Challenge to Evangelical Reception," paper presented at the annual meeting of the American Academy of Religion (San Francisco, California, November 19–22, 2011), and Tom Greggs, "Pessimistic Universalism: Rethinking the Wider Hope with Bonhoeffer and Barth," *Modern Theology* 26, no. 4 (October 2010): 495–510.

248. *Creation and Fall* (3:35). See also 3:57, 62–63, 70, 77, 136, 140.

The promise of the resurrection is ultimately how we will know that the words "In the beginning" were not simply anxious idolatry.

Further expounding on resurrection as the new event of God's "creation out of nothing" in a practical "Exercise in Homiletics" at Finkenwalde, Bonhoeffer admonished, "Christ's resurrection [is] not an individual event but rather the beginning of much more. Whoever denies [the] end also denies the beginning. One can only believe the one *in* the other." Thus, he summarizes, "Christ the Resurrected was indeed the beginning of the new world, the whole world thereby different and new."[249] Bonhoeffer goes on to unpack how, in the same way that "the beginning of our world is Adam" as "the initiator of sin," so Christ is the "initiator" of the resurrection in God's new world in which "our souls" will not "go to Christ in heaven" but "Christ comes to us on earth, remains true to earth!"[250]

Without slipping into escapism, this means for Bonhoeffer that "life only really begins when it ends here on earth, that all that is here is only the prologue before the curtain goes up."[251] From this perspective, even as the resurrection founds and fires love for life in the world as it is now, it also means that "death is grace, the greatest gift of grace that God gives to people who believe in him."[252] With both feet firmly planted in the earth, the "homesick children of the resurrection" anticipate and bear witness to the new beginning that God has promised to accomplish on the final/first day of resurrection—what Bonhoeffer calls from his prison cell "a magnificent and consummately consoling thought."[253] Prison is not the end; *shoah* is not the end; the power of death is not the end. God is making a new beginning, and thus we have hope, both for ourselves but especially for others in the midst of devastation.

Fourth, amid his claims about the resurrection as (1) the defeat of death and the affirmation of embodied life in the material world, (2) Christ's vicarious redemption of a new humanity that includes all people, and thus (3) God's promise of an ultimate new beginning beyond the limits of our present world, Bonhoeffer repeatedly acknowledges the present "hiddenness" of the resurrection, which remains a challenging conviction of faith that exceeds human proof or comprehension, just like the unconditioned beginning of creation and hermeneutics of revelation, which resist the waves of human thought that seek to get "behind" it.

---

249. Practical Exercise on 1 Corinthians 15:12–19 from 1936 (14:371, 373).
250. Bonhoeffer unpacks this analogy throughout his works. See "The Nature of the Church" from summer 1932 (11:294) and sermon outline on Revelation 1:9–20 from June 24, 1936 (14:643).
251. Sermon on Wisdom 3:3 from November 26, 1933 (13:335). Note *Sanctorum Communio* (1:213).
252. Sermon on Luke 21:28 from December 3, 1933 (13:337).
253. Letter to Bethge on December 19, 1943 (8:229). Note that here again Bonhoeffer explicitly distinguishes "resurrection" and "new creation" from "spiritualization" and "sublimation."

In his early Berlin lectures, Bonhoeffer calls the empty tomb "the impossible possibility" that is "the stumbling block of faith."[254] At Finkenwalde, Bonhoeffer freely admits that the resurrection is "anything but a self-evident notion or an eternal truth." Rather, it is the "impossible, distant, outlandish" event and promise of God that calls for our ultimate faith.[255] In a short essay attached to a March 1940 Confessing Church newsletter, Bonhoeffer describes the resurrection as "the new beginning that followed the end as a miracle from on high—not, like spring, according to a fixed law, but out of the incomparable freedom and power of God, which shatters death."[256] And Bonhoeffer voluntarily confesses that "the variety of the accounts reporting" the risen Jesus with his disciples in the Gospels "demonstrates perhaps nothing so clearly as the fact that we are unable to construct an image of the new life in the body of the risen one."

Although Bonhoeffer sees the report of the empty tomb in the Gospels as compelling testimony to the historicity of the resurrection, because had the tomb not been empty Bonhoeffer thinks this fact would have become "the foundation of anti-Christian polemic" from the outset, he remains content to agree that "there is no historical proof for the resurrection, but only a number of facts, in themselves highly peculiar and difficult for historians to interpret."[257] Thus, the resurrecting action of God in all of its "historicity" and "awesomeness" remains a "riddle" to science,[258] and Christ humbly "holds back any visible self-vindication" until the last day.[259]

As such, the resurrection is not a dogma to be foisted on others but a conviction of faith to be witnessed in one's way of life and radical hope for new life. Bonhoeffer remained content with a resolute but hermeneutically modest position: "The resurrection of Christ as well as the resurrection of man was and is conceivable by faith. God remains in His hiddenness."[260]

Fifth, Bonhoeffer nonetheless refuses to yield the challenging claim that, without hope in the truth of the resurrection, we must explicitly face the reality that "everything is lost." As we saw earlier, the "wheel of history" that has crushed the vulnerable cannot be rolled back by human power, and its horrors remain unredeemable. Christ's "revaluation," in which the weak and

---

254. "Lectures on Christology" from summer 1933 (12:359).
255. Letter to Rüdiger Schleicher on April 8, 1936 (14:170).
256. Reflection for Easter on "Resurrection" from March 1940 (16:473).
257. See "Lectures on Christology" (12:359).
258. Note Letter to Bethge on April 30, 1944 (8:366).
259. "The Ascension of Jesus Christ: A Reflection on Its Christological, Soteriological, and Parenetical Meaning" from April 1940 (16:475). See Sermon on Colossians 3:1–4 from June 19, 1932 (11:464): "But Christ came into the world not so that we should understand him but so that we should cling to him, so that we should simply let him pull us into the unbelievable event of the resurrection . . . he builds [our life] up new and good in that hidden world where the line of death that separates us from God has been taken away."
260. Essay "Concerning the Christian Idea of God" from 1932 (10:460).

the devastated of the world are prophetically valued and promised new life, becomes another wishful fantasy without the resurrection. If, however, the resurrection is true, then even death itself becomes "the great hope in God, the gate of honor and glory," providing a radically different interpretation to human suffering and the arc of history:

> Blessed are you Lazaruses of all the ages, for you shall be consoled in the bosom of Abraham. Blessed [are] you outcasts and outlaws, you victims of society, you men and women without work, you broken down and ruined, you lonely and abandoned, rape victims and those who suffer injustice, you who suffer in body and soul; blessed are you, for God's joy will come over you and be over your head forever. That is the gospel, the good news of the dawning of the new world, the new order, which is God's world and God's order. The dead hear, the blind see, the lame walk, and the gospel is preached to the poor.[261]

Thus, we see that for Bonhoeffer, the resurrection was not merely a matter of "hope" in the future but, as such, *a matter of justice* and *the tenability of ethical conviction* in a world whose history begins with Cain's "violent hands" and leaves ruins in its wake. If the resurrection is true and it is genuinely the case that "in death the rich man is no longer rich, and the poor man no longer poor" but both are "one and the same" because "after death something new begins, over which all the powers of the world of death have no more control,"[262] then justice is something real, important, and worthy of love and conviction. In the resurrection, justice is not merely a "social construct" or ideological "noble lie" used to manipulate and manufacture consent among the mass for immanent agendas. Justice is God's ultimate promise, which vindicates and restores the devastated.

For Bonhoeffer, the stakes for faith are high and demand an ultimate decision in response to God's new beginning or its illusion. If the resurrection is true, then we are right to believe in a "new world" with a "new order of value." If it is not, then "we lay in our blood, struck and cast down by our own sin,"[263] and "the world would be lost in death and damnation without hope."[264] Without the resurrection hope, this bloody picture is simply the end of that story in Bonhoeffer's analysis. With steely sobriety, Bonhoeffer wrote, "It is my firm conviction and also my experience in conversation with many people that today they cannot look the present straight in the eye and at the same time have energy for future tasks unless they believe in the Creator—and the

---

261. Sermon on Luke 16:19–31 from May 29, 1932 (11:445). See also Sermon on Romans 5:1–5 from September 3, 1938 (15:475).
262. Sermon on Luke 16:19–31 from May 29, 1932 (11:448).
263. Letter to the Finkenwalde Brothers on December 27, 1937 (15:23).
264. Reflection on "Resurrection" from March 1940 (16:473).

Redeemer."[265] Here Bonhoeffer sees the resurrection as a vital conviction for moral energy because it redeems the basic convictions that it is good to exist, that life in the world with others should be loved, and thus that personal life and responsibility matter eternally.

Finally, as I have just indicated, Bonhoeffer sees the resurrection as carrying fundamental and practical ethical, societal, and political implications. If it is the case that "life only really begins when it ends on earth"—that "not until the end of the world can there be something entirely new"[266]—then this means for Bonhoeffer that we can relax our grip on our "defiant grasping for earthly eternities," which all too often is tightly linked to totalistic "all or nothing" philosophies and the "idolization of death," which lead to euphemistic "factories of new humanity."

Bonhoeffer bluntly points to the incontrovertible fact that "where death is final, earthly life is all or nothing." And without the resurrection, Bonhoeffer believes this finality either leads to a desperate rage for order or to "a careless playing with life" mixed with "an indifferent contempt for life." For Bonhoeffer, this dynamic of desperation and indifference leads to a distinctively modern perversity: we claim "to build for eternity" and use "big words" about "a new humanity, a new world, a new society that will be created"—here again we are reminded of Hitler's proclamation of "new realities"—and yet "in that era life is worth nothing" and "all this newness consists only in the annihilation of existing life."

By contrast, Bonhoeffer sees the new beginning promised in the resurrection—*God's* promise and eschatological "practice" of new beginning—as pointing toward an alternative, fruitfully tensioned possibility for living in this world:

> [In this case] one demands no eternities from life. One takes from life what it offers, not all or nothing, but good things and bad, important things and unimportant, joy and pain. One doesn't cling anxiously to life, but neither does one throw it lightly away. One is content with measured time and does not attribute eternity to earthly things. One leaves to death the limited right that it still has. But one expects the new human being and the new world only from beyond death, from the power that has conquered death.[267]

The resurrection relaxes "all or nothing" philosophies, which drive toward final solutions, and grounds a grateful respect for mortal finitude and everyday life, without collapsing into resignation and passivity.

---

265. Letter to Christoph Bethge on November 17, 1941 (16:236–37).
266. "The Nature of the Church" from spring 1932 (11:293).
267. *Ethics* (6:91).

On the one hand, if Christ is raised and ultimate hope for a new beginning is real, then we receive powerful energy to serve and suffer for a better world in the way we have seen earlier.[268] In a letter from prison to Bethge, Bonhoeffer wrote,

> It's possible for a human being to manage dying, but overcoming death means resurrection. It is not through the *ars moriendi* [art of dying] but through Christ's resurrection that a new and cleansing wind can blow through our present world. . . . If a few people really believed this and were guided by it in their earthly actions, a great deal would change. . . . Do you find that most people don't know what they really live by? The *perturbatio animorum* [confusion of minds] spreads far and wide.[269]

In the same way that Bonhoeffer believed that an accurate understanding of baptism would have deconstructed racism and that the authentic practice of prayer would have extended one's loyalty beyond blood and nation to the scope of universal entry, so Bonhoeffer thought "a great deal would change" if "a few people" believed in the resurrection and lived in its wisdom and power.[270] Rather than merely practicing the "art of dying" for oneself, the resurrection motivates one to serve, sacrifice, and even give one's life for others in the path of Jesus for his enemies. The resurrection means that "Christians do not have an ultimate escape route out of their earthly tasks and difficulties" but rather must "drink the cup of earthly life to the last drop."[271] The resurrection insists that there is reason to lay down one's life in baptism; to pray and intercede for others; to humbly repent, confess, and freely give forgiveness to whoever asks; to serve, resist, and suffer for the oppressed; and courageously to give thanks and practice gratitude in every circumstance of life and thereby to give one's fundamental affirmation to the gift of life in time despite horrific evils.[272]

But, on the other hand, the resurrection means that we can surrender our rage to remake the world from the ground up. It means that we can abandon the "murderous law of never-ending beginnings" and pursue the proximate

---

268. Homiletical Exercise on Luke 21:25–36 from 1935–1937 (14:755): "[The message of Christ's return] gives the strength to suffer."

269. Letter to Bethge on March 24, 1944 (8:333).

270. Bonhoeffer had moved far beyond his much earlier and temporary view in "Basic Questions of a Christian Ethic" (1930) about "my people [*Volk*]" as a "divine order" because "God created peoples" (10:371).

271. See Letter to Bethge on May 20, 1944 (8:394), in which Bonhoeffer calls God's love the "*cantus firmus*" of the Christian life, which is not in competition with love for the earth or the "counterpoint" of divine love.

272. See Letter to Bethge on December 5, 1943 (8:213): "Only when one loves life and the earth so much that with it everything seems to be lost and at its end may one believe in the resurrection of the dead and a new world."

initiatives that we can with and for others before death.[273] Rather than trying to "create the kingdom of God" through "the Christianizing of culture and politics and upbringing," Bonhoeffer is able to affirm that "the treasure of the kingdom of God is *hidden*" and only God ultimately "affects this breakthrough, this miracle, this kingdom of the resurrection."[274] The human task is to serve and bear witness, not to capture, control, and coerce the world into God's kingdom.[275] Here all utopianism is rejected without collapsing into pessimism or cynicism. The drive of the human will toward omnipotence and totality, especially in technology and politics, can be relaxed and restrained without condemning or denying human agency and value. Thus, the resurrection provides a powerful challenge to nihilism in both its "passive" and "active" forms.[276]

According to Sigismund Payne Best, a British secret intelligence agent who was with Bonhoeffer on the day before his execution at Flossenbürg concentration camp (April 8, 1945), Bonhoeffer's final words, meant for "the Bishop of Chichester," were the following:

> This is for me the end, but also the beginning—with him I believe in the principle of our Universal Christian brotherhood which rises above all national hatreds and that our victory is certain.[277]

Bonhoeffer's last words encapsulate his entire theology and ethics of new beginning. When we freely give ourselves for others to the point of death, what appears to be "the end" is truly the secret of our new beginning. The end of the old life that grasps after itself and its survival is the beginning of the new life in being there for others. Having begun on such a path, even Nazi gallows are transfigured into the gateway of God's new beginning where the resurrection can shine most brightly.

Thus, we should interpret Bonhoeffer's last words not as an improvised message but as his essential testament, which energized and unified his entire life. Indeed, a survey of Bonhoeffer's corpus, stretching back at least to a sermon from November 22, 1926, indicates that these final words were perhaps

---

273. "Meditation on Psalm 119" (15:496). Bonhoeffer was worried that a continuous second guessing of the start one had made was a way of evading commitment and genuine self-sacrifice, especially in the midst of insecurity and danger. See Letter to the Finkenwalde Brothers from November 20, 1938 (15:82) and "Meditation on Psalm 119" (15:497), discussed in chapter 4.

274. "Thy Kingdom Come!" from November 1932 (12:291).

275. Bonhoeffer reaffirms this position several years later in his essay "'Personal' and 'Objective' Ethics" (summer 1942?), in which he writes (16:549): "The spirit and goal of Christ's dominion is not to Christianize the worldly order or turn it into a church but to liberate it for genuine worldliness."

276. See Nietzsche, *The Will to Power*, §§22–23, in which Nietzsche differentiates between passive nihilism ("decline and recession of the power of the spirit") and active nihilism ("a violent force of destruction").

277. Letter from S. Payne Best to George K. A. Bell on October 13, 1953 (16:468).

Bonhoeffer's personal mission statement, which he reworded throughout the two decades of his adult life and may have planned to confess on the day of his death.[278] "This is for me the end, but also the beginning"—it is hard to imagine a more compact crystallization of Bonhoeffer's ethics of new beginning.

Such was the confidence and final confession of Bonhoeffer about the new beginning of Christ based on the resurrection in the face of death for his self-giving service. Indeed, Bonhoeffer gave his final sermon for his fellow prisoners on April 8, 1945, the Sunday after Easter, on the text "With his wounds we are healed" (Isaiah 53:5) and "By his great mercy we have been born anew to a living hope through the resurrection of Jesus Christ from the dead" (1 Peter 1:3).[279] The next day, Bonhoeffer peacefully went to his execution and spoke his final words of new beginning.

In summary, then, as a practice of new beginning, witnessing the resurrection overcomes death and affirms embodied life on earth against escapism and despair; it climaxes Christ's life of vicarious representative action for all people; it ushers in the beginning of God's new world; it demands faith in the hiddenness of God; and it energizes action, vindicates ethics, and challenges totalistic philosophies that violently struggle for earthly eternities. The resurrection is God's privileged practice of new beginning and the consummation of our paradoxically passive action of new beginning in time.

CONCLUSION: "THE FOUNDATION IS DEEP AND SOLID AND GOOD"

In this long chapter, I have made the argument that for Bonhoeffer a genuine "new beginning" is not something we can make for ourselves by force of will. Instead, the new beginning is the miracle of Christ himself and the gifted opening of the self to welcome, wait on, and respond to others in love. This is what Bonhoeffer named "a new life in being there for others."

Next, I situated this understanding of newness within Bonhoeffer's concept of "revaluation." In the "new order of value" commenced by God with creation and Christ, what the self and society in the "old way" so often assume to be of ultimate value (for example, initiative, self-assertion, power, success, even religious piety) is "devalued," and what is often seen as valueless (for example, the child, the sinner, the sick, the oppressed, the racial minority, the dying) is recognized as bearing ultimate value. Thus, for Bonhoeffer, "The

---

278. See the appendix, in which I show how Bonhoeffer seemed to refine and rehearse his last words throughout his life and writings.

279. See Bethge, *Dietrich Bonhoeffer*, 926.

human being who loves because he has been made free by God's truth is the most revolutionary human being on earth. He is the overturning of all values; he is the explosive material in human society; he is the most dangerous human being."

I then discussed the crucial importance of practice or *exertitia* across Bonhoeffer's corpus. For Bonhoeffer, this new beginning following after the way of Christ is not the stuff of "fantasy" or "religious daydreaming"; it is not obvious or easy. To the contrary, it is "the hardest" and "most sacred work." The new beginning requires constant exercise and disciplined habituation, even as it begins with and is constantly powered by the gracious initiative of God. The paradox—"passive action"—is inhabited rather than overcome.

It is within this fundamental framework of Bonhoeffer's ethics of new beginning that I elaborated six practices of new beginning in Bonhoeffer's thought: (1) baptism; (2) prayer, intercession, and discernment; (3) repentance, confession, and forgiveness; (4) service, resistance, and suffering; (5) gratitude; and (6) witnessing God's own practical promise of resurrection. Throughout this discussion, I highlighted the "revaluating" and even revolutionary personal, social, and political implications of these practices, particularly with regard to dignifying individuals (especially those who are vulnerable and subject to devaluation) and limiting and rechanneling power within a robust framework of moral universalism. For Bonhoeffer, *the new beginning is not primarily an idea or problem to be figured out; it is a practical way of life in the world*. As he wrote, "Truth shall happen. . . . You will come to the light not by thinking, says Jesus, but through that which you do."[280]

In prison Bonhoeffer started writing a novel, in which a character named Heinrich asks the searching question, "Why lay bricks if the foundation is crumbling?"—an apt interrogation of Bonhoeffer's world and perhaps ours as well. Heinrich continues, "It's a miracle if you don't go mad, torn between despair and the urge to live, torn between hatred for everything alive and craving for wild pleasure."[281] This is the voice of the self torn from the origin and tempted to make its own beginnings, as we saw in chapter 3.

To this, Christoph replies,

If the foundation crumbles, it's all over. But you see, that's how it is. The foundation is deep and solid and good. You just have to build on it, not beside it, on the quicksand of so-called new ideas. . . . There must be some self-evident things in life, and you must have the courage to stand up for them. You can't start life all over every day, calling into question again everything you learned or gained the day before. What we consider self-evident has been tried through

---

280. Sermon on John 3:16–21 from February 20, 1940 (15:560).
281. From Scene 3 of Bonhoeffer's unfinished, untitled prison drama (7:67–69).

many generations and has stood up to life's tests hundreds and thousands of times.[282]

In Christoph's and Bonhoeffer's own analysis, "That's precisely what's wrong today. People act as if the world had only begun with them, so they question everything and thus never get around to laying one small brick that's theirs to fit into the structure of the whole."[283]

This moment of dialogue is a powerful display in miniature of Bonhoeffer's fundamental conviction, beset as we are with crumbling foundations and the divided drives of hatred and pleasure trapped in "the murderous law of never-ending beginnings." With Christoph, Bonhoeffer testifies, "The foundation is deep and solid and good. You just have to build on it, not beside it, on the quicksand of so-called new ideas."[284] Thus, we are empowered for the humble work of "laying one small brick" that is ours "to fit into the structure of the whole" as we wait for the fulfillment of God's final promise of new beginning and follow after him with the practices of new beginning described earlier.

In this chapter, I have attempted to excavate Bonhoeffer's practical, upbuilding vision of this "deep and solid and good" foundation, his ethics of new beginning. For Bonhoeffer, this foundation reaches back to the beginning of creation and opens onto "the dawn of the new world, the new order" of the resurrection. In all of its hope and challenge, this ethics offers us today "an entirely new way of being human and being good."[285]

> Dear brothers, our real crisis is not at all the doubt about the path we have begun but rather our failure of patience, of remaining below. We are still unable to imagine that God today really wants nothing new of us but solely that we stand the test in the old. That is too little for us, too monotonous, too modest. We still refuse to accept that God's cause is not always the cause of success and that we could really be "unsuccessful" even following the right path. But it is precisely here that it will become decisive whether we have started out in faith or in enthusiasm. . . . Remaining below for us means to stand in communion with the sufferings of Christ (2 Corinthians 1:6–7).[286]

---

282. From Scene 3 of Bonhoeffer's unfinished, untitled prison drama. This statement about "self-evident things," though in a fictional context, complicates and seemingly relaxes the almost exclusive dependence on revelation for ethics in Bonhoeffer's (earlier) thought, which we discussed in chapter 4.

283. From Scene 3 of Bonhoeffer's unfinished, untitled prison drama.

284. Bonhoeffer's position is beautifully revoiced by Elshtain in *Who Are We?*, 6. See also Jean Bethke Elshtain, *Sovereignty: God, State, and Self* (New York: BasicBooks, 2008), xvii.

285. *Ethics* (6:166).

286. Letter to the Finkenwalde Brothers on November 20, 1938 (15:82).

After the Beginning

The Problem of Morality, Divine Absence, and the Ethics of New Beginning after Devastation

I wait and always disappointment. I'm waiting for God.[1]

—Dietrich Bonhoeffer

God is calling me—unworthy and sinful that I am. I am longing to give all for souls. They will all think me mad—after so many years—to begin a thing which will bring me for the most part only suffering—but He calls me also to join the few to start the work. . . . All beginners have their many crosses.[2]

—Mother Teresa

In this conclusion, I aim to do two things. First, I will attempt to retrace the argument and findings of this book. Here I will return to the discussion in the introduction and chapters 1 and 2 of the ethics of new beginning after devastation in Nietzsche, Arendt, Glover, and Lear and show how I interpret the greater adequacy of Bonhoeffer's position. In my judgment, Bonhoeffer's ethics of new beginning reconstructed in chapters 3 through 5 is able to redeem and energize the fundamental convictions that it is good to exist, that finite life with others in the world should be loved, and that the scope of our moral consciousness and community should stretch to universal entry as our "overall take on human life" in a way that these four other options cannot.

Second, I will turn to the problem of Bonhoeffer's fundamentally *theological* new beginning and his searching question, "Where is room left for God in the world?" vis-à-vis the perceived absence of God in much contemporary

---

1. Notes from Tegel Prison, July 1944 (8:453).
2. Letter to Archbishop Périer on January 13, 1947, and Letter to Mother Pauline on November 9, 1948, in Mother Teresa, *Mother Teresa*, 51, 129.

experience, including the faith of an exemplary believer like Mother Teresa. This discussion is important because the absence of God would seem to destroy the ground of Bonhoeffer's ethics of new beginning or show it to be of merely parochial interest, and thus invalidate its claim to be a vital option in "the work of reconstruction" for ethics today.[3] If this is so, then we would be taken back to Nietzsche's claim that "the rug has been pulled out from under [our] right to Christian morality" and seemingly void the principles that it is good to exist, that life with others in the world should be loved, and that the scope of our moral consciousness and community should be extended to universal entry.

This will lead me to discuss three senses of the "death of God" in Bonhoeffer's thought as a response to this problem. I will then offer some concluding remarks on the persisting promise and challenge of Bonhoeffer's theological ethics of new beginning for the moral life today.

THE PROBLEM OF MORALITY AND
A NEW BEGINNING FOR ETHICS

In the introduction, I raised the "problem of morality" vis-à-vis the realities of horrific devastation in our world, which are brought to acute consciousness by the moral exercise of "universal entry." In universal entry, the state of one's mind and the scope of the moral community are opened and enlarged to welcome all others as intrinsically valuable and thus morally significant, especially the suffering, dying, and dead in the midst of catastrophe.

Thus, I asked: What could possibly justify and redeem the fundamental convictions that it is good to exist and that finite life in the world with others should be loved as our fundamental moral responsibility in light of an uncensored confrontation with reality? Is Nietzsche right that "pure thinking," which opens itself to "the sufferings of mankind," collapses with "a curse against existence"? Paradoxically, I suggested that serious reflection on ethics is in danger of destroying itself and raises Levinas's question of whether we are "duping ourselves with morality." This, of course, was precisely Nietzsche's claim.

Thus, universal entry presses on us the urgent question of whether it is possible for us to make a new beginning for our moral life in the world, to begin again after we have become devastated, confused, and perhaps hopelessly nihilistic in our "overall take on human life" and how we actually live. The problem of morality compels us to interrogate the question of the ethics of new beginning.

---

3. Schweiker, "Loose Morals: The Barbaric 20th Century," 36–38.

I then turned to look at four different thinkers and their respective ethics of new beginning. Each of these thinkers centered their work on an honest confrontation with devastating moral rupture and articulated a vision for making a new beginning.

Nietzsche

Friedrich Nietzsche's subversive ethics of new beginning focused on the "problem of morality" (that is, the claim that morality has no rightful claim on us), the "new philosopher," and his radical embrace of the will to power. All of this unfolds within Nietzsche's analysis of our "condemnation" to invent "new values" beyond good and evil in the wake of the death of God and the advent of nihilism.

In response to the apparent brutality and amorality of this position driven by "a sovereign disposition" and "great inventiveness,"[4] Nietzsche wrote, "That lambs dislike great birds of prey does not seem strange: only it gives no ground for reproaching these birds of prey for bearing off little lambs."[5] While we may not like this novel proposal and even find it reprehensible and terrifying, Nietzsche insists that this is where we find ourselves. In fact, Nietzsche argues that it is only our weakness and cowardice that prevent us from actively embracing the will to power for ourselves and making the new beginning that we want freed from empty inhibitions about truth and justice.

For Nietzsche, then, the ironic "ground" of the new beginning for "morality" and for human life in the world is precisely the insistence that the normative foundation of morality has collapsed and thus that we are free to create ourselves and the world according to the design of our will and its "new values," if only we are powerful enough to achieve this. It was on this basis that Nietzsche claimed that "morality will gradually perish now" and "the next century will bring the struggle for the domination of the earth—the *compulsion* to great politics."

Thus, Nietzsche's "ethics" of new beginning utterly rejects any notion of a universal morality that sources a vision of individual value and the love-worthiness of life in the world with others, especially for the weak, the vulnerable, and the dead. Indeed, it is this Christian moral realism and universalism that Nietzsche thinks has fallen apart with the "death of God" and led to us becoming weak and pitiful. This "decadence" is precisely the reason why Nietzsche makes his call for the "new philosopher" and his new beginning driven by the will to power.

---

4. Nietzsche, *The Will to Power*, II, §358.
5. Nietzsche, *On the Genealogy of Morals*, I, §13.

For Nietzsche, these historic liberal values, which Nietzsche thinks "commenced with Christianity," must be overthrown and left behind if we are truly to begin again in a "new" (but ultimately cyclical) way marked by greatness and overcoming. The weak may not *like* "birds of prey," who can "bear off little lambs," but this personal preference—this culturally constructed, arbitrary, and ultimately fear-based distaste—"gives no ground for reproaching" them. Thus, Nietzsche ecstatically exclaimed, "Oh! If you knew how soon, so soon now—things will be different!"

Nietzsche's new beginning was meant to change everything.

Arendt

With uncanny continuity, I then turned to Hannah Arendt's analysis of the breakdown of Western civilization and its morality "after all hopes have died" in the ruins of twentieth-century totalitarianism. There we discovered her claim that we must launch "the first consciously planned beginning" for ourselves and civilization without any appeals to God or nature. Arendt rooted this new beginning in a call for a new international law to protect the "dignity" of individuals in their natality and plurality, and thus the human "right to have rights." We then looked at Arendt's vision of *amor mundi* and her gratitude for the "anonymous chance" to perform great acts into the "chronicle" of human history, a "givenness" that Arendt believes makes it worthwhile for us to strive toward this new beginning.

Despite the complexity and insight of Arendt's action theory and vision of human natality, I argued that Arendt's ethics provides inadequate resources for being able to tell the difference between a normatively justified beginning and yet another act of arbitrariness or violence. Arendt's position seems in danger of falling into "perpetual revolution" or what Bonhoeffer called "the murderous law of never-ending beginnings," and thus an intensified despair.

Second, I argued that Arendt has an overoptimistic estimation of human agency and our capacity—historically laden and morally ruptured as she herself describes us as being—to make new beginnings spontaneously with our own autonomous wisdom and power. Arendt's picture of the natal agent appears unrealistic, ultimately leads to disappointment, and may unintentionally intensify the dangerous conditions that she saw leading to the breakdown of morality in the first place.

Third, Arendt's Greek "great man" vision of immortality/redemption as historical memory, which focuses on "one's own anonymous chance to perform something passionate and brave and austere . . . into man's enduring chronicle," ultimately offers strikingly little hope of a new beginning for the vast majority of the human family in its devastation. Thus, I worried that

Arendt's ethics fails to warrant a moral consciousness and community constituted by universal entry. We are not "all still here."

Thus, Arendt seemingly fails to justify and energize her grateful *amor mundi* as anything more than her own personal inclination or preference, as beautiful as it is. Arendt's ethics of new beginning never provides an adequate response to Nietzsche's "problem of morality" and the twentieth century's "holes of oblivion." We are left "after all hopes have died" with the "irresistible temptation" of seeing existence in the world with others as "lifeless, bloodless, meaningless, and unreal,"[6] especially when the scope of our moral consciousness is radically enlarged and intensified by the exercise of universal entry.

Even as she calls for a new law on earth that would protect the universal "dignity" of persons, I do not see how Arendt offers us an ethics and hope of new beginning that is able to warrant and sustain this universality without ultimately collapsing into a radicalized disenchantment and skepticism that leads to "the holes of oblivion."

Glover

I next argued that Jonathan Glover's call for "self-creation" and a "new start" for a moral order that extends beyond one's own group actually falls prey to Nietzsche's argument about the groundlessness and power-drivenness of so-called morality.

To be sure, Glover provides a practical account of a kind of moral sense theory, in which a certain understanding of human psychology—manifest in the normal person's pursuit of self-interest, the "moral resources" (a sense of moral identity), and the "human responses" (respect and sympathy)—grounds the normative claim of moral responsibility. He sees these responses and resources as leading us to move beyond narrowly selfish behavior. But Glover provides no grounds for explaining *why* we have any obligation or compelling motivation to abide by what he describes as our "natural" condition contra the will to power, brutality, and atrocity, patterns of personality and behavior that are so overwhelmingly documented in his historically masterful book. The only resource he seems to provide is the force of our own will to choose this way of life and enforce it on others—what *we* happen to "want." Here morality seems reducible to preference, prudence, and the power required to enforce our "creation" on others, which was exactly Nietzsche's point in his "question marking" of morality.

Moreover, Glover's ethics of new beginning also offers no resources for hope for the devastated and dead aside from the immanent picture of

---

6. Arendt, *The Origins of Totalitarianism*, xxvi.

self-creation and the tenuous new beginning for morality, which he hopes will extend beyond one's group. To be sure, in Glover's humane position, we are at liberty to feel sorrow and regret for the two hundred people who were killed in war every hour of the twentieth century, but seemingly nothing more. Against his intentions, Glover's painstaking research into human horror only intensifies Nietzsche's "problem of morality" and thus fails to provide an adequate new beginning for "humanity." We are left with the devastating maxim "never such innocence again" as we struggle for survival, face the inevitability of death, and remain haunted by the horrifying memory of how many millions of persons have been killed and are being killed right now on our planet.

Lear

Last, I looked briefly at Jonathan Lear's work in *Radical Hope: Ethics in the Face of Cultural Devastation*. At the risk of oversimplification, I argued that Lear's proposal of a new beginning for ethics after "the fate worse than death" amounts to an ethics of group/tribal identity and survival/success in which the one group's "radical hope" grounded in the poetic invention of a "new subjectivity" and another group's "devastation" (a new subjugation?) become indistinguishable. That is, I argued that Lear actually offers no normative "ethics" but remains trapped in Nietzsche's problem of morality and the (group's) will to power. Thus, Lear's "radical hope" is in danger of leading to an overoptimistic intensification of "devastation," primarily for others beyond one's own tribe or community of concern. For the dead, for outsiders, for enemies, Lear offers little to no "radical hope" in the face of "the fate worse than death."

The Stakes for Our Overall Take on Human Life

Taken together, in the ethics of new beginning formulated by these four thinkers, I do not find adequate resources to redeem and energize the moral principles that it is good to exist, that life in the world with others should be loved, and that our moral consciousness and community should extend to the scope of universal entry as our overall take on human life. If these options were the only ones available, I submit that the worry behind Levinas's question was real and that Nietzsche was right: we *are* "duping ourselves with morality" and "pure thinking" leads to "a curse against existence." Nietzsche's claim tenaciously holds:

> For the few, at least, whose eyes, whose *suspicion* in their eyes, is strong and sensitive enough for this spectacle, some sun seems to have set just now. . . .

What must collapse now that this belief [in "the Christian God"] has been undermined—all that was built upon it, leaned on it, grew into it; for example, our whole European morality.[7]

The implication is that any "ethics" of new beginning and the "hope" it might offer is ultimately reducible to the perennial story of the will to power.

Undoubtedly, this "will" can take numerous forms, as Glover pointed out, some more conventional and "civilized" than others, some more inclusive and optimistic than others. For example, we could advocate for the "evolution" of morality and universal "human rights" as "global citizens."[8] But in their grounds, these forms of "ethics" reduce to the same root: the finite human will's preference, prudence, and power—whether this is admitted or not. This, again, was precisely Nietzsche's radical point and what he meant by "the problem of morality" and its claim: "The origin of moral values is the work of immoral affects and considerations." In Nietzsche's position, even our *morality*—perhaps our morality *more than anything else*—is really the bastard child of the will to power. This is why Nietzsche was utterly serious when he asked, "Shouldn't moralists be—immoral?"[9]

Thus, we face again the radioactive intensity and force behind Nietzsche's maxim: "Even the boldest of us have but seldom the courage for what we really *know*," because we are "too afraid to reflect."[10] According to Nietzsche, what we really *know* when we muster the courage to *reflect* is this: "When [we] give up Christian faith, [we] pull the rug out from under [our] right to Christian morality as well."[11] And this means that our hope for a new beginning is baseless and the intrinsic value, love-worthiness, and universal scope of our moral life in the world with others collapse under the pressure of the new philosopher and his will to power.

Bonhoeffer

With these arguments in place, I turned in the body of this book to interpret Dietrich Bonhoeffer's account of moral rupture and his ethics of new beginnings as a critical yet constructive alternative possibility for redeeming and energizing these basic moral principles for our overall take on human life.

Chapter 3 focused on Bonhoeffer's evaluation of the human capacity to make new beginnings. In opposition to Nietzsche, Arendt, Glover, and Lear, Bonhoeffer is severely critical of and ultimately rejects the idea that humans

---

7. Nietzsche, *The Gay Science*, Book V, §343.
8. See de Waal, *The Bonobo and the Atheist*, 235–37.
9. Nietzsche, *Beyond Good and Evil*, §228.
10. Nietzsche, *Twilight of the Idols*, 2.
11. Nietzsche, *Twilight of the Idols*, IX:5, "Raids/Skirmishes of an Untimely Man."

are capable of autonomously making a new beginning for ourselves and society. Indeed, in both Bonhoeffer's critical interpretation of fallen human nature "torn from the origin" of God's free act of creation, as well as his historical analysis of Western society alienated from the "form of Christ," Bonhoeffer thinks that the human drive to initiate our own beginning is precisely the satanic temptation that continuously ruptures and devastates the self and our life together in society. This self-creation and autonomous initiative leads to "violent hands" and entraps us in "the murderous law of never-ending beginnings," which is all too often animated by the "spirit of annihilation" given the kinds of morally and historically ruptured creatures that we are. Here Bonhoeffer challenges and offends modernity's fundamental valuation of autonomous human wisdom and power and insists that "that other" must precede us and go before us in the beginning.

In chapter 4, I attempted to excavate Bonhoeffer's understanding of what could possibly justify and provide guidance for making a new beginning in light of his critical interpretation of human moral ontology and our historic moral tradition. When we begin again, how do we know that we are not simply perpetuating arbitrariness and violence as Nietzsche insisted?

For Bonhoeffer, a new beginning after rupture in these interrelated dimensions of personhood and history must commence with the initiative of God the Creator, Redeemer, and Reconciler. This means, paradoxically, that the first step of a justified new beginning for humanity must be the renunciation of the orientation that says, "Let me first" with its "good intentions" for obedience to the call of Jesus who says, "Follow me." This is what Bonhoeffer calls *Nachfolge* (following-after) and *Nachdenke* (thinking-after). Having "begun with Christ," Bonhoeffer envisions the truly human life, which always comes after the beginning and assumes the posterior posture of follower, as an unceasing responsiveness to the self-revealed will of God in Christ. And this will is concretized in the command of love for others, divine and human, which frees us from the "murderous law of never-ending beginnings" to be with and for others in bonds of love and service.

In the remainder of chapter 4, I unpacked Bonhoeffer's understanding of Christ's initiative to stand in our place on our behalf, what he calls *Stellvertretung* or the new "life-principle" of "one for the other." I then looked at the mutually limiting and empowering "divine mandates" for human institutional life (that is, marriage and family, church, culture, and government) and Bonhoeffer's interpretation of "new life" and "new beginning" as freely "being there for others" even to the point of death.

It is precisely this principle of the priority of the other person rooted in love that Bonhoeffer uses as the measure for his critique of the false starts of idolatrous religion and secular nihilism, which say, "Let me first" and have at their core "no risk taking for others," despite their "good intentions." Bonhoeffer's fundamentally theological account of beginnings rooted in creation and Christ, then, enables him to articulate a normative ground for new beginnings that simultaneously provides affirmation and guidance for the freedom of finite human agents, which liberate us from the arbitrary force of our own preferences, prudence, and power, while also demanding the full engagement of our thinking, feeling, and willing as responsible agents in the world.

In chapter 5, I elucidated Bonhoeffer's challenging vision of practices of new beginning rooted in his notion of radical "revaluation." In the transfigured vision of Bonhoeffer's revaluation, we encounter the most fundamental new beginning in "a new life in being there for others," especially for children, minorities, the sick, the persecuted and oppressed, and those sinners that the religious often see as damned and without worth. For Bonhoeffer, practices of new beginning, rather than being the satanic temptation that says, "Discover your beginning for yourself" are forms of waiting on transcendence, of welcoming and responding to divine and human others beyond the self's "ego-world." This is what Bonhoeffer calls "paradoxically passive action."

In this way, the self is gifted with a liberation from its self-enclosure and endless self-creation to be with and for others in bonds of love, service, and mutual responsibility. Here we looked specifically at Bonhoeffer's practices of baptism; prayer, intercession, and discernment; repentance, confession, and forgiveness; service, suffering, and political resistance; gratitude; and witness to "the new world of the resurrection." In each practice, we noted Christianity's "revolutionary protest" on behalf of the downtrodden and devalued, sourced in its moral universalism.

Taken together, the contention of these three chapters is that Bonhoeffer's ethics of new beginning is able to accomplish coherently what Nietzsche, Arendt, Glover, and Lear cannot in their respective a- or nontheological positions. Bonhoeffer offers us a compelling vision of the goodness of existence, the love-worthiness of finite life in the world with others, and thus a scope of moral consciousness and community that extends to universal entry without destroying itself.

Let me now further unpack Bonhoeffer's accomplishment and with it the warrant for the central claims of this book.

First, in Bonhoeffer's ethics of new beginning, it is good to exist because creation and all creaturely life are most fundamentally the miraculous gifts of a personal Creator, the one who Bonhoeffer names "that other." The gift of the beginning is freely given by God "to greatly increase the power" of what is other than God. Here the most basic description of reality for Bonhoeffer is not "being" or "facticity," which by themselves remain morally vacuous categorizations of objects and their totality. The most basic description of reality for Bonhoeffer is *gift*, which comes packed with intentionality, affirmation, and commitment to others, that is, *moral* reality. Here the particular facts of existence and the phenomena of the world in their totality, most radically encountered in human persons, are inherently valuable as expressions of divine initiative and care, what Bonhoeffer called God's "dominion and love." The creation is the open house of God's self-transcendent generosity and hospitality for others out of the impenetrable mystery of the beginning, after which we come and are dignified with the call to follow in this way of self-transcending, self-giving love with and for others in God's image.

For Bonhoeffer, then, as we have seen, no one is excluded from this community of creation and the call of Christ to "follow after" his new beginning. To the contrary, the moral life in the world becomes the practice of walking in Christ's path, undergoing his radical revaluation, and thereby committing ourselves to practices of welcoming, waiting on, and responding to others, particularly those who are weak, vulnerable, excluded, hated, or put to death. The world is the gift of God, and it is of such great worth that Christ would become one of us, give himself for us, and welcome us into his "new life" after we have rejected "that other," denied our finitude, and sought to be "like god," resulting in our "violated, silenced, dead, ego-world" animated by "the spirit of annihilation." Here a genuine new beginning is offered for all persons.

In parallel, Bonhoeffer's understanding of the resurrection, which simultaneously relativizes all "earthly eternities" and affirms finite life in the world, promises final justification and new life beyond the limits of proximate human justice and power. The resurrection means that even the value of a fallen, mortal creature's life can be vindicated and made new, bearing everlasting significance and love-worthiness. Here finite life is lived in hope for "the dawning of the new world" of God's redeeming power. Thus, the resurrection points again to the absolute threshold of God's own initiative to create a new beginning after which we follow in faith and self-transcendence without anesthetizing human agency or becoming subject to totalizing human possession and power.

As such, second, Bonhoeffer's ethics of new beginning fundamentally affirms and demands that our finite life in the world with others *should be loved*. Rather than attempting to escape creation, as in so much therapeutic religion and spirituality, or to "overcome" it, as in Nietzsche, or to instrumentalize it for our own purposes, as in the economy of consumerism, or merely to endure it, as in Stoicism, life in the world with others is a call—indeed, a command—to pass beyond our own self-enclosure, safety, and survival for a life that welcomes and responds to the lives of others in bonds of love and service. This way of love for Bonhoeffer is so fundamental and constitutive that it demands from the start a willingness to relinquish the primacy of personal happiness, expose one's self to suffering, and even the willingness to give one's life for God and others in their needs and sufferings, without collapsing into Nietzsche's *ressentiment*. Bonhoeffer argues that the other person, that "impenetrable You," is laden with the sacred significance of God's own love and sacrifice, which calls us into the "messianic event" that is not a new heroism or Nietzsche's "sovereign disposition" but an intercessory self that prayerfully affirms and shares the concerns of others even to the radical extent of political resistance and being willing to give up our own salvation for others. The beginning and end of life is found in love with and for others.

Thus, third, Bonhoeffer's ethics of new beginning is able to withstand and press forward in hope vis-à-vis the trial—indeed, the intentional embrace— of universal entry as the scope of our moral consciousness and community, despite its intense demands and concomitant sorrows. As we have seen, it is precisely the "person who appears so totally strange and incomprehensible to us" that should specially claim our love and responsibility. Bonhoeffer insists that in the distant one and the stranger "we hear the voice of Christ" calling us into moral community. This includes the "sinner" and "enemy," all of whom in the eyes of baptism and prayer are recognized and, in extreme situations, must be fought for as the beloved children of God for whom Christ died and calls into "the new order" of the resurrection.

For Bonhoeffer, then, this kind of theological-ethical orientation leads to new kind of community, what he calls "the church-community" or "the community that is there for others." This is a community whose Christological core is practiced in welcoming, waiting on, and serving others, the world of creation, and God. Bonhoeffer describes the members of this universal, antitribal community as "the waiting ones," who are "bound together" because "we encounter Christ in the brother, the German in the Englishman, the Frenchman in the German" in *enemies* who found themselves at war with one another.[12]

Rather than denying or deselecting the lives and devastations of others in all of their "foreignness" and suffering, Bonhoeffer's ethics of new beginning calls for a life of actively serving and searching for others in need, giving special attention to those we are accustomed to see as valueless and hopeless. This revaluation retrains us to focus our love for "the eternally disregarded, the eternally insignificant, the weak, ignoble, unknown, the least of these, the oppressed and despised, the houses of the prostitutes and tax collectors, the working, toiling, sinning masses"—for the people we encountered in the introduction: the baby girl buried in the jungle of the Central African Republic,

---

12. Untitled address at the International Youth Conference in Gland on August 29, 1932 (11:377).

the bloated bodies left to be scraped up by tractors on the roadside of Bentieu, the refugees of the Syrian civil war, Eyob walking alone on the streets of Addis Ababa with his brain throbbing through his cancer-eaten skull, the neighbor, stranger, and enemy on the Southside of Chicago. For Bonhoeffer, "Christianity preaches the infinite worth of that which is seemingly worthless and the infinite worthlessness of that which is seemingly so valued. What is weak shall become strong through God, and what dies shall live."[13]

Bonhoeffer's revaluating ethics of new beginning, then, calls for a radically inclusive, universal vision of moral consciousness and community in bonds responsibility and hope. Indeed, Bonhoeffer goes so far as to claim that the *Stellvertretung* of Christ, who has embraced and renewed "human nature," is so universal and efficacious that it will "also make the final non-believers healthy" such that "in this new life no one will be cursed." Thus, Bonhoeffer's "miraculous community of saints" is not ultimately composed of the members of a privileged group, tribe, or nation but every one whom God has welcomed in creation and Christ's new beginning.[14]

Thus, it is clear that Bonhoeffer's ethics of new beginning is not a form of Nietzsche's "impure thinking," which shields itself from cursing existence by selfishly denying, disregarding, or devaluing the suffering, devastation, and horror that afflict others. But neither is it overwhelmed and overthrown by it. To the contrary, Bonhoeffer's ethics of God's beginning and the new life in being there for others is perhaps the only solid and sustainable basis for this kind of radically universal morality in consciousness and practical community. Here serious, uncensored ethical reflection does not destroy itself but enters into an intensified, though sometimes lachrymose, love, witness, and responsibility.

If we follow Bonhoeffer's new beginning—or, rather, if we follow the beginning that Bonhoeffer repeatedly insisted could never be his own or our own but only given, received, and followed after with God—living a finite life of love within universal entry is not to be "duped by morality." It is rather to walk in the mysterious path of the divine beginning that opens the house of creation, greatly increases its power, and promises a new world through which we can live, die, and hope in community. In response to Camus's "but one truly serious philosophical question" of "judging whether life is worth living," Bonhoeffer's affirmation of the goodness of existence, the love-worthiness of life with others in the world, and the opening of the self and the moral community to the scope of universal entry answers with a sober, resolute, defiantly hopeful Yes.[15]

---

13. "Jesus Christ and the Essence of Christianity" from December 11, 1928 (10:352, 354).

14. Homiletical Exercise on Revelation 22:1–5 from 1935–1937 (14:767–68).

15. For a comparison of Camus's and Bonhoeffer's thought, see Arnaud Corbic, *Camus et Bonhoeffer: Recontre de Deux Humanismes* (Geneve: Labor et Fides, 2002).

Taken together, then, I am arguing that Bonhoeffer's ethics of new beginning provides a coherent, compelling moral vision in which the fundamental principles of our modern moral life—our "overall take on human life"—are not only redeemed but grounded, guided, and energized with conviction, gratitude, and hope. If we are compelled to believe that these founding principles of our liberal tradition are essential for a worthwhile way of inhabiting our planet in our time, then Bonhoeffer's ethics of new beginning—both with its counter-cultural claims and hope-giving promises—should be taken seriously, further investigated, and lived into. As I stated in the introduction, Bonhoeffer's ethics of new beginning can serve as "a paradigm now of what a plausible Future might be."[16]

In a profound sense, the question of which of these four ethics of new beginning we choose to follow as our orienting path is a matter of the kind of life and horizon within which we must live in the world. In his *A Secular Age*, Charles Taylor argues, "If you grasp our predicament without ideological distortion, and without blinders, then you see that going one way or another requires what is often called a 'leap of faith.'" Taylor continues to claim, "what pushes us one way or another" amounts to "what we might describe as our over-all take on human life, and its cosmic and (if any) spiritual surroundings."[17] In many ways, the concern at the core of this book has been precisely "our overall take on human life" and the question of whether we can remain committed to its goodness, love-worthiness, and universality.

My argument is that if we are compelled to believe—whether through a transcendent call of God or the voice of conscience or an abiding intuition or the relentless claim of grief before evil or the face of the other—that it is good to exist, that life in the world with others should be loved, and that we should not accept a morality that sustains itself by excluding others but rather opens toward the moral consciousness and community of universal entry, then Bonhoeffer's ethics of new beginning provides the only adequate resources for doing so without plunging into hypocrisy or Nietzsche's "curse against existence," at least among the thinkers I have considered in chapter 2 and earlier in this conclusion.

What is at stake is perhaps the greatest moral horror and death: to be alive in the world without a love that is able to embrace every other, especially the most brutally devastated others, and not let go in life and in death. Kierkegaard argued, "Wherever love is present, there is something infinitely profound! The true lover says: 'Hope all things; give up no man, for to give him up is to abandon your love for him—and if you do not give it up, then you hope. But if you abandon your love for him, then you yourself cease to

---

16. Auden, "The Garrison," in *W.H. Auden: Collected Poems*, 633–34.
17. See Taylor, *A Secular Age*, 550.

be a lover.'"[18] For Kierkegaard, the ultimate stake in our decision about God and ethics is whether we can continue to be lovers in the essence of who we are, or whether honesty demands that we abandon our identity as lovers with its demanding obligations and hopeful promises. Dostoevsky articulated the underside of this ultimate decision: "Fathers and teachers, I ponder 'What is hell?' I maintain that it is the suffering of being unable to love."[19]

The stakes could not be higher or more fundamental. Here what is at stake moves beyond an egocentric fear of nothingness in death or punishment in the afterlife to the moral horror of not being able to live as *lovers* with and for others in this world because our morality is too weak to sustain such a rigorous way of life, which demands that we "give up no man" and live as witnesses of a new beginning beyond human power. In this book, I have argued that Bonhoeffer gives us precisely this kind of heavy-grade, catastrophe-capable ethics of new beginning that can sustain our love and thus also our moral responsibility to the point of universal entry, now after the beginning in a time such as ours when seemingly "all hopes have died."

THE ABSENCE OF GOD, THE PROBLEM OF A THEOLOGICAL ETHICS, AND THE DEATH OF GOD IN BONHOEFFER'S THOUGHT

I hope that the argument of this book energizes fresh hope and moral responsibility with its ethics of new beginning. But a sobering challenge must be confronted now explicitly and, indeed, on every page of this book and every day of our lives. The life-giving claims of Bonhoeffer's ethics of new beginning may ring hollow or of merely parochial interest, because Bonhoeffer's position fundamentally depends on what Nietzsche, Arendt, Glover, and Lear vehemently denounced as dead or simply disregarded as irrelevant: *God* and *God's* beginning. More specifically, Bonhoeffer's ethics of new beginning depends on the *Christian* God of creation, Christ, and the promise of resurrection, which are three ways of naming the beginning in Bonhoeffer's thought. Bonhoeffer's position is fundamentally *theological* and could never even get started, much less sustain us to the end time, without God.

But it is not enough simply to invoke God and trump the a-theological moralists as if with a magic wand or *deus ex machina* that generates a normative ethics and hope beyond human power to suit our wishes and sooth

---

18. Kierkegaard, *Works of Love*, 239.
19. Fyodor Dostoevsky, *The Brothers Karamazov*, trans. Constance Garnett (New York: Barnes and Noble Classics, 2004), 297.

our anxieties. For many of us in the late modern world,[20] as thinkers like Charles Taylor, J. Hillis Miller, and others have described, God seems to have "disappeared"[21] or at least belief in God has become radically "fragilized" and "optional."[22] This is due to an existential experience of divine absence impinging on and, for Nietzsche at least, undermining our ethics, such that we are all "new philosophers" condemned to invention because "God is dead." In Nietzsche's estimation, "By now we all know something of this."[23]

Thus, facing this negative experience of divine absence does not require a turn to atheists or agnostics, which some believers, justifiably or not, might dismiss as willfully rebellious or close-minded. Instead, we need only turn to a "saint" like Mother Teresa, who is perhaps the most powerful and painful witness of divine absence in recent memory and thus a paradoxically Christian challenge to Bonhoeffer's theological ethics of new beginning.

In her posthumously published confessions *Come Be My Light*, we discover a prayer of Mother Teresa's from July 3, 1959—one of many stretched across some four decades—in which she agonizes,

Lord, my God, who am I that You should forsake me? The Child of your Love— and now become as the most hated one—the one—You have thrown away as unwanted—unloved. I call, I cling, I want—and there is no One to answer—no One on Whom I can cling—no, No One.—The darkness is so dark—and I am alone.—Unwanted, forsaken.—The loneliness of the heart that wants love is unbearable.—Where is my Faith?—even deep, down right in, there is nothing, but emptiness & darkness—My God—how painful is this unknown pain. It pains me without ceasing.—I have no Faith—I dare not utter the words & thoughts that crowd in my heart—& make me suffer untold agony. . . . When I try to raise my thoughts to Heaven—there is such convicting emptiness that those very thoughts return like sharp knives & hurt my soul.—Love—the word—it brings nothing.—I am told God loves me—and yet the reality of darkness & cold & emptiness is so great that nothing touches my soul.[24]

20. I do not mean to imply that this is a new or exclusively "modern" experience or that this is a universal experience. Documentation of the felt absence of God stretches from ancient Israel (for example, Psalms 22 and 88; Lamentations 3:8) and Jesus of Nazareth (for example, Matthew 27:46) to the sixteenth-century mystic St. John of the Cross in his *Dark Night of the Soul* and beyond. See Ingolf Dalferth, ed., *The Presence and Absence of God*, Claremont Studies in the Philosophy of Religion, Conference 2008 (Berlin: Mohr Siebeck, 2009).

21. For a study of this experience in nineteenth- and twentieth-century literature, see J. Hillis Miller, *The Disappearance of God: Five Nineteenth-Century Writers* (Cambridge, MA: Harvard University Press, 1963). Terrence Malick's 2012 film *To the Wonder* insightfully explores the themes of the presence and absence of God around the character of the priest, Father Quintana (Javier Bardem).

22. I borrow the language of "fragilization" from Taylor, *A Secular Age*, 303–4. For a discussion of divine absence in Taylor, see *A Secular Age*, 551–55.

23. Nietzsche, *Beyond Good and Evil*, I, §55.

24. Mother Teresa, *Mother Teresa*, 186. For somewhat similar passages in Bonhoeffer's works, see Address on John 19 from April 15, 1927 (9:519); Sermon on Luke 9:51–56 from late 1927 (9:550); Bible Study on Temptation from June 20–25, 1938 (15:412); Sermon on Romans 5:1–5 from

Mother Teresa's description is powerful and painful. She points to the experience of emptiness in the midst of service in which God's "love" as a "word" is no longer adequate but "brings nothing." Rhetoric is not enough and verges on sophistry in this agonizing experience. Something more is needed, a demand for a comforting, empowering presence of God, which nevertheless remains absent. Two months later, Mother Teresa continued her confession of godforsakenness:

> They say people in hell suffer eternal pain because of the loss of God—they would go through all that suffering if they had just a little hope of possessing God.—In my soul I feel just that terrible pain of loss—of God not wanting me—of God not being God—of God not really existing (Jesus, please forgive my blasphemies—I have been told to write everything). . . . If there be no God—there can be no soul.—If there is no soul then Jesus—You also are not true.—Heaven, what emptiness—not a single thought of Heaven enters my mind—for there is no hope. I am afraid to write all those terrible things that pass in my soul.—They must hurt You. In my heart there is no faith—no love—there is so much pain—the pain of longing, the pain of not being wanted.—I want God with all the powers of my soul—and yet there between us—there is terrible separation.[25]

It was on the basis of secret confessions like these that critics like Christopher Hitchens and others denounced Teresa's faith as pathological and delusional. Thus, her critics passionately argued that faith in an absent God should play no role in our interpretation of reality and quest to construct a renewed moral order for contemporary life.[26] If even one of the most globally recognized, self-sacrificial *believer's* "experience" of God was really "No One" and "nothing, but emptiness & darkness"—such that she could refer to God as "the Absent One," call heaven "an empty place,"[27] and groan "there is no hope"—why should God play any role in our ethics of new beginning after devastating moral and spiritual ruptures, what Nietzsche called "the problem of morality"?

Within the bounds of this book, this question must be delimited: Why does *Bonhoeffer* think otherwise, that ethics must—indeed, does and can—begin and end with God's own miraculous beginning in creation and Christ, after which we are called to follow and in which we may reliably hope despite our

September 3, 1938 (15:475); Confirmation Sermon on Mark 9:24 from April 9, 1938 (15:479); Notes from Tegel Prison, July 1944 (8:453).

25. Letter to Father Picachy from September 3, 1959, in Mother Teresa, *Mother Teresa*, 193.

26. See Christopher Hitchens, *The Missionary Position: Mother Teresa in Theory and Practice* (London: Verso, 1995); Hitchens, "Mother Teresa and Me," *Vanity Fair*, February 1995; and Hitchens, "Teresa, Bright and Dark" *Newsweek*, August 28, 2007.

27. Letter to Archbishop Périer, March 27, 1956, and February 28, 1957, in Mother Teresa, *Mother Teresa*, 165, 169.

devastations? What, if anything, does Bonhoeffer have to say about the felt absence of God in our world "after all hopes have died"?[28]

To sketch a tentative response to this question, I suggest that we excavate three senses of the statement "God is dead" in Bonhoeffer's thought and with which Bonhoeffer might have interpreted this disturbing phenomenon of divine absence vis-à-vis the problem of new beginnings for ethics, had his life and theological work not been cut short by his execution in 1945.

"God is dead"$_1$ (Idolatry): "We, who out of the faintheartedness of our own lives with their lack of a beginning and an end, cry out to a god who is but our own ego"

First, the statement "God is dead" for Bonhoeffer confronts us with the truth that we have worshiped imaginary idols of our own making and—often through experiences of technological advance, philosophical critique, and cultural rupture—discover their total emptiness and nonexistence. The "God" we want for ourselves is nothing. And the result of this "death" is a paradoxical experience of divine absence or "godlessness" in which the world is evacuated of "divine" presence and we find ourselves alone and left to our own resources. As in chapter 4, here we see again Bonhoeffer's critique of "religion" as fundamentally ambiguous and frequently pernicious, understood as the human attempt to manufacture and manipulate a "God" for our own purposes.[29]

For Bonhoeffer, God is not given to be grasped and used by human creatures—a mere "working hypothesis."[30] As we have seen in *Creation and Fall*, Bonhoeffer stated that "in the beginning" itself could be the first and most fundamental statement of human insecurity and ideology, which rejects the *living* God for "an illusion produced by the fainthearted imagination." He interrogates,

> What does it mean that in the beginning God is? Which God? Your God, whom you make for yourself out of your own need because you need an idol, because do you not wish to live without the beginning, without the end, because being in the middle causes you anxiety? In the beginning, God—that is just your lie, which is not better but even more cowardly than the lie of the evil one. . . . So what sort of statement are these first words of Scripture? An illusion produced by the fainthearted imagination of a person who is unable to live in the middle with pride or with resignation? And are we not all that person—we who out of

---

28. For an earlier interpretation of Bonhoeffer in comparison with Schleiermacher and Barth, see Carl E. Krieg, "The Presence and Absence of God" (PhD Diss., University of Chicago, 1971).

29. See chapter 4, note 158.

30. This is the context in which Bonhoeffer's statement to Bethge in his letter on July 16, 1944, must be interpreted (8:478–79).

the faintheartedness of our own lives, with their lack of a beginning and an end, cry out to a god who is but our own ego?[31]

In this first sense of "God is dead," then, Bonhoeffer paradoxically joins the ranks of the great modern critics of religion like Feuerbach, Marx, Nietzsche, and Freud and insists that most of us—including most Christians, it would seem—"cry out to a god who is but our own ego."[32] We cry out to a "God" to sooth our anxiety, who thus remains little more than a coping mechanism or spiritualized form of self-help inside our idolatrous ego-world without beginning.

Of course, as we have seen, Bonhoeffer's affirmation of this first sense of "God is dead" is not due to his embrace of "atheism" per se but because of his understanding of the transcendence of God and the miracle of revelation. (It is worth remembering that the early Christians were accused of "atheism" for rejecting the idols of the empire and embraced this reputation. Bonhoeffer would undoubtedly follow in this tradition happily.[33]) Thus Bonhoeffer writes, "The meaning [of ex nihilo revelation] for human religious life: There can be no point in human life when we can speak of God as our possession. . . . God is always the One who is to come; that is God's transcendence. One can only have God by expecting God."[34] This claim about the nonpossess-ability of God develops a basic principle that Bonhoeffer articulated in *Act and Being*: "Never is God at the disposal of human beings."[35]

These claims grow out of Bonhoeffer's insistence on the freedom of God or what he calls God's "eternal beginning" beyond human account or control. He writes, "The space that is open to God remains open to the end of time." Thus, on this basis, Bonhoeffer rejects "any general account given by religion" of God, which leads back to his most basic claim explicated in chapter

---

31. *Creation and Fall* (3:29).

32. See Bonhoeffer, quoted in Bergen, *Twisted Cross*, 1: "Those who claim to be building the church are, without a doubt, already at work on its destruction; unintentionally and unknowingly, they will construct a temple to idols." See also Hunter, *To Change the World*, 275.

33. See Justin Martyr, *First Apology* in *The Ante-Nicene Fathers: Translations of the Writings of the Fathers down to A.D. 325*, Vol. 1, ed. Alexander Roberts and James Donaldson (New York: Scribner's Sons, 1905), 165, and *The Martyrdom of Polycarp*, III.2 and XIII.2 in *The Apostolic Fathers*, Vol. II, trans. Kirsopp Lake, Loeb Classical Library (New York: The Macmillan Co., 1923), 317 and 329.

34. "The History of Twentieth-Century Systematic Theology" from winter 1931–1932 (11:229–30). What differentiates Bonhoeffer from a thinker like Jacques Derrida, amid important similarities worth exploring, is that Bonhoeffer actually believes the Messiah *has come* and *will come* again, unlike Derrida's structure of "messianicity" seemingly without a messiah or what Derrida calls "the disappearance of any originary presence" within the economy of "*différance*." See Jacques Derrida, *Dissemination*, trans. B. Johnson (Chicago: University of Chicago Press, 1981), 168, and *Margins of Philosophy*, trans. A. Bass (Chicago: University of Chicago Press, 1982), 67. See Simon Perry, *Resurrecting Interpretation: Technology, Hermeneutics, and the Parable of the Rich Man and Lazarus* (Eugene, OR: Pickwick Publications, 2012), 143.

35. *Act and Being* (2:81).

4: "We should begin with God's own beginning set for us. Nobody knows that in advance; we must each receive it as told us . . . to accept this is the beginning of all genuine theological thinking, to allow space for the freedom of the living God."

Thus, the conclusion for the existence of the human-fabricated "God" is clear: "God is Not-God" because "God as a concept" is merely "an object again."[36] If we interpret "religion" as Bonhoeffer does as the attempt to put God at our disposal, "God is dead." The "God" we want for ourselves is nothing but our own "divine *Doppelgänger*." This takes us back to one of Bonhoeffer's earliest claims about "religion":

> To violate religion means to believe that one possesses it. It is not we who possess God, but rather God who possesses us. It is not human beings who have God at their disposal, but God who has human beings at his disposal. To be religious means to recognize that one can never be religious; to have God means to realize that human beings can never have God.[37]

It was on this basis and with striking continuity that Bonhoeffer in prison welcomed the "development toward the world's coming of age [and its 'religionlessness'], which has cleared the way by eliminating a false notion of God."[38] Bonhoeffer believed that the modern critiques of philosophy, science, and culture could actually "free us to see the God of the Bible, who gains ground and power in the world by being powerless." Here Bonhoeffer interprets modern European incredulity toward God as a positive development, if it functions as a Nietzschean demolition of human idols. Thus, Bonhoeffer continues, "The world come of age is more god-less and perhaps just because of that closer to God than the world not yet come of age."[39]

Bonhoeffer's claim is striking and insightful: true believers should welcome "the world come of age" with its "death of God" because its "godlessness" is a precondition for actually moving "closer to God" over against religious ideology.

This letter, affirming the "elimination" of our "false notion of God," harkens back to and develops Bonhoeffer's thinking in his *Ethics* about "a promising Western godlessness that expresses itself in antireligious and antichurch terms." Here Bonhoeffer paradoxically thinks that this promising Western godlessness

---

36. "The History of Twentieth-Century Systematic Theology" from winter 1931–1932 (11:230–35).

37. Public lecture on "The Tragedy of the Prophets and Its Lasting Meaning" given in Barcelona on November 13, 1928 (10:336).

38. Note Bonhoeffer's earlier letter to Erwin Sutz on April 28, 1934 (13:135): "Nat. [*sic.*] Socialism has brought about the end of the church in Germany and has pursued it single-mindedly. We can be grateful to them."

39. Letter to Bethge on July 16, 1944 (8:478–79). Bonhoeffer made a similar point in a letter to Bethge on June 8, 1944 (8:430).

"thus preserves in a sure though negative way the heritage of genuine faith in God and of a genuine church." From this perspective, "the phenomenon of canceling church membership is not unambiguous" and may actually be a *good* development—"indeed even necessary in certain circumstances"[40]—provided that it reflects this "promising godlessness," which "makes room" for "genuine faith in God" by "eliminating" the empty idols we therapeutically worship.[41]

It must be underscored, then, that for Bonhoeffer this "death of God" and some of our resulting experiences of "God's" absence—what he called a world "come of age" "without God"—is fundamentally positive and to be pursued. This is why Bonhoeffer rejected the "the *salto mortale* [death-defying leaps] back to the Middle Ages" in the face of modernity.[42] His hope was that this modern religious crisis would push us to reject and reach beyond the "god who is but our own ego."

"God is dead"$_2$ (Crucifixion): "God consents to be pushed out of the world and onto the cross"

This condition points to the second sense of "God is dead" in Bonhoeffer's thought, which we can unpack more concisely. For Bonhoeffer, we have pushed the living God out of the world and onto the cross with our idolatry and "violent hands." Human beings—the creatures for whom in the beginning God took the initiative "to greatly increase power"—have become the killers of God.

Thus, the death of God in Christ is the disastrous dénouement of the human hatred of grace in God's beginning and the drive for our own divinized ego concealed in "the murderous law of never-ending beginnings." He writes in *Creation and Fall*, "with the death of Christ on the Cross the nihil negativum was taken into God's own being.—O great desolation! God, yes, God is dead."[43] With the violence of the cross, "the world exhausts its rage on the body of Jesus Christ,"[44] and Jesus becomes "the figure of misery and of pain . . . upon whom humanity's guilt has fallen, pushing Christ into shame and death under God's judgment."[45] In this way, Bonhoeffer argues that "the en-

---

40. Note Bonhoeffer's early statement from a sermon in 1928 (10:254): "Christianity conceals within itself a germ hostile to the church."

41. *Ethics* (6:124). See Martin Kuske, "Hopeless and Promising Godlessness," in *Bonhoeffer's Ethics: Old Europe and New Frontiers* (Kampen, The Netherlands: Kok Pharos Publishing House, 1991), 190–93.

42. Letter to Bethge on July 16, 1944 (8:478). Already in a 1925 school paper on the pneumatological interpretation of Scripture, Bonhoeffer wrote, "None of us can return to a pre-critical time" (9:294). See Feil, *The Theology of Dietrich Bonhoeffer*, 189.

43. *Creation and Fall* (3:35). Bonhoeffer appears to be quoting the hymn of Johannes Rist (1607–1667), "O Traurigkeit, O Herzeleid," which is quoted in Hegel's *Philosophy of Religion*.

44. *Ethics* (6:83).

45. *Ethics* (6:88).

tire world has become godless, and . . . no effort on its part can lift this curse from it." The cross of Christ shows humanity and our world its true "mark," which Bonhoeffer describes as "its unquenchable desire for its own deification," which pushes God out.[46]

This is the conceptual-historical framework in which Bonhoeffer's provocative but precise formulation from prison must be interpreted, as we saw at the end of chapter 4. There he argues, "we cannot be honest unless we recognize that we have to live in the world—'etsi deus non daretur' [as if there were no God]."[47] And rather than some begrudging or blasphemous admission, Bonhoeffer claims, "And this is precisely what we do recognize—before God! God himself compels us to recognize it."[48] The result follows the pattern we saw earlier under the first sense of "God is dead": "Thus our coming of age leads us to a truer recognition of our situation before God." As those who have "pushed [God] out of the world and onto the cross," we are now confronted by an agonizing divine absence, which is simultaneously a paradoxical promise of cruciform presence:

> God would have us know that we must live as those who manage their lives without God. The same God who is with us is the God who forsakes us (Mark 15:34!).[49] The same God who makes us to live in the world without the working hypothesis of God is the God before whom we stand continually. Before God, and with God, we live without God. God consents to be pushed out of the world and onto the cross;[50] God is weak and powerless in the world.[51]

For Bonhoeffer, this is the kind of world we live in: one in which God was not wanted and has been killed by "violent hands." These are the kinds of people we are and what we have done: those who have rejected and killed God. To think of where we are and who we have become any differently, argues Bonhoeffer,

---

46. *Ethics* (6:400–401).

47. See letter to Bethge on March 19, 1944 (8:325) and *Creation and Fall* (3:41, 90, 142). On Bonhoeffer's quotation of Grotius, see Kevin Lenehan, *"Etsi deus non daretur*: Bonhoeffer's Useful Misuse of Grotius' Maxim and Its Implications for Evangelization in the World Come of Age," *The Bonhoeffer Legacy: Australasian Journal of Bonhoeffer Studies* 1, no. 1 (2013): 34–60.

48. See Letter to Renate and Eberhard Bethge on Christmas Eve, 1943 (8:238): "One remains connected to [the absent one] through the emptiness to the extent it truly remains unfilled."

49. See *Ethics* (6:279).

50. See *Ethics* (6:88, 346): "It is the Christ who is unable to find shelter in the world, the Christ of the manger and the cross who is cast out of the world." In prison, Bonhoeffer frequently used this language of God being "pushed out of the world" on the cross. See letter to Bethge on May 29, 1944 (8:405–6); letter to Bethge on June 8, 1944 (426); letter to Bethge on June 30, 1944 (8:450); Notes from Tegel Prison, July 1944 (8:455); Tegel Prison Notes I from July–August 1944 (8:490). Toward the beginning of his career in a sermon on 1 Corinthians 15:17 from April 8, 1928 (10:487), Bonhoeffer wrote, "[Good Friday] is the day on which human beings—human beings who wanted to be like gods—kill the God who became human, the love that became person."

51. Letter to Bethge on July 16, 1944 (8:478–79). See Joseph Sittler, "The Cruciform Character of Human Existence," *The Chicago Lutheran Seminary Record* 54 (October 1949): 19.

would be denial and delusion. A pleasanter picture would be to fall back into "the faintheartedness of our own lives," into religion's "emotional daydreaming," into a "usable Christianity." We live in a world and we live lives burdened and shadowed by this catastrophe, this ultimate violence and spirit of annihilation, this horrific "Saturday" between Friday and Sunday, which has ripped a world torn from its origin *etsi deus non daretur*.

For Bonhoeffer, this is the "truer recognition of our situation before God." Unlike the idols of our own imagination, the living God paradoxically "consents to be pushed out of the world and onto the cross" such that "God is weak and powerless in the world."[52] Bonhoeffer's friend Eberhard Bethge provides a helpful gloss on Bonhoeffer's meaning when he writes, "Before and with the Biblical God we live without the Greek God . . . before and with the concretely crucified God on earth we live without the metaphysical triumphalist God . . . before and with the suffering God we live without the powerful God at our disposal."[53]

This second sense of "God is dead," then, would doubtlessly play a significant role in Bonhoeffer's analysis of the negative but paradoxically revelatory experience of the absence of God in many modern people's lives, including the life of a saint like Mother Teresa, especially after the "form of Christ" had been widely renounced in society. Bonhoeffer himself was not immune to the agony of an order of things that had pushed God out of the world and onto the cross, a world from which Bonhoeffer refused to distance himself and in which he thought the church had earned the "*damnamus*" for contributing to its decay. And thus he himself was able to write in a fragmentary note from prison, "I wait and always disappointment; I'm waiting for God."[54]

"God is dead"₃ (Self-giving): "Christ helps us not by virtue of his omnipotence but rather by virtue of his weakness and suffering"

But it is important to add immediately a third sense of "God is dead" in Bonhoeffer's thought vis-à-vis the problem of felt divine absence. For Bonhoeffer, the death of God means not only that we have fabricated empty idols that do not exist and thus that we have crucified the living God. It also means that God has willingly given Godself as a gift in our place and on our behalf for our new beginning in Christ's death. This act opens to the miracle of resur-

---

52. Sermon on Psalm 63:3 from October 4, 1931 (11:402): "We so often hear and say that religion makes people happy and harmonious and calm and content. That may be right about religion. For God himself, the living God, it is not true, but the very opposite. And that is how it now affects the life of our psalmist. Something within him has been ripped open."
53. Quoted in Christian Gremmels, "Editor's Afterword to the German Edition" (8:590).
54. Notes from Tegel Prison, July 1944 (8:453).

rection, which we explored in Bonhoeffer's practices of new beginning in chapter 5.

In the letter I quoted earlier where Bonhoeffer wrote, "God consents to be pushed out of the world and onto the cross; God is weak and powerless in the world," Bonhoeffer does not stop there but crucially continues, "and in precisely this way, and only so, is [God] at our side and helps us."[55] By willingly suffering with us and for us in our place, Jesus fulfills the messianic vocation described by the prophet Isaiah marked by "taking our infirmities and bearing our diseases" (Isaiah 53:4), what Bonhoeffer calls *Stellvertretung*. As the messianic servant, "Christ helps us not by virtue of his omnipotence but rather by virtue of his weakness and suffering."

For Bonhoeffer, this claim amounts to "the crucial distinction between Christianity and all religions." Whereas "human religiosity" only directs "people in need to the power of God in the world, God as deus ex machina," the God that Bonhoeffer thinks is "but our own ego," biblical faith does something different. It "directs people toward the powerlessness and suffering of God." Indeed, this is how God "helps" us, by going before us and setting the salvific precedent of self-giving love after which we are called to follow, even if this means suffering and death for us as well. This is the place where Bonhoeffer makes his famous statement "only the suffering God can help."[56] Thus, Bonhoeffer repeats his claim that "the world's coming of age," by "eliminating a false notion of God," actually "frees us to see the God of the Bible" for the first time, the God of "strange glory" who "gains ground and power in the world by being powerless."[57]

This letter follows the same pattern as Bonhoeffer's *Ethics*, where he argues that "the cross of reconciliation sets us free to live before God in the midst of the godless world, sets us free to live in genuine worldliness." Precisely in the world's "godlessness" (that is, the crucifixion of Jesus), the world has been "reconciled with God" through Christ's free act of sacrifice for us in our place.[58] This passage, in turn, merely develops Bonhoeffer's earlier claim in *Ethics* that "the abyss of the love of God . . . takes responsibility for godlessness, love for hate, the holy one for the sinner." God's love embraces, absorbs, and ultimately overwhelms violence and hate in Christ. If this is true, then "there is no more godlessness, hate, or sin that God has not taken upon himself, suffered, and atoned." In the wake of God's self-giving

---

55. See the poem "Christians and Heathens" from July 8, 1944 (8:461).
56. See *Life Together* (5:169–70).
57. Letter to Bethge on July 16, 1944 (8:478–79). It would be interesting and fruitful to compare Bonhoeffer's notion of God's "power . . . by being powerless" with Vaclav Havel's ideas in *The Power of the Powerless: Citizens against the State in Central Eastern Europe* (London: Routledge, 1985).
58. *Ethics* (6:400–401).

love, "there is no longer any reality, any world, that is not reconciled with God and at peace," at least from the point of view of the beginning and the end by faith.[59]

In each of these passages, Bonhoeffer's claim is that, as much as the cross was the ultimate atrocity committed by humanity against the Giver of life and thus the most horrifying evil, it was also the most radical manifestation of the love of God and thus a *felix culpa*, indeed, the fundamentally *new* beginning that fulfills the precedent of the first beginning: God willingly gives the free gift of God's self for others beyond their right or request for love and new life. Christ's life, death, and resurrection were all gratuitous grace.

The paradox of the death of Christ in Bonhoeffer's interpretation, then, is that God himself has freely embraced this suffering and death—being "pushed out of the world"—in our place and on our behalf. And it is this free initiative that opens the way of redemption for us, who left to ourselves are God's enemies. From this perspective, Bonhoeffer makes the revaluating argument that "suffering is holy" and "the suffering man is the likeness of God,"[60] at least insofar as we participate in the self-giving love of God with and for others.[61]

Thus, Bonhoeffer's paradoxical claim seems to be this: To live with the living God, the God of the beginning in creation and the new beginning made decisively on Christ's cross, is to live, suffer, and die with the one who allows himself to suffer, die, and be pushed out of the world. In order to bear witness to this God, indeed, to experience and live in the "strange" presence of this God, finite human creatures must also bear witness to and participate in God's suffering and death in the form of Christ.[62] With Christ, we are called to bear witness to the paradox of love that we live in a god-less world without God for others and, only in that way, in the presence of God.[63]

This is what Bonhoeffer means when he continues to develop his thought from prison in the same letter quoted earlier and here worth quoting at length:

"Christians stand by God in God's own pain"—that distinguishes Christians from heathens. "Could you not stay awake with me one hour?" Jesus asks in

---

59. *Ethics* (6:83).

60. Sermon on 2 Corinthians 12:9 from London 1934 (13:403).

61. Thus, amid his honest statements about living "without God" and "as if there were no God," Bonhoeffer is able to write in one of his last letters to Bethge from August 23, 1944 (8:515) that "God is near and present with us" and thus that we have "an utterly new life" because "nothing is impossible for God."

62. Sermon on 2 Corinthians 5:20 from October 22, 1933 (13:325) and *Ethics* (6:67).

63. See Kendal Walser Cox, "Liturgy, Kenosis, and Creation: Bonhoeffer and Lacoste on Being before God without God in the World," in *Ontology and Ethics: Bonhoeffer and Contemporary Scholarship*, ed. Adam C. Clark and Michael G. Mawson (Eugene, OR: Pickwick Publishing, 2013), 118–32.

Gethsemane. That is the opposite of everything a religious person expects from God. The human being is called upon to share in God's suffering at the hands of a godless world. Thus we must really live in that godless world and not try to cover up or transfigure its godlessness somehow with religion. Our lives must be "worldly," so that we can share precisely in God's suffering; our lives are *allowed* to be "worldly," that is, we are delivered from false religious obligations and inhibitions. . . . It is not a religious act that makes someone a Christian, but rather sharing in God's sufferings in the worldly life. That is *metanoia*, not thinking first of one's own needs, questions, sins, and fears but allowing oneself to be pulled into walking the path that Jesus walks, into the messianic event, in which Isa. 53 is now being fulfilled![64]

Based on this meditation, it seems probable that Bonhoeffer would interpret Mother Teresa and her agonized faith in an experientially absent God as an exemplar of this "staying awake" with Jesus in the Gethsemane of Calcutta's slums, not for an hour but for forty years. If Bonhoeffer would have any criticism for Teresa, it would likely be that she felt the need "to cover up" and keep secret her "blasphemous" experience of "godlessness" across her adult life, perhaps because of her own "religious inhibitions and obligations" as a pious missionary. I suspect that Bonhoeffer would both understand and critique this secrecy, and perhaps in some way help a faithful believer like Mother Teresa experience a more honest and less traumatic relationship with the God, who both loves us and seemingly abandons us as we follow the crucified Christ in our world torn from its origin.

With his repeated claim that the believer should be willing to give up his or her salvation for the other, Bonhoeffer would doubtlessly have affirmed Mother Teresa's paradoxical self-understanding as "a saint of darkness" and her private mission statement: "I will be continually absent from Heaven—to light the light of those in darkness on earth."[65]

"So Where Is Any Room Left for God?"

This third sense of "God is dead," then, provides Bonhoeffer's paradoxical and poignant answer to his pressing question in prison, "So where is any room left for God?" The "room" of God, the house of God's presence—however disturbing, undesirable, or even repulsive to sensibilities habituated in comfort, self-preservation, and self-promotion—is somehow found in "sharing in God's suffering at the hands of a godless world." God's

---

64. Letter to Bethge on July 16, 1944 (8:479). See *Ethics* (6:66, 241).

65. Mother Teresa, *Mother Teresa*, 230. It is worth noting that Bonhoeffer rejected any pursuit of "sainthood" and saw it as distracting from authentic faith and service. See Letter to Eberhard Bethge on July 21, 1944 (8:486).

presence is found in "being pulled along into the—messianic—suffering of God in Jesus Christ," in (re)discovering love for "what we exert ourselves to grow beyond" and "leave behind."[66] For Bonhoeffer, God's presence is given in suffering, in the self-giving love of the renewed intercessory self that begins again and welcomes, waits on, and responds to the sufferings and death of others in a world torn from its origin. This, as we have seen in chapter 5, is what Bonhoeffer called the "new life in being there for others."

This "room for God" clearly takes us back to the fundamental touchstone of Bonhoeffer's thought, which follows from his founding conviction that God loves the nothing in creation and gives his life for the enemy sinner in Christ's death. This is Bonhoeffer's radical revaluation, in which "Christianity preaches the infinite worth of that which is seemingly worthless and the infinite worthlessness of that which is seemingly so valued."[67] God is found where we often least expect God or assume that God is most absent.

Thus, if we ask in our late modern, godless world, "Where is any room left for God?," Bonhoeffer's life and writings compose an elegy of answers that flow out of his revaluating theological ethics of new beginning. God is found in a life of welcoming, waiting on, and responding to

children and . . . the morally and socially least of these, those viewed as less worthy[68]

the socially despised, the outcasts, the tax collectors, the deceivers, and the prostitutes[69]

the unrighteous, the foolish, the sinners[70]

the eternally disregarded, the eternally insignificant, the weak, ignoble, unknown, the least of these, the oppressed and despised . . . the houses of the prostitutes and tax collectors . . . the working, toiling, sinning masses[71]

Lazaruses of all the ages . . . you outcasts and outlaws, you victims of society, you men and women without work, you broken down and ruined, you lonely and abandoned, rape victims and those who suffer injustice, you who suffer in body and soul[72]

---

66. *Ethics* (6:84).
67. "Jesus Christ and the Essence of Christianity" from 1928 in Barcelona (10:352, 354).
68. "Jesus Christ and the Essence of Christianity" from 1928 in Barcelona (10:350).
69. "Jesus Christ and the Essence of Christianity" from 1928 in Barcelona (10:351).
70. "Jesus Christ and the Essence of Christianity" from 1928 in Barcelona (10:353).
71. "Jesus Christ and the Essence of Christianity" from 1928 in Barcelona (10:354).
72. Sermon on Luke 16:19–31 from May 29, 1932 (11:445).

the child, the fool, the crucified one—a strange assortment of people, of saviors of humanity, of revolutionaries[73]

poor people, ill people, insane people—people who cannot help themselves but who have just to rely on other people for help, for love for, for care[74]

a cripple, a hopelessly ill man, a socially exploited man, a coloured man in a white society, an untouchable.[75]

This claim must be clear: Bonhoeffer gives the surprising, unsettling, and ultimately inspiring answer that "Jesus Christ, God himself, speaks to us from every human being." The other person, "this enigmatic, impenetrable You," is truly "God's claim on us." Bonhoeffer argues that such a revaluated "gaze opens to the fullness of the divine life in the world." By following after Christ's beginning in love for all people, "life in the human community acquires its divine meaning."

The conclusion of this radical revaluation unveils, then, that "I am for you, you are for me God's claim, God himself," in some mysterious way. After this new beginning, we are welcomed into the trust that "God is with us long as there is community," even as we enter into the "messianic event" of Christ's death with and for others, and are sometimes left waiting with disappointment on God.[76] As he wrote from prison, bearing the penalty for his own practice of the theological ethics of new beginning in a totalitarian world torn from the origin, "our relationship to God is a new life in 'being there for others,' through participation in the being of Jesus. The transcendent is not the infinite, unattainable task, but the neighbor within reach in any given situation. God in human form! . . . 'the human being for others'! therefore the Crucified One."[77]

Bonhoeffer's argument about where God can be found in our world with all of its disturbing absence reverberates in Mother Teresa's own later confessions. Amid her excruciating spiritual agonies and godforsakeness, Mother Teresa also spoke about where she found "room for God" and thus how she was able to remain faithful to what she described earlier in her life as a call "to begin a thing which will bring me for the most part only suffering."[78] She testified to her private confessor, "When I walk through the slums or enter the dark holes, there Our Lord is always really present . . . the streets, Kalighat, slums & Sisters have become places where He lives His own life of

---

73. Sermon on John 8:32 from July 24, 1932 (11:467).
74. Sermon on 2 Corinthians 12:9 from London 1934 (13:402).
75. Sermon on 2 Corinthians 12:9 from London 1934 (13:403)
76. Sermon on Matthew 28:20 from April 15, 1928 (10:492, 494–95).
77. "Outline for a Book" (8:501).
78. Letter to Archbishop Périer on January 13, 1947, in Mother Teresa, *Mother Teresa*, 51.

love to the full."[79] Like Bonhoeffer, Mother Teresa went into these "slums" and "dark holes"—tangible instances of Arendt's "holes of oblivion" whose extreme suffering doubtlessly contributed to her excruciating experience of God's absence—with her eyes wide open. She knew and confessed, "All beginners have their many crosses."[80]

CONCLUSION: "THIS IS FOR ME THE END, BUT ALSO THE BEGINNING"

For Bonhoeffer, if we want to find God and thus the sourcing ground, guide, and energy of the ethics of new beginning, which can sustain our faith in the goodness of existence, the love-worthiness of life with others in the world, and thus our capacity to remain lovers who give up on no one within the scope of universal entry, this is the path. This revaluating, self-giving love even to the point of suffering and death is the way of the new beginning in a godforsaken world that has pushed the God of the beginning out for idols and the spirit of annihilation. This "new life in being there for others" is the "dawning of the new world" in our "old world" convulsed with "the advent of nihilism" (Nietzsche) "after all hopes have died" (Arendt) in which we know "never such innocence again" (Glover) and face "the fate worse than death" (Lear).

Perhaps this new beginning is the ethics that many late modern humans want least and resist most of all. We are immersed in a swirling ocean of consumerism, dogmatic secularism, religious fundamentalism, popular nihilism, institutionalized racism, pervasive logics of instrumentalism, and routine and numbing violence that destroy the lives of innumerable others. So many of the fundamental forces and structures of our global order tell us to use our powers of beginning for the sake of self-preservation and self-promotion—for the sake of ourselves and our tribe.

In our time after the beginning, Bonhoeffer's imaginative description of the Bible's beginning and the beginning of our world has enduring power: the place "where our most impassioned waves of thinking break, are thrown back upon themselves, and lose their strength in spray and foam."[81] This "new life in being there for others" is "the beginning that [we] want and cannot want,"[82] which humans torn from their origin rage against and build sophisticated religious, economic, cultural, military, and political systems to

---

79. Letter to Archbishop Périer from June 21, 1950, and November 17, 1956, in Mother Teresa, *Mother Teresa*, 168.

80. Letter to Mother Pauline on November 9, 1948, in Mother Teresa, *Mother Teresa*, 129.

81. *Creation and Fall* (3:25).

82. *Creation and Fall* (3:27).

suppress and subvert. In the face of decision and the call of responsibility, this is the new beginning that we sedate and stall with ambivalence and deferral posing as religious piety and moral seriousness.[83] We resist the beginning in which God's presence is found in the beginning to greatly increase the power of others, in practices of welcoming, waiting on, and serving "that which is seemingly worthless" out of a love that will "give up no man" and hopes self-transcendently in a new beginning that only God can initiate beyond human power for all of God's children in universal entry.

This call of love and responsibility remains the crux of Bonhoeffer's ethics of new beginning in our late modern world as it "looks for new and unprecedented itineraries,"[84] confronted as we are with the absence of God and the hope for a new beginning after all hopes have died. This hope and its new beginning is not ultimately a matter of the crashing waves of thought coming to secure stillness in a shimmering ocean of reasons. It is the loving risk of "a new life in being there for others" embraced by a "people who have been placed on the path and now cannot do otherwise"[85]—those who "see their brother's face as if they were seeing God's face," even in the face of Eyob.[86]

> This is for me the end, but also the beginning . . .
> I believe in the principle of our Universal Christian brotherhood
> which rises above all national hatreds
> and that our victory is certain.[87]

---

83. See Letter to the Finkenwalde Brothers from November 20, 1938 (15:82): "We think that we are acting particularly responsibly when every few weeks we reconsider the question of whether the path on which we've started was the right one. Here it's especially striking that such 'responsible examination' always commences just when serious difficulties become evident." See Kierkegaard, *Works of Love*, 35: "How remarkable! What struggle is so protracted, so terrifying, so involved as self-love's war to defend itself?"

84. Taylor, *A Secular Age*, 755. Note MacIntyre, *After Virtue*), xvi, and Gutierrez, *A Theology of Liberation*, 206.

85. "Meditation on Psalm 119" from winter 1939–1940 (15:498).

86. Sermon on Genesis 32:25–32; 33:10 from March 13, 1932 (11:432).

87. Bonhoeffer's last words given to Sigismund Payne Best for Bishop Bell on the day of his execution, April 9, 1945 (16:468).

Beginning Anew

I began this book by exploring the many ways in which beginning is fundamental to the world and human life. I then spent the next few hundred pages
exploring Bonhoeffer's ethics of new beginning after devastation in dialogue
with four other thinkers. I want to end now by offering a short summary of
the book's key claims and practical implications as we receive the gift and
responsibility of making new beginnings today.

We are all beginners who spend our entire lives making seemingly endless
beginnings. We discover how important our beginnings are as we remember
our births, grow in freedom, celebrate memorials, reflect on the origins of the
universe, suffer the anguish of evil initiatives, long for new beginnings, and
decide how best to practice our powers of beginning in our lives, relationships, and vocations in a suffering world. Our nature as beginners is essential
to our identity as singular persons and our freedom as moral agents. It is also
fundamental to our nature as storied creatures of memory and hope who live
our lives in the present between past and future with historical consciousness.

Beginning is the most precious gift of God to humanity. In it we discover
the gratuitous goodness of existence and that life in the world with others is
worthy of universal love. Our thinking becomes thanking.

But beginning is also perhaps the most pernicious temptation that we face
in life. In so many ways and circumstances, we lust to position ourselves as
autonomous beginners who can make our own beginnings for ourselves and
thus achieve the illusion of self-creation. We strive to be sovereign authors
who authorize our identity, governing narrative, and moral order with our
own authority.

Bonhoeffer passionately argues and our own experiences often powerfully
confirm that this temptation—*Discover your beginning for yourself!*—is dishonest, misleading, and often devastating. When we greedily grasp to possess

our beginnings and fabricate self-sufficiency, we forget how our lives are given to us as gifts before us from others by birth in a world we did not create. We deny our dependency and disregard how existence finds meaning and goodness in being shared with others. More often than we recognize or care to admit, our beginnings diminish and damage others, sometimes becoming violent and animated by a spirit of annihilation, as if we were the only ones in the world.

Paradoxically, our drive to make beginnings for ourselves terminally ages toward death, and our efforts to fabricate new lives and a new world frequently contribute to radicalizing the old lives and world that we resent, hate, and seek to remake anew. Thus, we find ourselves questioning whether it is good to exist, whether life in the world with others is worthy of love, and what our overall take on reality should be. We vertiginously travel a twilit valley of temptation between "impure thinking" and "a curse against existence."

Beginning is the most precious gift of God given to us as beginners. Beginning is also the most pernicious temptation we face in life.

After the devastations of our beginnings, how are we to begin again and rediscover the goodness and love-worthiness of life in the world with others?

To make a genuinely new beginning, Bonhoeffer argues that we must start by giving up our beginnings to God, who is the first and ultimate Beginner. Our first act must be to give back to God the most fundamental gift that we have received from Him: our beginning. This is the paradoxical, gift-giving way for making truly new beginnings rather than false starts that fatally age our lives and world toward devastation and death.

In Bonhoeffer's theology, God's beginning is most basically emplotted in the story of Scripture. In creation, God creates a beginning for literal nothings and nobodies as gift. In Christ, God takes on humanity and sacrificially makes a new beginning of redemption for sinners and enemies on the cross. And in the resurrection, God promises to make an ultimate new beginning for the dead and gone who have returned to nothing.

In these intensifying divine initiatives, we discover the radical love of God to welcome and renew finite human life and the material world. And through these divine initiatives, God's way of beginning provides precedents and an ever-clarifying plot to ground, guide, and energize our limited beginnings as finite moral agents in creation.

Thus, we are called by God to embrace the posterior posture of *followers*, those who make our beginning by answering Christ's call, "Follow me!" In Bonhoeffer's ethics, this call to a new beginning is grounded and guided by Christ's command of neighbor-love, which Christ himself embodies in his vicarious representative action for us. Our beginnings of neighbor-love then get enacted within God's mandates for institutional life in the family, education, culture, and politics. In the form of Christ, all of our beginnings are called to embody "a new life in being there for others."

But this new beginning is not easy. It requires strenuous, unceasing practice and discipline in the new, self-transcending life of welcoming, waiting upon, and responding to others in love and responsibility. If our prime temptation is to put ourselves first and to begin by and for ourselves, then our renewal and rehabilitation must take the form of "paradoxically passive action": putting others first through practiced initiatives of being there for others. This should not be misunderstood as acquiescence or blindly submitting to the abuse and violence of others. But giving priority to others and practically embodying Christ's form of service, sacrifice, and suffering for others is the only way to make a genuinely new beginning and thus also to cultivate the discernment for knowing when to resist the destructive beginnings of others.

In Bonhoeffer's ethics of new beginning, we discovered six beautiful practices that can provide guidance and energy for our lives as beginners today.

In baptism, we embrace "a grace-filled death" and receive God's miraculous gift of new birth and the promise of resurrection. The old self with its drive to begin for itself is crucified, and Christ's new life in being there for others is commenced. Thus, the waters of baptism should work as a healing antidote to racism, sexism, ablism, tribalism, and other forms of exclusion and violence. As we make a new beginning founded in God's will to redeem all people, we must also join God in resisting the structures and institutions of the old world that devastate God's beloved image-bearers.

In prayer, we practice listening for God and our neighbors. We relinquish the sovereign position of knowers and controllers, and we open ourselves up to others outside ourselves and beyond our agendas. We learn to attune ourselves to others and their needs and afflictions, and we intercede for them before God. In our speech and theology, as we listen and intercede, we begin to discern the new language of God that is right and relevant for our time and place. Thus, the practice of prayer works as a healing antidote to resentment, confusion, and hatred as we bathe in the cleansing waters of intercession not only for friends but also for enemies, those who offend, harm, and even seek to destroy our lives with their initiatives. The faces of the strange, far off, and offensive become familiar, near to us, and held in affection as we repeatedly lift them up to God.

In repentance, confession, and forgiveness, we practice "ultimate honesty" toward ourselves in our fallenness, fallibility, and failures. Self-deception and pride are relinquished, and we relearn to see ourselves humbly as sinners and "Christs," who are called by God to receive and give Christ's liberating forgiveness in community. The offenses and wrongs of the past are released, and the present opens to a new future retrained in honesty, kindness, and a commitment to the well-being of others. Through this repentant practice, mentalities and habits of superiority, exclusion, and hatred are broken and overcome with "a new brotherhood of guilt" and love.

In service, resistance, and suffering, we learn to live a practical life of help for others. This can take the most ordinary forms of assisting others in their daily needs and extend to the most extreme cases of opposing political violence to the point of tyrannicide. Throughout this practice, we are trained to renounce comfort, safety, and cowardly piety and to embrace a self-giving love for the needs of others, even to the point of personal sacrifice and suffering. In this way, we are prepared and stand ready to actively oppose powerful initiatives that glory in greatness, call for our allegiance, and promise a new order but only lead to violence and the devastation of God's mandates.

In gratitude, we learn to give thanks throughout our lives. Our memory is awakened to the blessings of our past. Our complaining is overcome with thankfulness and infused with generosity in community. Our vision of life is transfigured with a new mindfulness for the gifts of God in all things, and we discover the limits of responsible action. We tap into a wellspring of love for God and others even during times of hardship and suffering. Our will to live is strengthened when we are tempted to despair and can only see destruction. In gratitude, our thinking turns to thanking.

In witnessing the resurrection, we practice celebrating and embracing earthly life. We learn to recognize the eternal value of individuals. We are given new hope to endure suffering and times of devastation. We are energized with confidence to face the fact that we are dying and with the courage to oppose ideologies that promise "earthly eternities." We retrain ourselves to trust that God will be faithful to his promise of making a new beginning for our world freed from hatred, violence, suffering, and evil. We grow in grit to make good of our beginnings in baptism, prayer, service, repentance, and gratitude. We experience joy that in our end is our beginning for eternity as we live a new life in being there for others, even to the point of death.

For Bonhoeffer and for us today, these practices of new beginning must start with Christians in our local communities and then extend far beyond them for the common good. The new beginning of Christ is not obvious or easy, and it is all too often overtaken by our statement "Let me first" with our good intentions. Often without even recognizing it, our new beginning of following after Christ detours into the old paths of indifference, exclusion, hatred, and violence against others.

We confront a sobering historical case of how the church can easily follow false starts and be animated by "the spirit of annihilation" in the disturbing facts that few Christians in Bonhoeffer's Nazi Germany had the courage to resist Hitler, the majority of German theologians gave their oath of allegiance to Hitler, and a prominent Christian journal published a celebration of Hitler's fiftieth birthday in which it proclaimed: "The *Führer*, powerfully fighting his way through old worlds, seeing with his mind's eye what is new and compelling its realizations, is named on those few pages of world history that are reserved for the initiators of a new epoch. . . . The figure of the *Führer* has brought a new obligation for the church too."[1]

In the wake of devastating experiences of poverty, humiliation, and insecurity between the World Wars, German Christians forgot and conveniently reinterpreted the revaluating meanings of baptism, prayer, repentance, service, gratitude, and witness to the resurrection. And thus, rather than pressing deeper into Christ's sovereign call to a new life in being there for others, the majority of Christians were silent, complicit, or actively loyal to a murderous regime that annihilated over six million of their neighbors. The church, which claimed Christ's name and believed itself to be following Christ's founding command "Follow me!," often did not even realize that it had embraced the satanic temptation of making its own beginning and joined its hands with the violent hands of Cain.

This example from recent history must seize and sober us as beginners today in the twenty-first century, confronted as we are by old and new anxieties, animosities, and dangers of annihilation, both local and global. As Peter Maas warned in *Love Thy Neighbor: A Story of War*, "When the call of the wild comes, the bonds of civilization turn out to be surprisingly weak, professors turn into nutcases, and everything that a generation built up can be destroyed in a day or two, often by the generation that built it."[2]

If we are not vigilant, the waters of baptism will dry, and we will carry on with our old undead lives of suspicion, resentment, ethnocentrism, nationalism, and violence. Prayer will routinize into a mindless piety that stops listening for God and interceding for others, especially those who are different, offensive, or opposed to us. Repentance will be privatized, confession of sin will fall silent, and forgiveness will sedate our guilty consciences. If we are not vigilant, our service will grow lazy, get shifted onto others, and become an excuse to privilege the powerful without suffering. Gratitude will mutate into impure thinking that forgets others, overlooks suffering, and justifies narcissism, consumerism, and hedonism. Witnessing the resurrection will transform into spiritualized escapism, indifference to the value of others' earthly lives, and a religious justification for triumphalist ideologies promising earthly eternities and ecological destruction.

---

1. Quoted in Bethge, *Dietrich Bonhoeffer*, 648.
2. Peter Maas, *Love Thy Neighbor: A Story of War* (New York: Knopf Doubleday, 1997), 15.

If we are not vigilant, Christians who claim the name of Christ will continue living as loyal initiates of the old way and our churches as institutions of the old world. If we are not vigilant, we too will remain silent, give our oaths of allegiance, and join those who promise "new realities" in a "new epoch" but only leave behind fields of corpses and the wreckage of war. The result is what Bonhoeffer called "useable Christianity" and a "church-not-worthy-to-be-church"—an antichurch of "no risk-taking for others." Thus, if we are not vigilant, "Christians" will perversely lend doubt to the convictions that it is good to exist, that life with others in the world should be loved, and that this goodness and love should pulse as the heart of our overall take on human life for all people.

The Yale legal scholar Jack Balkin observed, "In almost every creedal community—every community that organizes itself around a set of practices and beliefs inherited from the past—a return to origins and to basic principles is a standard method for urging reform, and especially radical reform."[3] That is very much the intention of this book.

Beginning is wondrous. It is the most precious gift that we have received from God by nature as beginners. But it is also the most pernicious temptation that we face in life. To make a genuinely new beginning, we must repeatedly regift our beginnings to God and answer Christ's command "Follow me!" Rather than another badge of identity within the security of our religious tribe, Christ must remain our sovereign Beginner who endlessly leads us back into a new life in being there for others without excuse or exclusion. Thus, we must work out our beginnings with fear and trembling, knowing that it is God who began before us and God who promises never to stop until he begins all things again in the new world of the resurrection.

In any other initiative, we are condemned to the murderous law of never-ending beginnings. But following after the divine initiative of Christ, we may begin again in life and love without end—universal entry, the open house of heaven.

And it is only the beginning of the new life, an eschatological prolepsis, where the You reveals itself to the I as another I, as heart, as love, as Christ.[4]

---

3. Balkin, *Living Originalism*, 97.
4. *Sanctorum Communio* (1:213).

Appendix

Bonhoeffer's Last Words

A Personal Testament and Theological Summary?

In chapter 5, I suggested that Bonhoeffer's last words—"This is for me the end, but also the beginning"[1]—may have been a personal mission statement for Bonhoeffer and something he planned to say at his death. Here I show how frequently this idea (with direct linguistic or merely conceptual connection) appears throughout Bonhoeffer's work from 1926 to 1945.

Address for a children's worship service on November 22, 1926 (9:507): "[Jesus] told us that everything is *not at an end when we die; instead, everything really begins anew.*"

Barcelona sermon on August 26, 1928 (10:519): "Lord, teach me that my days will end and that my life has a final goal and that I must then depart . . . *the end of the world—is the beginning of something new, of eternity.*"

"The Theology of Crisis and Its Attitude toward Philosophy and Science" from Union Theological Seminary 1930–1931 (10:476): "*Here at the end we stand again where we stood in the beginning* [with God]."

"The Right to Self-Assertion" from February 4, 1932 (11:257): "The church believes in all seriousness, in a time of the deepest ideological division, that it can and may stand there *where ideologies reach their end and something new and ultimate begins.*"

---

1. See Letter from S. Payne Best to George K. A. Bell on October 13, 1953 (16:468). Bethge, *Dietrich Bonhoeffer*, 927, records Bonhoeffer's last words to Best as, "This is the end—for me the beginning of life." According to Best, "He gave me this message twice in the same words, holding my hand firmly in his and speaking with emotional earnestness." See Best, *The Venclo Incident: A True Story of Double-Dealing, Captivity, and a Murderous Nazi Plot* (New York: Hutchinson & Co., 1950), 200.

Creation and Fall, 1933 (3:21): "The new is the real end of the old; the new, however, is Christ. . . . Only the church, which knows the end, knows also the beginning. . . . The church therefore *sees the beginning only in dying, from the viewpoint of the end.*"

London sermon on November 26, 1933 (13:334–35): "*That life only really begins when it ends here on earth*, that all that is here is only the prologue before the curtain goes up—that is for the young and old alike to think about."

London sermon from 1934 (13:400) [originally in English]: "Man's plans are crossed by God's way and this crossing *points to that place* in the world where all human desires, ideas and ways were crossed by God's way—it points to the Cross . . . —*man's end—God's beginning*; man's crucifixion—God's kingdom."

Sermon draft on September 1935 (14:772–73): "But in reality, that [dying] is *not death but life. Only there do we really begin to live.* . . . 'The beginning, the end, O Lord, are yours' [Fritz Reuter]."

Bible study on Temptation at a retreat in Zingst, June 20–25, 1938 (15:401): "But precisely here, *where the human being loses everything, where hell reveals openly all its horror, life has begun for the believer.*"

Reflections on Easter from 1940 in newsletter of the Pomeranian Council of Brethren (16:473–74): "But God, who alone accomplished salvation for us— 'all this is from God' (2 Cor. 5:18)—*raised Christ from the dead. That was the new beginning that followed the end as a miracle from on high.*"

Untitled, unfinished novel from prison between 1943–1944 (7:157): "'*This is the end*,' he said softly. A deep, calm voice behind me said, '*Perhaps it's a better beginning.*'"

Letter to Eberhard Bethge on August 21, 1944 (8:515): "What is certain is that in suffering lies hidden the source of our joy; *in dying, [lies hidden] the source of our life.*"

In Paul Lehmann's letter to Timothy Lehmann on July 17, 1939 (15:253), Paul writes, "*The times of the end are really the time of the only possible beginning.*" Because this letter was about Bonhoeffer and written immediately after Bonhoeffer's decision to return to Germany, which Bonhoeffer discussed with Lehmann, it is conceivable that Lehmann is borrowing language that Bonhoeffer may have used to describe his momentous decision. This is all the more likely because we have evidence (discussed earlier) that Bonhoeffer made similar statements in mid-1938 and early 1940 before and after Bonhoeffer's decision and Lehmann's letter.

It is on the basis of these thirteen pieces of evidence that I propose that Bonhoeffer's final words—"This is for me the end, but also the beginning"—on April 8, 1945, may have been premeditated and encapsulate the heart of Bonhoeffer's theological vision. This confession evokes the devastation of sin ("the end"$_1$) and the costly ("come and die") nature of Christ's call to follow ("the end"$_2$), as well as the promise of new beginnings when we embrace the "new life in being there for others" ("the beginning"$_1$) and hope in Christ's resurrection ("the beginning"$_2$). This seems all the more likely if Bonhoeffer said these words *twice* to Best moments before his death, as Best attests, which indicates that Bonhoeffer wanted Best to remember his final message exactly.

Bibliography

WRITINGS OF DIETRICH BONHOEFFER

The following is a chronological list of Bonhoeffer's writings referred to in this study. The number at the end of each entry refers to the volume in which the work can be found. See "Citations and Abbreviations" at the beginning of this book for bibliographic information on each volume.

Diary from 1924 (9).

Seminar paper on "Luther's Feelings about His Work as Expressed in the Final Years of His Life Based on His Correspondence of 1540–1546" from summer 1925 (9).

Seminar paper "Can One Distinguish between a Historical and a Pneumatological Interpretation of Scripture, and How Does Dogmatics Relate to This Question?" from the summer of 1925 (9).

Sermon on Psalm 127:1 from May 20, 1926 (9).

Sermon on Luke 17:7–10 on October 18, 1925 (9).

Paper "The Holy Spirit according to Luther" from February 1926 (9).

Sermon on James 1:21–25 from summer of 1926 (9).

Paper on "Frank's View of Spirit and Grace" from November 19, 1926 (9).

Address on Luke 12:35ff from November 22, 1926 (9).

Children's Address on Psalm 23:7 from November 29, 1926 (9).

Address on John 19 from April 15, 1927 (9).

Sanctorum Communio: A Theological Study of the Sociology of the Church accepted on July 18, 1927, by Reinhold Seeberg for Bonhoeffer's licentiate in theology at the University of Berlin; first published in abbreviated form on September 2, 1930 (1).

Catechetical Exam on Matthew 8:5–13 from November 10, 1927 (9).

Sermon on Luke 9:51–56 from late 1927 (9).

Journal from 1928 (10).

Sermon on Romans 11:6 from March 11, 1928 (10).

Sermon on 1 Corinthians 15:17 from April 8, 1928 (10).

Sermon on Matthew 28:20 from April 15, 1928 (10).

Sermon on Matthew 7:1 from June 24, 1928 (10).

Sermon on Psalm 62:2 from July 15, 1928 (10).

Sermon on 1 Corinthians 12:26–27 on July 29, 1928 (10).

Sermon from Barcelona on July 29, 1928 (10).

Sermon on Matthew 5:8 from August 12, 1928 (10).

Sermon on 1 John 2:17 from August 26, 1928 (10).

Sermon on Luke 17:33 from October 21, 1928 (10).

Lecture "The Tragedy of the Prophetic and Its Lasting Meaning" from November 13, 1928 (10).

Sermon on Revelation 3:20 from December 2, 1928 (10).

Lecture "Jesus Christ and the Essence of Christianity" on December 11, 1928 (10).

Lecture "Basic Questions of a Christian Ethic" from February 1929 (10).

Letter to Helmut Rößler from February 23, 1930 (10).

Catechesis in the Second Theological Examination on the Fifth Petition of the Lord's Prayer from June 29, 1930 (10:560).

Examination paper "What Is Paul's View on Earthly Suffering?" from July 5, 1930 (10:386).

Seminar paper on "The Theology of Crisis and Its Attitude toward Philosophy and Science" from 1930–1931 (10).

Act and Being: Transcendental Philosophy and Ontology in Systematic Theology accepted as Bonhoeffer's Habilitationsschrift at the University of Berlin on July 12, 1930; published in September 1931 (2).

Sermon for the Second Theological Examination on 1 Thessalonians 5:16–18 from July 20, 1930 (10).

Lecture on "The Anthropological Question in Contemporary Philosophy and Theology" from July 31, 1930 (10).

Paper on "The Character and Ethical Consequences of Religious Determinism" from 1930–1931 (10).

Lecture on "War" from 1930–1931 (10).

Essay "The Theology of Crisis and Its Attitude to Philosophy and Science" from 1930–1931 (10).

Letter to Paul Lehmann on August 23, 1931 (11).

"Report on a Conference of the World Alliance in Cambridge" from September 1931 (11).

Sermon on Psalm 63:3 from October 4, 1931 (11).

Letter to Erwin Sutz on October 8, 1931 (11).

Letter to Helmut Rößler on October 18, 1931 (11).

Sermon on Luke 12:35–40 from November 29, 1931 (11).

Student notes from lecture course "The History of Twentieth-Century Systematic Theology" given at the University of Berlin during the winter semester of 1931–1932 (11).

"Draft for a Catechism" published in 1932 (11).

"On Karl Heim's *Glaube und Denken*" published in 1932 (12).

"Concerning the Christian Idea of God" from 1932 (10).

Lecture course on "The Nature of the Church" given at the University of Berlin in the spring of 1932 (11).

Lecture on "The Right to Self-Assertion" from February 4, 1932 (11).

Sermon on Luke 4:3–4 from February 4, 1932 (11).

Sermon on Matthew 24:6–14 from February 21, 1932 (11).

Seminar "Is There a Christian Ethic?" given at the University of Berlin during the summer semester of 1932 (11).

Sermon on Genesis 32:25–32; 33:10 from March 13, 1932 (11).

Sermon on 2 Chronicles 20:12 on May 8, 1932 (11).

Letter to Erwin Sutz on May 17, 1932 (11).

Sermon on Luke 16:19–31 from May 29, 1932 (11)

Sermon on Colossians 3:1–4 from June 19, 1932 (11).

"On the Theological Foundation of the Work of the World Alliance" from July 26, 1932 (11:361).

"Welcoming Address" in Ciernohorské Kúpele from July 1932 (11).

Sermon on John 8:32 from July 24, 1932 (11).

Untitled address at the International Youth Conference in Gland on August 29, 1932 (11).

Baptism sermon on Ephesians 5:14 from October 1932 (11).

Essay on "Thy Kingdom Come! The Prayer of the Church-Community for God's Kingdom on Earth" from November 1932 (12).

Sermon on Revelation 2:4–5, 7 from November 6, 1932 (12).

"Personal Confession (according to the Large Catechism)" from December 21, 1932 (14).

Lecture course on Dogmatic Exercise on "Theological Anthropology" given at the University of Berlin in the winter of 1932–1933 (12).

Lecture course "Theological Anthropology" given at the University of Berlin in the winter of 1932–1933 (12).

Lecture course "Creation and Sin" given at the University of Berlin in the winter of 1932–1933; published as *Creation and Fall: A Theological Exposition of Genesis 1–3* in autumn of 1933.

Dietrich Bonhoeffers Hegel-Seminar 1933: Nach den Aufzeichnungen von Ferenc Lehel (International Bonhoeffer Forum 8). Edited by Ilse Tödt. Munich: Chr. Kaiser, 1988.

Student Notes from Lecture Course "Review and Discussion of New Publications in Systematic Theology" from the winter semester of 1932–1933 (12:201).

Discussion paper for the Ecumenical Conference in Dassel on "The Concept of Confession from the Standpoint of the Concept of Truth" from 1933 (12).

Essay "The Church and the Jewish Question" from 1933 (12).

"What Is Church?" from January 1933 (12).

Sermon on Matthew 8:23–27 from January 15, 1933 (12).

"The Führer and the Individual in the Younger Generation" from February 1933 (12).

"Lectures on Christology" given at the University of Berlin during the summer of 1933 (12).

Draft of "The Bethel Confession" from August 1933 (12).
Letter to Julie Bonhoeffer on August 20, 1933 (12).
Sermon on 2 Corinthians 5:20 from October 22, 1933 (13).
Sermon on 2 Corinthians 5:10 from November 19, 1933 (13).
Sermon on Wisdom 3:3 from November 26, 1933 (13).
Essay "What Should a Student of Theology Do Today?" from November 1933 (12).
Sermon on Luke 21:28 from December 3, 1933 (13).
Sermon on Luke 1:46–55 from December 17, 1933 (13).
Sermon on 2 Corinthians 12:9 from London 1934 (13).
"Beginning with Christ," Sermon on Luke 9:57–62 from January 1, 1934 (13).
Letter to Karl-Friedrich Bonhoeffer on January 13, 1934 (13).
Letter to Erwin Sutz on April 28, 1934 (13).
"The Church and the Peoples of the World" for Fanø Conference from summer of
    1934 (13).
Letter to Julie Bonhoeffer on May 22, 1934 (13).
Sermon on 1 Corinthians 2:7–10 from May 27, 1934 (13).
Baptismal Homily on Joshua 24:15 from June 1934 (13).
Letter to Hildegard Lämmerhirdt from July 1934 (13).
Letter to George Bell on July 31, 1934 (13).
Letter to Bishop Ammundsen from August 8, 1934 (13).
Letter to Erwin Sutz on September 11, 1934 (12).
Sermon on 1 Corinthians 13:1–3 from October 14, 1934 (13).
Sermon on 1 Corinthians 13:4–7 from October 21, 1934 (13).
Sermon on 1 Corinthians 13:8–12 from October 28, 1934 (13).
Bonhoeffer's Homiletical Exercise on Mark 4:26–29 from 1935 (14).
"Morning blessing. Devotion" from summer 1935 (14).
Sermon on Psalm 42 from June 2, 1935 (14).
Letter to Leonard Hodgson from July 18, 1935 (14).
"Homily for Personal Confession on Proverbs 28:13" from summer 1935 (14).
Essay on "The Confessing Church and the Ecumenical Movement" from August
    1935 (14).
Lecture on "Contemporizing the New Testament" from August 23, 1935 (14).
Sermon on Matthew 18:21–35 from November 17, 1935 (14).
"Second Letter from Finkenwalde" from November 29, 1935 (14).
"Lecture on Catechesis" from late 1935 (14).
"Lecture on Pastoral Care" from 1935–1936 (14).
Homiletical Exercise on Luke 21:25–36 from 1935–1937 (14).
Homiletical Exercise on Revelation 22:1–5 from 1935–1937 (14).
"Baptismal Homilies" from 1936–1937 (14).
"Lecture on Homiletics" from 1936 (14).
Theses on "Personal Confession and Lord's Supper" from 1936 (14).
Practical Exercise on 1 Corinthians 15:12–19 from 1936 (14).
Practical Exercise on 1 Corinthians 15:20–28 from 1936 (14).
"Notes on the Concept of 'Sin'" from January 9, 1936 (15).
"Lecture on Catechesis" from January 1936 (14).

Letter to Elizabeth Zinn from January 27, 1936 (14).

Student notes on lecture section on Service to God and Service to One Another from early 1936 (14).

Statement on February 28, 1936, "From the Preachers' Seminary to the Provisional Administration of the German Evangelical Church" (14).

Letter to Philipp Cromwell from early 1936 (14).

Letter to Ernst Cromwell on March 27, 1936 (14).

"On the Question of Church Communion" from April 1936 (14).

Wedding sermon on 1 Thessalonians 5:16–18 from April 15, 1936 (14).

"Statement at Pentecost!" from 1936 (14).

Letter to Rüdiger Schleicher on April 8, 1936 (14).

"The Reconstruction of Jerusalem according to Ezra and Nehemiah" from April 21, 1936 (14).

"Guide to Daily Meditation" from May 22, 1936 (14).

Sermon outline on Revelation 1:9–20 from June 24, 1936 (14).

Letter to Wolfgang Staemmler on June 27, 1936 (14).

Wedding Sermon on John 13:34 from July 18, 1936 (14).

Letter to Bethge on July 31, 1936 (14).

Presentation on "The Inner Life of the German Evangelical Church" from August 5, 1936 (14).

Lecture on "Concrete Ethics in Paul" from October 1936 (14).

Lecture "Confirmation Instruction Plan" likely from October 1936 (14).

Sermon on Revelation 2:1–7 from October 25, 1936 (14).

Lecture fragment on the "Doctrine of the Holy Spirit" from late 1936 (14).

Student notes from Bonhoeffer's outline on "Funeral Homilies" from 1936–1937 (14).

Transcription of Lecture on the Catalogue of Vices from 1937 (14).

Lecture on "Congregational Development and Church Discipline in the New Testament" from March 1937 (14).

Sermon on Matthew 26:45b–50 from March 14, 1937 (14).

"The Space of the Church Proclamation and of Its Confession" from April 18–September 11, 1937 (14).

Sermon on Psalm 58 from July 11, 1937 (14).

Publication of *Discipleship* in November 1937 (4).

Letter to Karl-Friedrich Bonhoeffer on November 29, 1937 (14).

Letter to the Finkenwalde Brothers on December 27, 1937 (15).

Homiletical Exercise on 2 Timothy Chapter 3 from 1938 (15).

"Lecture on Pastoral Counseling" from March 1938 (15).

Bible Study on Temptation from June 20–25, 1938 (15).

Confirmation Sermon on Mark 9:24 from April 9, 1938 (15).

"The Letter to Timothy. Chapter 1" from summer 1938 (15).

Bible Study on Temptation from June 1938 (15).

Untitled Notes on the Concept of Temptation from June 1938 (15).

Untitled Bible Study on Temptation from June 1938 (15).

Life Together written between September and October 1938 (5); published in 1939.

Sermon on Romans 5:1–5 from September 3, 1938 (15).

"Exercises in Pastoral Epistles" from 1938 (15).

Lecture on "Our Path According to the Testimony of Scripture" from October 26, 1938 (15).

Letter to the Finkenwalde Brothers on November 20, 1938 (15).

"Notes on Death" from 1938–1939 (15).

Notes on the Concept of "Gratitude" from winter 1938–1939 (15).

"Theological Letter on Christmas" from 1939 (15).

Draft for a Worship Service on 2 Corinthians 2:14, 6:10, 6:1 on February 25, 1939 (15).

Diary from New York from summer 1939 (15).

Diary from New York in June 1939 (15).

Letter from Paul Lehmann to Timothy Lehmann on July 17, 1939 (15).

"Protestantism without Reformation" from August 1939 (15).

"Meditation on Christmas" from December 1939 (15).

"Meditation on Psalm 119" from 1939–1940 (15).

Prayerbook of the Bible published in 1940 (5).

Lecture outline on "Theology and the Congregation" from 1940 (16).

"*On the Lord's Supper*: A Guide to the Study of Article 7 of the Lutheran Formula of Concord" from 1940 (15).

Sermon on John 10:11–16 from January 1940 (15).

Sermon for the Lector on Matthew 2:13–23 from January 1940 (15).

Sermon on John 3:16–21 from February 20, 1940 (15).

Reflection on "Resurrection" from March 1940 (16).

Letter to Ruth Roberta Stahlberg on March 23, 1940 (16).

"The Ascension of Jesus Christ: A Reflection on Its Christological, Soteriological, and Parenetical Meaning" from April 1940 (16).

Reflection "On Gratitude among Christians" from July 26, 1940 (16).

Sermon on Isaiah 9:6–7 from Christmas 1940 (16).

Letter to Paula Bonhoeffer on December 28, 1940 (16).

Ethics (unfinished) written from 1940–1943 (6).

Essay "State and Church" probably from 1941 (16).

Essay "The Best Physician" from January 1941 (16).

Letter to Bethge from February 14, 1941 (16).

"Thoughts on William Paton's Book *The Church and the New Order*" from September 1941 (16).

Letter to Erwin Sutz on September 21, 1941 (16).

Letter to Christoph Bethge on November 17, 1941 (16).

"Co-Report on the 'Reflection on the Question of Baptism' in Reference to the Question of Infant Baptism" from 1942 (16).

"'Personal' and 'Objective' Ethics" likely from the summer of 1942 (16).

Letter to the Leibholz Family from May 21, 1942 (16).

Letter to Gustav Seydel on June 23, 1942 (16).

Letter to Bethge from June 25, 1942 (16).

Letter to Ernst Wolf on September 13, 1942 (16).

Letter to Max Diestel on November 5, 1942 (16).

Finkenwalde Circular Letter from December 1942 (16:378).

"After Ten Years" from Christmastime 1942 (8).

Letter to Maria von Wedemeyer on January 17, 1943 (16).

Letter to Maria von Wedemeyer on January 24, 1943 (16).

Letter to Maria von Wedemeyer on March 24, 1943 (16).

Wedding Sermon for Renate and Eberhard Bethge on May 15, 1943 (8).

Letter to Manfred Roeder on June 10, 1943 (16).

Letter to Maria von Wedemeyer on August 9, 1943 (92).

Letter to Bethge on November 18, 1943 (8).

Letter to Bethge on November 21, 1943 (8).

Letter to Bethge on November 26, 1943 (8).

Letter to Bethge on December 5, 1943 (8).

Letter to Bethge on December 19, 1943 (8).

Letter to Bethge on December 22, 1943 (8:236)

Letter to Renate and Eberhard Bethge on December 24, 1943 (8).

Letter to Maria von Wedemeyer from December 24, 1943 (92).

Untitled prison drama from Christmas 1943 (7).

Letter to Renate and Eberhard Bethge on Christmas Eve, 1943 (8).

Undated letter to Maria von Wedemeyer in 1944 (92).

"Outline for a Book" from 1944 (8).

Letter to Maria von Wedemeyer from January 2, 1944 (92).

Letter to Renate and Eberhard Bethge on January 23, 1944 (8).

Letter to Bethge on February 1, 1944 (8).

Letter to Bethge from February 12, 1944 (8).

Letter to Bethge on March 9, 1944 (8).

Letter to Bethge from March 19, 1944 (8).

Letter to Bethge on March 24, 1944 (8).

Letter to Bethge on April 11, 1944 (8).

Letter to Bethge on April 22, 1944 (8).

Letter to Maria von Wedemeyer from April 23, 1944 (92).

Letter to Bethge on April 30, 1944 (8).

"Thoughts on the Day of Baptism of Dietrich Wilhelm Rüdiger Bethge" from May 1944 (8).

Letter to Bethge on May 5, 1944 (8).

Letter to Bethge on May 16, 1944 (8).

Letter to Bethge on May 20, 1944 (8).

Letter to Bethge on May 29, 1944 (8).

Letter to Bethge on June 8, 1944 (8).

Daily Text Meditation from June 7–8, 1944 (16).

Poem on "The Past" from June 1944 (92).

Letter to Bethge on June 27, 1944 (8).

Letter to Bethge from June 30, 1944 (8).

"Exposition on the First Table of the Ten Words of God" from June or July 1944 (16).

Prison poem "Night Voices" from April–July 1944 (8).

Poem "Christians and Heathens" from July 8, 1944 (8).

Letter to Bethge on July 16, 1944 (8).

Letter to Bethge on July 21, 1944 (8).
Letter to Bethge on July 28, 1944 (8).
Notes from Tegel Prison, July 1944 (8).
Tegel Prison Notes I from July–August 1944 (8).
Tegel Prison Notes II from July–August 1944 (8).
"Outline for a Book" from early August 1944 (8).
Letter to Bethge on August 10, 1944 (8).
Letter to Bethge from August 23, 1944 (8).
Bonhoeffer's last words on April 8, 1945 (16).
S. Payne Best, letter to George K. A. Bell on October 13, 1953 (16).
The Collected Sermons of Dietrich Bonhoeffer: Volume 1. Edited by Isabel Best. Minneapolis, MN: Fortress Press, 2012.
The Collected Sermons of Dietrich Bonhoeffer: Volume 2. Edited by Victoria Barnett. Minneapolis, MN: Fortress Press, 2017.
The Bonhoeffer Reader. Edited by Clifford Green and Michael DeJonge. Minneapolis, MN: Fortress Press, 2013.

SECONDARY WORKS WITH REFERENCE TO BONHOEFFER

Barker, H. Gaylon, "Editor's Introduction to the English Edition," in *Theological Education at Finkenwalde: 1935–1937*. Edited by H. Gaylon Barker and Mark Brocker. Translated by Douglas Stott. Minneapolis, MN: Fortress Press, 2013.
Barnes, Kenneth C. "Dietrich Bonhoeffer and Hitler's Persecution of the Jews." In *Betrayal: German Churches and the Holocaust*, edited by Robert Ericksen and Susannah Heschel. Minneapolis, MN: Fortress Press, 1999.
Barth, Frederike. *Die Wirklichkeit des Guten: Dietrich Bonhoeffers "Ethik" and ihr philosophischer Hintergrund*. Tübingen: Mohr Siebeck, 2011.
Benktson, Benkt-Erik. *Christus und die Religion: Der Religionsbegriff bei Barth, Bonhoeffer und Schleiermacher*. Stuttgart: Valver, 1967.
Bethge, Eberhard. *Dietrich Bonhoeffer: A Biography*. Revised edition. Minneapolis, MN: Fortress Press, 2000.
———. "Turning Points in Bonhoeffer's Life and Thought." In *Bonhoeffer in a World Come of Age*, edited by Peter Vorkink. Philadelphia, PA: Fortress Press, 1968.
Blackburn, Vivienne. *Dietrich Bonhoeffer and Simone Weil: A Study in Christian Responsiveness*. Bern: Peter Lang AG, European Academic Publishers, 2004.
Brocker, Mark S. "The Community of God, Jesus Christ, and Responsibility: The Responsible Person and the Responsible Community in the Ethics of Dietrich Bonhoeffer." PhD Diss., University of Chicago, 1996.
Brown, Petra. "Bonhoeffer, Schmitt, and the State of Exception." *Pacifica: Australasian Theological Studies* 26, no. 3 (2013): 246–64.
Busch, Kirsten Nielsen, Ralf Karolus Wüstenberg, and Jens Zimmermann, eds. *Dem Rad in die Speichen fallen: das Politische in der Theologie Dietrich Bonhoeffers*. Gütersloh: Gütersloher Verlag, 2013.

Butler, William Warren. "A Comparison of the Ethics of Emil Brunner and Dietrich Bonhoeffer: With Special Attention to the Orders of Creation and the Mandates." PhD Diss., Emory University, 1970.

Corbic, Arnaud. *Camus et Bonhoeffer: Recontre de Deux Humanismes.* Geneve: Labor et Fides, 2002.

Cox, Kendal Walser. "Liturgy, Kenosis, and Creation. Bonhoeffer and Lacoste on Being before God without God in the World." In *Ontology and Ethics: Bonhoeffer and Contemporary Scholarship*, edited by Adam C. Clark and Michael G. Mawson. Eugene, OR: Pickwick Publishing, 2013.

Christian, Albini. *Il Male: Risvegliare L'umano in Hannah Arendt e Dietrich Bonnhoeffer.* Cengia VR, Italy: Gabrielli Editori, 2016.

Dahill, Lisa. "Probing the Will of God: Bonhoeffer and Discernment." *Dialog* 41, no. 1 (Spring 2002): 42–49.

———. *Reading from the Underside of Selfhood: Bonhoeffer and Spiritual Formation.* Princeton Theological Monograph Series 95. Eugene, OR: Pickwick Publications, 2009.

DeJonge, Michael P. "Bonhoeffer's Concept of the West." In *Bonhoeffer and Politics.* Frankfurt: Peter Lang, 2011.

———. *Bonhoeffer's Reception of Luther.* New York: Oxford University Press, 2017.

———. *Bonhoeffer's Theological Formation: Berlin, Barth, and Protestant Theology.* New York: Oxford University Press, 2012.

Destrempes, Sylvain. *Thérèse de Lisieux et Dietrich Bonhoeffer: Kénose et Altérite.* Paris: Cerf, 2002.

"Dietrich Bonhoeffer (1906–1945)—Jesus Christ and the Restoration, Preservation and Reconciliation of Creation." In *Creation and Salvation*, Volume 2: *A Companion on Recent Theological Movements* (Studien zur Religion und Umwelt), edited by Ernst M. Conradie. Zurich: LIT Verlag, 2012.

Dreß, Walter. "Religiöses Denken und christliche Verkündigung in der Theologie Dietrich Bonhoeffer." In *Theologia Viatorum* 14 (1997–1998): 35–61.

Elliston, Clark. *Dietrich Bonhoeffer and the Ethical Self: Christology, Ethics, and Formation.* Minneapolis, MN: Fortress Press, 2016.

Elshtain, Jean Bethke. *Sovereignty: God, State, and Self.* New York: BasicBooks, 2008.

———. *Who Are We? Critical Reflections and Hopeful Possibilities.* Grand Rapids, MI: Eerdmanns, 2000.

Feil, Ernst. *The Theology of Dietrich Bonhoeffer.* Translated by Martin Rumscheidt. Philadelphia, PA: Fortress Press, 1985.

Floyd, Wayne Jr. "Christ, Creation, and Concreteness in the Early Bonhoeffer." *Union Seminary Quarterly Review* 39 (1984): 101–14.

———. *Theology and the Dialectics of Otherness: On Reading Bonhoeffer and Adorno.* Lanham, MD: University Press of America, 1988.

Frick, Peter. "Nietzsche and Bonhoeffer." In *Bonhoeffer's Intellectual Formation: Theology and Philosophy in His Thought* (Religion in Philosophy & Theology), edited by Peter Frick. Tubingen: Mohr Siebeck, 2008.

Geyer, Alan. "Creation and Politics in Bonhoeffer's Thought." *Church and Society* (July/August 1995): 93–100.

Green, Clifford. *Bonhoeffer: A Theology of Sociality.* Grand Rapids, MI: Eerdmans, 1999.

———. "Pacifism and Tyrannicide: Bonhoeffer's Christian Peace Ethic." *Studies in Christian Ethics* 18, no. 3 (December 2005): 31–47.

———. "Two Bonhoeffers on Psychoanalysis." In *A Bonhoeffer Legacy*, edited by A. J. Klassen. Grand Rapids, MI: Eerdmans, 1981.

Gregersen, Niels Henrik. "The Mysteries of Christ and Creation: 'Center' and 'Limit' in Bonhoeffer's *Creation and Fall* and *Christology* Lectures." In *Mysteries in the Theology of Dietrich Bonhoeffer: A Copenhagen Bonhoeffer Symposium*, edited by Kirsten Busch, Ulrik Nissen, and Christiane Tietz, 135–58. Göttingen: Vandenhoeck and Ruprecht, 2007.

Gregor, Brian. "Following-After and Becoming Human: A Study of Bonhoeffer and Kierkegaard." In *Becoming Human, Being Human: Dietrich Bonhoeffer and Social Thought*, edited by Jens Zimmermann and Brian Gregory. Eugene, OR: Wipf and Stock, 2010.

———. "Shame and the Other: Bonhoeffer and Levinas on Human Dignity and Ethical Responsibility." In *Ontology and Ethics: Bonhoeffer and Contemporary Scholarship*, edited by Adam C. Clark and Michael G. Mawson. Eugene, OR: Pickwick Publishers, 2013.

Greggs, Tom. "Pessimistic Universalism: Rethinking the Wider Hope with Bonhoeffer and Barth." *Modern Theology* 26, no. 4 (October 2010): 495–510.

———. *Theology Against Religion: Constructive Dialogues with Bonhoeffer and Barth.* London: T & T Clark, 2011.

Gremmels, Christian. "Religionless Christianity." In *Encyclopedia of Christianity Online*. Brill Online, 2012.

de Gruchy, John. *Confessions of a Christian Humanist.* Minneapolis, MN: Fortress Press, 2006.

———. "The Reception of Bonhoeffer's Theology." In *The Cambridge Companion to Dietrich Bonhoeffer*, edited by John de Gruchy. New York: Cambridge University Press, 1999.

———. "Resistance, Democracy, and New Realities: Bonhoeffer's Political Witness Then and Now." Paper presented at XI International Bonhoeffer Congress, Sigtuna, Sweden, June 27–July 1, 2012.

de Gruchy, John, Stephen Plant, and Christiane Tietz, eds. *Dietrich Bonhoeffers Theologia heute: Ein Weg zwischen Fundamentalismus und Säkularismus?* Gütersloher Verlagshaus, 2009.

Hand, Robert. "Dietrich Bonhoeffer on Prelapsarian Anthropology: Creation, 'Freedom,' and Boundaries." *Crux* (Regent College, Vancouver) 42, no. 3 (Fall 2006): 37–50.

Harrison, Peter. *The Fall of Man and the Foundations of Science.* Cambridge: Cambridge University Press, 2007.

Hauerwas, Stanley. "Dietrich Bonhoeffer." In *The Blackwell Companion to Political Theology*, edited by Peter Scott and William Cananaugh. Malden, MA: Blackwell Publishing, 2004.

Hennecke, Susanne. "Reading Bonhoeffer's *Creation and Fall* from a Gender-Theoretical Perspective." *Sino-Christian Studies* 6 (December 2008).

Kahl, Brigitte. "Church for Others: Bonhoeffer, Paul, and the Critique of Empire." In *Interpreting Bonhoeffer: Historical Perspectives, Emerging Issues*, edited by Clifford Green and Guy Carter. Minneapolis, MN: Fortress Press, 2013.

Kaltenborn, Carl-Jürgen. *Adolf von Harnack als Lehrer Dietrich Bonhoeffers*. Berlin: Evangelische Verlag Anst., 1973.

Kirkpatrick, Matthew. *Attacks on Christendom in a World Come of Age: Kierkegaard, Bonhoeffer, and the Question of "Religionless Christianity."* Princeton Theological Monographs. Eugene, OR: Pickwick Publications, 2011.

———. "Bonhoeffer, Kierkegaard, and the Teleological Suspension of the Ethical: The Beginning or End of Ethics." In *Ontology and Ethics: Bonhoeffer and Contemporary Scholarship*, edited by Adam C. Clark and Michael G. Mawson. Eugene, OR: Pickwick Publications, 2013.

———, ed. *Engaging Bonhoeffer: The Impact and Influence of Bonhoeffer's Life and Thought*. Minneapolis, MN: Fortress Press, 2016.

Krieg, Carl E. "The Presence and Absence of God." PhD Diss., University of Chicago, 1971.

Kuske, Martin. "Hopeless and Promising Godlessness." In *Bonhoeffer's Ethics: Old Europe and New Frontiers*. Kampen, The Netherlands: Kok Pharos Publishing House, 1991.

de Lange, Fritz. *Waiting for the Word: Dietrich Bonhoeffer on Speaking about God*. Translated by Martin N. Walton. Grand Rapids, MI: Eerdmans, 2000.

Lenehan, Kevin. *"Etsi deus non daretur*: Bonhoeffer's Useful Misuse of Grotius' Maxim and Its Implications for Evangelization in the World Come of Age." *The Bonhoeffer Legacy: Australasian Journal of Bonhoeffer Studies* 1, no. 1 (2013): 34–60.

Lovin, Robin. "The Mandates in an Age of Globalization." In *Ontology and Ethics: Bonhoeffer and Contemporary Scholarship*, edited by Adam C. Clark and Michael G. Mawson. Eugene, OR: Pickwick Publishing, 2013.

Marsh, Charles. "Eric Metaxas's Bonhoeffer Delusions." October 18, 2018. www.religionandpolitics.org.

———. "Human Community and Divine Presence: Bonhoeffer's Theological Critique of Hegel." *Scottish Journal of Theology* (Winter 1992).

———. *Reclaiming Dietrich Bonhoeffer*. New York: Oxford University Press, 1994.

———. *Strange Glory: A Life of Dietrich Bonhoeffer*. New York: Knopf, 2014.

Mathewes, Charles T. *Evil and the Augustinian Tradition*. New York: Cambridge University Press, 2007.

———. "A Tale of Two Judgments: Bonhoeffer and Arendt on Evil, Understanding, and Limits, and the Limits of Understanding Evil." *Journal of Religion* 80, no. 3 (July 2000).

McBride, Jennifer. *The Church for the World: A Theology of Public Witness*. Reprint edition. New York: Oxford University Press, 2014.

McGarry, Joseph. "Dietrich Bonhoeffer and *Apocatastasis*: A Challenge to Evangelical Reception." Paper presented at the annual meeting of the American Academy of Religion. San Francisco, California, November 19–22, 2011.

Metaxas, Eric. *Bonhoeffer: Pastor, Martyr, Prophet, Spy: A Righteous Gentile vs. the Third Reich*. Nashville, TN: Thomas Nelson, 2010.

Moses, John A. "Bonhoeffer's Germany: The Political Context." In *The Cambridge Companion to Dietrich Bonhoeffer*, edited by John de Gruchy. New York: Cambridge University Press, 1999.

Nickson, Ann L. *Bonhoeffer on Freedom: Courageously Grasping Reality*. Ashgate New Critical Thinking in Religion, Theology, and Biblical Studies. London: Ashgate, 2002.

Nielson, Paul George. "The Concepts of Responsibility and Vocation in the Theological Ethics in Dietrich Bonhoeffer." PhD Diss., University of Chicago, 1998.

Nissen, Ulrik Becker. "Being Christ for the Other." *Studia Theologica* 64, no. 2 (December 2010): 177–98.

Pangritz, Andreas. *Karl Barth in the Theology of Dietrich Bonhoeffer*. Translated by Barbara and Martin Rumscheidt. Grand Rapids, MI: Eerdmans, 2000.

———. "Mystery and Commandment in Leo Baeck's and Dietrich Bonhoeffer's Thinking." *European Judaism: A Journal for the New Europe* (Autumn 1997): 44–57.

Plant, Stephen, and Ralf K. Wüstenberg, eds. *Religion, Religionlessness and Contemporary Western Culture: Explorations in Dietrich Bonhoeffer's Thought*. Frankfurt am Main: Peter Lang, 2008.

Pugh, Jeffrey C. *Religionless Christianity: Dietrich Bonhoeffer in Troubled Times*. London: T & T Clark, 2008.

Rasmussen, Larry. "Bonhoeffer: Ecological Theologian." In *Bonhoeffer and Interpretive Theory: Essays on Methods and Understanding*, edited by Peter Frick. Frankfurt am Main: Peter Lang, 2013.

———. *Earth Community, Earth Ethics*. Maryknoll, NY: Orbis, 1997.

———. *Earth-Honoring Faith: Religious Ethics in a New Key*. New York: Oxford University Press, 2015.

Reynold, Dianne. *The Doubled Life of Dietrich Bonhoeffer: Women, Sexuality, and Nazi Germany*. Eugene, OR: Cascade, 2016.

Robinson, Marilynne. *The Death of Adam: Essays on Modern Thought*. London: Picador, 2005.

Rosner, Brian. "Bonhoeffer on Disappointment." In *The Consolation of Theology*, edited by Brian Rosner. Grand Rapids, MI: Eerdmans, 2008.

Schliesser, Christine. *Everyone Who Acts Responsibly Becomes Guilty: Bonhoeffer's Concept of Accepting Guilt*. Louisville, KY: Westminster John Knox Press, 2008.

Schmitz, Florian. *"Nachfolge": zur Theologie Dietrich Bonhoeffers*. Göttingen: Vandenhoeck & Ruprecht, 2013.

———. "Only the Believers Obey, and Only the Obedient Believe: Notes on Dietrich Bonhoeffer's Biblical Hermeneutics with Reference to Discipleship." In *God Speaks to Us: Dietrich Bonhoeffer's Biblical Hermeneutics*, edited by Ralf K. Wüstenberg and Jens Zimmermann. Frankfurt: Peter Lang, 2013.

Schödl, Albrecht. *"Unsere Augen sehen nach dir": Dietrich Bonhoeffer im Kontext einer aszetischen Theologie*. Leipzig: Evangelische Verlagsanstalt, 2006.

Schwerin Rowe, Terra. *Toward a Better Worldliness: Ecology, Economy, and the Protestant Tradition*. Minneapolis, MN: Fortress Press, 2017.

Scott, Peter Manley. "Postnatural Humanity? Bonhoeffer, Creaturely Freedom and the Mystery of Reconciliation in Creation." In *Mysteries in the Theology of Dietrich Bonhoeffer: A Copenhagen Bonhoeffer Symposium*, edited by Kirsten Busch, Ulrik Nissen, and Christiane Tietz. Göttingen: Vandenhoeck and Ruprecht, 2007.

Strohm, Christian. *Theologische Ethik im Kampf gegen den Nationalsoziailsmus*. München: C. Kaiser, 1989.

Tietz-Steiding, Christiane. *Bonhoeffers Kritik der verkrümmten Vernunft. Eine erkenntnistheoretische Untersuchung*. Tübingen: Mohr Sibeck, 1999.

Tietz, Christiane, and Jens Zimmermann, eds. *Bonhoeffer, Religion and Politics*. Fourth International Bonhoeffer Colloquium. Frankfurt: Peter Lang, 2012.

Tödt, Heinz Eduard. "Conscience in Dietrich Bonhoeffer's Ethical Theory and Practice." In *Bonhoeffer's Ethics: Old Europe and New Frontiers*. Kampen, The Netherlands: Kok Pharos Publishing House, 1991.

van den Heuvel, Steven C. *Bonhoeffer's Christocentric Theology and Fundamental Debates in Environmental Ethics*. Eugene, OR: Pickwick, 2017.

van Hoogstraten, Hans-Dirk. "Europe as Heritage: Christian Occident." In *Bonhoeffer's Ethics: Old Europe and New Frontiers*. Kampen, The Netherlands: Kok Pharos Publishing House, 1991.

von Uwe, Gerrens. *Medizinisches Ethos und Theologische Ethik: Karl und Dietrich Bonhoeffer in der Auseinandersetzung um Zwangssterilisation und "Euthanasie" im Nationalsozialismus*. München: Oldenbourg, 1996.

Weikart, Richard. "Scripture and Myth in Dietrich Bonhoeffer." *Fides et Historia* 25 (1993): 12–25.

———. "So Many Bonhoeffers." *Trinity Journal* 32 NS (2011): 69–81.

Weizsäcker, Carl Friedrich von. "Thoughts of a Non-Theologian on Dietrich Bonhoeffer's Theological Development." *Ecumenical Review* 29, no. 2 (April 1976): 156–73.

Wüstenberg, Ralf K., and Jens Zimmermann, eds. *God Speaks to Us: Dietrich Bonhoeffer's Biblical Hermeneutics*. International Bonhoeffer Interpretations. Frankfurt am Main: Peter Lang GmbH, Internationaler Verlag der Wissenschaften, 2013.

Young III, Josiah Ulysses. *No Difference in Fare: Dietrich Bonhoeffer and the Problem of Racism*. Grand Rapids, MI: Eerdmans, 1998.

Zerner, Ruth. "Dietrich Bonhoeffer and the Jews: Thoughts and Actions, 1933–1945." *Jewish Social Studies* 37, no. 2–4 (Summer–Fall 1975): 235–50.

Zimmermann, Jens. "Finitum Capax Infiniti or the Presencing of Christ: A Response to Stephen Plant and Robert Steiner." In *God Speaks to Us: Dietrich Bonhoeffer's Biblical Hermeneutics*, edited by Ralf Wüstenberg and Jens Zimmerman. Frankfurt: Peter Lang, 2013.

Zimmermann, Jens, et al. *Bonhoeffer and Continental Thought: Cruciform Philosophy*. Indiana Series in the Philosophy of Religion. Indianapolis, IN: Indiana University Press, 2009.

OTHER WORKS CITED

Adkins, Arthur. "Cosmogony and Order in Ancient Greece." In *Cosmogony and Ethical Order*, edited by Robin W. Lovin and Frank E. Reynolds. Chicago: University of Chicago Press, 1985.

Agamben, Giorgio. "*Auctoritas* and *Potestas*." In *State of Exception*, translated by Kevin Attell. Chicago: University of Chicago Press, 2005.

Alexander, Michelle. *The New Jim Crow: Mass Incarceration in the Age of Colorblindness*. New York: New Press, 2012.

Andolsen, Barbara Hilkert. "Agape in Feminist Ethics." In *Feminist Theological Ethics*, edited by Lois K. Daly. Louisville, LA: Westminster John Knox Press, 1994.

Angehrn, Emil, ed. *Anfang und Ursprung: Die Frage nach dem Ersten in Philosophie und Kulturwissenschaft*. Berlin: de Gruyter, 2007.

Arendt, Hannah. *Between Friends: The Correspondence of Hannah Arendt and Mary McCarthy 1949–1975*. Edited by Carol Brightman. New York: Harvest Books, 1996.

———. *Between Past and Future: Eight Exercises in Political Thought*. New York: Penguin, 2006.

———. *Eichmann in Jerusalem: A Report on the Banality of Evil*. New York: Penguin Books, 2006.

———. *The Human Condition*. Second edition. Chicago: University of Chicago Press, 1998.

———. "Labor, Work, Action." In *The Portable Hannah Arendt*, edited by Peter Baehr. New York: Penguin, 2000.

———. *Lectures on Kant's Political Philosophy*. Edited by Ronald Beiner. Chicago: University of Chicago Press, 1992.

———. *The Life of the Mind*. Edited by Mary McCarthy. One-volume edition. New York: Harcourt, 1978.

———. *Love and Saint Augustine*. Edited by Judith Chelius Stark and Joanna Vecchiarelli Scott. Chicago: University of Chicago Press, 1996.

———. *Men in Dark Times*. New York: Harcourt, 1968.

———. *On Revolution*. New York: Viking, 1969.

———. *On Violence*. New York: Harcourt, 1972.

———. *The Origins of Totalitarianism*. New York: Schocken Books, 2004.

———. *The Promise of Politics*. Edited by Jerome Kohn. New York: Schocken Books, 2005.

———. "Some Questions of Moral Philosophy." In *Responsibility and Judgment*, edited by Jerome Kohn. New York: Schocken Books, 2005.

———. "Tradition and the Modern Age." In *Between Past and Future: Eight Exercises in Political Thought*. New York: Penguin, 2006.

———. "The Tradition of Political Thought." In *The Promise of Politics*, edited by Jerome Kohn. New York: Schocken Books, 2005.

———. "What Is Authority?" In *The Portable Hannah Arendt*, edited by Peter Baehr. New York: Penguin, 2000.

———. "What Is Freedom?" In *The Portable Hannah Arendt*, edited by Peter Baehr. New York: Penguin, 2000.

Aristotle. *Nicomachean Ethics*. Loeb Classical Library. Translated by H. Rackham. Cambridge, MA: Harvard University Press, 1926.

———. *Politics*. Loeb Classical Library. Translated by H. Rackham. Cambridge, MA: Harvard University Press, 1932.

Auden, W. H. *W.H. Auden: Collected Poems*. Edited by Edward Mendelson. New York: Random House, 1976.

Augustine. *City of God*. Translated by Henry Bettenson. New York: Penguin Books, 2003.

———. *Confessions*. Translated by Henry Chadwick. New York: Oxford University Press, 1998.

———. *On Christian Teaching*. Translated by R. P. H. Green. New York: Oxford University Press, 1997.

Baldwin, James. *Baldwin: Collected Essays*. Edited by Toni Morrison. New York: The Library of America, 1998.

Bales, Kevin. *Disposable People: New Slavery in the Global Economy*. Berkley, CA: University of California Press, 1999.

Balkin, Jack. *Constitutional Redemption: Political Faith in an Unjust World*. Cambridge, MA: Harvard University Press, 2011.

———. *Living Originalism*. Cambridge, MA: Harvard University Press, 2011.

Bauman, Zygmunt. *Does Ethics Have a Chance in a World of Consumers?* Cambridge, MA: Harvard University Press, 2009.

Bellah, Robert. *Religion in Human Evolution: From the Paleolithic to the Axial Age*. Cambridge, MA: Harvard University Press, 2011.

Benhabib, Seyla. "Judgment and the Moral Foundations of Politics in Arendt's Thought." *Political Theory* 16, no. 1 (February 1998): 29–51.

Benson, Bruce Ellis. *Pious Nietzsche: Decadence and Dionysian Faith*. Bloomington, IN: Indiana University Press, 2008.

Bergen, Doris L. *Twisted Cross: The German Christian Movement in the Third Reich*. Chapel Hill: University of North Carolina Press, 1996.

Best, S. Payne. *The Venclo Incident: A True Story of Double-Dealing, Captivity, and a Murderous Nazi Plot*. New York: Hutchinson & Co., 1950.

Best, S., and D. Kellner. *Postmodern Theory: Critical Interrogations*. Basingstoke and London: Macmillan Press, 1991.

Biemann, Asher D. *Inventing New Beginnings: On the Idea of Renaissance in Modern Judaism*. Stanford, CA: Stanford University Press, 2009.

Birmingham, Peg. "The An-Archic Event of Natality and 'the Right to Have Rights.'" *Social Research* 74, no. 3, Hannah Arendt's Centenary: Political and Philosophical Perspectives, Part I (Fall 2007): 763–76.

Bodin, Jean. *On Sovereignty*. Translated by Julian Franklin. New York: Cambridge University Press, 2008.

Boulton, Wayne, Thomas Kennedy, and Allen Verhey, eds. *From Christ to the World: Introductory Readings in Christian Ethics*. Grand Rapids, MI: Eerdmans, 1994.

Bouteneff, Peter C. *Beginnings: Ancient Christian Readings of the Biblical Creation Narratives*. Grand Rapids, MI: Baker Academic, 2008.

Boutros, Haugen and Victor. *The Locust Effect: Why the End of Poverty Requires the End of Violence*. New York: Oxford University Press, 2014.

The Brilliance, "Does Your Heart Break?" from *Brother*, original copyright of Integrity Music (Colorado Springs, CO: 2015).

Brookes, David. "The Art of Presence." *New York Times*, January 20, 2014.

Brown, William. *The Ethos of the Cosmos: The Genesis of Moral Imagination in the Bible*. Grand Rapids, MI: Eerdmans, 1999.

Brueggemann, Walter. *The Prophetic Imagination*. Second edition. Minneapolis, MN: Fortress Press, 2001.

Burrell, David B., et al. *Creation and the God of Abraham*. New York: Cambridge University Press, 2010.

Camus, Albert. *The Myth of Sisyphus*. Translated by Justin O'Brien. New York: Vintage, 1991.

———. *Notebooks: 1942–1951*. Chicago, IL: Marlowe & Company, 1994.

———. *The Rebel: An Essay on Man in Revolt*. Translated by Anthony Bower. New York: Vintage International, 1991.

Cane, Lucy. "Hannah Arendt on the Principles of Political Action." *European Journal of Political Theory* 14 (January 2015): 55–75.

Cavanaugh, William, and James K. A. Smith. *Evolution and the Fall*. Grand Rapids, MI: Eerdmans, 2017.

Collier, Paul. *The Bottom Billion: Why the Poorest Countries Are Failing and What Can Be Done About It*. New York: Oxford University Press, 2008.

Cone, James. *God of the Oppressed*. Revised edition. Maryknoll, NY: Orbis, 1977.

Cunningham, Connor. *Genealogy of Nihilism: Philosophies of Nothing and the Difference of Theology*. London; New York: Routledge, 2002.

Danielson, Dennis Richard, ed. *The Book of the Cosmos: Imagining the Universe from Heraclitus to Hawking*. Cambridge, MA: Perseus Publishing, 2000.

Dalferth, Ingolf. "The Idea of Transcendence." In *The Axial Age and Its Consequences*, edited by Hans Joas and Robert Bellah. Cambridge, MA: Belknap Press of Harvard University Press, 2012.

———, ed. *The Presence and Absence of God*. Claremont Studies in the Philosophy of Religion, Conference 2008. Berlin: Mohr Siebeck, 2009.

de Beauvoir, Simone. *The Second Sex*. New York: Knopf, 1993.

Derrida, Jacques. *Dissemination*. Translated by B. Johnson. Chicago: University of Chicago Press, 1981.

———. *Margins of Philosophy*. Translated by A. Bass. Chicago: University of Chicago Press, 1982.

Descartes, Rene. *Meditations on First Philosophy*. In *The Philosophical Writings of Descartes*, Volume 2. Translated by John Gottingham, Robert Stoothoff, and Dugald Murdoch. New York: Cambridge University Press, 1984.

de Waal, Frans. *The Bonobo and the Atheist: In Search of Humanism among the Primates*. New York: W. W. Norton & Company, 2013.

Doniger, Wendy. "Ethical and Nonethical Implications of the Separation of Heaven and Earth in Indian Mythology." In *Cosmogony and Ethical Order*, edited by Robin W. Lovin and Frank E. Reynolds. Chicago: University of Chicago Press, 1985.

Dostoevsky, Fyodor. *The Brothers Karamazov*. Translated by Constance Garnett. New York: Barnes and Noble Classics, 2004.

———. *Notes from Underground / The Double*. Translated by Jessie Coulson. New York: Penguin, 1972.

Drozdek, Adam. *Greek Philosophers as Theologians: The Divine Arche*. Burlington, VT: Ashgate, 2007.

Dupré, Louis. *Passage to Modernity: An Essay in the Hermeneutics of Nature and Culture*. New Haven, CT: Yale University Press, 1993.

Edemariam, Yohannes. "From an Ancient Cloud: Getting by in Ethiopia's Slums." *Harper's Magazine*, May 2007.

Ehrhardt, Arnold. *The Beginning: A Study in the Greek Philosophical Approach to the Concept of Creation from Anaximander to St. John*. Manchester: University of Manchester Press, 1968.

Elshtain, Jean Bethke. *Democracy on Trial*. New York: BasicBooks, 1995.

———. *Public Man, Private Woman: Women in Social and Political Thought*. Princeton, NJ: Princeton University Press, 1981.

———. *Sovereignty: God, State, and Self*. New York: BasicBooks, 1995.

Engels, Friedrich. *The Dialectics of Nature*. Translated by Clemens Dutt. Moscow: Progress Publishers, 1964.

The Epistle to Diognetus. In *The Apostolic Fathers*, Volume 2. Translated by Kirsopp Lake. Cambridge, MA: Harvard University Press, 1985.

Ericksen, Robert. *Theologians under Hitler: Gerhard Kittel, Paul Althaus, and Emanuel Hirsch*. New Haven, CT: Yale University Press, 1985.

Fagenblat, Michael. A *Covenant of Creatures: Levinas's Philosophy of Judaism*. Stanford, CA: Stanford University Press, 2010.

Falk, Darrel. "Human Origins: The Scientific Story." In *Evolution and the Fall*, ed. William Cavanaugh and James K. A. Smith. Grand Rapids, MI: Eerdmans, 2017.

Fekade Azeze. "Abba Gubanna." In *Encyclopedia Aethiopica*, Volume 1. Edited by Siegberg Uhlig. Wiesbaden: Harrasowitz, 2003.

Fishbane, Michael. *Biblical Myth and Rabbinic Myth-Making*. New York: Oxford University Press, 2005.

Foucault, Michel. *The Archaeology of Knowledge and the Discourse on Language*. New York: Vintage, 1982.

Freud, Sigmund. *Civilization and Its Discontents*. Translated by Joan Riviere. New York: Doubleday, 1958.

Funkenstein, Amos. *Theology and the Scientific Imagination*. Princeton, NJ: Princeton University Press, 1986.

Gadamer, Hans-Georg. *Truth and Method*. Second revised edition. New York: Continuum, 1989.

Getachew, Indrias. "Ethiopia: Steady Increase of Street Children Orphaned by AIDS." UNICEF, January 2006.

Gillespie, Michael. *Nihilism before Nietzsche*. Chicago: University of Chicago Press, 1996.

Glover, Jonathan. *Humanity: A Moral History of the Twentieth Century*. Second edition. New Haven, CT: Yale University Press, 2012.

Goldberg, Jeffrey. "A Matter of Black Lives." *The Atlantic*, September 2015.

Goldoni, Marco, and Christopher McCorkindale, ed. *Hannah Arendt and the Law*. Oxford: Hart Publishing, 2012.

Gushee, David. *The Sacredness of Human Life: Why an Ancient Biblical Vision Is Key to the World's Future*. Grand Rapids, MI: Eerdmans, 2013.

Gutiérrez, Gustavo. *A Theology of Liberation*. Translated by Caridad Inda and John Eagleson. Maryknoll, NY: Orbis Books, 1973.

———. *On Job: God-Talk and the Suffering of the Innocent*. Translated by Matthew J. O'Connell. Maryknoll, NY: Orbis Books, 1987.

Hadot, Pierre. *Philosophy as a Way of Life: Spiritual Exercises from Socrates to Foucault*. Edited by Arnold Davidson. New York: Wiley-Blackwell, 1995.

Harari, Yuval Noah. *Homo Deus: A Brief History of Tomorrow*. New York: HarperCollins, 2017.

———. *Sapiens: A Brief History of Humankind*. London: Vintage, 2011.

Harries, Karsten. *Infinity and Perspective*. Cambridge, MA: MIT Press, 2001.

Havel, Vaclav. *The Power of the Powerless: Citizens against the State in Central Eastern Europe*. London: Routledge, 1985.

Hegel, G. W. F. *Hegel's Science of Logic*. Translated by A. V. Miller and edited by H. D. Lewis. Amherst, NY: Humanity Books, 1999.

———. *Lectures on the Philosophy of Religion* [1827]. One-volume edition. Edited by Peter C. Hodgson. New York: Oxford University Press, 2006.

Heidegger, Martin. *Being and Time*. Translated by Joan Stambaugh. Albany, NY: SUNY, 1996.

———. "What Is Metaphysics?" In *Basic Writings*, edited by David Farrell Krell. New York: HarperCollins, 1993.

Heidel, Alexander, ed. *The Babylonian Genesis*. Chicago: University of Chicago Press, 1963.

Hesiod. *Theogony, Works and Days. Testimonia*. Cambridge, MA: Loeb Classical Library, 2007.

Hitchens, Christopher. "Mother Teresa and Me." *Vanity Fair*, February 1995.

———. *The Missionary Position: Mother Teresa in Theory and Practice*. London: Verso, 1995.

———. "Teresa, Bright and Dark." *Newsweek*, August 28, 2007.

Hobbes, Thomas. *Leviathan*. Edited by C. B. Macpherson. New York: Penguin, 1985.

Huidobro, Vicente. "Epoch of Creation." In *Manifestos Manifest*, translated by Gilbert Alter-Gilbert. Los Angeles, CA: Green Integer, 1999.

Hunter, James Davidson. *To Change the World: The Irony, Tragedy, & Possibility of Christianity in the Late Modern World*. New York: Oxford University Press, 2010.

Insole, Christopher. *Kant and the Creation of Freedom*. New York: Oxford University Press, 2013.

———. *The Politics of Human Frailty: A Theological Defense of Liberalism*. London: SCM Press, 2004.

James, William. *The Varieties of Religious Life*. New York: Penguin Classics, 1985.

Jenkins, Willie. *The Christian Imagination: Theology and the Origins of Race.* New Haven, CT: Yale University Press, 2011.

Joas, Hans. "The Axial Age Debate as Religious Discourse." In *The Axial Age and Its Consequences*, edited by Robert Bellah and Hans Joas. Cambridge, MA: Belknap Press of Harvard University Press, 2012.

———. *Do We Need Religion? On the Experience of Self-Transcendence.* Boulder; London: Paradigm Publishers, 2008.

———. *The Genesis of Values.* Chicago: University of Chicago Press, 2001.

———. *The Sacredness of the Person: A New Genealogy of Human Rights.* Washington, DC: Georgetown University Press, 2013.

Kampowski, Stephan. *Arendt, Augustine, and the New Beginning: The Action Theory and Moral Thought of Hannah Arendt in the Light of Dissertation on St. Augustine.* Grand Rapids, MI: Eerdmans, 2008.

Kangas, David. *Kierkegaard's Instant: On Beginnings.* Bloomington, IN: Indiana University Press, 2007.

Kant, Immanuel. *The Critique of Pure Reason.* Edited and translated by Paul Guyer and Allen W. Wood. New York: Cambridge University Press, 2006.

Keene, Sam. *Faces of the Enemy: Reflections of the Hostile Imagination.* New York: Harper & Row, 1991.

———. *In the Absence of God: Dwelling in the Presence of the Sacred.* Danvers, MA: Harmony Books, 2010.

Kierkegaard, Søren. *The Concept of Anxiety: A Simple Psychologically Orienting Deliberation on the Dogmatic Issue of Hereditary Sin.* Edited and translated by Reidar Thomte. Princeton, NJ: Princeton University Press, 1980.

———. *Eighteen Upbuilding Discourses.* Edited and translated by Howard V. Hong and Edna H. Hong. Princeton, NJ: Princeton University Press, 1990.

———. *Fear and Trembling.* Edited and translated by Howard V. Hong and Edna H. Hong. Princeton, NJ: Princeton University Press, 1983.

———. *Journals and Papers*, Volume 2. Bloomington, IN: Indiana University Press, 1970.

———. *Philosophical Fragments.* Translated by Edna and Howard Hong. Princeton, NJ: Princeton University Press, 1985.

———. *Repetition.* Translated by Walter Lowrie. Princeton, NJ: Princeton University Press, 1946.

———. *The Sickness Unto Death: A Christian Psychological Exposition for Upbuilding and Awakening.* Edited and translated by Howard V. Hong and Edna H. Hong. Princeton, NJ: Princeton University Press, 1983.

———. *Works of Love.* Translated by Howard and Edna Hong. New York: Harper-Perennial, 2009.

King, Jr., Martin Luther. *Strength to Love.* Minneapolis, MN: Fortress Press, 2010.

Krauss, Lawrence. *A Universe from Nothing: Why There Is Something Rather than Nothing.* New York: Free Press, 2012.

Lear, Jonathan. *Open Minded: Working Out the Logic of the Soul.* Cambridge, MA: Harvard University Press, 1998.

——. *Radial Hope: Ethics in the Face of Cultural Devastation*. Cambridge, MA: Harvard University Press, 2006.

Levenson, Jon. *Creation and the Persistence of Evil: The Jewish Drama of Divine Omnipotence*. Princeton, NJ: Princeton University Press, 1988.

Levinas, Emmanuel. "God and Philosophy." In *Emmanuel Levinas: Basic Philosophical Writings*, edited by Adriaan T. Peperzak, Simon Critchley, and Robert Bernasconi. Bloomington, IN: Indiana University Press, 1996.

——. "Is Ontology Fundamental?" In *Emmanuel Levinas: Basic Philosophical Writings*, edited by Adriaan T. Peperzak, Simon Critchley, and Robert Bernasconi. Bloomington, IN: Indiana University Press, 1996.

——. *Otherwise than Being or Beyond Essence*. Translated by Alphonso Lingis. Pittsburgh, PA: Duquesne University Press, 1998.

——. *Totality and Infinity*. Translated by Alphonso Lingis. Pittsburgh, PA: Duquesne University Press, 1969.

Levine, Donald N. *Interpreting Ethiopia: Observations of Five Decades*. Edited by Andrew DeCort. Los Angeles, CA: Tsehai Press, 2014.

——. *Wax and Gold: Tradition and Innovation in Ethiopian Culture*. Chicago: University of Chicago Press, 1965.

Lewis, C. S. *Collected Letters*, Volume 2. Edited by Walter Hooper. London: HarperCollins, 2004.

——. *The Weight of Glory and Other Addresses*. Grand Rapids, MI: Eerdmans, 1965.

Lincoln, Abraham. "First Inaugural Address." In *The Collected Works of Abraham Lincoln*, edited by Rob B. Basler. 9 vols. New Brunswick, NJ: Rutgers University Press, 1953.

Locke, John. *A Letter Concerning Toleration*. Edited by James Tully. Indianapolis, IN: Hackett, 1983.

——. *Two Treatises of Government*. Edited by Peter Laslett. New York: Cambridge University Press, 1988.

Lonergan, Bernard. "Mission and the Spirit." In *A Third Collection: Papers by Bernard J. F. Lonergan, S.J.*, edited by Frederick E Crow. New York: Geoffrey Chapman, 1985.

Lovin, Robin W., and Frank E. Reynolds. *Cosmogony and Ethical Order*. Chicago: University of Chicago Press, 1985.

Maas, Peter. *Love Thy Neighbor: A Story of War*. New York: Knopf Doubleday, 1997.

Machiavelli, Niccolo. *The Prince: A Revised Translation, Backgrounds, Interpretations, Marginalia*. Second edition. Edited by Robert M. Adams. New York: W. W. Norton & Company, 1992.

MacIntyre, Alasdair. *After Virtue*. Third edition. Notre Dame, IN: University of Notre Dame Press, 2007.

——. *Whose Justice? Which Rationality*. Notre Dame, IN: University of Notre Dame Press, 1989.

Mandela, Nelson. *Long Walk to Freedom: The Autobiography of Nelson Mandela*. New York: Little, Brown and Company, 1995.

Mann, Thomas. *Joseph and His Brothers*. Translated by John E. Woods. New York: Knopf, 2005.

Mannermaa, Tuomo. *Two Kinds of Love: Martin Luther's Religious World.* Translated by Kirsi I. Stjerna. Minneapolis, MN: Fortress Press, 2010.

Marion, Jean-Luc. *In Excess: Studies of Saturated Phenomena.* Translated by Robyn Horner and Vincent Berraud. New York: Fordham University Press, 2002.

Markell, Patchen. "Anonymous Glory." *European Journal of Political Theory* 16, no. 1 (2017): 77–99.

———. "The Rule of the People: Arendt, Arché, and Democracy." *American Political Science Review* 100, no. 1 (February 2006): 1–14.

Marx, Karl. *Early Writings.* Introduced by Lucio Colletti, translated by Rodney Livingston and Gregor Benton. New York: Vintage Books, 1975.

Marx, Werner. *Reason and World: Between Tradition and Another Beginning.* The Hague, Netherlands: Martinus Nijhoff, 1971.

Martyr, Justin. *First Apology.* In *The Ante-Nicene Fathers: Translations of the Writings of the Fathers down to A.D. 325,* Volume 1. Edited by Alexander Roberts and James Donaldson. New York: Scribner's Sons, 1905.

The Martyrdom of Polycarp. In *The Apostolic Fathers,* Volume II. Translated by Kirsopp Lake. The Loeb Classical Library. New York: Macmillan, 1923.

Mendes-Flohr, Paul. *Love, Accusative and Dative: Reflections on Leviticus 19:18.* Syracuse, NY: Syracuse University Press.

Middleton, J. Richard. *The Liberating Image: The* Imago Dei *in Genesis* 1. Grand Rapids, MI: Brazos Press, 2005.

Miles, Margaret. *"Volo ut sis*: Arendt and Augustine." *Dialog* 41, no. 3 (Fall 2002): 221–30.

Miller, J. Hillis. *The Disappearance of God: Five Nineteenth-Century Writers.* Cambridge, MA: Harvard University Press, 1963.

Moltmann, Jürgen, "European Political Theology," in *The Cambridge Companion to Political Theology,* eds. Craig Hovey and Elizabeth Phillips (New York: Cambridge University Press, 2015), 3–22.

Moyn, Samuel. *Christian Human Rights.* Philadelphia, PA: University of Pennsylvania Press, 2015.

Mulhall, Stephen. *Philosophical Myths of the Fall.* Princeton, NJ: Princeton University Press, 2005.

Munhall, Patricia, et al. *The Emergence of Man into the 21st Century.* Sudbury, MA: Jones and Bartlett Publishers, 2002.

Murdoch, Iris. *The Sovereignty of Good.* New York: Routledge, 2001.

Nicklas, Tobias, and Korinna Zamfir, eds. *Theologies of Creation in Early Judaism and Ancient Christianity.* New York: De Gruyter, 2010.

Nietzsche, Friedrich. *The Antichrist.* In *The Portable Nietzsche.* Edited and translated by Walter Kaufmann. New York: Penguin, 1982.

———. *Beyond Good and Evil.* Edited by Rolf-Peter Horstmann and Judy Norman, translated by Judith Norman. New York: Cambridge University Press, 2005.

———. *The Gay Science.* Translated by Walter Kaufmann. New York: Vintage, 1974.

———. *Human, All Too Human: A Book for Free Spirits.* Translated by Marion Faber. Lincoln: University of Nebraska Press, 1986.

———. *On the Genealogy of Morals.* Edited and translated by Walter Kaufmann. New York: Vintage, 1969.

———. *Thus Spoke Zarathustra.* In *The Portable Nietzsche.* Edited and translated by Walter Kaufmann. New York: Viking Penguin, 1982.

———. *Twilight of the Idols.* Translated by Thomas Common. Mineola, NY: Dover, 2004.

———. *The Will to Power.* Translated and edited by Walter Kaufmann and R. J. Hollingdale. New York: Vintage, 1968.

North, Michael. *Novelty: A History of the New.* Chicago: University of Chicago Press, 2013.

Paul, Annie Murphy. *Origins: How the Nine Months Before Birth Shape the Rest of Our Lives.* New York: Free Press, 2010.

Payne, Thomas. *Common Sense.* Mineola, NY: Dover Publications, 1997.

Perry, Simon. *Resurrecting Interpretation: Technology, Hermeneutics, and the Parable of the Rich Man and Lazarus.* Eugene, OR: Pickwick Publications, 2012.

Peters, Edward. "What Was God Doing before He Created the Heavens and the Earth?" *Augustiniana* 34 (1984).

Phillips, Elizabeth. *Political Theology: A Guide for the Perplexed.* New York: T & T Clark, 2012.

Pippin, Robert. *Modernism as a Philosophical Problem: On the Dissatisfactions of European High Culture.* Malden, MA: Wiley-Blackwell, 1999.

Pizer, John. *Toward a Theory of Radical Origin: Essays on Modern German Thought.* Lincoln: University of Nebraska Press, 1995.

Plato. *Republic*, Volume 1: Books 1–5. Loeb Classical Library. Translated by Christopher Emlyn-Jones and William Preddy. Cambridge, MA: Harvard University Press, 2013.

———. *Republic*, Volume 2. Loeb Classical Library. Translated by Christopher Emlyn-Jones and William Preddy. Cambridge, MA: Harvard University Press, 2013.

———. *Theaetetus.* In *Plato: Complete Works.* Edited by John Cooper. Indianapolis, IN: Hackett Publishing Company, 1997.

Pope Francis. *Laudato Si: On Care for Our Common Home.* Washington, DC: United States Conference of Catholic Bishops, 2015.

Postman, Neil. *Amusing Ourselves to Death.* New York: Penguin, 2005.

Reventlow, Henning Graf, and Yair Hoffman, eds. *Creation in Jewish and Christian Tradition.* London: Sheffield Academic Press, 2002.

Rhee, Helen, ed. *Wealth and Poverty in Early Christianity.* Minneapolis, MN: Fortress Press, 2017.

Ricoeur, Paul. "Emplotment: A Reading of Aristotle's *Poetics.*" In *Time and Narrative*, translated by Kathleen McLaughlin and David Pellauer, 31–49. Chicago: University of Chicago Press, 1990.

Robinson, Matthew R. *Redeeming Relationships, Relationships that Redeem: Free Sociability and the Completion of Humanity in the Thought of Friedrich Schleiermacher.* Tübingen: Mohr Siebeck, forthcoming.

Robson. Mark. *Ontology and Providence in Creation: Taking ex nihilo Seriously.* New York: Continuum, 2012.

Rosenzweig, Franz. "The New Thinking." In his *Philosophical and Theological Writings*, translated and edited by Paul Franks and Michael Morgan. Indianapolis, IN: Hackett, 2000.

——. *The Star of Redemption*. Translated by William Hallo. Notre Dame, IN: University of Notre Dame Press, 2002.

Sade, "King of Sorrows," from *Lovers Rock*. Las Angeles, CA: Epic Records, 2000.

Said, Edward. *Beginnings: Intentions and Methods*. London: Granta Books, 19997.

Schmitz, Kenneth L. *The Gift: Creation*. Milwaukee, MN: Marquette University Press, 1982.

Scholder, Klaus. *The Church and the Third Reich*, Volume 1: *1918–1934*. Philadelphia, PA: Fortress Press, 1988.

——. *The Church and the Third Reich*, Volume. 2: *The Year of Disillusionment 1934, Barmen, and Rome*. Philadelphia, PA: Fortress Press, 1988.

Schweiker, William. "Loose Morals: The Barbaric 20th Century." *The Christian Century* 120, no. 10 (May 17, 2003): 36–38.

——. "On Religious Ethics." In *The Blackwell Companion to Religious Ethics*, edited by William Schweiker. Malden, MA: Blackwell, 2008.

——. "A Preface to Ethics: Global Dynamics and the Integrity of Life." *Journal of Religious Ethics* 32, no. 1 (2004): 13–37.

——. *Responsibility and Christian Ethics*. New York: Cambridge University Press, 1995.

——. *Theological Ethics and Global Dynamics: In the Time of Many Worlds*. Malden, MA: Blackwell, 2004.

Shepherd, Andrew. *The Gift of the Other: Levinas, Derrida, and a Theology of Hospitality*. Cambridge, UK: James Clark & Co., 2014.

Smail, Daniel Lord. *Deep History and the Brain*. Berkeley, CA: University of California Press, 2008.

——, ed. *Deep History: The Architecture of Past and Present*. Berkley, CA: University of California Press, 2011.

Smith, D. L. *Less than Human: Why We Demean, Enslave, and Kill*. New York: St. Martin's Press, 2011.

Smith, Mark. *The Priestly Vision of Genesis 1*. Minneapolis, MN: Fortress Press, 2009.

Siedentop, Larry. *Inventing the Individual: The Origins of Western Liberalism*. London: Penguin Books, 2015.

Sittler, Joseph. "The Cruciform Character of Human Existence." *The Chicago Lutheran Seminary Record* 54 (October 1949).

——. "The Sittler Speeches." In *Center for the Study of Campus Ministry Yearbook 1977–78*. Edited by Phil Schroader. Valparaiso, IN: Valparaiso University, 1978.

Song, Robert. *Christianity and Liberal Society*. Oxford: Oxford University Press, 1997.

Sontag, Susan. *Regarding the Pain of Others*. New York: Picador, 2003.

Sori, Darsema. "Letter from Qilinto Prison." *Addis Standard*, January 17, 2017. http://addisstandard.com/letter-qilinto-prison-will-not-falter-journalist-darsema-sori/.

Stark, Rodney. *The Rise of Christianity: How Christianity Led to Freedom, Capitalism, and Western Success*. New York: Random House, 2005.

Steiner, George. *Grammars of Creation*, Originating in the Gifford Lectures for 1990. New Haven, CT: Yale University Press, 2001.

Sturm, Douglous. "Cosmogony and Ethics in the Marxian Tradition." In *Cosmogony and Ethical Order*, edited by Robin W. Lovin and Frank E. Reynolds. Chicago: University of Chicago Press, 1985.

Taylor, Charles. *A Secular Age*. Cambridge, MA: Belknap Press of Harvard University Press, 2007.

———. *Modern Social Imaginaries.* Durham, NC: Duke University Press, 2004.

———. "What Was the Axial Revolution?" In *The Axial Age and Its Consequences*, edited by Robert Bellah and Hans Joas. Cambridge, MA: Belknap Press of Harvard University Press, 2012.

Teferra, Sehin. "Agency and Sisterhood: A Feminist Analysis of Ethiopian Sex Workers' Experience of, and Resistance to, Violence." Unpublished doctoral dissertation, SOAS, University of London, 2015.

Teresa. *Mother Teresa: Come Be My Light: The Private Writings of the "Saint of Calcutta."* Edited by Brian Kolodiejchuk. New York: Doubleday, 2007.

Thucydides. *The Peloponnesian War*. Translated by John H. Finley Jr. New York: Random House, 1951.

Tillich, Paul. *The Courage to Be*. New Haven, CT: Yale University Press, 2000.

Tolkien, J. R. R. *The Lord of the Rings*. Single-volume edition. New York: Houghton Mifflin, 1993.

van der Kolk, Bessel. *The Body Keeps the Score: Brain, Mind, and Body in the Healing of Trauma.* New York: Penguin Books, 2015.

Vanier, Jean. *Community and Growth*. Revised edition. Mahwah, NY: Paulist Press, 1989.

Walton, John. *Genesis 1 as Ancient Cosmology*. Winona Lake, IN: Eisenbrauns, 2011.

Walzer, Michael. *Interpretation and Social Criticism*. Cambridge, MA: Harvard University Press, 1987.

Williams, Reggie. *Bonhoeffer's Black Jesus: Harlem Renaissance Theology and an Ethic of Resistance*. Waco, TX: Baylor University Press, 2014.

Williams, Rowan. *Being Christian: Baptism, Bible, Eucharist, Prayer*. Grand Rapids, MI: Eerdmans, 2014.

Wittgenstein, Ludwig. *Philosophical Investigations*. Translated by G. E. M. Anscombe. New York: Macmillan Publishing: 1958.

Wolynn, Mark. *It Didn't Start with You: How Inherited Family Trauma Shapes Who We Are and How to End the Cycle.* New York: Penguin, 2016.

Wright, Joanne H. *Origin Stories in Political Thought: Discourses on Gender, Power, and Citizenship*. Toronto: University of Toronto Press, 2004.

Yates, Joshua. "The New Cosmopolitans & The Problem of the Good World." University of Virginia: Unpublished, 2009.

Yearley, Lee. "Freud as Creator and Critic of Cosmogonies and Their Ethics." In *Cosmogony and Ethical Order*, edited by Robin W. Lovin and Frank E. Reynolds. Chicago: University of Chicago Press, 1985.

Yeats, W. B. *Collected Poems*. New York: Macmillan, 1953.

Zinn, Howard. *A People's History of the United States*. New York: Harper, 2005.

Author Index

Subject Index

About the Author

Andrew DeCort (PhD, University of Chicago) is director of the Institute for Christianity and the Common Good (www.iccgood.org) and lecturer in ethics and public theology at the Ethiopian Graduate School of Theology. Follow his writing at www.andrew-decort.com.

Made in the USA
Middletown, DE
03 April 2025

73749274R00176